COUPLES COPING WITH STRESS

This is the first book that reviews both empirical and clinical applications of how couples jointly cope with stress—dyadic coping—around the globe. The Systemic-Transactional Stress Model (STM), developed by co-editor Guy Bodenmann, is used as a consistent framework so readers can better appreciate the contrasts and similarities across the fourteen cultures represented in the book. Written by scholars from the particular culture, each chapter provides a conceptual review of the dyadic coping research conducted in their specific cultures, and also provides empirical and clinical recommendations. Additional contributions include how to measure dyadic coping, so others can apply the STM model in other contexts. The latest treatment approaches for therapy and prevention are also highlighted, making this book ideal for professionals interested in expanding their cultural competence when working with couples from various backgrounds.

Highlights include:

- How couples in different cultures deal with stress and how values and traditions affect dyadic stress and coping.
- Global applications, especially to couples in the regions highlighted in the book— the U.S. (including one chapter on Latino couples in the U.S.), Australia, China, Germany, Greece, Hungary, Italy, Japan, Kenya, Nigeria, Pakistan, Portugal, Romania, and Switzerland.
- Factors encountered in examining dyadic coping using the STM Model including measurement and assessment issues.
- Suggestions for making treatment, prevention, and intervention programs for couples more effective.

Ideal for relationship researchers, psychologists, mental health counselors, social workers, and advanced students who work with couples dealing with stress. This book is also appropriate for advanced courses on interpersonal processes, close relationships, stress and coping, multicultural issues in marriage and family therapy or counseling, or family systems, taught in a variety of social science disciplines.

Mariana K. Falconier is Associate Professor and Clinical Director of the Center for Family Services at Virginia Polytechnic Institute and State University.

Ashley K. Randall is Assistant Professor of Counseling and Counseling Psychology at Arizona State University.

Guy Bodenmann is Professor of Clinical Psychology at the University of Zurich.

COUPLES COPING WITH STRESS

A Cross-Cultural Perspective

Edited by
Mariana K. Falconier, Ashley K. Randall,
& Guy Bodenmann

Routledge
Taylor & Francis Group

NEW YORK AND LONDON

First published 2016
by Routledge
711 Third Avenue, New York, NY 10017

and by Routledge
2 Park Square, Milton Park, Oxfordshire OX14 4RN

Routledge is an imprint of the Taylor & Francis Group, an informa business

Library of Congress Cataloging in Publication Data
Names: Falconier, Mariana K., editor. | Randall, Ashley K., editor. | Bodenmann, Guy, editor.
Title: Couples coping with stress: a cross-cultural perspective/edited by Mariana K. Falconier, Ashley K. Randall, & Guy Bodenmann.
Other titles: Couples coping with stress (Routledge)
Description: New York, NY: Routledge, 2016. | Includes bibliographical references and index.
Identifiers: LCCN 2015046750| ISBN 9781138906631 (hardback: alk. paper) | ISBN 9781138906655 (pbk.: alk. paper) | ISBN 9781315644394 (ebook: alk. paper)
Subjects: LCSH: Marital psychotherapy. | Couples. | Stress (Psychology) | Adjustment (Psychology)
Classification: LCC RC488.5 .C64342 2016 | DDC 616.89/1562—dc23
LC record available at http://lccn.loc.gov/2015046750

ISBN: 978-1-138-90663-1 (hbk)
ISBN: 978-1-138-90665-5 (pbk)
ISBN: 978-1-315-64439-4 (ebk)

Typeset in Bembo and Stone Sans
by Florence Production Ltd, Stoodleigh, Devon, UK

CONTENTS

ABOUT THE EDITORS

Dr. Mariana K. Falconier obtained her bachelor's degree in Psychology from Universidad de Buenos Aires, Argentina and her master's degree in Marriage and Family Therapy and her doctoral degree in Family Studies from the University of Maryland in the U.S. She is an associate professor and Clinical Director in the Marriage and Family Therapy Program at Virginia Polytechnic Institute and State University. Her research, which has been published and presented in the U.S. and internationally, has focused on dyadic coping processes in couples, with particular attention to economic stress and Latinos' immigration stress. In collaboration with Dr. Celia Hayhoe she developed the program TOGETHER to help couples improve their coping, communication, and financial management skills. She has been responsible for teaching the graduate course *Multicultural Issues in Marriage and Family Therapy* for several years at Virginia Tech. Dr. Falconier has been an active clinician and supervisor for the last twenty years and holds a license as a marriage and family therapist in Virginia (LMFT) and Maryland (LCMFT) and a license as a psychologist in Argentina. She has extensive experience in individual, couple, and family therapy with immigrant populations, particularly Latinos and French-speaking African immigrants in the U.S. She is a clinical fellow and approved supervisor by the American Association of Marriage and Family Therapy (AAMFT).

Dr. Ashley K. Randall is an assistant professor in Counseling and Counseling Psychology at Arizona State University. She received her doctoral degree in Family Studies and Human Development from the University of Arizona. Dr. Randall was the recipient of a Fulbright Fellowship in 2007, where she conducted research at the Institute for Family Research and Counseling in Fribourg, Switzerland. Dr. Randall's research uses a multi-method approach to examine how couples cope with stress in the context of their relationship, and resulting implications for mental health outcomes. She has presented and published both nationally and internationally on these topics. Dr. Randall serves on the editorial board for *Emotion*, the *Journal of Couple and Relationship Therapy*, and *The Counseling Psychologist*, and is a board member of the International Association for Relationship Research.

Dr. Guy Bodenmann is a professor of Clinical Psychology at the University of Zurich. Professor Bodenmann is well known for his research on stress and coping in couples and his development of the systemic-transactional stress and coping model. Many of his studies focus on the role of dyadic coping for couples functioning. He is author of sixteen books, one of which is *Couples Coping with Stress* (co-authored with Kayser & Revenson, 2005), and more than 200 articles in scientific journals. He developed the Couples Coping Enhancement Training (CCET) and the coping-oriented couple therapy (COCT) approach. He is the director of the Clinical Training Program for Psychotherapy in Children and Adolescents, director of the Clinical Training Program for Couple Therapy, and director of the Postgraduate Training for School Psychology. He is also the president of the Academy of Behavioral Therapy in Children and Adolescents.

ABOUT THE CONTRIBUTORS

Sara Magalhães Albuquerque is a Ph.D. student at the University of Coimbra and University of Lisbon. She received her master's degree in Clinical Psychology at the Faculty of Psychology and Educational Sciences of the University of Coimbra, Portugal. She is currently undertaking a project entitled 'Dyadic interdependence after a child's death: Influence of individual and interpersonal factors in the individual and marital adjustment.'

Zara Arshad recently obtained a Master of Science degree in Human Development from Virginia Polytechnic Institute and State University. She has clinical experience working with individuals, couples, and families of various racial/ethnic and socio-economic backgrounds. While acquiring her master's degree, her research focused on the experiences of non-Muslim, Caucasian Licensed Marriage and Family Therapists working with South Asian and Middle Eastern Muslim clients.

Melissa G. Bakhurst obtained her bachelor's degree in Psychology from the University of Melbourne and is currently a Ph.D. student at the University of Queensland, Australia. Her research project has involved tailoring the Couple CARE relationship education program for use with serving military personnel and their partners, and evaluating the program through a randomized controlled trial.

Susana Costa Ramalho is a clinical psychologist and psychotherapist. She obtained a Master of Science degree in Stress and Well-Being at the Faculty of Psychology and Educational Sciences, University of Lisbon (Portugal), and she is currently a Ph.D. candidate at the Faculty of Psychology, University of Lisbon and University of Coimbra. Her research focuses on the domains of well-being and human relationships, namely the couple ones, studying social, cognitive, and contextual factors, which may promote satisfying and healthy relationships.

Silvia Donato is a researcher in Social Psychology and a faculty member at Università Cattolica del Sacro Cuore-Milano, where she teaches 'Methods and Techniques on Family and Community Interventions.' She is a member of the Catholic University Centre for Family Studies and Research at the UCSC. She is a trainer and member of the scientific committee of the postgraduate course on family preventive intervention: the 'Family Enrichment Programs.' Her research focuses primarily on the study of stress and coping in couples, with particular attention to the role of dyadic coping for partners' well-being, in both everyday life and illness, as well as the intergenerational transmission of coping competences. Her interests extend to partners' interpersonal perceptions, partners' support in response to positive events, scale psychometrics, and the evaluation of preventive psychosocial interventions.

Dr. William K. Halford obtained his Ph.D. from Latrobe University in Australia. He served as Professor of Clinical Psychology at Griffith University until 2008 and has taught at the University of Queensland since 2009. Dr. Halford's research focuses on couple and family relationships. He was a pioneering voice in introducing couple-based cognitive therapy strategies to assist in the management of individual problems. Dr. Halford has given numerous keynote addresses and in 2009 received the President's Award from the Australian Psychological Society for distinguished contribution to psychology.

Dr. Philipp Y. Herzberg is a professor for Personality Psychology and Psychological Assessment at the Helmut Schmidt University (the University of the Federal Armed Forces) in Hamburg, Germany. His research interests include dyadic assessment, the role of personality in relationships, the person-centered approach to personality, and personality and health. His most recent publications have appeared in *Anxiety, Stress, & Coping*, *European Journal of Personality*, *Journal of Research in Personality*, and *Psychological Assessment*. He is currently an associate editor of the *Journal of Individual Differences*.

Dr. Danika N. Hiew received her Ph.D. in Psychology from the University of Queensland, Australia in 2014. Her doctoral research focused on the communication and relationship standards of Chinese, Western, and intercultural Chinese-Western couples. As part of her research, Danika developed and validated the first measure of Chinese and Western couple relationship standards, and observed and coded the communication of 123 couples. Danika is also a practicing psychologist who works with individuals and couples coping with a variety of psychological and physical health conditions, and family and couple relationship difficulties.

Dr. Peter Hilpert obtained his Ph.D. in Clinical Psychology from the University of Zurich. During his doctoral studies, which included an annual visiting position at the University of California, Los Angeles, he focused on couples' interactions in clinical psychology. Currently he is at the University of Washington as a visiting scientist examining intra- and interpersonal regulation processes during real-time interactions.

Dr. Nazia Iqbal received her Ph.D. from Quaid-I-Azam University in Islamabad, Pakistan. She currently teaches at the International Islamic University in Islamabad. Her research interests include dyadic coping, adult attachment, conflict resolution, communication competence, social support, and marital satisfaction among Pakistani couples.

Dr. Jeffrey B. Jackson is an assistant professor in the Marriage and Family Therapy Program at Polytechnic Institute and State University. He obtained his Ph.D. in Marriage and Family Therapy from Brigham Young University. He is a Licensed Marriage and Family Therapist (LMFT), and an American Association for Marriage and Family Therapy (AAMFT) Approved Supervisor. His research interests include relationship quality and stability, ambiguous loss, disability, clinical outcome research, and meta-analytic methods.

Laura E. Jiménez-Arista is currently a Ph.D. student in the Counseling Psychology Program at ASU. She obtained certification as a National Certified Counselor (NCC) through the National Board for Certified Counselors (NBCC). Her research interests include couples and relationships, stress and coping, and psychotherapy outcome. Her clinical experience includes work at community mental health settings providing counseling and psychotherapy to individuals, couples, and families in both English and Spanish. Ms. Jiménez-Arista is the recipient of the Mexican National Council for Science and Technology scholarship award, a five-year academic award for doctoral studies granted to scholars with outstanding academic and professional history.

Dr. Evangelos C. Karademas is an associate professor at the Department of Psychology, University of Crete, Greece. He teaches Health Psychology at a pregraduate level at the University of Crete as well as at post-graduate programs at the Universities of Crete and Athens. He has authored one book and edited five more. He has also authored/co-authored more than ninety scientific articles and chapters in international and local journals and editions. His research interests include self-regulation and health, adaptation to chronic illness, quality of life, the role of stress, and related factors in health and illness.

Dr. Akiko Kawashima is currently an assistant professor in the School of Social Welfare at Tokyo University of Social Welfare. Dr. Kawashima has authored a number of scientific papers on marital quality, emphasizing its effects on children's mental health. Her present collaborative research program includes a large-scale longitudinal study that is being conducted in Japan. This investigation focuses on family members' mental health from a developmental psychopathological perspective.

Dr. Karen Kayser is the Dr. Renato LaRocca Endowed Chair of Oncology Social Work at the University of Louisville, USA. Her research is in psychosocial oncology with an emphasis on couples and families coping with cancer-related stress. She conducts research in the United States and internationally, including the countries of India, China, Switzerland, Italy, and Australia. She developed the program *Partners in Coping* (PIC), which is a couple-based psychosocial intervention to assist couples coping with breast cancer. Results of the trial have been disseminated in peer-reviewed journals, online trainings, national and international workshops, and the book, *Helping Couples Cope With Women's Cancers: An evidence-based approach for practitioners* (with Scott, 2008). She is the editor of the *Journal of Psychosocial Oncology*. In 2012 she received the American Cancer Society's Quality of Life Award by the Association of Oncology Social Work.

Charles Kimamo was among the first two students to obtain a Ph.D. in the Department of Psychology, University of Nairobi, Kenya. He is a Clinical/Developmental Psychologist. He has a background in both Education and Nursing. His Ph.D. was on the psychosocial determinants of problem behavior in adolescence. He has been teaching in the University of Nairobi since 1994 and one of his research interests is in gender harmony.

Rebekka Kuhn received a master's degree in Clinical and Health Psychology at the University of Fribourg in Switzerland. Her research focuses on health, couples, stress, and dyadic coping. She is currently completing her doctoral studies at the University of Zurich. In addition she works as a trainer and assistant for CCET, a prevention program focused on dyadic coping.

Dr. Tai Kurosawa is an assistant professor at Ibaraki Christian University, Japan. His research interest includes relationship-focused coping, work–family spillover, and coparenting. He is a clinical psychologist who specializes in the field of family therapy. He got a student submission award from International Association for Relationship Research in 2012.

Dr. Alexandra Marques Pinto is Professor of Educational Psychology at the Faculty of Psychology and researcher at the Center of Research in Psychology of the Lisbon University. Her research and publications focus on two main domains: psychology of stress and coping—studying social, cognitive, and contextual factors, which may prevent pathological reactions and promote constructive responses to chronic and acute stress experiences; and well-being promotion programs—the design or adaptation, implementation (in school, family, and workplace settings), and evaluation of well-being promotion programs.

Dr. Ivone Martins Patrão is an associate professor, holds a doctoral degree in Health Psychology (ISPA-IU, 2008), and is a Master of Science in both Health Psychology (ISPA-IU, 2001) and Clinical Psychology (ISPA-IU, 1999). She received the Health Ministry Award in 2011 for the Primary Health Care Work-group and the Future Hospital Award in 2011 for the project BeCAMeHealth —Multifamily interventions. She is a family and couples' therapist, clinical psychologist at the Primary Health Care (Lisbon), researcher and university teacher at ISPA—IU (Department of Clinical and Health Psychology).

Dr. Tamás Martos is a psychologist and associate professor at the Institute of Mental Health Semmelweis University in Budapest, Hungary. He received his Ph.D. in 2010. In addition to lecturing in psychology, he serves as a psychodrama group leader and a family therapist. His research interests include the role of motivational processes and goal constructs in healthy human functioning, positive psychology, and systemic aspects of couples' functioning. He currently runs a research project on the long-term pursuits of goals in married and cohabiting couples.

Dr. Isabel Narciso Davide is an associate professor at the University of Lisbon, Department of Psychology and a family therapist. Her main research and pedagogic areas are: Family Psychology (e.g., marital satisfaction, couple intimacy, parental educative patterns, adoptive families, children in social care, adolescence, and self-destructive trajectories) and systemic interventions with families and communities (couple and family therapy).

Dr. Fridtjof W. Nussbeck is currently a professor teaching research methods and evaluation in the Department of Psychology for Bielefeld University in Bielefeld, Germany. He obtained his Doctorate of Psychology at Trier University in Germany. From 2002 to 2008 he taught at Landau University, the University of Geneva, and the Free University of Berlin with a focus on psychometrics and multitrait–multimethod analysis. His current research interests include dyadic data analysis and relationship satisfaction.

Marta Figueiredo Pedro received her European Doctorate in Family Psychology from the University of Lisbon, and during this period she was a research visitor at Cardiff University. She is currently a lecturer of Family Studies in the Faculty of Psychology, University of Lisbon, teaching child, couple, and family assessment, and therapy as well as supervising the clinical work of postgraduate students.

Her research interests include marital and family relationships, with a focus on the association between aspects of marital functioning, marital conflict, parenting, and children's psychological well-being. She also works as a clinical psychologist in Portugal, developing clinical practice with children, adolescents, and families.

Dr. Marco Daniel Pereira is an associate researcher at the Faculty of Psychology and Educational Sciences of the University of Coimbra (Portugal). He received his Ph.D. degree in Health Psychology at the University of Coimbra in 2008. His general area of research is clinical and health psychology. His current research interests include adult attachment and dyadic interdependence in the adjustment to different contexts of adversity (e.g., death of a child, HIV serodiscordancy, and postpartum depression). He has published more than sixty papers in peer-reviewed journals and ten book chapters.

Dr. Tracey A. Revenson is a professor of Psychology at Hunter College and the Graduate Center of the City University of New York where she heads the Ph.D. area in Health Psychology & Clinical Science. Dr. Revenson is well known for her research on stress and coping processes among individuals, couples, and families facing serious physical illness. She is the co-author or co-editor of ten volumes, including the *Handbook of Health Psychology*, *Couples Coping with Stress* (coauthored with Kayser & Bodenmann), and *Caregiving in the Illness Context*. She serves as senior associate editor of the journal *Annals of Behavioral Medicine* and is on the editorial board of the journal *Health Psychology*. Dr. Revenson is a past president of the Division of Health Psychology of American Psychological Association. In 2013 she was awarded the Nathan Perry Award for Career Contributions to Health Psychology by the American Psychological Association.

Dr. Maria Teresa Ribeiro is Associate Professor of the Faculty of Psychology at the University of Lisbon where, besides teaching and publishing, she conducts research (at the Center of Research in Psychology at the University of Lisbon) and provides guidance on masters and Ph.D. theses in Clinical Psychology, Family Psychology, and Family Intervention.

Dr. Pagona Roussi is an associate professor in the School of Psychology of the Aristotle University of Thessaloniki in Greece. She received her Ph.D. in Organic Chemistry from Imperial College, London University and her Ph.D. in Clinical Psychology from Temple University. Using the Cognitive-Social Health Information Processing model as a theory-based framework, she has studied the concepts of flexibility in perceptions of control and coping and their relationship to distress, how individuals process information about cancer threats and risk-reduction options, as well as the impact of interventions on affective and behavioral outcomes. She has been a visiting professor at the Fox Chase Cancer Center/Temple Health. She has published about forty journal papers and chapters.

Dr. Petruţa P. Rusu is a lecturer at the Faculty of Educational Sciences, 'Ştefan cel Mare' University of Suceava, Romania. She completed her master and doctoral degrees in Couple and Family Psychology at the Al. I. Cuza University of Iaşi, Romania. Dr. Rusu was awarded a post-doctoral fellowship to conduct research at the Department of Clinical Psychology: Children/Adolescents & Couples/Families, University of Zurich, Switzerland, under the supervision of Professor Guy Bodenmann. Her research focuses on family issues in Romanian couples: relationship stress, dyadic coping, family financial strain, family religiosity, and partner's well-being.

Dr. Viola Sallay is a psychologist and Assistant Professor at the Institute of Mental Health, Semmelweis University in Budapest, Hungary. She received her Ph.D. in 2014. Her Ph.D. thesis discussed qualitative grounded theory research of emotional self-regulation processes in the family home. She works also as a family therapist.

Dr. Susan Sierau is a research associate at the Department of Child and Adolescent Psychiatry, Psychotherapy, and Psychosomatics at the University of Leipzig. She is an experienced researcher with particular interest in the topics of developmental psychopathology, partnerships, and family processes. Currently, Dr. Sierau is conducting a research project on pathways from early maltreatment to internalizing symptoms and disorders.

Rita Tóth-Vajna is a psychologist and Ph.D. student at the doctoral program of the Institute of Mental Health, Semmelweis University in Budapest, Hungary. Her doctoral research focuses on the relational dynamics of couples and the psychometric properties of the Couples Rorschach test.

Dr. Ana M. Vedes is a post-doctoral research fellow at the University Children's Hospital of Zurich, Department of Psychiatry and Psychosomatics. She received her Ph.D. in Family Psychology and Interventions by the Universities of Lisbon and Coimbra, in 2014. During her doctoral studies she was awarded a four-year Ph.D. fellowship by the Portuguese Foundation for Science and Technology and did an internship at the Department of Clinical Psychology, Children/Adolescents and Couples/Families, of the University of Zurich, under supervision of Prof. Dr. Guy Bodenmann. Her research focuses mainly on intra- and interpersonal mechanisms related with dyadic coping and their implications for interventions with committed individuals and couples; the role of we-ness and we-appraisals for close relationships and for families coping with different types of stressors. As a clinical psychologist she has experience in working with individuals, couples, and families, and is an Emotionally-Focused Therapist (EFT) trainee. In her practice, she bridges EFT with coping-oriented approaches.

Kelsey J. Walsh is currently a doctoral student of Counseling Psychology at Arizona State University. She is a Licensed Associate Counselor (LAC) in Arizona, and a National Certified Counselor (NCC). She has clinical experience working with diverse individuals, groups, and families across the lifespan, and has developed a focus of working with emerging adults. Her research interests include the influence of relationships on well-being, how individuals experience and cope with stress, and academic success in undergraduates, which also serves as her focus of teaching.

Feng Xu received his master's degree from Beijing Normal University with the research field of sports psychology and mental health. He is currently completing his doctoral studies under the direction of Dr. Guy Bodenmann at the University of Zurich. His research focuses on Chinese couples' relationship satisfaction under stressful circumstances and the impact of dyadic coping on couples' marital functioning. He is particularly interested in cross-cultural comparisons between Chinese and Western couples and among Chinese couples in different cultural contexts.

He has been involved in both cross-sectional and longitudinal studies. His affiliation also includes Guangdong Construction Vocational Technology Institute, China.

FOREWORD

Love—this desire or need we have to connect, to nurture, and to be nurtured—is powerful, and our perpetuation as a species demands that it be universal. So many of the uplifting experiences, which we have or learn about every day attest to these simple facts, and yet each day also brings us face to face with another simple fact: compassion, comfort, and nurturing are sometimes in short supply, even within the intimate relationships where we might expect it to be unusually strong and enduring. We cannot blame modern life entirely for the plight of our relationships, of course, yet neither can we dismiss the idea that our ability to connect and stay connected is affected by the many responsibilities, commitments, and demands, which we each face as we lead our lives and long for authenticity and purpose.

Couples Coping with Stress: A Cultural Perspective begins not just with the idea that stress can intrude into our relationships, but with the even better idea that stress and responses to stress can and should be conceived explicitly as a dyadic process—a team sport of sorts. This is a far better idea because it goes well beyond the common notion that communication is all that matters in relationships, and because it draws our attention to our relationships as dynamic systems, partly under our control, but often destabilized by all manner of stresses and strains that life sends our way. In this way, *Couples Coping with Stress* marks a critical moment in our scientific efforts to understand relationships, as it fully acknowledges that two otherwise identical relationships, situated in different circumstances, will grow to become markedly and perhaps irrevocably different.

If we take seriously the idea that circumstances matter to our relationships, then we cannot proceed by simply asserting this and administering a few questionnaires to show that we were right all along. We have to ask, how does this universal experience of love manifest itself in different cultural settings? To find out, we need to start thinking about all of the ways in which cultural circumstances differ and begin to wonder about exactly how those differences might operate to make relationships better and worse. And this is the second point on which *Couples Coping with Stress* excels, as it embeds intimate connection explicitly in a range of different cultural contexts. The complexity here is staggering—we are just beginning to learn about stress in relationships, much less about how stress and relationships are individually and jointly affected by culture— but the editors and authors of this book prove to be excellent guides. Thanks to their unusually fine set of chapters, the curious reader will learn a great deal not just about diverse cultures, and not just about how couples in different cultures enact mutual support, but about the very essence of love itself.

Thomas Bradbury
Los Angeles, California

FOREWORD

When couples form their relationships they commonly begin with a vision that being together will be a source of numerous rewards, whether those be meeting emotional needs or establishing a partnership in achieving instrumental goals such as a comfortable home and financial security. That's not to suggest that members of couples are routinely naïve about the fact that over the course of their life together they will face a variety of challenges and obstacles, but the amount of time that they spend thinking individually about how they will cope with the stressors they may encounter most likely is limited. Sooner or later, those challenges do occur, and as described so effectively by the chapter authors in *Couples Coping with Stress: A Cultural Perspective*, the ways in which a couple responds to them have major consequences for their individual physical and psychological well-being, as well as the quality of their relationship.

Researchers and clinicians have long recognized that some forms of coping with stressors have positive effects, whereas some other approaches can be ineffective at best or even harmful. However, until recently most attention has been paid to coping at the individual level, even though for decades couple and family therapists have conceptualized intimate relationships as social systems in which the members mutually influence each other. The ground breaking theoretical, empirical, and clinical work on dyadic coping reviewed in this volume finally takes our understanding of coping to a systemic level, and the findings clearly indicate the advantages of dyadic coping for individual and relational well-being. A major strength of the book's chapters is their demonstration of both common elements across diverse cultures and socio-political environments, and significant variation in how stressors are experienced, what factors determine how couples cope, and what consequences result from those efforts. The reader can compare across the chapters that each describes couples' experiences in a different country, with two complementary take-home messages. On the one hand, couples around the world universally face a range of stressors to which they must respond effectively in order to flourish, and whether a stressor initially affects one or both partners, there is great potential for unsettling 'spillover' into the relationship. On the other hand, culture shapes meanings, which members of couples attach to life experiences; for example, a family member's illness may be perceived as a distressing burden among members of one culture but be accepted as a reasonable challenge in another. For researchers, this poses a problem of how to be culturally sensitive in asking people about stressors and how acceptable they consider various ways of coping. For clinicians, it requires educating oneself about belief systems, values, and traditions in a culture before venturing to intervene to enhance couples' coping. The chapters in this book provide an excellent resource for such efforts. The book is unique in that the same Systemic-Transactional Model is applied across all chapters, guiding the review of literature on stressors and how couples cope with them, and the same measure of dyadic coping is used. The authors frequently are reporting the first studies of dyadic coping to be conducted in a country, and they provide a guide for the design and implementation of sound cross-cultural research. This is a wonderful model for culturally sensitive research. Similarly, each chapter has sections on implications for practice (e.g., the design of relationship education programs that will be appropriate for members of a particular culture) and implications for research. Thus, this is an important book. It provides an overview of cutting edge work on dyadic coping and the promise of enhancing partners' abilities to navigate life challenges together and increase their chances of achieving their initial dreams for their relationship.

Norman B. Epstein
College Park, Maryland

PREFACE

We live in a world where, unfortunately, couples and families are facing an increasing number of stressors every day. Understanding how couples can cope with the variety of stressors they face, in an attempt to mitigate any deleterious effects on individual and relational well-being, is of critical importance. Beginning in the 1990s, researchers began to focus increasingly on how partners' experience of stress affects their own and their partners' outcomes. From these theoretical contributions and research activities emerged the new field of *dyadic stress and coping*, and the *systemic transactional model of dyadic coping* (STM; Bodenmann, 1995).

For a long time, research, utilizing the STM to help understand how couples can cope with stress, has been conducted in several Western countries, specifically in Europe and the United States. Recently, there has been an increasing interest in studying stress and coping processes in other countries and cultural contexts. The goal of this book is to bring together the international research applying the STM approach to understand how couples cope with stress in various cultural contexts. To do this, we present research from fourteen geographical regions, each of them focusing on a specific cultural group of couples: American, Latino couples in the U.S., Swiss, Portuguese, German, Italian, Greek, Hungarian, Romanian, Pakistani, Chinese, Japanese, African, and Australian couples. Each of these fourteen chapters is authored by a scholar from a specific country and addresses the relevance, appropriateness, and use of dyadic coping in their specific culture supported by the conceptual and empirical literature. Additionally, each chapter provides a conceptual review from empirical studies that have been conducted on dyadic coping in this cultural context to be able to provide clinical and programmatic recommendations. Furthermore, we have included a chapter on the measurement of dyadic coping for future research on dyadic coping applying the STM model to other cultural applications.

This book is the first to bring together dyadic coping researchers from different countries, while integrating empirical knowledge accumulated in each country to support the discussion of cultural considerations. Given this, the content in this book is relevant and of interest to social scientists and mental health professionals alike, who wish to expand their knowledge on how couples cope with stress in a specific culture. Specifically, this book will serve as an important resource for researchers interested in dyadic coping as it will provide them with an understanding of the advances in dyadic coping in different countries, measurement issues in studying dyadic coping, the applicability of STM cross-culturally to study dyadic coping, and areas of study that need further examination. Additionally, the book will help mental health professionals working with couples expand their cultural competence to be able to work with couples with different cultural backgrounds. Furthermore, this book can be used as a reference book for those interested in couples' stress and coping processes and/or multicultural issues related to interpersonal processes. As such, this book would be appropriate for undergraduate or graduate courses in the social sciences related to the study of stress and coping, close relationships, and interpersonal processes across cultures.

ACKNOWLEDGMENTS

Editing a book that brings together scholars from different parts of the world with diverse cultural backgrounds has been an incredibly enriching and exciting experience. However, this work could never have been completed without the enthusiasm and openness to collaborate from each of the contributing authors. Unlike many other edited books, our book utilizes the same conceptual model throughout the different chapters and is consistent in the way the content is presented. This organizational consistency was achieved through an ongoing collaboration with all contributors to whom we are immensely grateful for their patience, flexibility, and willingness to cross cultural bridges to finish this book.

There are a few specific individuals whom we would like to acknowledge. We would like to thank Amy Wu and Brionne Porter, graduate students in the Marriage and Family Therapy Master's Program at Virginia Polytechnic Institute and State University, for her countless hours dedicated to administrative support and editing. With an international group of thirty-five authors and three editors, Amy's effort in checking not only format but also language across all chapters was simply invaluable. We would also like to thank Debra Riegert, Senior Editor at Routledge/Taylor & Francis, for all her help and guidance throughout this process. We would also like to thank the reviewers who provided input on our original book plan including Norman B. Epstein, University of Maryland, Carolyn E. Cutrona, Iowa State University, and one anonymous reviewer.

Lastly, and certainly not least, we would like to acknowledge all the participants across the world who made this research possible. We hope that the content in this volume and subsequent future directions will be enriching to their lives.

INTRODUCTION

Mariana K. Falconier, Ashley K. Randall,
and Guy Bodenmann

For decades theorists and practitioners focused on how individuals experience and respond to stress (e.g., Lazarus & Folkman, 1984), while limited attention was given to the effects of stress on intimate relationships and each partner's role in the coping process. However, in the 1990s researchers began to focus increasingly on stress and coping in the context of couple relationships, examining in particular the ways in which partners' stress affected one another, the effects of stress and individual coping strategies on intimate relationships, and partners' strategies to assist each other cope with stress. This new focus resulted in the emergence of a new research and clinical field known as *dyadic stress and coping* and the development of conceptual models such as Coyne and Smith's relationship focused coping model (RFCP; 1990), DeLongis and O'Brien's empathic coping model (ECM; 1991), Revenson's congruence coping model (CCM; 1994), and Bodenmann's systemic-transactional model (STM; 1995). Since the late 1990s, and particularly in the last ten years, the stress and dyadic coping field has grown significantly as evidenced by the number of research studies and publications as well as the organization of the bi-annual international conferences on dyadic coping research, one of which resulted in the first book on dyadic stress and coping: *Couples Coping with Stress: Emerging Perspectives on Dyadic Coping* (2005).

Despite some similarities across the various dyadic coping approaches, Bodenmann's STM model is perhaps the most comprehensive framework to understand stress and coping in couples for its inclusion not only of how one partner could assist or undermine the other partner's coping process, but also of how partners could cope conjointly and communicate about their stress to each other. Because of this, the STM and the Dyadic Coping Inventory (DCI; Bodenmann, 2000), the self-report questionnaire designed to measure dyadic coping, were soon adopted by researchers all around the world, expanding the STM approach beyond the Swiss frontiers where it had been developed. As of today STM research has been conducted in thirty-five countries and the DCI has been translated into twenty-four languages. Although many studies have been conducted based on the STM in Western countries (Europe, U.S.) there is increased interest in studying stress and coping processes in other countries and cultural contexts. Thus the main aim of this book is to give a synopsis of this emerging research and to reflect on specific aspects regarding dyadic coping in various cultures. The book is unique in presenting dyadic coping research conducted on all five continents.

Given the wide application of the STM framework, the goal of this book is to bring together the international research applying the STM approach to understand how couples cope with stress in various cultural contexts. In doing so, it becomes possible to appreciate the cultural variations in what couples experience as stressful, the extent to which partners rely on various dimensions on dyadic coping, and the role of dyadic coping in couples' relationship functioning across the world. In addition to making evident the role of cultural factors in dyadic coping, the book highlights the influence of the socio-political-economic contextual factors in stress and coping and the extent to which STM can be used to study dyadic coping and promote effective coping behaviors in relationship education programs or couple therapy.

The first chapter of this book presents an introduction to the STM approach by providing a very detailed description of the way in which the STM conceptualizes stress and coping processes in couples, the various factors affecting dyadic coping, and the different dyadic coping dimensions. The chapter also describes the evolution of STM from a model that was originally developed to explain the spillover effects of everyday stress on couples' functioning to a model that has been used to understand dyadic coping with severe health conditions and critical life events with the incorporation of the concept of 'we-stress' or 'we-disease.' The chapter also discusses applications of the dyadic coping in stress prevention and clinical interventions for couples derived from STM concepts such as the Couples Coping Enhancement Training (CCET; Bodenmann & Shantinath, 2004) and the Coping-Oriented Couple Therapy (COCT; Bodenmann, 2010). The second chapter discusses the role of cultural factors in the STM approach and presents value orientations that may influence stress and coping in couples, which include individualism versus collectivism, low- versus high-context communication, and traditional versus non-traditional couples' functioning. The focus of this chapter is to highlight the potential role of culture in the stress and coping processes of couples and serves as a framework for the various cultural chapters that follow in the book. The third chapter focuses on the measurement of dyadic coping, with particular attention to the DCI, the most widely used measure of dyadic coping (Falconier, Jackson, Hilpert, & Bodenmann, 2015). In addition to describing the DCI and how it has been used cross-culturally, this chapter also introduces other measurements of dyadic coping and provides guidelines for assessing dyadic coping in a culturally sensitive way.

After these three introductory chapters on STM, the role of culture in STM, and the measurement of dyadic coping, the book includes fourteen chapters, each of them focusing on a specific cultural group of couples: American, Latino couples in the U.S., Swiss, Portuguese, German, Italian, Greek, Hungarian, Romanian, Pakistani, Chinese, Japanese, African, and Australian. The goal of each of these chapters is to present a synthesis of the research that has been conducted using the STM in the specific cultural group, while highlighting the cultural character-istics that may explain some of the research findings. Additionally, the authors present all of the existing interventions that have been derived from the STM approach and used with these diverse populations and provide clinical and research recommendations. Despite the similar organizational structure, there are wide variations across these fourteen chapters due not only to cultural differences, but also to the different directions and level of development of the stress and dyadic coping research conducted in each geographic region. It is important to note that the authors of these chapters have been invited to contribute to this book because they are the scholars who have conducted STM research with those populations, and also share the cultural background of the populations they write about.

The book concludes with two chapters, the first written by Karen Kayser and Tracey Revenson, two pioneers in the field of dyadic stress and coping. In their chapter, they provide guidelines for integrating culture into research and practice related to dyadic stress and coping. Their guidelines regarding the key cultural dimensions, which should be included in research and practice reflect the integration of the knowledge gained from the STM research around the world and presented in the fourteen cultural chapters of this book as well as from their own cross-cultural research on dyadic coping in couples dealing with breast cancer. The last chapter of the book is meant to be a final reflection, which summarizes the role of STM in research and dyadic coping in culturally diverse populations and invites scholars and practitioners to continue to work on applying the STM to various stressors and populations.

Even though the cultural chapters can be read in any order, we recommend reading the first three chapters before reading any other chapter in the book. Similarly, the last two chapters should be read after reading all of the cultural chapters so that the integration that these last two chapters propose can be understood.

References

Bodenmann, G. (1995). A systemic-transactional conceptualization of stress and coping in couples. *Swiss Journal of Psychology, 54*(1), 34–49.

Bodenmann, G. (2000). *Stress und Coping bei Paaren.* Göttingen: Hogrefe.

Bodenmann, G. (2010). New themes in couple therapy: The role of stress, coping, and social support. In D. H. Baucom, K. Hahlweg, & M. Grawe-Gerber (Eds.), *Enhancing couples: The shape of couple therapy to come* (pp. 142–156). Cambridge: Hogrefe.

Bodenmann, G., & Shantinath, S. D. (2004). The Couples Coping Enhancement Training (CCET): A new approach to prevention of marital distress based upon stress and coping. *Family Relations, 53*(5), 477–484.

Coyne, J. C., & Smith, D. A. (1991). Couples coping with a myocardial infarction: A contextual perspective on wives' distress. *Journal of Personality and Social Psychology, 61*(3), 404–412.

DeLongis, A., & O'Brien, T. (1990). An interpersonal framework for stress and coping: An application to the families of Alzheimer's patients. In M. A. P. Stephens, J. H. Crowther, S. E. Hobfoll, & D. L. Tennenbaum (Eds.), *Stress and coping in later-life families* (pp. 221–239). New York: Hemisphere Publishing Corp.

Falconier, M. K., Jackson, J., Hilpert, J., & Bodenmann, G. (2015). Dyadic coping and relationship satisfaction: A meta-analysis. *Clinical Psychology Review, 42*, 28–46.

Lazarus, R. S., & Folkman, S. (1984). *Stress, appraisal, and coping.* New York: Springer.

Revenson, T. A. (1994). Social support and marital coping with chronic illness. *Annals of Behavioral Medicine, 16*(2), 122–130.

Revenson, T. A., Kayser, K., & Bodenmann, G. (Eds.) (2005). *Couples coping with stress: Emerging perspectives on dyadic coping.* Washington DC: American Psychological Association.

1

COPING IN COUPLES

The Systemic Transactional Model (STM)

Guy Bodenmann, Ashley K. Randall, and Mariana K. Falconier

Origin of the Systemic Transactional Model (STM)

Individual-Oriented Stress and Coping Theories

Coping with stress has historically been viewed as an individual phenomenon. Specifically, psychodynamic theories focusing on the regulation of intrapsychic conflicts (e.g., Haan, 1977), stimulus-oriented approaches focusing on the impact of critical life events on humans (e.g., Dohrenwend & Dohrenwend, 1974), as well as reaction-oriented theories (e.g., Selye, 1974) emphasizing endocrine and physiological reactions of individuals under stress were typically individual-oriented. In addition to these theories, Lazarus and Folkman's (1984) prominent and internationally recognized *transactional theory of stress* is also in line with the individualistic conceptualization of stress and coping. In this theory, personal appraisals of characteristics of the situation (i.e., significance for the person, characteristics of the situation such as representing threat, loss, damage, challenge) and one's own available resources to respond to these demands are evaluated by the individual. The individual's appraisals of the situation will determine a) whether this situation is perceived as stressful (or not), and b) the intensity of the stress experienced. Once the event has been appraised, the individual reacts both physiologically and psychologically (i.e., stress emotions), and engages in stress-related behavior (e.g., approach or avoidance behavior). Therefore, the experience of stress is a result of the transaction between the individual and his/her environment (Lazarus & Folkman, 1984). Although this approach ascertains that, for example, dysfunctional individual coping may have detrimental effects on the social environment, and thus coping is viewed as embedded in social context, stress and coping are still conceptualized as an individual affair.

From Individual to Dyadic View of Stress and Coping

Starting in the early 1990s, theoretical approaches aimed to expand traditional individual approaches to stress and coping to specifically understand stress and coping as a systemic issue. Specifically, the *Systemic Transactional Model* (STM) by Bodenmann (1995) as well as other approaches in the early 1990s (relationship-focused coping by Coyne & Smith, 1991; empathic coping model by DeLongis & O'Brien 1990; congruence approach by Revenson, 1994) or the 2000s (developmental contextual model of dyadic coping, Berg & Upchurch, 2007; relational-cultural coping model by Kayser, Watson, & Andrade, 2007) are the first known theories that started to perceive stress and coping as a social process rooted in close relationships, with a specific focus on the romantic partner. The assumption of interdependence between romantic partners (Kelley et al., 1983), which views partners as having a strong and frequent mutual influence on each other across multiple life domains, became a key feature of dyadic coping. Therefore, in the context of stress, one partner's experience of adversity is not limited to himself/herself, but affects the experience and well-being of the romantic partner as well. Folkman (2009) praised this extension of the original transactional theory by stating that 'dyadic coping is more than the sum of two individuals' coping responses' (p. 73). The assertion that one partner's stress and coping experiences are not independent of their partner's stress and coping represents a relational and interdependent process and is a cornerstone of modern dyadic coping concepts (Acitelli & Badr, 2005; Bodenmann, 1995, 1997, 2005; Kayser, 2005; Lyons, Mickelson, Sullivan, & Coyne, 1998; Revenson, 1994, 2003; Revenson & Lepore, 2012; Revenson, Kayser, & Bodenmann, 2005).

Different dyadic coping models have been proposed. One line of research emphasized *congruence or discrepancy* between the partners' coping efforts by analyzing the effects of similar versus different individual coping strategies (e.g., problem- versus emotion-focused coping) of the partners facing a stressful event (e.g., Revenson, 1994). Congruence or discrepancy in individual coping strategies such as problem-solving, rational thinking, seeking social support, escape into fantasy, distancing, and passive acceptance are analyzed on a dyadic level.

Coyne and Smith (1991) expanded upon Lazarus' transactional approach (Lazarus & Folkman, 1984) by considering partners' coping contribution to the other partner's well-being. Originally, this approach was developed in the context of couples dealing with one partner's severe health problems, where the ill partner's health-related stress was defined as a shared fate. Coping in this context represents a 'thoroughly dyadic affair' where a mutual exchange of taking and giving occurs. Coyne and Smith (1991) distinguished three forms of relationship-focused coping: (1) active engagement (e.g., involving the partner in discussions, inquiring how the partner feels, and instrumental or emotional engagement in active problem-solving), (2) protective buffering (e.g., providing emotional relief to the partner, withdrawing from problems, hiding concerns from the partner, denying worries, suppressing anger, and compromising), and (3) overprotectiveness (e.g., dominant, aggressive, or submissive strategies to avoid strong emotional involvement).

Along similar lines, DeLongis and O'Brien (1990) proposed the concept of empathic coping, which encompasses: a) taking the other's perspective, b) experiencing the other's feelings, c) adequately interpreting the feelings underlying the other's non-verbal communication, and d) expressing caring or understanding in a non-judgmental helpful way. A significant conceptual contribution of this approach is that coping extends beyond the goal of solving a specific individual problem and focuses on the benefits for the relationship of shared, responsive coping. This approach also identifies a set of highly destructive coping strategies (e.g., criticism, ignoring, confrontation, or minimizing the frequency of contacts), which predict relationship dissolution in highly dysfunctional couples.

Berg and Upchurch (2007) proposed a developmental contextual model of dyadic coping that is theoretically close to the systemic transactional model (STM; Bodenmann, 2005) regarding shared appraisals and common dyadic coping, but enlarges this model regarding the context of severe chronic disease. The model embeds the coping process in a developmental and historical perspective regarding the different stages of dealing with disease across the lifespan (young couples, middle-aged couples, late adulthood couples) and historical times. Berg and Upchurch (2007) suggest that dyadic coping may vary according to these factors, especially the stage of disease (anticipatory coping, coping with initial symptoms, coping with treatment, daily management), but also socio-cultural aspects (health-related beliefs, access to healthcare, perception of symptoms, role division, individualistic versus collectivistic orientation etc.). Dyadic coping is further shaped by gender, marital quality, illness ownership, and illness severity. Thus, a complex set of variables is considered in the prediction of dyadic coping in the context of chronic illness.

Systemic Transactional Model (STM) of Stress and Coping in Couples

The STM model (Bodenmann, 1995, 1997, 2005) is based upon these above mentioned assumptions (e.g., interdependence between partners' stress and coping processes) and postulates that one partner's daily stress experiences, his/her behavior under stress and well-being have a strong and frequent impact upon their partner's experiences in a mutual way (Kelley et al., 1983). Thus, stressors directly or indirectly can always affect both partners in a committed close relationship. As such, even if a situation concerns primarily one partner, his/her stress reactions and coping affect the other and turn into dyadic issues, representing the cross-over of stress and coping from one partner to the other.

According to STM, partners' well-being is strongly intertwined, and their happiness is dependent on one another. In this approach a romantic relationship is compared to a couple rowing on the lake. Their boat can only advance if both partners row synchronically and with the same strength; otherwise it turns around in a circle and does not make any progress in moving forward. Therefore, STM emphasizes the interdependence and mutuality between partners, meaning that the stress of one partner always also affects the other one, but also that the resources of one partner expand the resources of the other, creating new synergies. This is true with regard to stress from daily hassles (e.g., work stress) and more severe stressors (e.g., dealing with a chronic illness). For example, one partner's stress from his/her day at work, can negatively affect the other partner in the evening if the stressed partner was not able to successfully cope with the stress on his/her own (Randall & Bodenmann, 2009). Often the stressed partner comes home upset, withdrawn, or preoccupied, and this negative mood can spill over into the relationship causing the non-stressed partner to experience stress as well (Neff & Karney, 2007; Story & Bradbury, 2004; Westman & Vinokur, 1998). A similar stress spillover process can be observed if one partner has a severe illness (e.g., cancer, heart disease), has lost a beloved person, or has to care for an elderly parent.

Appraisal Processes in STM

The original individual-oriented transactional stress theory (Lazarus & Folkman, 1984) differentiated between two individual-oriented appraisals: (1) *primary appraisals*, which are defined as the evaluations of the significance of the situation for one's well-being, and (2) *secondary appraisals*, which are defined as the evaluation of the demands of the situation and one's resources to respond to these demands. Bodenmann (1995) expanded the concept of primary and secondary appraisals by including an interpersonal aspect, which focuses on different evaluations of both partner's independent appraisals as well as their joint appraisal.

Within the primary appraisals STM differentiates four forms: 1a-appraisal corresponds to the original primary appraisal by Lazarus and Folkman (1984) evaluating the significance of the situation and its profile for the individual (e.g. threat, loss, damage, challenge). 1b-appraisal means the evaluation of Partner B's appraisal by Partner A (and vice versa). In the 1c-appraisal, the partners evaluate whether the other may have recognized one's appraisal of his/her appraisal; while the 1d-appraisal consists of a comparison of one's own and the partner's appraisal examining potential congruence or discrepancy, resulting in a we-appraisal. In the secondary appraisals, STM proposes three different appraisals: 2a-appraisal means one's own evaluation of one's own resources in response to the situation's demands. 2b-appraisal stands for the partner's evaluation of the other's resources, and in the 2c-appraisal partners evaluate congruence or discrepancies in appraisals, resulting in we-appraisals regarding resources. These appraisals lead to individual, couple-related, or joint goals and finally result in individual, partner-oriented coping (supportive, delegated, negative dyadic coping), or common dyadic coping (see Figure 1.1). These different forms of dyadic coping will be described in more detail below.

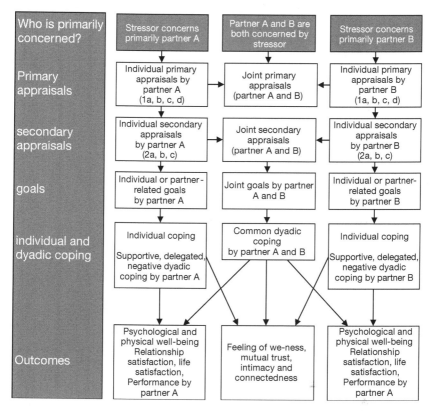

FIGURE 1.1 Appraisals and goals in the STM

Bodenmann, 2000

Among the different forms of appraisals, joint appraisals (we-stress) gained increased attention. Studies show that joint appraisals (i.e., appraisals by both partners) are significantly linked to dyadic coping and dyadic adjustment in couples in which one partner was diagnosed with cancer (e.g., Checton, Magsamen-Conrad, Venetis, & Greene 2014; Magsamen-Conrad, Checton, Venetis, & Greene, 2014). For example, in couples where one partner was suffering from a chronic disease, Checton and colleagues (2014) found that dyadic appraisals were positive predictors of partner's support, but also of patient's own health condition management. Manne, Siegel, Kashy, and Heckman (2014) further support these findings in women diagnosed with early-stage breast cancer. Shared awareness of cancer-specific relationship impact predicted higher levels of mutual self-disclosure and higher mutual responsiveness. These findings support the notion that we-appraisals are beneficial for patients and partners in their adjustment to illness, while discrepancies in appraisals are associated with higher depressive symptoms in partners (McCarthy & Lyons, 2015). As will be shown below, we-appraisals and we-disease are important aspects of STM.

Factors Affecting the Dyadic Coping Process

The types of coping partners may engage in depend on various factors including (a) the locus of stress origin (Partner A, Partner B, both Partner A and B, or external factors such as circumstances or chance), (b) the direct or indirect involvement of Partner A, Partner B, or both, (c) the general and situational resources of both partners, (d) their individual-oriented, partner-oriented, and couple-oriented goals, (e) their situational and general motivation (e.g., commitment for the relationship) as well as (f) aspects of timing such as whether the stressor affects both partners at the same time or wheather a partner experiences the stress subsequent to his/her partner. When external factors are responsible for stress occurrence, dyadic coping might be more likely (external attribution) than when one partner caused the stress by imprudence, incompetence, or inanity. However, dyadic coping is also likely when one partner caused the stress by his/her inadequate behavior (which would generally lower the likelihood of dyadic coping), but the other partner has partner-related goals ('I care about my partner independently of why he/she is in this situation') or couple-oriented goals ('I am only happy when my partner is happy as well, thus I have to engage in dyadic coping to smooth his/her stress'). In sum, cognitive, motivational, and situational processes are complex and dynamic and affect whether partners rely on dyadic coping and what forms of dyadic coping they choose.

The Process of Dyadic Coping

STM assumes that partners express their stress verbally and/or non-verbally and with implicit or explicit requests for assistance. These expressions of stress are then perceived and decoded by the responding partner within the primary and secondary appraisals described above (see Figure 1.1). He/she may either fail to respond, ignore or dismiss what his/her stressed partner has expressed, engage in his/her own stress communication or offer dyadic coping that reflects his/her own reaction to the partner, the relationship, and the stressor. The stressed partner may then provide additional details, feel better or worse, ask for advice, or propose a new plan for solving the problem, as the conversation unfolds. The partner's dyadic coping reactions may be positive or negative. Positive dyadic coping is thought to restore some degree of homeostasis for the individual and for the couple in the face of the challenge, whereas negative dyadic coping is an attempt to regulate stress by expressing negativity (see Figure 1.2).

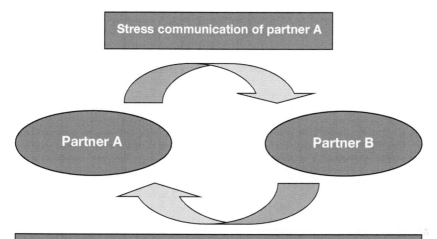

FIGURE 1.2 Stress Communication and Dyadic Coping

Bodenmann, 2000

Forms of Dyadic Coping

Dyadic coping includes partner-oriented behaviors (e.g., supportive or delegated dyadic coping) or couple-oriented behaviors (e.g., common dyadic coping), according to individual and dyadic appraisals and goals.

Dyadic coping can be positive or negative in nature, and can be further distinguished regarding its focus on emotion regulation (emotion-focused) or problem-solving (problem-focused) (see Figure 1.3). Emotion-focused supportive dyadic coping includes behaviors that intend to support the partner in regulating his/her emotions and to ease stress arousal. Problem-focused supportive dyadic coping includes support, which is judged accommodating for the partner to resolve the practical part of the stressor. Delegated dyadic coping includes taking over some of the partner's tasks in order to reduce his/her stress. Furthermore, three forms of negative dyadic coping are distinguished: hostile dyadic coping, ambivalent dyadic coping, and superficial dyadic coping (see Table 1.1). Negative dyadic coping is likely to occur when the supporting partner is stressed or she/he is not motivated or unable to support the stressed partner due to low relationship commitment, negative attributions about the partner (e.g., he/she caused the stress and is to blame for the bad outcome), poor personal emotional resources, negative

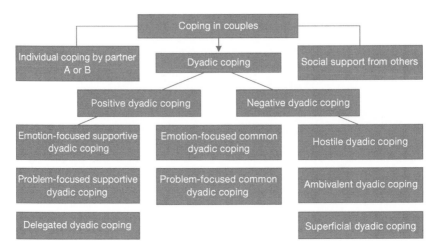

FIGURE 1.3 Forms of coping in couples

Bodenmann, 2000

mood, or difficult personality traits (e.g., lack of empathy, egoism, dominance, intolerance, etc.). Often negative dyadic coping is observed in situations where support is provided by necessity or coercion rather than voluntarily. Often it might be a sign of exhaustion after a long period of unidirectional support towards the other with no rewarding feedback and no balanced equilibrium between giving and receiving.

Apart from supportive, delegated, and negative dyadic coping, STM also includes common dyadic coping. Common dyadic coping means a symmetric or complementary involvement of both partners in a shared coping process. Common dyadic coping can be expressed by either talking together about the stress and its meaning for each partner, trying to reframe the stress together, searching jointly for more information, mutual efforts to calm down, praying together or sharing emotional or physical intimacy. STM predicts common dyadic coping to occur when the stressor affects both partners, typically at the same time, and when both partners perceive that their own personal resources may contribute to the coping process. The notion of common dyadic coping goes beyond classical partner support. Not only reciprocal consequences of each partner's stress, coping, and support are considered, but coping itself is defined as a real interdependent process involving both partners in more or less symmetric or complementary roles. Common dyadic coping is the result of the appraisal that the stressor concerns both partners, and is primarily caused by external conditions (external stress). This 'we' approach assumes that both partners jointly manage their shared stress and engage in dyadic coping to maintain the quality of their relationship or the well-being of both partners.

TABLE 1.1 Forms of dyadic coping

Form	Different expressions	Goals
Stress communication (stress-related self-disclosure)	Problem-oriented or matter-of-fact description of stress, verbal implicit or explicit emotion-focused stress communication	Seeking for partner's attention and interest in one's stress experience, asking for concrete support in problem-solving or emotion regulation
Supportive dyadic coping (problem-oriented)	Helping the partner to seek for more information, helping the partner to resolve a practical problem by assisting him/her, searching for practical solutions with the partner, giving the partner helpful advices	Reduction of problem-oriented stress by resolving the concrete problem in assisting the partner's own efforts
Supportive dyadic coping (emotion-oriented)	Empathy, understanding, showing solidarity with the partner, helping the partner to reframe the situation, helping the partner to calm down, helping the partner to believe in him/herself, physical tenderness (neck massage, holding)	Reduction of emotional stress arousal and bad mood in the partner in assisting the partner's own efforts
Delegated dyadic coping	Taking over tasks and duties that normally the partner does in order to reduce his/her burden	Reduction of stress arousal and bad mood by relieving the partner
Common dyadic coping (problem-oriented)	Joint search for information, joint search for solutions of the problem, mutual engagement in problem-solving	Solution of a practical problem that concerns both partners
Common dyadic coping (emotion-oriented)	Joint relaxation, joint solidarity, joint reframing of the situation, joint spiritual coping, mutual self-disclosure and sharing negative emotions, mutual tenderness (massages, physical contact)	Sharing negative emotions in an attempt to regulate them jointly

continued . . .

TABLE 1.1 Continued

Form	Different expressions	Goals
Negative dyadic coping (hostile)	Expressing reluctance to help, blaming the partner for creating the stress, criticizing how the partner has responded to the stress, ridicularizing the partner's stress, expression of disparagement, distancing, mocking, sarcasm, open disinterest, or minimizing the seriousness of the partner's stress	Attempt to minimize or avoid future support provision
Negative dyadic coping (ambivalent)	Providing support to the partner but in an unwilling and unmotivated way, making the partner feel that provision of support is a burden for the partner	Goal to support the partner but with low own energy and limited own resources
Negative dyadic coping (superficial)	Support is provided in a insincere way, the partner provides support but with no motivation, no authentic empathy, and no real understanding (asking questions about the partner's feelings without listening or support that lacks empathy and real commitment)	Provision of support without personal implication, interest in calming the partner down for having one's own peace.

Functions of Dyadic Coping

Dyadic coping has two main functions, a stress-related and a relationship-related function (Bodenmann, 2005). The stress-related function is to reduce the stress, which affects primarily one partner and spills over to the other partner or, which affects both partners at the same time (we-stress). This aspect is closely related to maintaining or restoring the general well-being of both partners. Dyadic coping becomes relevant if individual coping was not successful in reducing one's negative emotions or in solving the problem. The fact that dyadic coping fosters the feeling of 'we-ness' among partners, their mutual trust and intimacy, and strengthens partners' mutual attachment and commitment may, however, be the most important function (Cutrona, 1996).

Expansion of STM

STM was initially developed in the context of everyday stress (see also Chapter 5). One of its aims was to predict how couples cope together when facing daily hassles, and under which conditions couples engage, in which concrete form of coping when extra-dyadic stress spills over to the dyad. Thus, in the beginning, most studies assessed dyadic coping in community samples examining how couples cope together and what this means for their relationship functioning or well-being (Bodenmann, 2005). The initial model was then adapted and enlarged in the context of chronic illness in the contextual model of dyadic coping (Berg & Upchurch, 2007) and the 'we-disease' approach by Kayser and colleagues (2007). We-disease means that both partners consider the disease of one as a problem of both, a stress that affects both, and requires coping contributions from both.

To date, the STM has been expanded upon and applied to a variety of other contexts. First, within the different forms of dyadic coping, common dyadic coping received increased attention as this form of dyadic coping is uniquely considered in STM, except from the developmental-contextual model by Berg and Upchurch (2007), where collaborative coping plays an important role as well. Second, STM has been adapted to couples coping with severe stressors such as critical life events (e.g., death of a child; Bergstraesser, Inglin, Hornung, & Landolt, 2014) or partner's severe health conditions (e.g., cancer; Badr, Carmack, Kashy, Cristofanilli, & Revenson, 2010; Kayser et al., 2007; Regan et al., 2014; chronic obstructive pulmonary disease; Meier, Bodenmann, Mörgeli, & Jenewein, 2011). Third, while many studies addressed the role of dyadic coping for relationship functioning (e.g., Bodenmann, Meuwly, & Kayser, 2011; Falconier, Jackson, Hilpert, & Bodenmann, 2015; Herzberg, 2013; Merz, Meuwly, Randall, & Bodenmann, 2014; Papp & Witt, 2010; Randall, Hilpert, Jiménez-Arista, Walsh, & Bodenmann, 2015) or well-being (e.g., Bodenmann et al., 2011; Falconier, Nussbeck, Bodenmann, Schneider, & Bradbury, 2015), most recent studies focus on mediating variables within the dyadic coping process, such as motivational aspects like communal goals (Koranyi, Hilpert, Langner, Job, & Bodenmann, 2014), approach-avoidance goals (Kuster et al., 2014), or the assumption that dyadic coping increases the feeling of 'we-ness' (Vedes, Bodenmann, Nussbeck, Randall, & Lind, 2014).

Common Dyadic Coping and We-Stress or We-Disease

The concept of 'we-stress' (Bodenmann, 1995; Lyons et al., 1998) is originally inherent in the STM, while 'we-disease' is an expansion of the model in the context of severe illness (Badr et al., 2010; Kayser et al., 2007). It emphasizes a relational dimension of illness and offers a new perspective on support and coping processes in dyads dealing with severe stressful events. In the concept of 'we-stress' or 'we-disease' couples are viewed as facing daily hassles or severe life stressors as shared 'we-events' and 'we-experiences' rather than as individual problems of one partner requiring support from the other. Apart from stressors affecting both partners similarly (e.g., birth of a child, quarrels with neighbors, financial strain), the notion of 'we-stress' or 'we-disease' assumes that common dyadic coping is likely to occur in situations that primarily concern one partner (disease) but has a serious impact on the other as well.

Thus, STM has evolved from a concept describing couples' coping with daily hassles (Bodenmann, 1995) to a broad theoretical framework for understanding couples' management of critical life events (Kayser et al., 2007). Based on this expansion, the STM has important implications for clinicians' understanding of disorders and therapeutic interventions. While currently a patient's partner is usually involved only sporadically in the therapeutic process, and typically is thought of as supporting the ill partner in psycho-educational programs (i.e., supportive dyadic coping, delegated dyadic coping), the extension of STM suggests that the therapist should not only involve the patient's partner in providing support to the patient, but the therapist should invite both partners to engage in common dyadic coping, as both are suffering from the stressor (i.e., the illness). STM also suggests that both partners have resources to deal jointly with the disease or mental illness (Bodenmann & Randall, 2013) and that their goal must be to jointly overcome the situation ('we-disease'). This approach has already shown to be beneficial in the context of couples where one partner had been diagnosed with severe depression (Bodenmann et al., 2008) as well as in the context of breast cancer where common dyadic coping revealed to be more effective than supportive or delegated dyadic coping (Rottmann et al., 2015).

This new focus of STM means that the model has to be adapted in the context of severe stressors regarding common dyadic coping, eventually requiring more detailed categories of common dyadic coping according to the stage of the illness (Berg & Upchurch, 2007), contextual factors (e.g., family situation with or without children, general life situation, stage of the close relationship, etc.), and perception congruence (e.g., Iafrate, Bertoni, Margola, Cigoli, & Acitelli, 2012; Donato et al., 2014) as well as regarding common dyadic coping (e.g., fighting together for overcoming the disease, finding together a conciliatory conclusion of the life one shared together in the case of terminal illness, etc.).

Intercultural Aspects in STM

The original STM did not explicitly consider cultural aspects as a focal point in the conceptualization of stress and coping. Rather, the model was assumed to be applicable in all couples of Western societies, regardless of couples' age (which has been supported by the study by Landis, Peter-Wight, Martin, & Bodenmann, 2013), sexual orientation (which has been supported in a study by Meuwly, Feinstein, Davila, Nuñes, & Bodenmann, 2013; Randall, Totenhagen, Walsh, Adams, & Tao, submitted) or gender (Bodenmann, 2000). However, as STM received international attention and researchers all over the world started to investigate stress and coping processes based on STM, the question of intercultural application becomes relevant, as the Dyadic Coping Inventory (DCI; Bodenmann, 2008) has been translated into twenty-one languages (e.g., Chinese, Danish, Dutch, English, French, Italian, Japanese, German, Greek, Hebrew, Hindi, Hungarian, Indonesian, Persian, Polish, Portuguese, Romanian, Russian, Spanish, Thai, and Urdu). The short version of the DCI is even available in thirty-five languages, among others also several African languages (see Chapter 16). This intercultural application of STM potentially requires cultural adaptations or at least a cultural embedment of the model as shown in this volume and particularly in Chapter 2.

Conclusion

STM (Bodenmann, 2005) has played an important role in expanding a traditionally individual-oriented view of stress and coping (e.g., Lazarus & Folkman, 1984), into a more current view of stress and coping that takes into consideration the mutual interdependence between partners' experiences. The notion that one partner's stress always affects his/her partner, and thus forms of dyadic coping may add to individual coping efforts, is an important insight, which is also relevant for relationship researchers and therapists working with couples and families. The STM offers a theoretical framework for the investigation of these processes and clinical implications as it is evident in the notion of 'we-stress' or 'we-disease;' two concepts, which received increased attention in the last decade and may be considered as the most important outcomes of this approach.

While originally STM was developed in the context of everyday stress, and dyadic coping was viewed as an additional form of stress management in couples' coping with daily hassles, the model moved progressively into a theoretical framework for couples dealing with severe stressors such as chronic diseases, mental disorders, and severe critical life events. Especially in the context of chronic disease (e.g., cancer) or mental disorders (e.g., depression), STM represents an important expansion of the classical view of disorders where the partner with a diagnosis is the patient and the other, typically the healthy partner, who should support recovery processes in the patient. STM no longer defines roles of a patient and a partner, but views the patient and his/her partner as two members of a couple who are both affected by the stressor, both suffering and both needing to share their resources in order to effectively cope with the situation (Bodenmann & Randall, 2013). This implies that the partner should be involved in clinical treatments of physical illness as well as mental disorders as much as possible, in order to validate his/her suffering likewise but also in order to allow both partners to engage in common dyadic coping and to strengthen partners' synergies. Common dyadic coping revealed to be more effective than supportive dyadic coping (Rottmann et al., 2015), indicating that support processes in couples dealing with a severe health condition has to be reconsidered.

STM seems in general robust and widely applicable in different fields of research (e.g., psychological, medical, and social science), with different types of couples (e.g., young, middle aged, and elderly couples), as well as with heterosexual and same-sex couples. Dyadic coping has revealed to be a robust and significant predictor of relationship satisfaction in community couples (Falconier & Jackson et al., 2015) as well as in couples dealing with cancer (Traa, de Vries, Bodenmann, & den Oudsten, 2015). Repeatedly, dyadic coping has been found to be a significant predictor of partners' well-being (Bodenmann et al., 2011; Falconier, Nussbeck et al., 2015).

Based on these empirical findings, and additional findings presented throughout this book, increasing dyadic coping skills may be an important area for future direction for those working with distressed couples or couples dealing with a chronic disease or psychological disorder. The Couples Coping Enhancement Training (CCET; Bodenmann & Shantinath, 2004) or the Coping-Oriented Couple Therapy (COCT; Bodenmann, 2010) are interventions that address these issues and strengthen couples' stress-related self-disclosure as well as their dyadic coping repertoire by means of the three-phase-method (for more information see Chapter 5). Several studies support the usefulness and effectiveness of this approach (see Chapter 5 for more information). Another program, TOGETHER (Falconier, 2015) addresses STM in an attempt to strengthen couples deal with financial strain. Thus, the STM seems fruitful within research context as well as clinical work.

References

Acitelli, L. K., & Badr, H. J. (2005). My illness or our illness? Attending to the relationship when one partner is ill. In T. A. Revenson, K. Kayser, & G. Bodenmann (Eds.) (2004), *Couples coping with stress: Emerging perspectives on dyadic coping* (pp. 121–136). Washington DC: American Psychological Association.

Badr, H., Carmack, C. L., Kashy, D. A., Cristofanilli, M., & Revenson, T. A. (2010). Dyadic coping in metastatic breast cancer. *Health Psychology, 29*(2), 169–180.

Berg, C. A., & Upchurch, R. (2007). A developmental-contextual model of couples coping with chronic illness across the adult life span. *Psychological Bulletin, 133*, 920–954.

Bergstraesser, E., Inglin, S., Hornung, R., & Landolt, M. A. (2015). Dyadic coping of parents after the death of a child. *Death Studies, 39*(3), 128–138.

Bodenmann, G. (1995). A systemic-transactional conceptualization of stress and coping in couples. *Swiss Journal of Psychology/Schweizerische Zeitschrift Für Psychologie/Revue Suisse de Psychologie, 54*(1), 34–49.

Bodenmann, G. (1997). Dyadic coping: A systemic-transactional view of stress and coping among couples: Theory and empirical findings. *European Review of Applied Psychology, 47*, 137–141.

Bodenmann, G. (2000). *Stress und Coping bei Paaren*. Göttingen: Hogrefe.

Bodenmann, G. (2005). Dyadic coping and its significance for marital functioning. In T. A. Revenson, K. Kayser, & G. Bodenmann (Eds.) (2005), *Couples coping with stress: Emerging perspectives on dyadic coping* (pp. 33–49). Washington DC: American Psychological Association.

Bodenmann, G. (2008). Dyadisches Coping Inventar: Testmanual. [Dyadic Coping Inventory: Manual]. Bern, Switzerland: Huber.

Bodenmann, G. (2010). New themes in couple therapy: The role of stress, coping, and social support. In D. H. Baucom, K. Hahlweg, & M. Grawe-Gerber (Eds.), *Enhancing couples: The shape of couple therapy to come* (pp. 142–156). Cambridge: Hogrefe.

Bodenmann, G., & Shantinath, S. D. (2004). The Couples Coping Enhancement Training (CCET): A new approach to prevention of marital distress based upon stress and coping. *Family Relations, 53*(5), 477–484.

Bodenmann, G., & Randall, A. K. (2013). Close relationships in psychiatric disorders, *Current Opinion in Psychiatry, 26*(5), 464–467.

Bodenmann, G., Meuwly, N., & Kayser, K. (2011). Two conceptualizations of dyadic coping and their potential for predicting relationship quality and individual well-being: A comparison. *European Psychologist, 16*(4), 255–266.

Bodenmann, G., Plancherel, B., Beach, S. R. H., Widmer, K., Gabriel, B., Meuwly, N., . . . Schramm, E. (2008). Effects of coping-oriented couples therapy on depression: A randomized clinical trial. *Journal of Consulting and Clinical Psychology, 76*, 944–954.

Checton, M. G., Magsamen-Conrad, K., Venetis, M. K., & Greene, K. (2014). A dyadic approach: Applying a developmental-conceptual model to couples coping with chronic illness. *Health Education & Behavior, 42*(2), 257–267.

Coyne, J. C., & Smith, D. A. (1991). Couples coping with a myocardial infarction: A contextual perspective on wives' distress. *Journal of Personality and Social Psychology, 61*(3), 404–412.

Cutrona, C. E. (1996). *Social support in couples: Marriage as a resource in times of stress*. Thousand Oaks: Sage Publications.

DeLongis, A., & O'Brien, T. (1990). An interpersonal framework for stress and coping: An application to the families of Alzheimer's patients. In M. A. P. Stephens, J. H. Crowther, S. E. Hobfoll, & D. L. Tennenbaum (Eds.), *Stress and coping in later-life families* (pp. 221–239). New York: Hemisphere Publishing Corp.

Dohrenwend, B. S., & Dohrenwend, B. P. (Eds.). (1974). *Stressful life events: Their nature and effects*. New York: Wiley.

Donato, S., Parise, M., Iafrate, R., Bertoni, A., Finkenauer, C., & Bodenmann, G. (2014). Dyadic coping responses and partners' perceptions for couple satisfaction: An actor-partner interdependence analysis. *Journal of Social and Personal Relationships, 32*(5), 580–600.

Falconier, M. K. (2015). TOGETHER—A couples' program to improve communication, coping, and financial management skills: Development and initial pilot-testing. *Journal of Marital and Family Therapy, 41*(2), 236–250.

Falconier, M. K., Jackson, J., Hilpert, J., & Bodenmann, G. (2015). Dyadic coping and relationship satisfaction: A meta-analysis. *Clinical Psychology Review, 42*, 28–46.

Falconier, M. K., Nussbeck, F., Bodenmann, G., Schneider, H., & Bradbury, T. (2015). Stress from daily hassles in couples: Its effects on intradyadic stress, relationship satisfaction, and physical and psychological well-being. *Journal of Marital and Family Therapy, 41*(2), 221–235.

Folkman, S. (2009). Commentary on the special section 'theory-based approaches to stress and coping': Questions, answers, issues, and next steps in stress and coping research. *European Psychologist, 14*(1), 72–77.

Haan, N. (1977). *Coping and defending: Process of self-environment organization.* New York: Academic Press.

Herzberg, P. Y. (2013). Coping in relationships: The interplay between individual and dyadic coping and their effects on relationship satisfaction. *Anxiety, Stress, & Coping, 26*(2), 136–153.

Iafrate, R., Bertoni, A., Margola, D., Cigoli, V., & Acitelli, L. K. (2012). The link between perceptual congruence and couple relationship satisfaction in dyadic coping. *European Psychologist, 17*(1), 73–82.

Kayser, K. (2005). Enhancing dyadic coping during a time of crisis: A theory-based intervention with breast cancer patients and their partners. In T. A. Revenson, K. Kayser, & G. Bodenmann (Eds.) (2005), *Couples coping with stress: Emerging perspectives on dyadic coping* (pp. 175–194). Washington DC: American Psychological Association.

Kayser, K., Watson, L. E., & Andrade, J. T. (2007). Cancer as a 'we-disease': Examining the process of coping from a relational perspective. *Families, Systems, & Health, 25*(4), 404–418.

Kelley, H. H., Berscheid, E., Christensen, A., Harvey, J. H., Huston, T. L., Levinger, G., . . . Peterson, D. R. (Eds.). (1983). *Close relationships.* New York: W. H. Freeman.

Koranyi, N., Hilpert, P., Langner, O., Job, V., & Bodenmann, G. (2014). The mechanics of dyadic coping: Increased preferences for communal goals in response to a stressed intimate partner. Manuscript submitted for publication.

Kuster, M., Backes, S., Brandstätter, V., Nussbeck, F., Bradbury, G., Sutter-Stickel, D., & Bodenmann, G. (2014). *Approach-avoidance motivation and stress, communication of stress, and dyadic coping in couples.* Manuscript submitted for publication.

Landis, M., Peter-Wight, M., Martin, M., & Bodenmann, G. (2013). Dyadic coping and marital satisfaction of older spouses in long-term marriage. *GeroPsych: The Journal of Gerontopsychology and Geriatric Psychiatry, 26*(1), 39–47.

Lazarus, R. S., & Folkman, S. (1984). *Stress, appraisal, and coping.* New York: Springer.

Lyons, R. F., Mickelson, K. D., Sullivan, M. J. L., & Coyne, J. C. (1998). Coping as a communal process. *Journal of Social and Personal Relationships, 15*(5), 579–605.

McCarthy, M. J., & Lyons, K. S. (2015). Incongruence between stroke survivor and spouse perceptions of survivor functioning and effects on spouse mental health: A mixed-methods pilot study. *Aging & Mental Health, 46*(1), 46–54.

Magsamen-Conrad, K., Checton, M. G., Venetis, M. K., & Greene, K. (2014). Communication efficacy and couples' cancer management: Applying a dyadic appraisal model. *Communication Monographs*, 1–22.

Manne, S. L., Siegel, S., Kashy, D., & Heckman, C. J. (2014). Cancer-specific relationship awareness, relationship communication, and intimacy among couples coping with early-stage breast cancer. *Journal of Social and Personal Relationships, 31*, 314–334.

Meier, C., Bodenmann, G., Mörgeli, H., & Jenewein, J. (2011). Dyadic coping, quality of life, and psychological distress among chronic obstructive pulmonary disease patients and their partners. *International Journal of Chronic Obstructive Pulmonary Disease*, 583.

Merz, C. A., Meuwly, N., Randall, A. K., & Bodenmann, G. (2014). Engaging in dyadic coping: Buffering the impact of everyday stress on prospective relationship satisfaction. *Family Science, 5*(1), 30–37.

Meuwly, N., Feinstein, B. A., Davila, J., Nuñez, D. G., & Bodenmann, G. (2013). Relationship quality among Swiss women in opposite-sex versus same-sex romantic relationships. *Swiss Journal of Psychology, 72*(4), 229–233.

Neff, L. A., & Karney, B. R. (2007). Stress crossover in newlywed marriage: A longitudinal and dyadic perspective. *Journal of Marriage and Family, 69*(3), 594–607.

Papp, L. M., & Witt, N. L. (2010). Romantic partners' individual coping strategies and dyadic coping: Implications for relationship functioning. *Journal of Family Psychology, 24*(5), 551–559.

Randall, A. K., & Bodenmann, G. (2009). The role of stress on close relationships and marital satisfaction. *Clinical Psychology Review, 29*(2), 105–115.

Randall, A. K., Hilpert, P., Jiménez-Arista, L. E., Walsh, K. J., & Bodenmann, G. (2015). Dyadic coping in the U.S.: Psychometric properties and validity for use of the English version of the Dyadic Coping Inventory. *Current Psychology*. Advanced online publication.

Randall, A. K., Totenhagen, C. J., Walsh, K. J., Adams, C. B., & Tao, C. (submitted). Coping with gay-related stress: Effects of supportive dyadic coping on anxiety in female same-sex couples. *Journal of Lesbian Studies*.

Regan, T. W., Lambert, S. D., Kelly, B., McElduff, P., Girgis, A., Kayser, K., & Turner, J. (2014). Cross-sectional relationships between dyadic coping and anxiety, depression, and relationship satisfaction for patients with prostate cancer and their spouses. *Patient Education and Counseling, 96*(1), 120–127.

Revenson, T. A. (1994). Social support and marital coping with chronic illness. *Annals of Behavioral Medicine, 16*(2), 122–130.

Revenson, T. A. (2003). Scenes from a marriage: Examining support, coping, and gender within the context of chronic illness. In J. Suls & K. A. Wallston (Eds.), *Social psychological foundations of health and illness* (pp. 530–559). Malden: Blackwell.

Revenson, T. A., & Lepore, S. J. (2012). Coping in social context. In A. Baum, T. A. Revenson, & J. E. Singer (Eds.), *Handbook of health psychology* (2nd ed, pp. 193–217). New York: Psychology Press.

Revenson, T. A., Kayser, K., & Bodenmann, G. (Eds.) (2005). *Couples coping with stress: Emerging perspectives on dyadic coping*. Washington DC: American Psychological Association.

Rottmann, N., Hansen, D. G., Larsen, P. V., Nicolaisen, A., Flyger, H., Johansen, C., & Hagedoorn, M. (2015). Dyadic coping within couples dealing with breast cancer: A longitudinal, population-based study. *Health Psychology, 34*, 486–495.

Selye, H. (1974). *Stress Sans Détresse*. Montréal: La Presse.

Story, L. B., & Bradbury, T. N. (2004). Understanding marriage and stress: Essential questions and challenges. *Clinical Psychology Review, 23*(8), 1139–1162.

Traa, M. J., de Vries, J., Bodenmann, G., & den Oudsten, B. L. (2015). Dyadic coping and relationship functioning in couples coping with cancer: A systematic review. *British Journal of Health Psychology, 20*(1), 85–114.

Vedes, A., Bodenmann, G., Nussbeck, F. W., Randall, A., & Lind, W. (2014). *The role of we-ness in mediating the association between dyadic coping and relationship satisfaction.* Manuscript submitted for publication.

Westman, M., & Vinokur, A. (1998). Unraveling the relationship of distress levels within couples: Common stressors, emphatic reactions, or crossover via social interactions? *Human Relations, 51,* 137–156.

2

CULTURAL CONSIDERATIONS IN UNDERSTANDING DYADIC COPING ACROSS CULTURES

Mariana K. Falconier, Ashley K. Randall, and Guy Bodenmann

The Importance of the Cultural Context

In the broadest sense, culture refers to a set of worldviews, beliefs, values, practices, and traditions that are shared by a group of people. Culture manifests in different ways, from observable artefacts (e.g., dress code and art) to values and assumptions regarding the nature of reality, time, space, and human nature, activity, and relationships (Schein, 1984). Individuals do not only co-construct cultural contexts but they are also affected by them. As such, aspects of culture are internalized by individuals, shaping their thoughts, feelings, behaviors, and worldviews (Ho, 1995). Although the smallest groups (e.g., a couple or a family) can develop their own 'culture,' this term is mostly associated with particular ethnic groups (Wong, Wong, & Scott, 2006). Ethnic groups are, in many cases, associated with particular nations; as such, we may refer to the 'Portuguese' culture or the 'Romanian' culture. Nonetheless, those cultures can also be grouped together forming a larger cultural group, mainly due to their common cultural characteristics. This is the case when we refer to continental and hemispheric groupings such as the 'Asian' culture, the 'Latino' culture, the 'European' culture, the 'African' culture or the 'Eastern' and 'Western' cultures. Despite the fact that individuals may belong to various cultural groups (e.g., work, religion, socio-economic class, etc.), this book will address culture as defined by the association with a particular ethnic group (e.g., Portuguese couples).

Much debate has surrounded the value, use, and definition of the term culture (Spencer-Oatey, 2012). For example, by 1952 Kroeber and Kluckhon had already found at least 164 different definitions of the term culture (as cited by Spencer-Oatey, 2012); however, the challenges involved in defining and using the term culture probably lie in the nature of the construct. To begin with, it is difficult, if not impossible, to fully describe all aspects of a specific culture and include all of its beliefs, values, and practices. It is in this regard that any description of a specific culture should always be considered incomplete as it will inevitably leave out some aspect of consideration. Second, even if we were able to fully describe a culture, cultures are fluid and dynamic (Wong, Wong, & Scott, 2006); they are socially constructed and transmitted through the family and the community, resulting in continuous change (Wong et al., 2006). In fact, in today's world in which the Internet is quickly opening windows into other cultures and other ways of living and viewing the world, cultural transformations are occurring at a much more rapid speed than before. Third, cultural descriptions often create a perception of homogeneity, which may hide important within-group differences. For example, Latinos are often described as a collective group mostly because they speak Spanish and share many common worldviews and traditions coming from their indigenous people and their colonial ties to Spain. Nevertheless, significant variation does exist within this vast group depending on country of origin, socio-economic status, educational level, and religious beliefs among other characteristics (Falicov, 2014). Lastly, and most importantly, one of the greatest challenges in describing cultures is the risk of perpetuating stereotypes that may be no longer true or representative of the whole ethnic group and that can reinforce prejudices and discrimination (McGoldrick, Giordano, & García-Preto, 2005). These challenges not only have contributed to the debate around definitions and uses of the word culture, but they also remind us of the inherent limitations of any description and discussion of cultures.

Cultural differences exist because of the physical environments, socio-economic contexts, historical events, religious beliefs, and historical philosophies that have shaped their development of different worldviews and traditions (Wong et al., 2006). These differences can be observed in differing attitudes, beliefs, expectations, ideals, norms, gender roles, stereotypes, and values (Triandis, 1988), which may play out particularly within the dynamics associated with close relationships. By ignoring cultural differences, we are ignoring contextual factors and assuming universal ways of living, working, eating, celebrating, partnering, parenting, communicating, loving, and dealing with death. As such, learning about different cultural characteristics has been recommended and encouraged to promote cultural sensitivity, and reduce prejudice (e.g., McGoldrick et al., 2005; Sue & Sue, 2008).

Considering that individuals internalize cultural worldviews, which shape their beliefs, assumptions, attributions, and expectations about themselves, others, and the world around them, we should expect variations across cultures in what individuals experience as stressful and how they deal with those stressful situations. Nonetheless, for several years, the stress and coping literature did not take into consideration cultural differences. Even though theoretical models of individual coping such as Lazarus and Folkman's (1984) transactional stress theory acknowledged the role of the environment, the field focused primarily on assessing the type and frequency of stressful events and coping strategies, without attending to contextual variables such as culture (Chun, Moos, & Cronkite, 2006). As the stress and coping field evolved, dyadic coping models, such as the relationship-focused coping model (RFCM; Coyne & Smith, 1991; O'Brien, DeLongis, Pomaki, Puterman, & Zwicker, 2009), the congruence-coping model (CCM; Revenson, 1994), the developmental-contextual coping model (DCCM; Berg & Upchurch, 2007), or the systemic-transactional model (STM; Bodenmann, 1997) attended to some aspects of the individual's immediate context by focusing on the romantic partner (for an overview of these models, see Chapter 1). Although most of these models acknowledged the cultural context as influencing the stress and coping process in couples (e.g., Berg & Upchurch, 2007; Falconier, 2013; Kayser, Watson, & Andrade, 2007), with the exception of a small qualitative study on couples coping with breast cancer, which incorporated both CCM and STM elements (Kayser, Cheung, Rao, Chan, Chan, & Lo, 2014), STM is the only dyadic coping conceptual model that has been applied and used in research in different cultures around the world. As of the time of writing this book STM research had been completed in at least thirty-five different cultures, placing STM in relation to other dyadic coping models in a unique position to understand cultural differences and similarities in stress and coping processes in couples. While this book presents the research and applications of STM in different cultural contexts, this chapter presents a conceptual framework to integrate culture into the STM approach by discussing the way in which cultural factors may affect stress perception and communication, supporting the partner, and/or coping conjointly. The chapter first describes some broad cultural differences, which have been identified in the cross-cultural and individual coping literature and then, discusses their potential role in the stress and coping process as conceptualized by STM. However, it is the final chapter in this book that provides guidelines on the specific cultural dimensions, which should be examined when studying dyadic stress and coping across cultures.

Overview of Cultural Differences

Before discussing the ways in which cultural factors may affect stress and coping processes in a couple's relationship, we will provide a general overview of cultural characteristics that are relevant for the discussion of similarities and differences in the experience of stress and coping responses across cultures, particularly in the context of couples' relationships. These characteristics include individualism versus collectivism, high- versus low-context communication, and couples' relationship functioning.

Individualism vs Collectivism

Individualism and collectivism have been used to refer to two different cultural orientations, which differ in their prioritization of the individual versus the group

(Hofstede, 1980; Triandis, 1988). These two orientations have provided a framework to understand most of the cultural differences observed in psychological phenomena, and are powerful organizing principles, which affect self-construal and the relationship between self and others (Marcus & Kitayama, 1991). Individualistic societies view the individual as the central unit of society and, therefore, prioritize the individual's needs over the group's needs (Chun et al., 2006; Triandis, 1988). As such, this cultural orientation values independence, autonomy, self-reliance, self-determination, and self-differentiation. As a result, individual goals, initiative, achievement, and competition are promoted. In individualistic contexts people should be able to choose with whom to form a relationship and terminate unsatisfactory relationships. By contrast collectivism prioritizes the group's needs and harmony over the individual's needs and happiness (Chun et al., 2006; Triandis, 1988). The individual's interdependence on others in the group is emphasized, and the individual views himself or herself as holding duties and responsibilities for the existence and well-being of the group (e.g., family, community, brotherhood, etc.). Relationships are viewed as involving specific obligations and duties established by groups such as families and communities rather than as a contract established by two individuals to meet their individual needs.

Several Western countries (e.g., United States, Germany, Switzerland, Australia, etc.) have been characterized as individualistic cultures whereas Eastern countries (e.g., China, Pakistan, Japan, Greece, or Romania, etc.) and several Latin American countries (e.g., Panama, Ecuador, Bolivia, Peru, Mexico, Cuba, etc.) have been described as collectivistic (Hofstede, Hofstede, & Minkov, 2010). Despite these common characterizations, many societies, which used to be described as collectivistic such as Japan or China, have been increasingly incorporating individualistic practices in the last decades (e.g., institutionalized care for the elderly) as a result of changing political and economic conditions and their closer contact with individualistic cultures (Lee & Mock, 2005; see Chapter 14 and 15 for more information).

Communication

Communication within cultures differs greatly based on the emphasis placed upon verbal communication and expression of emotions. Hall's (1976) distinction between low- and high-context communication has been used to identify different communication styles across cultures (Gudykunst et al., 1996). Low-context communication relies more on the explicit verbal code for the transmission and communication of messages with less dependence on contextual cues such as gestures or relational characteristics. Western European individualistic cultures tend to exhibit more low-context communication and they depend on explicit, verbal language to communicate and interpret thoughts and feelings (Kim, Pan, & Park, 1998; Shibusawa, 2005). Moreover, clinical interventions to cope with negative emotions such as sadness, anger, or resentment consist in naming and talking about these emotions (Thomas & McKay, 2015). In contrast to these overt, explicit verbal communications of thoughts and emotions, high-context communication depends more on the relational and contextual aspects of communication, which reduces the exchange and reliance on the verbal code for expression and interpretation of messages (Hall, 1976). High-context communication has been found more often in Eastern collectivistic cultures (Feng & Burleson, 2006; Shibusawa, 2005).

Couples' Relationships

Across cultures, striking differences also exist in couples' relationships with respect to their formation, functioning, termination, gender role orientation, communication, and relationship with the extended family. Variations in marriage formation range from individual, free choice of a partner for a love marriage (as seen in Western European cultures), to entering a marriage fully arranged by parents or grandparents (as seen in many Asian cultures) (Lee & Mock, 2005). Western European marriage may be viewed as the union of two individuals who have decided by themselves to enter a contractual relationship, which allows for an increasing legal recognition of same-sex marriages (Saez, 2011). Within Western European cultures, couples' relationships are partnerships where both partners communicate as equals and negotiate all aspects of their life together (e.g., Rabin, 2002). As such, both partners participate to different extents in all aspects of family life including household chores, raising children, or providing for the family, among others. In these relationships open, honest communication is encouraged and used to resolve conflict and differences so that growth can happen. In those contexts, the spousal subsystem is considered to be the most important one in the family structure and clear boundaries and differentiation from family of origin are encouraged and viewed as healthy.

Even though many Asian, African, and Latino marriages share similarities with Western European marriages, for many of these couples their marriage may also be regarded as the union of two families, which will keep close contact with the couple and will inform and guide their decisions (Lee & Mock, 2005; Ngazimbi, Daire, Soto, Carlson, & Munyon, 2013). Furthermore, in many Asian (e.g., Chinese, Pakistani) and African families (e.g., Kenyan) spouses are not expected to negotiate their roles but rather to perform specific roles, which are either socially or family assigned according to gender (Kamya, 2005; Lee & Mock, 2005). In these cultures marriage is structured following a traditional gender role orientation in which the man should be the breadwinner and the woman is expected to take care of the household, the children, and the elderly (Hiew, Halford, & Liu, 2014; Kamya, 2005). In these families the primary relationship in the family is not the husband–wife relationship but the parent-child dyad (Lee & Mock, 2005) (for a further discussion of cultural variations in gender roles and family boundaries, see

Chapter 18). Consistent with these views in many Asian and African cultures same-sex marriages are not allowed as marriage is only accepted for heterosexual relationships (Saez, 2011).

Culture and Stress

From an STM perspective (Bodenmann, 1995; see Chapter 1 for more information), cultural contexts influence whether and to what extent situations are considered stressful, and whether the stressor is viewed as concerning only one partner (individual stressor) or both partners (common stressor). In the same way that personal and relational factors impact the experience of stress, within STM culture can be viewed as a contextual factor affecting all levels of appraisals made by partners regarding the kinds of demands posed by a situation (primary appraisal) and the resources available to deal with the situation (secondary appraisal).

As an illustration of the influence of culture in the primary and secondary appraisals of the stress experience in couples (see Chapter 1), let us first consider the differences between individualistic and collectivistic societies and how these differences may affect couples' appraisals of demands of caring for an elderly parent. In an individualistic environment, the demands associated with elderly care may be perceived as limiting independence and interfering with the achievement of individual goals (e.g., financial, social). In addition, there may be fewer resources available to deal with those demands in individualistic environments such as family and community support to share caring responsibilities and work policies may be less understanding of such demands. In this context the responsibility of caring for an elderly parent is more likely to be viewed as an individual stressor that concerns only the adult child. By contrast, in many collectivistic contexts caring for the elderly is culturally expected and viewed positively, as the younger generation's duty to 'give back' to the older generations who cared for them before (Zhan & Montgomery, 2003). The Confucian concept of filial piety, which is present in many Asian cultures (see Chapters 14 and 15 for more information), involves the duty to revere and respect one's parents (Hwang, 1999) and contributes to this expectation of children taking care of their elderly parents. In other words, by caring for their elderly parents the younger generations may feel that they are fulfilling their social and family roles. Due to this generational responsibility and value for interdependence, it is possible that couples living in collectivistic cultures may view caring for an elderly parent or family member as a joint responsibility, versus the sole responsibility of one partner. Couples in collectivistic cultures may also find family resources more readily accessible to meet the demands associated with such caring responsibilities, whereas access to social support in individualistic cultures (e.g., community, family, and friends) depends on the couple's level of social embedment. In short, individualistic and collectivistic cultural orientations may affect whether caring for an elderly parent is viewed as an individual or a common stressor and whether and to what extent the situation is experienced as stressful. The highlighted differences should serve as an example of the extent to which the role of culture can contribute to partners' perceiving a situation as stressful and as an individual or a dyadic matter.

Culture and Coping

Cultural factors may not only affect which situations and to what extent they are perceived as stressful, but also the way people cope with those circumstances. As Mortenson and colleagues (2009) have noted, '*how* people react to an upsetting event, experience and express emotion, and seek support may vary -perhaps substantially- across cultures' (p. 209). Therefore, it is plausible to think that culture affects all the variables that the STM of dyadic coping includes: communication of stress, providing support to one's partner, and coping jointly, all of which could be affected by cultural values and expectations.

Stress Communication

Considering cultural differences in communication (Hall, 1976), it is likely that communication between romantic partners, especially under times of distress, can be affected by the larger cultural context. Within cultures that are characterized as low-context cultures, such as American, Swiss, German, and Australian, partners tend to avoid 'mind-reading,' and stressed partners usually communicate verbally and explicitly to the other partner about their stress and need for support or help (Falconier & Esptein, 2011). Conversely, in high-context cultures, such as Chinese, Japanese, Pakistani, etc. partners may perhaps communicate their stress to their partners in non-verbal ways such as gestures, silence, physical discomfort, behaviors (Kim et al., 1998). High-context cultures depend on the ability of the non-stressed partner to observe non-verbal indicators of stress and the need for support, whereas in low-context communication cultures stress communication depends on the stressed partner's ability to communicate clearly about their experience of stress and the need for assistance.

In addition to differences in communication styles, cultures hold diverse attitudes regarding help seeking, which can also affect the stress communication process between the partners. Various studies indicate that individuals in collectivistic cultures are less likely to disclose a problem and seek support than people in individualistic cultures. Mortenson and colleagues (2009) found that European Americans viewed seeking support as a coping mechanism more favorably than Chinese. Two studies (Mojaverian & Kim, 2013; Taylor, Sherman, Kim, Jarcho, Tagaki, & Dunagan, 2004) reported that Asian and Asian American individuals are less likely than European Americans to seek social support for coping with stress. Interestingly, Asian and Asian Americans reported significantly higher levels of distress and cortisol levels after explicitly requesting support from close people, as compared to European Americans (Taylor et al., 2004). Taken together, these findings suggest that individuals who identify with collectivistic values may not feel comfortable with seeking support, which is understandable given the preference for not communicating one's own individual struggles in an attempt to maintain group harmony (Markus & Kitayama, 1991). As Yeh and colleagues (2005) have noted, 'forbearing one's problems in order to minimize or avoid interpersonal conflict is a common way in which members of collectivistic cultures may deal with problems' (p. 62). Therefore, if in collectivistic cultures disclosing a problem and seeking help may be viewed as affecting relationships negatively, it is also likely that partners refrain from communicating their stress to each other and from actively seeking support from each other for the sake of the relationship's harmony.

In marked contrast to this collective orientation, in individualistic-oriented cultures communicating stress and explicitly asking for help is acceptable as 'a person is encouraged to explicitly signal personal needs and actively draw on social relationships for meeting them' (Taylor et al., 2007, p. 832). Relationships serve personal, individual needs and can be terminated if those needs are not met. In that context partners will view their romantic relationship as a place where their need for support can be expressed and help can be sought.

Providing Support to One's Partner

Once a partner has communicated—either verbally or non-verbally—their stress to their partner, there are a number of ways their partner can respond (dyadic coping; Bodenmann, 1997), which can depend on their cultural context. For example, within individualistic-oriented cultures, a partner's support may follow after an explicit verbal communication of an experience of stress and of a request for support. In the collectivistic-oriented cultures, the non-stressed partner may volunteer help without any explicit verbalization of stress or request for assistance. It has been argued that in collectivistic cultures individuals may provide support more spontaneously without a request than in individualistic contexts (Mortenson et al., 2009) because receiving this unsolicited support 'may affirm the self as interdependent, as this support is freely given by the provider and may be interpreted as genuine care and concern for the recipient' (Mojaverian & Kim, 2013, p. 89).

Regardless of whether the partner's support is solicited or unsolicited, cultural factors also influence the type of support provided. Research on individual coping shows that individuals in collectivistic cultures tend to rely more on emotion-focused rather than on problem-focused coping strategies, while the opposite is true in individualistic cultures (for a review of studies see Chun et al., 2006). This difference in individual coping strategies between individualistic and collectivistic orientations has been attributed to differences in individuals' perceptions regarding their possibilities of changing environmental conditions (Aldwin, 2007; Lam & Zane, 2004). In individualistic cultures people aim at changing the external conditions and mastering the environment, which invites more action- and problem-oriented strategies (Lam & Zane, 2004). By contrast in collectivistic cultures, individuals are more fatalistic and focus more on coping strategies that seek to modify themselves instead of the environment, which would explain the use of emotion-focused coping or even cognitive avoidance strategies (Kuo, 2013). This line of research suggests that partners in couples with a collectivistic orientation may be more likely to provide emotion-focused than problem-focused supportive dyadic coping while the opposite may happen for couples with an individualistic orientation (K. K. Dion & K. L. Dion, 1993).

In addition to individualism and collectivism, gender role orientation is another factor that can influence the type of support provided by the partner. The more traditional the culture is in gender role orientation, the more likely that women will be viewed as responsible for the emotional aspects in the couple's relationship and the more the men will be regarded as responsible for instrumental tasks (see, for example, Chapters 5 and 13). Consequently, in cultures with a more traditional gender role orientation, women may tend to engage more frequently in emotional supportive dyadic coping whereas men may tend to engage in problem-focused dyadic coping. On the other hand, cultures with a more liberal gender role orientation may expect both partners to engage in either type of supportive dyadic coping (see for example Chapters 6 and 8).

Common Dyadic Coping

In addition to partners' individual coping responses, another strategy that the communication stress process may trigger in couples is the joint coping response, which STM refers to as *common dyadic coping* (see Chapter 1). Partners tend to engage in common dyadic coping when stressors affect both partners and/or when partners believe that they may both contribute to the coping process. Although no empirical evidence exists on whether couples in different cultures perceive the same stressor as individual or common to the couple, it is possible that partners in collectivistic environments are more likely to experience the challenges that have originated in the other partner (e.g., unemployment, illness) as their own and the stressor becomes a 'we' problem (Yeh et al., 2006), given the focus on social harmony (see Chapter 13 for an example). This line of thinking would suggest that for couples in collectivistic cultures common dyadic coping might be a frequent coping strategy. Additionally, common dyadic coping seems to be consistent with the elements of *collective coping*, a coping strategy that has been identified as unique and different from the intra-individual coping responses found mostly in individualist societies (Kuo, 2103). Collective coping has been described as having two distinctive elements: engaging others in the coping process and prioritizing the well-being of other group members when coping (Moore & Costantine, 2005). Common dyadic coping could be seen as a collective type of coping for it involves both partners and the well-being of the couple and not just the individual is prioritized. This could explain why common dyadic coping has been found in collectivistic cultures such as the Latino ones to be associated more strongly with positive relationship outcomes than other forms of dyadic coping (see Chapter 3).

Even though common dyadic coping seems to be consistent with collectivistic values, we believe that it is also in line with individualistic cultures, which view the couple's relationship as an equal partnership. In this cultural context tasks and responsibilities (childcare, household, financial, etc.) are less gendered and shared between partners. Therefore, it could be expected that challenges arising in any of the shared areas of the couple's life are experienced as common stressors and are dealt with by common dyadic coping.

Conclusion

The goals of this chapter were to conceptualize the role of the cultural context in the STM approach and discuss the way in which some of the cultural orientations (i.e., individualism versus collectivism, high- versus low-context communication, and variations in couples' relationships) may influence stress and coping in couples as conceptualized by STM. While we recognize that other cultural dimensions may exist (for example see discussion on personal control in Chapter 18), the dimensions presented in this chapter were aimed to illustrate the role culture plays in the study of stress and coping, and highlight the importance of including culture as a key contextual variable in such studies. As such, each of the following chapters in this book presents STM research and applications in various cultural contexts. These chapters illustrate the way in which stress and dyadic coping are affected by various cultural elements, cultural variations in the effects of dyadic coping on relational functioning, and the dyadic coping dimensions, which are more culturally relevant (e.g., common dyadic coping over supportive dyadic coping).

References

Adams, G. (2005). The cultural grounding of personal relationship: Enemyship in North American and West African worlds. *Journal of Personality and Social Psychology, 88*, 948–968.

Aldwin, C. M. (2007). *Stress, coping, & development: An integrative perspective* (2nd ed.). New York: The Guilford Press.

Allendorf, K. (2013). Schemas of marital change: From arranged marriages to eloping for love. *Journal of Marriage and Family, 75*, 453–469.

Berg, C. A., & Upchurch, R. (2007). A social contextual model of couples coping with chronic illness across the adult life span. *Psychological Bulletin, 133*, 920–954.

Bodenmann, G. (1997). Dyadic coping—a systemic-transactional view of stress and coping among couples: Theory and empirical findings. *European Review of Applied Psychology, 47*, 137–140.

Chun, C., Moos, R. H., & Cronkite, R. C. (2006). Culture: A fundamental context for the stress and coping paradigm. In P. T. P. Wong & L. C. J. Wong (Eds.), *Handbook of multicultural perspectives on stress and coping* (pp. 29–53). New York: Springer.

Coyne, J. C., & Smith, D. A. F. (1991). Couples coping with a myocardial infarction: A contextual perspective on wives' distress. *Journal of Personality and Social Psychology, 61*, 404–412.

Dion, K. K., & Dion, K. L. (1993). Individualistic and collectivistic perspectives on gender and the cultural context of love and intimacy. *Journal of Social Issues, 49*, 53–69.

Falconier, M. K. (2013). Traditional gender role orientation and dyadic coping in immigrant Latino couples: Effects on couple functioning. *Family Relations, 62*, 269–283.

Falconier, M. K., & Epstein, N. B. (2011). Couples experiencing financial strain: What we know and we can do. *Family Relations, 60*, 303–317.

Falconier, M. K., Nussbeck, F., & Bodenmann, G. (2013). Immigration stress and relationship satisfaction in Latino couples: The role of dyadic coping. *Journal of Social and Clinical Psychology, 32*, 813–843.

Falicov, C. J. (2014). *Latino families in therapy* (2nd ed.). New York: The Guilford Press.

Feng, B., & Burleson, B. R. (2006). Exploring the support-seeking process across cultures: Toward an integrated analysis of similarities and differences. *International and Intercultural Communication Annual, 28*, 243–266.

Gudykunst, W. B., Matsumoto, Y., Ting-Toomey, S., Nishida, T., Kim, K., & Heyman, S. (1996). The influence of cultural individualism-collectivism, self construals, and individual values on communication styles across cultures. *Human Communication Research, 22*, 510–543.

Hall, E. T. (1976). *Beyond culture*. New York: Doubleday.

Ho, D. Y. F. (1995). Internalized culture, culturocentrism, and transcendence. *The Counseling Psychologist, 23*, 4–24.

Hofstede, G. (1980). Culture and organizations. *International Studies of Management & Organization, 10*(4), 15–41.

Hofstede, G., Hofstede, G. J., & Minkov, M. (2010). *Cultures and organizations: Software of the mind* (3rd ed.). New York: McGraw-Hill.

Hwang, K. K. (1999). Filial piety and loyalty: Two types of social identification in Confucianism. *Asian Journal of Social Psychology, 2*, 163–183.

Kamya, H. (2005). African immigrant families. In M. McGoldrick, J. Giordano, & N. García-Preto (Eds.), *Ethnicity and family therapy* (pp. 101–116). New York: The Guilford Press.

Kayser, K., Watson, L. E., & Andrade, J. T. (2007). Cancer as a 'we-disease': Examining the process of coping from a relational perspective. *Families, Systems & Health, 25*, 404–418.

Kayser, K., Cheung, P. K. H., Rao, N., Chan,Y. C. L., Yu Chan, Y., & Lo, P. (2014). The influence of culture on couples coping with breast cancer: A comparative analysis of couples from China, India, and the United States. *Journal of Psychosocial Oncology, 32*, 264–288.

Kim, D., Pan, Y., & Park, H. S. (1998). High- versus low-context culture: A comparison of Chinese, Korean, and American cultures. *Psychology and Marketing, 15*, 507–521.

Kim, H. S. (2002). We talk, therefore we think? A cultural analysis of the effect of talking on thinking. *Journal of Personality and Social Psychology, 83*, 828–842.

Kim, H. S., & Sherman, D. K. (2007). 'Express yourself': Culture and the effect of self-expression on choice. *Journal of Personality and Social Psychology, 92*, 1–11.

Kim, H. S., Sherman, D. K., Ko, D., & Taylor, S. E. (2006). Pursuit of happiness and pursuit of harmony: Culture, relationships, and social support seeking. *Personality and Social Psychology Bulletin, 32,* 1595–1607.

Kuo, B. C. H. (2013). Collectivism and coping: Current theories, evidence, and measurements of collective coping. *International Journal of Psychology, 48,* 374–388.

Lam, A. G., & Zane, N. W. (2004). Ethnic differences in coping with interpersonal stressors: A test of self-construals as cultural mediators. *Journal of Cross Cultural Psychology, 35*(4), 446–459.

Lazarus, R. S., & Folkman, S. (1984). *Stress, appraisal, and coping.* New York: Springer.

Lee, E., & Mock, M. R. (2005). Asian families: An overview. In M. McGoldrick, J. Giordano, & N. García-Preto (Eds.), *Ethnicity and family therapy* (pp. 269–289). New York: The Guilford Press.

McGoldrick, M., Giordano, J., & García-Preto, N. (2005). Overview: Ethnicity and family therapy. In M. McGoldrick, J. Giordano, & N. García-Preto (Eds.), *Ethnicity and family therapy* (pp. 1–40). New York: The Guilford Press.

Markus, H. R., & Kitayama, S. (1991). Culture and the self: Implications for cognition, emotion, and motivation. *Psychological Review, 98,* 224–253.

Mojaverian, T., & Kim, H. S. (2013). Interpreting a helping hand: Cultural variation in the effectiveness of solicited and unsolicited social support. *Personality and Social Psychology Bulletin, 39,* 88–99.

Moore, J. L., & Constantine, M. G. (2005). Development and initial validation of the Collectivistic Coping Styles Measure with African, Asian, and Latin American international students. *Journal of Mental Health Counseling, 27,* 329–347.

Moos, R. H. (1984). Context and coping: Toward a unifying conceptual framework. *American Journal of Community Psychology, 12,* 5–25.

Mortenson, S. T., Burleson, B. R., Feng, B., & Liu, M. (2009). Cultural similarities and differences in seeking social support as a means of coping: A comparison of European Americans and Chinese and an evaluation of the mediating effects of self-construal. *Journal of International and Intercultural Communication, 2,* 208–239.

Ngazimbi, E. E., Daire, A. P., Soto, D., Carlson, R. G., & Munyon, M. D. (2013). Marital expectations and marital satisfaction between African Immigrant and United States born married couples. *Journal of Psychology in Africa, 23,* 317–322.

O'Brien, T. B., DeLongis, A., Pomaki, G., Puterman, E., & Zwicker, A. (2009). Couples coping with stress: The role of empathic responding. *European Psychologist, 14,* 18–28.

Rabin, C. (2002). *Equal partners—Good friends: Empowering couples through therapy.* New York: Routledge.

Revenson, T. A. (1994). Social support and marital coping with chronic illness. *Annals of Behavioural Medicine, 16,* 122–130.

Saez, N. (2011). Same-sex marriage, same-sex cohabitation, and same-sex families around the world: Why 'same' is so different? *Journal of Gender, Social Policy, & the Law, 19,* 1–55.

Schein, E. (1984). Coming to a new awareness of organizational culture. *Sloan Management Review, 25,* 3–16.

Schwartz, L., Elk, R., & Teggin, A. F. (1983). Life events in Xhosas in Cape Town. *Journal of Psychosomatic Research, 27,* 223–232.

Shibusawa, T. (2005). Japanese families. In M. McGoldrick, J. Giordano, & N. García-Preto (Eds.), *Ethnicity and family therapy* (pp. 339–348). New York: The Guilford Press.

Spencer-Oatey, H. (2012). *What is culture? A compilation of quotations.* GlobalPAD Core Concepts. Available at GlobalPAD Open House. Available from www.go.warwick.ac. uk/globalpadintercultural

Sue, D. W., & Sue, D. (2008). *Counseling the culturally diverse: Theory and practice* (5th ed.). New York: Wiley.

Taylor, S. E., Welch, W. T., Kim, H. S., & Sherman, D. K. (2007). Cultural differences in the impact of social support on psychological and biological responses. *Psychological Science, 18,* 831–837.

Taylor, S. E., Sherman, D. K., Kim, H. S., Jarcho, J., Tagaki, K., & Dunagan, M. S. (2004). Culture and social support: Who seeks it and why? *Journal of Personality and Social Psychology, 87,* 354–362.

Thoma, N. C., & McKay, D. (Eds.) (2015). *Working with emotion in cognitive-behavioral therapy: Techniques for clinical practice.* New York: The Guilford Press.

Triandis, H. C. (1988). Collectivism vs. individualism: A reconceptualization of a basic concept in cross-cultural psychology. In G. K. Verna & C. Bagely (Eds.), *Cross-cultural studies of personality, attitude, and cognition* (pp. 60–95). London: Macmillan.

Wong, P. T. P., Wong, L. C. J., & Scott, C. (2006). Beyond stress and coping: The positive psychology of transformation. In P. T. P. Wong & L. C. J. Wong (Eds.), *Handbook of multicultural perspectives on stress and coping* (pp. 1–26). New York: Springer.

Yeh, C. J., Arora, A. K., & Wu, K. A. (2006). A new theoretical model of collectivistic coping. In P. T. P. Wong & L. C. J. Wong (Eds.), *Handbook of multicultural perspectives on stress and coping* (pp. 55–72). New York: Springer.

Zhan, H. J., & Montgomery, R. J. V. (2003). Gender and elder care in China: The influence of filial piety and structural constraints. *Gender and Society, 17,* 209–229.

3

MEASURING DYADIC COPING ACROSS CULTURES

Fridtjof W. Nussbeck and Jeffrey B. Jackson

Introduced in the early 1990s, the concept of dyadic coping (DC) enlarged the focus of coping in couples from an individual perspective to a more systemic perspective (see Chapter 1). This broader view of DC allows coping in couples to be conceptualized as an interdependent process, incorporating the notion of strong and frequent mutual influence between partners (Bodenmann, 1995). As such, one partner's experiences of stress can spill over to the other partner and both partners can jointly engage in coping activities to manage individual and shared stressors (Revenson & Lepore, 2012). Congruent with the systemic notion that the whole is greater than the sum of the parts (White & Klein, 2002), DC within couples is more than just the sum of two individual coping processes; DC is the complex transactional interconnection between each partner's efforts to manage stressors, combined efforts to manage stressors, and each partner's perceptions of those efforts (Revenson, Kayser, & Bodenmann, 2005; see Chapter 1). Therefore, it is important that measures of DC accurately and appropriately capture this complex process.

Several different theoretical models have been developed for conceptualizing DC: the *Congruence Model* of DC (Revenson, 1994), the *Developmental Contextual Coping Model* (Berg & Upchurch, 2007), the *Relationship Focused Coping Model* (Coyne & Smith, 1991; DeLongis & O'Brien, 1990), and the Systemic Transactional Model (STM; Bodenmann, 1995; see Chapter 1). According to the STM, DC is typically initiated through stress communication. That is, one partner verbally and/or non-verbally discloses being stressed. The other partner may then react to this stress communication in various ways, highlighting the systemic conceptualization of DC.

Dyadic Coping Instruments

Different inventories have been developed to measure the DC process based on several existing theoretical conceptualizations of DC. These DC instruments include the *Collaborative Coping Questionnaire* (CCQ; Berg, Johnson, Meegan, & Strough, 2003), the *Relationship Focused Coping Scale* (RFCS; Buunk, Berkhuysen, Sanderman, Nieuwland, & Ranchor, 1996; Coyne & Smith, 1991), the *Empathic Responding Scale* (ERS; O'Brien & DeLongis, 1996), a protective buffering observational coding system (PBOCS; Langer, Rudd, & Syrjala, 2007), and the *Dyadic Coping Inventory* (DCI; Bodenmann, 2008).

According to a meta-analysis of DC as a predictor of relationship satisfaction (Falconier, Jackson, Hilpert, & Bodenmann, 2015), compared to the other DC measures, the DCI has more DC dimensions, has been more widely used (multiple countries, translated into multiple languages), and has been more frequently used. The results of the meta-analysis indicated that as of the end of 2013 there were seventy-two independent samples of data on DC from which scholarly reports had been generated. Furthermore, one of the major findings of the meta-analysis was that the DCI was the instrument that had been the most widely used. In fact, 73 percent of the existing DC studies were based on data collected using the DCI, with 24 percent collected using the RFCS, and the remaining 3 percent collected using the CCQ, ERS, and PBOCS. Given the extensive implementation of the DCI for measuring DC in scholarly research, we have focused our discussion of measuring DC on the DCI.

Dyadic Coping Inventory

The DCI is a self-report measure developed to measure the eight dimensions or subscales of DC conceptualized by the STM (Bodenmann, 2005). There are six dimensions that measure reactions to one's partner's stress and two dimensions that measure common DC between partners. The DCI dimensions can be aggregated into positive DC behaviors and negative DC behaviors. Positive DC as a reaction to one's partner's stress consists of (1) emotion-focused supportive DC (e.g., being emotionally or physically close to the partner), (2) problem-focused supportive DC (e.g., giving advice or lending help), and (3) delegated DC (e.g., freeing resources of one's partner by taking over some of her or his tasks that do not relate to the stressor, like doing the dishes for the stressed partner). Positive DC as joint effort comprise (4) emotion-focused common DC (e.g., mutual efforts to calm down or share emotional or physical intimacy), and (5) problem-oriented common DC (e.g., joint searching for information, joint efforts to solve the situation). Conversely, negative DC behaviors consist of (6) hostile DC (e.g., open disinterest), (7) ambivalent DC (e.g., supporting the partner unwillingly), and (8) superficial DC (e.g., pretending to be interested without listening). Additionally, the DCI measures stress communication, which can be conceptualized as a prerequisite to evoke a DC reaction. In order to capture the systemic and dynamic aspect of DC behaviors, the DCI incorporates not only a self-report perspective, it also captures perspectives about one's partner's behavior. That is, respondents report how they perceive their own behavior (DC by self), their partner's behavior (DC by partner), and their joint efforts (common DC). Additionally, the partners evaluate their DC efforts in terms of satisfaction with and effectiveness of their DC behavior as a couple.

Development of the DCI

The original (i.e., German) version of the DCI (Bodenmann, 2000) contained 55 five-point Likert-scale items (1 = *very rarely*, 5 = *very often*); however, based on factor analysis results, the DCI was subsequently reduced to 41 items and then again to 37 items. The validation of the German 37 item version[1] (Bodenmann, 2008; Gmelch et al., 2008) was based on data from 2,399 individuals (1,327 females and 1,072 males) and 724 couples (i.e., 724 females and 724 males) who had been in a romantic relationship for at least 9 months. The DC by self, DC by partner, and common DC scores for the problem-focused and emotion-focused dimensions of DC were collapsed for parsimony. All of the items demonstrated satisfactory standardized loading parameters on the corresponding scales (all standard loading parameters > .56). Associations between DCI domains did not exceed the correlation (*r*) of .71, indicating that the different domains were sufficiently distinct from each other.

The current version of the DCI (see Table A1 in the Appendix for the English version; for the German version see Bodenmann, 2008) assesses: (a) stress communication with four items, (b) supportive DC with five items (three for emotion-focused supportive DC and two for problem-focused DC), (c) delegated DC with two items, (d) negative DC with four items (two for hostile and one for ambivalent and superficial DC), and (e) common DC with five items (two for problem-focused common DC and three for emotion-focused common DC). Since common DC consists of behaviors characterizing the couple's joint efforts, common DC can be measured by responses by both partners or only one partner. All other dimensions are measured in a self-perspective (coping by self) and a partner perspective (coping by partner). Figure 3.1 depicts the theoretically derived internal structure of the DCI separately for DC by self, DC by partner, and common DC.[2] The last two items assessing satisfaction with and the effectiveness of DC behaviors within the couple are not displayed, as they do not reflect behaviors but the evaluation of the whole process of DC.

The Dyadic Coping Inventory in Different Cultures

The DCI has been used to collect data from various populations across the world. In addition to the validation of the original version of the DCI in German

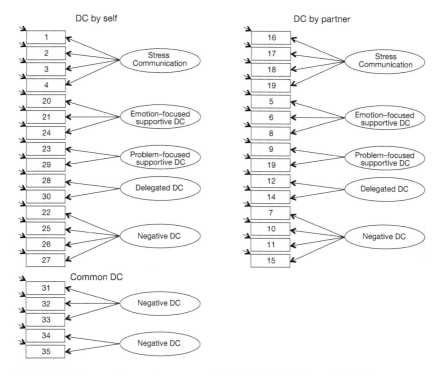

FIGURE 3.1 Supposed internal structure of the DCI for DC by self, DC by partner, and common DC. Numbers indicate the DCI items

(Bodenmann, 2008; Gmelch et al., 2008; Ledermann et al., 2010), the DCI has been translated and validated for the following languages:[3] English (Randall, Hilpert, Jiménez-Arista, Walsh, & Bodenmann, 2015), French (Ledermann et al., 2010), Greek (Roussi & Karademas, see Chapter 10), Hungarian (Martos, Sallay, Mihaela, & Józsa, 2012), Italian (Donato et al., 2009; Ledermann et al., 2010), Portuguese (Vedes, Nussbeck, Bodenmann, Lind, & Ferreira, 2013), and Spanish (Falconier, Nussbeck, & Bodenmann, 2013). Factor analytic models, internal consistency scores, and correlations between different scales in all of these validation studies indicated sound psychometric properties for the DCI for the respective samples. There are ongoing efforts to validate the DCI in other languages and cultures (see subsequent chapters).

It is important to clarify the difference between language, culture, and nationality with regard to the validation of the DCI. For example, the Greek and Hungarian DCI validations cover language, culture, and nationality given that the Greek and Hungarian languages and culture are almost exclusively associated with Greece and Hungary respectively. Conversely, the DCI has been used across different cultures and countries with the same language. For instance, the validation of the Spanish version of the DCI consisted of Spanish speaking immigrants from North, Central, and South American countries living in the United States; therefore although all participants spoke the Spanish language, there was substantial variation across culture and nationality. Similarly, the English version of the DCI has been validated in Australia, Canada, and the United States. In order to evaluate the commonalities and differences between the different validation studies of the DCI, we first present recommendations for questionnaire translation and cultural adaptation, discuss measurement invariance, and outline a prototypical validation strategy for the DCI.

Self-Report Measure Cultural Validity and Translation

Cultural validity is one of the major factors that should be considered in cross-cultural measurement, as validity can be compromised by cultural bias (Sindik, 2012). Construct bias—"the degree to which research instruments fail to accurately account for cultural variation in the meaning attributed to the concepts purportedly measured" is a significant issue, which is often overlooked in the process of adapting a measure to another culture, race, nationality, or other groups of people with a unique identity that differs from the group of people with whom the measure was originally developed (Linville, Todahl, & O'Neil, 2014, p. 100).

For instance, a DC behavior that is perceived positively in one culture might be perceived negatively in another culture. Consider the following DCI item: *I tell my partner openly how I feel and that I would appreciate his/her support.* In many Western European cultures, assertiveness (i.e., open expression of stress and requests for help) between partners is valued and espoused as an ideal; in many other cultures, assertiveness between partners may not only be devalued, it may be disrespectful or violate certain gender roles and expectations (Furnham, 2006). Relatedly, with the DCI item *I ask my partner to do things for me when I have too much to do,* it may be culturally acceptable within romantic relationships for women in some cultures to ask men for help (or vice versa) and it may be culturally unacceptable in other cultures.

Because of potential nuanced and considerable differences in perception, behavior, and experience between groups of people with divergent identities, it is important to (1) norm and adapt established measures for use with different cultural groups who speak the language of the established measures and (2) translate established measures in culturally sensitive ways. Furthermore, because the translation of an existing measure with established sound psychometric properties to a different language can threaten construct validity (Okazaki & Sue, 1995), we briefly summarize recommended *ideal* procedures for the translation of measures (see Herrera, Del Campo, & Ames, 1993). At least two translators with expertise in both the relevant languages and associated relevant cultures should translate the original measure independently from one another. After the initial translation is completed, the translators should combine their independent translations, resolving differences by coming to a consensus on the most linguistically and contextually sound solutions. Then, an expert in the language into which the original measure is being translated should edit the translation for clarity and grammar. Next, researchers should audio record multiple bilingual individuals from various backgrounds back translating the new translation into the original language. A translator with expertise in both the relevant languages and associated relevant cultures should listen to the audio recordings and refine the translation as necessary to more accurately convey the items in the original measure in contextually adapted ways. Finally, researchers should field test the translated measure with the target population and evaluate the reliability of the translated measure, identifying potential differences between translation issues and extraneous variables (see Geisinger, 1994; Herrera et al., 1993; and Okazaki & Sue, 1995 for more details on measure-translation and adaptation).

The translation procedures we have summarized represent recommended ideals for measure translation. Future research on the DCI and other DC measures should seek to employ these recommended procedures to increase cultural validity. For information on how the DCI has been translated into other languages and culturally adapted for other cultures, reference the subsequent chapters in this book and the published validation studies.

Measurement Invariance

Measurement invariance and especially factorial invariance (a specific type of measurement invariance), is a prerequisite for comparing constructs across different groups such as cultures or nations (Meredith, 1993). Factorial invariance implies that the same set of items is related to the same underlying latent variable (e.g., DCI dimension) for any given group; therefore, specific DCI domains can be compared across groups since their respective behavioral manifestations are identical. In other words, common DC cannot be compared across groups if items of delegated DC also measure common DC in one group but not in the other group (violation of factorial invariance); if delegated DC items were to measure common DC in one group and not in the other group, the concept of common DC would differ with respect to its behavioral manifestation as well as its internal structure in the two groups. Hence, satisfying the statistical property of factorial invariance hence guarantees that DCI scores and associations of DCI scores with other constructs can be compared across cultures. Additionally, measures can show strong factorial invariance or strict measurement invariance. Strong factorial invariance implies that the factor loadings are identical across groups. Strict measurement invariance implies that factor loadings and intercepts of confirmatory factor analysis (CFA) models are identical across groups. In the context of cross-cultural psychology, measures rarely have strong factorial invariance and strict measurement invariance; however, in most cases, only factorial invariance is needed to prove the interpretability of the desired constructs across cultures.

Prototypical Validation Process

The internal structure of the DCI is based on the STM. Hence, the internal structure of the DCI can be directly translated into a CFA model (see Figure 3.1), which automatically guarantees factorial invariance with other language versions. A CFA model can be used to determine if (a) items intended to measure the same construct load highly on the same factor, (b) items intended to measure different constructs load on different factors, and, most importantly, (c) the factorial (internal) structure can explain the associations found in the data (i.e., the goodness of fit for a given psychometric model).

In validation studies, it is very informative to build CFA-models in consecutive steps. First, if data from couples are to be analyzed, data of only one group of partners (female or male partners) should be considered because non-independence can artificially distort the factor structure (Kenny, Kashy, & Cook, 2006). Second, the three agents of DC need to be differentiated: (a) DC by self (what I do), (b) DC by partner (what my partner does), and (c) common DC (what we do). Within the submodels for DC by self and DC by partner, the model building process could start with the two forms of supportive DC (problem- and emotion-focused DC) in order to identify if these two domains can be separated or if they should be collapsed. The internal structure of the submodel is validated if the model fits the data, the loading pattern indicates large and significant standardized loadings, and the correlation between the two latent variables is not extremely high, then problem- and emotion-focused DC are two separate domains; if the correlation is extremely high, these two domains should be collapsed. In the following steps, latent factors (DC domain) are added stepwise (i.e., one at a time) to identify items that do not fit into the model and subscales that cannot be disentangled in readily interpretable models. Immediately specifying the complete submodel of DC by self is also possible but much more complex to interpret—especially in cases when there is poor model fit. Next, the submodels for partner reports and the common DC facets are specified following the same rationale. Finally, the three submodels are combined, yielding the total structure of the DCI for one individual.

We strongly recommend specifying the CFA models for partners separately because each partner represents a distinct source of information and it is crucial to investigate the internal structure for each source of information. Additionally, we also recommend specifying a CFA model for the DCI strongly grounded in the STM (see Figure 3.1). Researchers can adapt the DCI and collapse latent variables if they are interested in broader concepts; however, for validation purposes it is important to know if the theoretical assumptions can be reflected in the empirical application of the questionnaire.

Comparing Validation Studies

In all of the above mentioned DCI validation studies, the researchers based their analyses on theoretical assumptions of the underlying internal structure of the

DCI. In all but three studies, the researchers relied on the DCI structure with (a) problem-focused DC, (b) emotion-focused DC, (c) problem-focused common DC, and (d) emotion-focused common DC. In those three differing studies (i.e., Donato et al., 2009; Gmelch et al., 2008; and Ledermann et al., 2010), these domains were collapsed into supportive (for DC by self and DC by partner) and common DC. The domains of stress communication, delegated DC, and negative DC have been identified in all language groups.

Internal Structure

It is important to note that across all validation studies the DCI showed factorial invariance for its scales in most language groups except for stress communication. That is, the same sets of items formed the same theoretically meaningful set of factors for all of the domains except stress communication. With respect to stress communication, we found a consistent pattern that in some studies (i.e., Italian by Donato et al., 2009, German, and Portuguese) all four items of stress communication by self (items 1–4) loaded onto one factor and all four items of stress communication by partner (16–19) loaded onto another separate factor, whereas in other studies (i.e., Italian by Ledermann et al., 2010, English, French, Greek, and Spanish) only two items for DC by self (item 1: *I let my partner know that I appreciate his/her practical support, advice, or help* and item 4: *I tell my partner openly how I feel and that I would appreciate his/her support*), and only two items for DC by partner (item 16: *My partner lets me know that he/she appreciates my practical support, advice, or help* and item 19: *My partner tells me openly how he/she feels and that he/she would appreciate my support*) formed stress communication (i.e., models with item 2 [*I ask my partner to do things for me when I have too much to do*] and item 3 [*I show my partner through my behavior when I am not doing well or when I have problems*], as well as item 17 [*My partner asks me to do things for him/her when he has too much to do*] and item 18 [*My partner shows me through his/her behavior that he/she is not doing well or when he/she has problems*] did not fit the data or did not load on the factor; see Table A1 in the Appendix).

Items 1 and 4 cover open verbal communication about one's feelings and the expression of appreciation, whereas item 2 is related to delegated DC and item 3 covers aspects of emotional disclosure, which may be expressed verbally or non-verbally. It seems to be the case that in some language groups these differing item contents are more closely related than in others. In the Spanish validation study (Falconier et al., 2013), the behavioral component of items 2 and 3 was identified as a possible reason why these items did not load with the other stress com-munication items; no explanation was given in the other validation studies in which items 2 and 3 did not load with the other stress communication items. Interestingly, in the German validation study (Gmelch et al., 2008), exploratory factor analysis (EFA) indicated items 2 and 17 cross-loading with delegated DC by self and by partner, respectively. In addition, results from the Portuguese validation study (Vedes et al., 2013) also included weak factor loadings for items 2 and 17, representing further evidence of a potential issue with cultural validity in some languages or cultures. Stress communication was the only domain for which there was a consistent pattern with factor loading problems across the DCI validation studies. For all other scales, there were a few items that did not load well for only one language or culture (e.g., items 15 and 26 in the Spanish version had low loadings [Falconier, 2013], and items 9 and 24 in the English version were removed due to poor loadings [Randall et al., 2015]). Overall, the DCI has a stable internal structure with respect to the DC domains across languages and cultures.

Reliability

Having determined comparable factorial structures across the different language groups, reliability estimates of the different DC domains can be compared. Table 3.1 gives an overview about the reliability estimates. The Italian validation study (Donato et al., 2009) was not included as it covers the forty-one-item version of the DCI (i.e., the Dyadic Coping Questionnaire [DCQ], Bodenmann, 2000). Donato and colleagues (2009) reported ρ_C (Bagozzi & Yi, 1994) as a measure of internal consistency (reliability), stating that all internal consistency estimates are $\rho_C \geq .59$.

The reliability estimates vary to a large extent between domains of DC and also across the different language groups. Surprisingly, there are no large differences between the estimates for stress communication ($.63 < \alpha < .84$ for DC by self and DC by partner), although in some studies only two items were aggregated whereas in other studies four items were aggregated. With regard to problem-focused DC, there were rather low reliability scores across validation studies for DC by self ($.45 < \alpha < .75$) yet there were acceptable reliability scores for DC by partner ($.68 < \alpha < .84$). For all other domains, the reliability scores ranged from acceptable to very high, with the exception of negative DC in the French validation study. Overall, reliability was comparable across the validation studies, implying that the DCI can be used and compared across the associated language and cultural groups.

Correlations of DC Domains

The degree to which the DCI domain subscales correlated with each other indicated discriminant validity of the domains for each of the validation studies; that is, participants differentiated between the different subscales. Moreover, the correlations of DC domains were comparable in size across all of the validation studies. After systematically reviewing the correlation matrices in the validation studies, we did not identify large differences in correlations between stress

TABLE 3.1 Published reliabilities (Cronbach's α) for the DC domains of the DCI in different language groups

Language	1st author (year)	Sample	Sample size	Stress Communica-tion	Emotion-focused DC	Problem-focused DC	Supportive DC	Delegated DC	Negaive DC	Emotion-focused common DC	Problem-focused common DC	Common DC
English	Randall (2015)	Women	664	0.68/0.74	0.78/0.84	0.45/0.80		0.80/0.87	0.73/0.77	0.77	0.91	
		Men	274	0.77/0.72	0.82/0.86	0.54/0.68		0.80/0.80	0.81/0.81	0.79	0.87	
French	Ledermann (2010)	Mixed	198	0.64/0.78			0.82/0.84	0.89/0.81	0.53/0.50			.76
German	Gmelch/ Bodenmann (2008)	Women	2,399	0.77/0.79			0.82/0.88	0.82/0.84	0.72/0.76			0.80
	Gmelch/ Bodenmann (2008)	Men	2,399	0.74/0.76			0.82/0.87	0.80/0.77	0.74/0.71			0.74
	Ledermann (2010)	Mixed	216	0.80/0.82			0.76/0.82	0.86/0.81	0.61/0.66			0.70
Greek	Roussi (2016)	Women	144	0.69/0.79	0.86/0.84	0.60/0.78		0.79/0.82	0.68/0.62	0.88	0.69	
		Men	144	0.65/0.65	0.81/0.86	0.62/0.74		0.68/0.67	0.70/0.69	0.88	0.77	

continued . . .

TABLE 3.1 Continued

Language	1st author (year)	Sample	Sample size	Stress Communication	Emotion-focused DC	Problem-focused DC	Supportive DC	Delegated DC	Negative DC	Emotion-focused common DC	Problem-focused common DC	Common DC
Hungarian	Martos (2012)	Women	296	0.63/0.77			0.80/0.89	0.80/0.70	0.77/0.82			0.78
		Men	177	0.68/0.68			0.81/0.86	0.78/0.83	0.71/0.82			0.72
		Mixed	473	0.67/0.76			0.81/0.88	0.88/0.88	0.75/0.82			0.76
Italian	Ledermann (2010)	Mixed	378	0.78/0.75			0.86/0.89	0.73/0.76	0.62/0.67			0.68
Portuguese	Vedes (2013)	Women	462	0.64/0.78	0.73/0.92	0.63/0.81		0.75/0.84	0.77/0.80	0.83	0.80	
		Men	143	0.73/0.77	0.81/0.88	0.75/0.84		0.82/0.70	0.75/0.81	0.88	0.80	
Spanish	Falconier (2013)	Women	113	0.64/0.72	0.78/0.90	0.55/0.75		0.82/0.81	0.60/0.59	0.91	0.92	
		Men	113	0.84/0.69	0.80/0.82	0.70/0.76		0.88/0.68	0.64/0.71	0.82	0.95	

Note. Only the 1st author of the study is listed. Gmelch et al. (2008) and Bodenmann et al. (2008) used the same data set. Mixed: the study did not report internal consistency scores for female and male partners separately. Entries in the cells indicate internal consistency scores for perception of DC by self/perception of DC by partner. Empty cells indicate that the corresponding factor was not specified in the study.

communication and other DCI domain subscales, independent from the fact that stress communication was either measured by two or four items. Hence, measurements of stress communication based on two items appear to capture comparable information to measurements of stress communication based on four items.

Criterion Validity

DCI domains were positively related to both individual coping (Bodenmann, 2008; Falconier et al., 2013; Randall et al., 2015, Roussi & Karademas, Chapter 10) and positive communication patterns (Ledermann et al., 2010). With the exception of negative DC, the DCI domains seem to reflect functional interpersonal behavior in different cultures. Due to the nature of the DC construct, relationship satisfaction measures have frequently been used to investigate the criterion validity of the DCI.

DCI and Relationship Satisfaction

Recently, Falconier, Jackson, Hilpert, and Bodenmann used meta-analytic procedures to investigate the association between DC as measured by the DCI and relationship satisfaction. A thorough search for relevant samples yielded a total of 50 independent samples from 43 studies. The majority of included sample reports were published (69 percent), in journal articles (60 percent), and in English (60 percent). All of the identified sample reports were completed within seven years between 2006 and 2013. The identified samples were from eleven different countries (Austria, Canada, Germany, Indonesia, Israel, Italy, Netherlands, Portugal, Romania, Switzerland, and the United States), indicating that the concept of DC resonates with researchers from varying nations, cultures, and backgrounds in ways that transcend their differences.

Most of the sample data were obtained from cross-sectional study designs (88 percent), with substantially less sample data obtained from longitudinal study designs (12 percent). Roughly two thirds of the studies (64 percent) were completed with German speaking participants. The average sample size was 172 and the combined total participants for all included samples was 15,237 (8,440 females; 6,464 males). The participants in the included samples were predominately middle class Europeans with some level of college education. The average age of female participants was 37.3 years ($SD = 8.1$; range $= 19.0—68.0$) and the average age of male participants was 39.7 years ($SD = 8.7$; range $= 19.7 - 68.0$). The average relationship duration was 14.6 years ($SD = 8.1$; range $= 0.9 - 42.0$).

Overall, the association magnitude between total DC and relationship satisfaction was large, and the association magnitudes between the DC dimensions and relationship satisfaction were at least medium and predominantly large. The interpretation of correlational effect size magnitude can be guided by the following established ranges: small ($r \leq 0.10$), medium ($0.11 \leq r \geq 0.39$), and large ($r \geq 0.40$; Lipsey & Wilson, 2001).

The aggregated zero-order correlation (r) for total DC (aggregation of all of the DCI subscales) with relationship satisfaction was 0.50, indicating that relationship satisfaction was highly associated with DC as measured by the DCI. DC by partner ($r = 0.50$) and common DC ($r = 0.54$) were more strongly associated with relationship satisfaction than DC by self ($r = 0.38$). The supportive DC ($r = 0.50$) and negative DC ($r = -0.42$) dimensions were more strongly related to relationship satisfaction than delegated DC ($r = 0.31$) and stress communication ($r = 0.33$). The evaluation of DC was more strongly associated with relationship satisfaction ($r = 0.68$) than any other dimension of DC. Positive DC ($r = 0.46$) and negative DC ($r = -0.42$) were similarly associated with relationship satisfaction, yet opposite in direction. Across all samples, total DC and all associated DC dimensions were strongly related with relationship satisfaction regardless of gender, age, relationship length, education level, and nationality.

These findings not only support that DC is highly predictive of relationship quality (Falconier et al., 2015), they also underscore the utility of using the DCI to assess DC among couples experiencing stress. By identifying the efforts partners make to manage stressors and how those efforts are perceived within the couple, clinicians and relationship educators can assist partners through (a) identifying and increasing effective coping efforts, (b) identifying and decreasing ineffective coping efforts, and (c) shifting perceptions of partner coping efforts.

Congruence, Reciprocity, and Equity in the DCI

Measuring DC in a dyadic perspective (i.e., both DC by self and DC by partner) allows for additional uses of couples' data. If both partners in a couple complete the DCI, researchers may use the dyadic data structure to calculate measures of congruence, reciprocity, and equity (Gmelch & Bodenmann, 2007; Iafrate, Bertoni, Margola, Cigoli, & Acitelli, 2012). The congruence index reflects the degree to which both partners agree upon one partner's behavior (e.g., DC by self as perceived by the wife and DC by partner as perceived by the husband). The congruence index provides important information about the fit between both partners' perceptions of one partner's DC efforts and skills. In therapeutic or counseling settings, this information may be especially helpful in revealing discrepancies in couples' perceptions of their interactions. The reciprocity index reflects the degree to which degree both partners view the give and take in their relationship (e.g., DC by self as perceived by the wife compared to DC by self as perceived by the husband). If the reciprocity index reveals an imbalance in giving and taking, it may point to relationship problems such as commitment. The equity index refers to the within-partner perception of giving and taking (i.e., DC by self as perceived by the wife compared with DC by partner as perceived by the wife). If the equity index is imbalanced, it indicates that at least one partner perceives that he/she is either giving more than receiving or the converse (Hatfield, Utne, & Traupmann, 1979). All three indices may be conceived as indicators of agreement in addition to potential sources of relationship satisfaction depending upon how well one's own behavior and one's partner's behavior fit into one's conceptualization of an ideal relationship.

Observational Measurement of DC

Besides self-report questionnaire data, researchers can also use observational methods to assess DC behaviors of one or both partners. In general, the primary advantage of observational data is that they allow for the analysis of processes and dynamics of social interactions. Moreover, they are free from self-report biases such as self-deception and social desirability. The *System zur Erfassung des dyadischen Copings* (SEDC; System for assessing observed DC; Bodenmann, 2000) is an observational coding system for capturing dyadic interactions. As for any other behavioral coding system, the analysis of observed DC behaviors requires thorough coder training and accurate coding schemes.

To fully assess DC, researchers have to establish three observational situations. First, common DC can only be evaluated if both partners perceive a shared stressor; accordingly, in an observational situation the couple may be asked to discuss a shared stressor (e.g., birth of a child, illness of one partner, moving, financial strain). Second, DC as a reaction to one partner's stress can only be evaluated if the couple discusses a specific situation in which one partner was stressed (e.g., occupational work load, disagreement with a friend) or if stress is experimentally induced for one partner (e.g., Bodenmann, 2000; Meuwly, Bodenmann, Germann, Bradbury, Ditzen, & Heinrichs, 2012). Third, researchers interested in both partners' DC skills need to repeat the second situation by having the couple discuss a stressor only experienced by the other partner or experimentally introduce a stressor for the other partner. These situations allow for the study of stress communication in the stressed partner and response behavior (emotion- and problem-oriented verbal and non-verbal supportive DC) by the other partner.

The SEDC differentiates between six forms of stress communication (i.e., factual stress communication, neutral description of emotion-focused stress, latent emotion-focused stress, implicit emotion-focused stress, explicit emotion-focused stress communication, and non-verbal emotion-focused stress communication) and ten forms of support (i.e., problem-focused supportive DC, verbal emotion-focused supportive DC, non-verbal emotion-focused supportive DC, emotion-focused common DC, problem-focused common DC, active and interested listening, non-verbal hostile DC, verbal hostile, ambivalent DC, and superficial DC). Therefore, observational coding may shed light on specific mechanisms of coping reactions within a couple. Researchers may, for example, investigate if it is beneficial for a relationship if partners promptly react to a stress communication by the other partner. We recommend using observational measurements of DC for research questions that are specifically related to the *dynamic process* of DC.

Conclusion

In recent years, the concept of DC has been intensively researched. The DCI has been translated into various languages and successfully been used to explain relationship satisfaction in many cultures. In this chapter, we introduced the most important aspects with respect to the translation and validation of the DCI and other such measures. As for any construct that is researched across different cultures, it is necessary to ensure that constructs make sense given the context of the various cultures and languages (*cultural validity*) and measure those constructs with sound methods and psychometric properties (*factorial invariance*). With respect to stress communication, we found that the four items intended to measure a one-dimensional factor did not always psychometrically fit into one single scale across languages and cultures. Based upon the correlation patterns reported in the various studies, we concluded that it is very likely that stress is communicated between partners across cultures and languages; however, additional research is needed to identify if stress communication could principally be measured only with the two items that loaded together across cultures and languages or if the other two items should be reformulated in such a way that they measure stress communication more effectively and load with the other two items.

Although there is an increasing number of validation studies of the DCI and DCI scales, it is important to note that DCI translations should not only show comparable properties with respect to their internal structure, but should be similarly embedded in the nomological net across cultures. If there are differences with respect to associations within the DCI or to other constructs, researchers have to investigate if these differences are due to cultural differences or due to inconsistent translations of the DCI. Hence, researchers have to rule out inconsistent translations as a source of differential findings following the guidelines previously provided. Although the collection and coding of observational data tends to be more cumbersome than self-report questionnaires, because DC is an interpersonal and dynamic process, observational measurement is an important and relevant methodology for assessing DC interaction patterns. For example, researchers could investigate if there are different patterns of DC processes (e.g., if the partner reacts promptly to a stress communication) that predict relationship satisfaction or stability. Consequently, we recommend that DC be increasingly studied through observational measurement in future research.

Notes

1   The German version of the DCI was validated in the German speaking part of Switzerland. Approximately 80 percent of the participants were Swiss; the majority of the remaining participants were Austrian and German.

2   Although the DCI contains items reflecting the various domains of DC, researchers may also collapse some of the domains yielding (a) four scales of DC by self (i.e., stress communication, supportive DC, delegated DC, and negative DC), (b) four scales of DC by partner (i.e., stress communication, supportive DC, delegated DC, and negative DC), and (c) one scale reflecting common DC behavior. Accordingly, emotion- and problem-oriented supportive DC are often collapsed. Researchers interested in focusing on functional aspects of DC can collapse supportive, delegated, and common DC into positive DC. However, collapsing these scales blurs differences in individual behavior (either partner or both partners) and couple behavior (the joint efforts of both partners).

3   Levesque, Lafontaine, Caron, and Fitzpatrick (2014) also validated an English version of the DCI in Canada using a different psychometric model. Instead of focusing on the agent (self, partner, or couple) and the DCI domain as done in all other validation studies, the authors proposed a structure with three scales capturing (1) the DC by self, (2) by partner, and (3) common DC as global measures and four additional scales capturing (4) stress communication, (5) supportive, (6) delegated, and (7) negative DC by *both* partners (one common factor for one's own behavior and partner's behavior). Hence, their statistical model reflects some variations in the underlying STM assumptions of the DCI.

References

Bagozzi, R. P., & Yi, Y. (1994). Advanced topics in structural equation models. In R. P. Bagozzi (Ed.), *Advanced methods of marketing research* (pp. 1–51). Oxford, UK: Blackwell.

Berg, C. A., & Upchurch, R. (2007). A social contextual model of couples coping with chronic illness across the adult life span. *Psychological Bulletin, 133*, 920–954.

Berg, C. A., Meegan, S. P., & Deviney, F. P. (1998). A socio-contextual model of coping with everyday problems across the lifespan. *International Journal of Behavioral Development, 22*, 239–261.

Berg, C. A., Johnson, M. M., Meegan, S. P., & Strough, J. (2003). Collaborative problem solving interactions in young and old married couples. *Discourse Processes, 15*, 33–58.

Bodenmann, G. (1995). A systemic-transactional conceptualization of stress and coping in couples. *Swiss Journal of Psychology, 54*, 34–49.

Bodenmann, G. (2005). *Stress und Copingbei Paaren [Stress and coping in couples]*. Göttingen, Germany: Hogrefe.

Bodenmann, G. (2008). *DCI—Dyadisches Coping Inventar, Manual [The Dyadic Coping Inventory Manual]*. Bern, Goettingen: Huber & Hogrefe Testverlag.

Buunk, B. P., Berkhuysen, M. A., Sanderman, R., Nieuwland, W., & Ranchor, A. V. (1996). Actievebetrokkenheid, beschermendbufferenenoverbescherming. Meetinstrumentenvoor de rol van de partner bijhartrevalidatie [The role of the partner in heart disease: Active engagement, protective buffering, and overprotection]. *Gedrag and Gezondheid: Tijdschrift voor Psychologie and Gezondheid, 24*, 304–313.

Campell, D. T., & Fiske, D. W. (1959). Convergent and discriminant validation by the multitrait-multimethod matrix. *Psychological Bulletin, 56*, 81–105.

Carver, C. S. (1997). You want to measure coping but your protocol's too long: Consider the Brief COPE. *International Journal of Behavioral Medicine, 4*, 92–100.

Christensen, A., & Sullaway, M. (1984). *Communication patterns questionnaire*. Unpublished Manuscript. Los Angeles: University of California.

Coyne, J. C., & Smith, D. A. F. (1991). Couples coping with a myocardial infarction: A contextual perspective on wives' distress. *Journal of Personality and Social Psychology, 61*, 404–412.

DeLongis, A., & O'Brien, T. (1990). An interpersonal framework for stress and coping: An application to the families of Alzheimer's patients. In M. A. P. Stephens, J. H. Crowther, S. E. Hobfoll, & D. L. Tennenbaum (Eds.), *Stress and coping in later-life families* (pp. 221–240). New York: Hemisphere Publishing Corporation.

Dohrenwend, S., & Dohrenwend, B. P. (1974). *Stressful life events: Their nature and effects.* New York: Wiley.

Donato, S., Iafrate, R., Barni, D., Bertoni, A., Bodenmann, G., & Gagliardi, S. (2009). Measuring dyadic coping: The factorial structure of Bodenmann's Dyadic Coping Questionnaire in an Italian sample. *Testing, Psychometrics, Methodology in Applied Psychology, 16*, 25–47.

Falconier, M. K., Nussbeck, F. W., & Bodenmann, G. (2013). Dyadic coping in Latino couples: Validity of the Spanish version of the Dyadic Coping Inventory. *Anxiety, Stress, & Coping, 26*, 446–466.

Falconier, M. K., Jackson, J. B., Hilpert, P., & Bodenmann, G. (2015). Dyadic coping and relationship satisfaction: A meta-analysis. *Clinical Psychology Review, 42*, 28–46.

Fiske, V., Coyne, J. C., & Smith, D. A. (1991). Couples coping with myocardial infarction. An empirical reconsideration of the role of overprotectiveness. *Journal of Family Psychology, 5*, 4–20.

Furnham, A. (2006). Assertiveness in three cultures: Multidimensionality and cultural differences. *Journal of Clinical Psychology, 35*, 522–527.

Geisinger, K. (1994). Psychometric issues in testing students with disabilities. *Applied Measurement in Education, 7*, 121–140.

Gmelch, S., & Bodenmann, G. (2007). Dyadisches coping in selbst- und fremdwahrnehmung als prädiktoren für partnerschaftsqualität und befinden [Dyadic coping in self- and partner perception as a predictor of relationship quality and well-being]. *Zeitschrift für Gesundheitspsychologie, 15*,177–186.

Gmelch, S., Bodenmann, G., Meuwly, N., Ledermann, T., Steffen-Sozinova, O., & Striegl, K. (2008). Dyadisches Coping Inventar (DCI): Ein Fragebogen zur Erfassung des partnerschaftlichen Umgangs mit Stress [Dyadic coping inventory: A questionnaire to assess dyads dealing with stress]. *Zeitschrift fuer Familienforschung, 20*, 185–202.

Hatfield, E., Utne, M. K., & Traupmann, J. (1979). Equity theory and intimate relationships. In R. L. Burgess & T. L. Houston (Eds.), *Social exchange in developing relationships.* New York: Academic Press.

Hemphill, R. C. (2013). *Disease-related collaboration and adjustment among couples coping with type 2 diabetes.* Dissertation Abstracts International: The Sciences and Engineering, B 75/08 (E).

Hendrick, S. S. (1988). A generic measure of relationship satisfaction. *Journal of Marriage and the Family, 50*, 93–98.

Herrera, R. S., DelCampo, R. L., & Ames, M. H. (1993). A serial approach for translating family science instrumentation. *Family Relations, 42*, 357–360.

Kenny, D. A., Kashy, D. A., & Cook, W. L. (2006). *Dyadic data analysis.* New York: The Guilford Press.

Langer, S. L., Rudd, M. E., & Syrjala, K. L. (2007). Protective buffering and emotional desynchrony among spousal caregivers of cancer patients. *Health Psychology, 26*, 635–643.

Lazarus, R. S., & Folkman, S. (1984). *Stress, appraisal, and coping.* New York: Springer.

Ledermann, T., Bodenmann, G., Gagliardi, S., Charvoz, L., Verardi, S., Rossier, J., Bertoni, A., & Iafrate, R. (2010). Psychometrics of the Dyadic Coping Inventory in three language groups. *Swiss Journal of Psychology, 69*, 201–212.

Levesque, C., Lafontaine, M. F., Caron, A., & Fitzpatrick, J. (2014). Validation of the English version of the Dyadic Coping Inventory. *Measurement and Evaluation in Counseling and Development, 47,* 215–225.

Linville, D., Todahl, J. L., & O'Neil, M. E. (2014). Using questionnaires in clinical couple and family research. In R. B. Miller & L. N. Johnson (Eds.), *Advanced methods in family therapy research: A focus on validity and change* (pp. 94–111). New York: Routledge.

Lipsey, M. W., & Wilson, D. B. (2001). *Practical meta-analysis.* Thousand Oaks, CA: Sage.

Lord, F. M., & Novick, M. R. (1968). *Statistical theories of mental test scores.* Reading: Addison-Welsley Publishing Company.

Martos, T., Sallay, V., Mihaela, N., & Józsa, P. (2012). Párkapcsolati megküzdés és jóllét–a Páros Megküzdés Kérd_ív magyar változata [Dyadic coping and well-being—the Hungarian version of the Dyadic Coping Inventory]. *Psychiatria Hungarica, 27,* 446–458.

Meredith, W. (1993). Measurement invariance, factor analysis and factorial invariance. *Psychometrika, 58,* 525–543.

Messick, S. (1995). Validity of psychological assessment: Validation of inferences from persons' responses and performances as scientific inquiry into score meaning. *American Psychologist, 50,* 741–749.

Meuwly, N., Bodenmann, G., Germann, J., Bradbury, T. N., Ditzen, B., & Heinrichs, M. (2012). Dyadic coping, insecure attachment, and cortisol stress recovery following experimentally induced stress. *Journal of Family Psychology, 26,* 937–947.

O'Brien, T. B., & DeLongis, A. (1996). The interactional context of problem-focused, emotion-focused, and relationship-focused coping: The role of the Big Five personality factors. *Journal of Personality, 64,* 775–813.

Okazaki, S., & Sue, S. (1995). Methodological issues in assessment research with ethnic minorities. *Psychological Assessment, 7*(3), 367–375.

Randall, A. K., Hilpert, P., Jiménez-Arista, L. E., Walsh, K. J., & Bodenmann, G. (2015). Dyadic coping in the U.S.: Psychometric properties and validity for use of the English version of the dyadic coping inventory. *Current Psychology.* Advanced online publication.

Revenson, T. A. (1994). Social support and marital coping with chronic illness. *Annals of Behavioural Medicine, 16,* 122–130.

Revenson, T. A., & Lepore, S. J. (2012). Coping in social context. In A. Baum, T. A. Revenson, & J. Singer (Eds.), *Handbook of health psychology* (pp. 193–218). New York: Taylor & Francis.

Revenson, T. A., Kayser, K., & Bodenmann, G. (Eds.) (2005). *Emerging perspectives on couples' coping with stress.* Washington DC: American Psychological Association.

Selye, H. (1974). *Stress without distress.* New York: Lippincott & Crowell.

Simmons, C., & Lehmann, P. (2012). *Tools for Strengths' Based Assessment and Evaluation.* New York: Springer.

Sindik, J. (2012). Data analysis strategies for reducing the influence of the bias in cross-cultural research. *Collegium Antropologicum, 36*(1), 31–37.

Spanier, G. B. (1976). Measuring dyadic adjustment: New scales for assessing the quality of marriage and similar dyads. *Journal of Marriage and Family, 38,* 15–28.

Suls, J., Green, P., Rose, G., Lounsbury, P., & Gordon, L. (1997). Hiding worries from one's spouse: Associations between coping via protective buffering and distress in male post-myocardial infarction patients and their wives. *Journal of Behavioral Medicine, 20,* 333–349.

Vedes, A., Nussbeck, F. W., Bodenmann, G., Lind, W., & Ferreira, A. (2013). Psychometric properties and validity of the Dyadic Coping Inventory in Portuguese. *Swiss Journal of Psychology, 72,* 149–157.

White, J. M., & Klein, D. M. (2002). *Family theories* (2nd ed.). Thousand Oaks, CA: Sage.

4

DYADIC COPING AMONG COUPLES IN THE U.S.

*Laura E. Jiménez-Arista, Kelsey J. Walsh,
and Ashley K. Randall*

Introduction

The United States (U.S.) is considered to be the 'most diverse nation in the world' (Sue & Sue, 2008, p. 59). According to the U.S. Census Bureau (2014), racial/ethnic minority individuals (e.g., African American or Black, American Indian, and Alaska Native, Asian American, and Hispanic or Latino) make up about 37 percent of the U.S. population. Given this diversity, understanding how stress can affect the 'American Couple' can be quite challenging, as there may be additional racial and ethnic variables at play (see Chapter 5 as an example). In this chapter, we first present unifying themes in American culture, which may affect the types of stressors couples in the U.S. may face. Second, we review empirical studies conducted in the U.S. on stress and dyadic coping, as conceptualized by the systemic-transactional model (Bodenmann, 1995; see Chapter 1 for review). Lastly, we analyze the suitability of applying the systemic-transactional model (STM) of dyadic coping to couples in the U.S., and conclude with recommendations for future practice and research.

Review of the Literature

Couples' Relationships in the U.S.

Understanding Relationships in an Individualistic Society

The U.S. broadly embodies traits and values that lend to its classification as an individualistic society (e.g., Sue & Sue, 2008). Individualistic societies, like the U.S., value individual goals, rather than the goals of the entire society, by fostering the importance of distinct personal characteristics, such as independence and autonomy (i.e., making life decisions individually and freely) (Sue & Sue, 2008). In addition to the focus on individualism, political and social movements in the U.S., such as the women's rights and civil rights movements, continue to shape the views of human roles and values over time as social climates change (e.g., Amato, 2009, 2014; Finkel, Hui, Carswell, & Larson, 2014). Together, the individualistic nature and social movements of the U.S. influence the function and roles intimate partners have within their romantic relationship.[1] While the institutionalization of marriage has always been an important cultural construct in the U.S. (Amato, 2009, 2014; Finkel et al., 2014), the forms and functions of marriage have changed throughout history. Throughout the nineteenth century, marriage in the U.S. was conceptualized as an institution (Strong & Cohen, 2014), which was based on meeting practical needs (e.g., achieving security) and sacrificing personal needs to maintain the marriage. As the U.S. became industrialized in the beginning of the twentieth century, a new type of marriage, referred to as the breadwinner-homemaker model, began where companionship and teamwork were emphasized, and marriage was considered a life-long commitment (Hernandez, 1993). Beginning in the 1970s, individualist marriages (Cherlin, 2004) or self-expressive marriage (Finkel et al., 2014) emerged from the concept of expressive individualism (Bellah, Madsen, Sullivan, Swidler, & Tipton, 1985), placing importance on love and intimacy in relationships (Cherlin, 2004; Dion & Dion, 1993; Finkel et al., 2014); relationship ideals that currently persist today. According to the individualistic and self-expressive perspective, committed intimate relationships and marriages serve as a vehicle for individuals achieving higher level needs, such as self-fulfillment and self-actualization (Berscheid, 2010). Importantly, intimate relationships that were not historically recognized in society before the 1970s, such as same-sex relationships and cohabiting partners, are becoming more accepted (Amato, 2009).

Historical models of intimate relationships (e.g., Burgess & Locke, 1945; Hernandez, 1993) have also attempted to explain the roles partners may play in their romantic relationship. Gender roles have traditionally defined partner's roles, wherein women typically held feminine roles in their romantic relationships, assuming more relational, domestic, and nurturing functions within the family; whereas men held more masculine roles, such as working to financially support and provide for the family (Berscheid, 2006; Dion & Dion, 1993; Ickes, 1993). Although some partners may still adhere to these traditional gender roles, increased political rights for women starting in the 1950s have shaped the notions of what roles women and men should play in their romantic relationship (Berscheid, 2006; Bolzendahl & Myers, 2004). Generally speaking, roles within romantic relationships are now viewed as more egalitarian, allowing partners to establish more equal roles, and hold equal power and responsibility in their relationships (Amato, 2009; Rodman Aronson & Buchholz, 2001). Partners are seen as having an equal responsibility to make the relationship work (Schwartz, 1994), which is of extreme importance when partners are experiencing distress. As such, if partners are considered to hold equal responsibility in the success of the relationship, then it could be argued they also share equal responsibility for managing stress together, a central theme in dyadic coping (Bodenmann, 1995).

Demise of Romantic Relationships: Stress in the U.S.

According to the American Psychological Association (APA, 2014a), close to half of the marriages in the U.S. end in divorce, and the tendency to divorce has been increasing over the last sixty years (Amato, 2015). Additionally, the relationships of partners who choose to cohabitate appear to disintegrate more rapidly (Amato, 2015). Although many reasons may account for the high divorce rate and relationship disintegration, such as years of marriage, age at marriage, or unplanned premarital pregnancy (e.g., Amato, 2015; Gottman, 1994), divorce is especially prevalent during highly stressful times, as stress can negatively impact couples' adaptive processes to cope with stressors (Neff & Karney, 2009; Randall & Bodenmann, 2009).

About 75 percent of the U.S. population reports symptoms related to stress (APA, 2014b). For years, Americans have reported moderate to high levels of stress with a significant proportion (about 20–30 percent) reporting extreme stress impacting their physical and mental health (APA, 2011, 2012, 2013). Although the recent APA report (2014b) indicates that average stress levels seem to be decreasing, some groups, such as women, parents, younger people (Millennials and Gen Xers), and low-income individuals, have higher levels of stress than what is considered healthy. In particular, parents reported higher stress related to money compared to non-parents, and about 41 percent of adults who are married or cohabitating indicated that stress has affected their relationship (APA, 2014b). Furthermore, experts contend that high levels of stress and ineffective coping methods may contribute to perpetuating unhealthy styles of living for future generations (APA, 2013). Therefore, it is important to understand the common causes and impact of stress on both individual and relational well-being, as well as ways in which the couples can cope with stress.

Causes of Stress

The dyadic stress and coping literature has differentiated stressors that come from the environment (*external* stressors), such as work or social influences, from stressors that come from dynamics inside the relationship (*internal* stressors), such as incompatibilities and differences in partners' needs and desires (Bodenmann, 1995, 2005; Randall & Bodenmann, 2009). Not surprisingly, the 'Stress in America' reports published by APA (2010, 2012, 2013, 2014b) identify that the most common stressors people in the U.S. face are related to money and finances, work, family responsibilities, and health issues (external stressors). Particularly, money has been identified as the top source of stress, which is most pertinent to parents, women, low-income individuals, and young generations (APA, 2014b).

Factors Associated with the Experience of Stress

Although main sources of stress may be similar among men and women, women are more likely to report higher levels of stress compared to men (APA 2010, 2012, 2014b). Women report greater concerns related to money, whereas men report issues related to work as a primary source of stress (APA 2014b, APA 2010). Experts suggest that women may have increased levels of stress due to their difficulties balancing house work and paid work, and their tendencies to be concerned for others (e.g., Mirowsky & Ross, 1989). Stress levels in the U.S. have also been found to differ by community type (APA, 2010). According to APA, individuals living in urban settings felt less able to manage stress and cited work and money as stressors more frequently endorsed than people living in suburbs or rural areas.

In addition to gender and geographic location, it is important to note how minority status in the U.S. (including ethnic/racial, sexual, and disability minorities, as well as economically disadvantaged individuals) may affect the experiences of stress. Ethnic and racial minority couples face oppression and discrimination, which may influence how they experience and deal with stress (Hays, 1996; King, 2005). Furthermore, acculturation stress has been related to issues such as drinking and intimate partner violence (Caetano, Ramisetty-Mikler, Vaeth, & Harris, 2007). LGBT couples may experience other sources of stress such as heterosexism, stigmatization, work discrimination, and marriage and parenting restrictions (Meyer, 2003). One recent issue that has dominated the U.S. is the legalization of same-sex marriage, which has immense implications on the rights of parenting, adoption, hospital visitation, and insurance policy restrictions (Carroll, 2010; Hunter, 2012). As such, same-sex couples often face the dual problem of developing good relationships while dealing with stigmatization at the same time (Mohr & Daly, 2008). Disability status of a child or spouse is another factor that may affect stress in couples, leading to depression, fatigue, anger, or resentment (e.g., Marini, Glover-Graf, & Millington, 2011). Finally, poverty is a major factor in stress as reports show money as the top source of stress (APA, 2014b). Due to the severe recession in the U.S. in past years, low-income individuals have undergone high stress since they face unemployment, home loss, frequent change in residency, and lack of access to health insurance and medical care (Eckholm, 2010). Low-income couples, severely impacted by the U.S. recession, have been further affected by stress that has implications for the couple's well-being, including experience of violence (e.g., Cunradi, Caetano, & Schafer, 2002; Matjasko, Niolon, & Valle, 2013).

Taken together, research has shown that couples experience a majority of external stress that may or may not immediately affect both partners in the relationship. However, researchers suggest that although stress may first be experienced by one partner, the effects of stress can spill over into the relationship causing stress for both partners (Falconier, Nussbeck, Bodenmann, Schneider, & Bradbury, 2015; Story & Repetti, 2006). Specifically, stress can cause decreased quality time with one's partner. As such, the interpersonal approach of dyadic stress conceptualizes all individual stress as dyadic stress, which suggests that stress affects both partners within the relationship (Bodenmann, 1995; 2008).

Effects of Stress

Compared to single women, married women reported higher levels of stress, being less effective managing stress, feeling irritable or angry, and experiencing more fatigue (APA, 2010). Additionally, stress has shown to impact sex and relationship satisfaction (Bodenmann, Ledermann, & Bradbury, 2007). In a study about stress in America, 40 percent of respondents reported having less sex than usual as a response to stress (NPR, 2014). Furthermore, the experience of external stress has been found to be related to angry or withdrawn marital behavior (Schulz, Cowan, Cowan, & Brennan, 2004), which has implications for the ways in which partners interpret and process marital perceptions (Neff & Karney, 2004). Researchers have also shown that the experience of daily, chronic (stable factors), and acute (temporary events) stress can affect well-being. For instance, daily stressors have been negatively related to marital quality (Harper, Schaalje, & Sandberg, 2000), and chronic stressors have been associated with lower levels of marital satisfaction, which decrease over time (Karney, Story, & Bradbury, 2005). In contrast, if chronic stress is low, acute stressors can have positive effects on the relationship, as experiencing these events may help the couple to reestablish closeness and relationship efficacy (Karney, Story, & Bradbury, 2005).

The research we have presented thus far has highlighted how stress can have negative effects on both partners (dyadic stress). As dyadic stress generates joint appraisals and efforts from both partners, coping with stress can also be seen as a joint effort between partners (Bodenmann, 2005). Conceptualized by the systemic-transactional model (Bodenmann, 1995, 1997, 2005), dyadic coping takes into account the dynamic interplay of the origin of the stress, the goals of each partner, and the couples' coping resources (see Chapter 1 for a review). Therefore, partners' experience of stress and coping involves common concerns, emotional intimacy, and the maintenance of the close relationship (Bodenmann, 2005; Randall & Bodenmann, 2009).

The systemic-transactional model (STM) shows theoretical utility in explaining how couples in the U.S. can cope with stress (Bodenmann, 1995, 1997, 2005). The model focuses on what one partner does for the other one and also what couples do conjointly, which is consistent with the general make-up of romantic relationships: based on a give-and-take agreement and egalitarian in nature (e.g., Amato, 2009; Aronson & Buchholz, 2001). Despite the relevance of the STM model, only a handful of studies in the U.S. have used this theoretical framework to understand the role of stress and coping in couples' relationships, which we review below.

Dyadic Coping in Couples in the U.S.: Review of Literature

Coping and Relationship Functioning

Several studies have utilized aspects of the STM (Bodenmann, 1995, 1997, 2005) to examine how stress and coping are related to *individual* (e.g., attachment style) and *dyadic-level* (e.g., relationship quality) variables. Using the STM framework, two empirical studies in the U.S. have examined the relation between adult attachment styles and dyadic coping. Chow and colleagues (2014) examined interpersonal coping styles in 123 heterosexual couples and found that secure individuals engaging in positive dyadic coping (i.e., validating one's partner, providing emotional support) endorsed feeling closer to their partner; whereas insecure individuals who engaged in negative dyadic coping (i.e., criticizing one's partner, using sarcasm) reported feeling more distant. In another study, Fuenfhausen and Cashwell (2013) found that attachment insecurity (anxiety and avoidance) and dyadic coping explained a significant portion of the differences in marital satisfaction among a sample of 191 graduate-level counseling and counseling psychology students. Furthermore, dyadic coping was strongly correlated with marital satisfaction and served as a partial mediator for the association between both martial satisfaction and attachment avoidance, and marital satisfaction and attachment anxiety. These studies show the importance of utilizing dyadic coping to manage stress in relationships, which can be particularly beneficial for insecurely attached individuals.

Dyadic coping has also been applied to understanding general relationship functioning. Using a sample of 100 young adult heterosexual couples living in the U.S., Papp and Witt (2010) examined whether dyadic coping would be related to relationship satisfaction and individual well-being. Positive dyadic coping (i.e., support, empathy, joint problem solving) was associated with participants' own relationship satisfaction (actor effects), and for female participants, with their partners' relationship satisfaction (partner effects). While the authors found that the partner effects were more consistent for the female participants than the male participants, the results provide support for the STM model as dyadic coping was found to be more predictive of relationship satisfaction than individual coping strategies. More recently, in their validation of the English version of the Dyadic Coping Inventory (Bodenmann, 2008), Randall, Hilpert, Jiménez-Arista, Walsh, and Bodenmann (2015) found a positive association between dyadic coping and relationship satisfaction, supporting the association between STM and relationship functioning. Taken together, the reviewed research supports notions associated with romantic relationships (e.g., Berscheid, 2010), described in detail above.

Dyadic Coping in Same-Sex Relationships

To date, research has primarily focused on understanding the role external stressors have on relationship well-being in heterosexual couples (see Randall & Bodenmann, 2009 for a review). Same-sex couples' experiences of common external stressors on a daily basis have been found to be negatively associated with relationship satisfaction in the U.S. (Totenhagen, Butler, & Ridley, 2012); however, there is still a dearth of literature in this area. To our knowledge, only two studies exist that aim to understand the link between stress and dyadic coping in LGBT individuals and same-sex couples, using the STM framework. In her dissertation, Weaver (2014) explored perceptions of stress and dyadic coping of 391 heterosexual and 201 lesbian and gay U.S. individuals, and found that heterosexual participants endorsed higher perceptions of stress; however, lesbian and gay participants reported using positive dyadic coping significantly more than the heterosexual individuals. While lesbian and gay individuals may experience more daily stress, engaging in positive dyadic coping decreases their perception of stress. Another study conducted by Randall and colleagues (*in press*) examined how forms of supportive dyadic coping could buffer symptoms of anxiety as a result of experiencing workplace minority stress. Results showed that when individuals reported their partners provided high levels of supportive dyadic coping, work discrimination stress was no longer associated with increased anxiety; however, results were only marginally significant for emotion-focused supportive dyadic coping. Taken together, these two studies highlight the benefit dyadic coping can have on stress experienced by same-sex couples.

Health Issues

One important area of research utilizing the STM framework with U.S. couples focuses on how partners cope with health issues (e.g., Badr, Carmack, Kashy, Cristofanilli, & Revenson, 2010; Berg et al., 2008; Feldman & Broussard, 2005, 2006; Johnson, Anderson, Walker, Wilcox, Lewis, & Robbins, 2013; Kayser, Watson, & Andrade, 2007), specifically Type 2 diabetes and cancer. In their study of 117 married U.S. couples with one partner diagnosed with Type 2 Diabetes, Johnson and colleagues (2013) examined how couples' relationship functioning impacted dietary and exercise adherence for the diabetic participants. The authors found that couples who engaged in higher common dyadic coping (coping together with one's partner) endorsed higher levels of both relationship satisfaction and diabetes efficacy, and more closely adhered to dietary and exercise requirements.

One larger area of research has focused on evaluating the *Partners in Coping Program* (PICP; Kayser, 1998), a psychosocial program based on the STM which teaches individual- and partner-related coping skills (e.g., communication skills and social support) for U.S. women battling breast cancer. Feldman and Broussard

(2005, 2006) applied this program and the STM framework to explore men's adjustment to their partner's breast cancer diagnosis in two studies in the U.S. In their first study of seventy-one male partners of breast cancer patients, mutuality, education level, and previous treatment for depression were all significant predictors of both common and positive dyadic coping, while mutuality was negatively associated with both hostile dyadic coping and avoidance coping. Their second study of these seventy-one individuals revealed that a negative style, such as hostile dyadic coping, was a significant predictor of how intrusive the male participants saw their partner's diagnosis in their lives.

In another PICP study of breast cancer patients in the U.S. and their husbands, Kayser and colleagues (2007) used a qualitative approach to examine how ten couples coping with cancer described their stress related to their diagnosis. The authors suggested that couples follow Lazarus and Folkman's (1984) cyclical coping pattern (i.e., appraising the stress, responding and validating it, coordinating coping strategies, and finding the benefits). Three relational qualities, awareness, authenticity, and mutuality, were identified as playing an important role in the coping process and in distinguishing those couples who responded to the disease as a couple and those who disengaged or avoided the impact of this stressor (Kayser et al., 2007). Indeed, couples who engaged in mutual responsive dyadic coping utilized both problem-focused and emotion-focused coping strategies and saw the illness as a 'we-disease,' while couples who engaged in avoidance primarily used problem-focused coping strategies and viewed the breast cancer as an individual stressor. Adaptive patterns of mutual responsiveness included appraising the illness as a dyadic stressor ('our' stress) first, and then attending each other's emotional and physical needs. Couples who adopted a mutual responsiveness pattern identified several benefits, such as building individual strength and resilience, and increasing relationship closeness (Kayser et al., 2007).

Similarly, Badr and colleagues (2010) explored the effects of dyadic coping in U.S. couples coping with breast cancer. Results revealed that couples who engaged in more positive dyadic coping (e.g., using joint efforts to solve problems) over a period of 3 and 6 months, and in less negative dyadic coping (e.g., engaging in avoidance and withdrawal), exhibited greater dyadic adjustment (i.e., relationship functioning and marital satisfaction). Conversely, individuals who used more negative dyadic coping showed greater cancer-related distress (e.g., intrusive thoughts and avoidance). Finally, using a collaborative coping framework in a U.S. study of fifty-nine prostate cancer patients and their partners, Berg and colleagues (2008) found an association between coping and better mood (as conceptualized by the Positive and Negative Affect Scale). Collectively, the research examining dyadic coping in health related issues highlights how when couples jointly cope with their health related stressors (i.e., hold egalitarian roles in coping), this allows the patient to maintain important health regimens, while experiencing an increase in relationship functioning and marital satisfaction during a stressful time (e.g., Berscheid, 2010; Cherlin, 2004; Finkel et al., 2014; Sue & Sue, 2008).

Summary

Although research on utilizing the STM framework to understand stress and coping among U.S. couples is relatively new, the existent literature points to the importance of the STM framework in explaining how couples can cope together to ameliorate the negative effects of stress in the following ways. First, the studies consistently show that dyadic coping is associated with relational satisfaction (e.g., Fuenfhausen & Cashwell, 2013; Papp & Witt, 2010; Randall et al., 2015). These findings are comparable with similar research in other cultures (e.g., Bodenmann, 1997; Bodenmann & Cina, 2005; Bodenmann, Meuwly, & Kayser, 2011) and support the conceptualization that romantic relationships serve as a mechanism for individuals to meet higher level needs, such as life satisfaction. Second, several positive dyadic coping styles (e.g., mutual responsiveness or joint efforts) used by couples coping with chronic illnesses were associated with multiple benefits such as strength, resilience, relationship closeness, confidence to follow self-care regimes, medical treatment adherence, collaboration in decisions, greater dyadic adjustment, and better mood (e.g., Badr et al., 2010; Berg et al., 2008; Johnson et al., 2013; Kayser et al., 2007). Conversely, negative dyadic coping styles, such as hostile or avoidant, were associated with illness, perceptions of intrusiveness, and individual rather than dyadic stress approaches (e.g., Feldman & Broussard, 2005; Kayser et al., 2007). Third, the positive effects of dyadic coping (e.g., strength, resilience, or better mood) were ultimately associated with the individual and the couple's functioning and wellness. Fourth, relational characteristics (e.g., relationship awareness, authenticity, mutuality, collaboration, couple identity, and attachment) may enable dyadic coping (e.g., Chow et al., 2014; Feldman & Broussard, 2005; Kayser et al., 2007) and correspond to the ideals of egalitarian relationships in the U.S. culture. In sum, these findings suggest that examining dyadic coping from the STM framework has important implications for clinicians and relationship researchers who aim to understand how couples in the U.S. can cope with various stressors.

Measuring Dyadic Coping

While the application of the STM of dyadic coping has great utility for understanding stress and couples in the U.S., the dearth of literature may be related to the lack of validated self-report measures assessing dyadic coping in couples in the U.S. To address this gap, the authors recently conducted a validation study of the English version of the Dyadic Coping Inventory (Bodenmann, 2008; see Chapter 3 for more information on the DCI). This instrument was validated using a sample of 938 individuals in committed relationships in the U.S. (Randall et al., 2015). The results showed that the factorial structure of the DCI using a U.S. sample is comparable with previous validation studies in other languages (Bodenmann, 2008; Falconier, Nussbeck, & Bodenmann, 2013; Ledermann et al., 2010; Vedes et al., 2013). In addition, the psychometric results indicated that the DCI was both reliable and valid to assess couples' coping resources, and the measurement invariance results suggested that this version can be used for comparisons across cultures. Considering these findings, the validated English version of the DCI (Randall et al., 2015) may prompt more researchers and clinicians in the U.S. to utilize the STM theory when examining issues related to dyadic stress and coping.

Implications for Practice

Despite the high divorce rate (APA, 2014a), an increasing number of couples seek therapy in order to address issues and improve the relationship (Christensen, Wheeler, Doss, & Jacobson, 2012). Some statistics indicate that over 700,000 couples are seen just by family therapists alone per year (American Association for Marriage and Family Therapy, 2014). Couples' stress models, such as the stress-divorce model proposed by Bodenmann (Bodenmann et al., 2007), explain how external stress affects relationship quality and increases the likelihood of divorce. Literature on dyadic coping in the U.S. highlights the positive associations of dyadic coping with relationship satisfaction and quality (e.g., Badr et al., 2010; Fuenfhausen & Cashwell, 2013; Papp & Witt, 2010); hence, preventive and remedial interventions in couples' therapy can incorporate current research findings to improve satisfaction and quality. For example, interventions can integrate facilitative factors found in dyadic coping such as relationship awareness, authenticity (i.e., honesty and openness), and mutuality (i.e., a sense of we-ness) (Kayser et al., 2007). These factors may promote couples' communication, dyadic coping, and ultimately, the couple's well-being. Additionally, clinicians working with couples can identify elements that may hinder dyadic coping such as avoidance, withdrawal, anxiety, and negative emotionality (Badr et al., 2010; Fuenfhausen & Cashwell, 2013). TOGETHER is an example of an intervention that is built upon the STM framework (Falconier, 2015). TOGETHER assists individuals in coping with financial stressors by teaching couples dyadic coping skills through didactics and homework (for more information see Chapter 5). This program has been found to be effective in reducing partners' financial strain, by increasing their skills in both financial management and dyadic coping strategies (Falconier, 2015). This research suggests that incorporating elements of dyadic coping into interventions designed to address specific stressors may be beneficial for relational well-being.

Healthcare

Dyadic coping has been shown to decrease stress related to health issues, like chronic illness (Badr et al., 2010; Johnson et al., 2013; Kayser et al., 2007). Partners can learn how to jointly manage illness concerns at an early stage and avoid future distress. These strategies can also be employed therapeutically with couples who have been facing distress for a long time due to chronic illness, so interventions can specifically focus on helping caregivers share concerns and avoid burnout (e.g., Badr et al., 2010). It is recommended that clinicians take into account the severity of the chronic illness (e.g., terminal clients), because caregivers might need to take a more active role in the dyadic coping process (Badr et al., 2010). Further, specific coping strategies have been successful in couples coping with cancer (i.e., problem-focused and emotion-focused strategies), and they can be taught and put into practice in couple's therapy. When developing interventions, clinicians should also take into account that dyadic coping does not only alleviate stress and improve relationship satisfaction, but it may also facilitate improvement in physical health; because dyadic coping has been related to confidence to adhere to medical treatments (Johnson et al., 2013).

Implications for Research

Given the impact of dyadic coping on well-being (e.g., Badr et al., 2010; Fuenfhausen & Cashwell, 2013; Papp & Witt, 2010), several opportunities for future research can be identified. First, it would be relevant to understand how dyadic coping behaviors develop and change across time. For example, understanding not only how dyadic coping can be fostered in couples, but also how this process advances longitudinally across the relationship life course. While some studies used longitudinal data (e.g., Badr et al., 2010; Bodenmann, Pihet, & Kayser, 2006), having more continuous assessments of the stress and dyadic coping process can offer potential benefits, such as: 1) obtaining a comprehensive picture of patterns of change in dyadic coping, 2) identifying critical periods including periods of early change, and 3) providing clinicians information about areas that should be of focus in couple's counseling. Furthermore, examining associations between patterns of change in dyadic coping and relational outcomes (i.e., marital functioning or medical treatment adherence) can also be examined in order to identify what type of patterns (i.e., trajectories) are related to better outcomes. Second, researchers can continue to examine differences in dyadic coping behaviors based on role (e.g., patient/caregiver). For instance, prior research found differences in female and male reports of dyadic coping in terms of spillover effects and prediction of marital quality (Papp & Witt, 2013). Additionally, other differences in the way patients and caregivers experience the dyadic process were also found (Badr et al., 2010). Separate analyses of patterns of change in dyadic coping by role would provide insight for couples' therapists. Finally, it is important that new research takes into account the enormous diversity in the U.S., which includes, but is not limited to, ethnic and racial diversity, contrasts in socio-economic status, and sexual identities. The pronounced cultural difference among ethnic groups in the U.S. adds specific considerations for understanding the dyadic coping process, especially for minority groups. Socio-economic disparities should also be taken into account in future research, as poverty and socio-economic factors exert influence on couple's well-being (Cunradi, Caetano & Schafer, 2002). Lastly, examining how dyadic coping may buffer LGBT couples' experience of specific minority stressors (e.g., Meyer, 2003) is an important area for future research. In summary, factors related to diversity in dyadic coping are worth exploring as they will assist relationship researchers and professionals in clinical practice to work together to develop culturally sensitive interventions, which promote dyadic coping and successful relational outcomes.

Conclusion

Individuals in the U.S. face unhealthy levels of stress, which has negative effects on both individual and relational well-being (APA, 2014b; Falconier et al., 2014; Randall & Bodenmann, 2009). The systemic-transactional model of dyadic coping (Bodenmann, 1995, 1997, 2005), which involves the interplay of each partner's goals and coping resources, represents an instrumental framework for studying dyadic coping and developing couples' interventions in the U.S., given that romantic partners have equal responsibility to make their relationship work (Schwartz, 1994). As noted above, dyadic coping has been found to be an effective strategy for dealing with the deleterious effects of stress by increasing resilience (Kayser et al., 2007), and medical treatment adherence (Johnson et al., 2013), and relational satisfaction and quality (Badr et al., 2010; Fuenfhausen & Cashwell, 2013; Papp & Witt, 2010). Future research on dyadic coping in the U.S. should focus on the individual and relational predictors associated with engaging in dyadic coping, as well as any between-partner effects associated with this process. Furthermore, an increased focus on race/ethnicity, and sexual identities, and the intersection of multiple minority identities should be incorporated to represent the diverse makeup of couples in the United States.

Note

1   With the increasing diversity in the U.S. we acknowledge that not all individuals, and subsequently romantic couples, living in the U.S. may identify with these general principles.

References

Amato, P. R. (2009). Institutional, companionate, and individualistic marriage: A social psychological perspective on marital change. In H. E. Peters & C. M. Kamp Dush (Eds.), *Marriage and family: Perspectives and complexities* (pp. 75–90). New York: Columbia University Press.

Amato, P. R. (2014). Tradition, commitment, and individualism in American marriages. *Psychological Inquiry, 25*(1), 42–46.

Amato, P. R. (2015). *President's report: Studying divorce and couple relationships—difficult times for family scholars.* Retrieved from www.ncfr.org/ncfr-report/current-issue/presidents-report-studying-divorce-and-couple-relationships-difficult-time

American Association for Marriage and Family Therapy. (2014). *Marriage and family therapists: The friendly mental health professionals.* Retrieved from www.aamft.org/iMIS15/AAMFT/Content/consumer_updates/Marriage_and_Family_Therapists.aspx

American Psychological Association. (2010). *Stress in America findings* [Data file]. Retrieved from www.apa.org/news/press/releases/stress/

American Psychological Association. (2011). *Stress in America: Our health risk connection* [Data file]. Retrieved from www.apa.org/news/press/releases/stress/

American Psychological Association. (2012). *Stress in America: Missing the healthcare connection* [Data file]. Retrieved from www.apa.org/news/press/releases/stress/

American Psychological Association. (2013). *Stress in America: Are teens adopting adults' stress habits?* [Data file]. Retrieved from www.apa.org/news/press/releases/stress/

American Psychological Association. (2014a). *Marriage & divorce.* Retrieved from www.apa.org/topics/divorce/

American Psychological Association. (2014b). *Stress in America: Paying with our health* [Data file]. Retrieved from www.apa.org/news/press/releases/stress/

Aronson, M. R., & Buchholz, E. S. (2001). The post-feminist era: Still striving for equality in relationships. *The American Journal of Family Therapy, 29,* 109–124.

Badr, H., Carmack, C. L., Kashy, D. A., Cristofanilli, M., & Revenson, T. A. (2010). Dyadic coping in metastatic breast cancer. *Health Psychology, 29*(2), 169–180.

Bellah, R. N., Madsen, R., Sullivan, W. M., Swidler, A., & Tipton, S. M. (1985). *Habits of the heart: Individualism and commitment in American life.* Berkeley, CA: University of California Press.

Berg, C. A., Wiebe, D. J., Butner, J., Bloor, L., Bradstreet, C., Upchurch, R., . . . Patton, G. (2008). Collaborative coping and daily mood in couples dealing with prostate cancer. *Psychology and Aging, 23*(3), 505–516.

Berscheid, E. (2006). The changing reasons for marriage and divorce. In M. A. Fine & J. H. Harvey (Eds.), *Handbook of divorce and relationship dissolution* (pp. 613–618). Mahwah, NJ: Lawrence Erlbaum Associates, Publishers.

Berscheid, E. (2010). Love in the fourth dimension. *The Annual Review of Psychology, 61,* 1–25.

Bodenmann, G. (1995). A systemic-transactional conceptualization of stress and coping in couples. *Swiss Journal of Psychology, 54*(1), 34–49.

Bodenmann, G. (1997). The influence of stress and coping on close relationships: A two-year longitudinal study. *Swiss Journal of Psychology, 56*(3), 156–164.

Bodenmann, G. (2005). Dyadic coping and its significance for marital functioning. In T. A. Revenson, K. Kayser, & G. Bodenmann (Eds.), *Couples coping with stress: Emerging perspectives on dyadic coping* (pp. 33–50). Washington DC: American Psychological Association.

Bodenmann, G. (2008). *Dyadisches Coping Inventar (DCI). Testmanual* [Dyadic Coping Inventory (DCI). Test manual]. Bern, Göttingen: Huber & Hogrefe.

Bodenmann, G., & Cina, A. (2005). Stress and coping among stable-satisfied, stable-distressed, and separated/divorced Swiss couples: A 5-year prospective longitudinal study. *Journal of Divorce & Remarriage, 44*(1–2), 71–89.

Bodenmann, G., Pihet, S., & Kayser, K. (2006). The relationship between dyadic coping, marital quality and well-being: A two year longitudinal study. *Journal of Family Psychology, 20,* 485–493.

Bodenmann, G., Ledermann, T., & Bradbury, T. N. (2007). Stress, sex, and satisfaction in marriage. *Personal Relationships, 14*, 407–425.

Bodenmann, G., Meuwly, N., & Kayser, K. (2011). Two conceptualizations of dyadic coping and their potential for predicting relationship quality and individual well-being. *European Psychologist, 16*, 255–266.

Bolzendahl, C. I., & Myers, D. J. (2004). Feminist attitudes and support for gender equality: Opinion change in women and men, 1974–1998. *Social Forces, 82*(2), 759–790.

Caetano, R., Ramisetty-Mikler, S., Vaeth, P. A. C., & Harris, T. R. (2007). Acculturation stress, drinking, and intimate partner violence among Hispanic couples in the US. *Journal of Interpersonal Violence, 22*(11), 1431–1447.

Carroll, L. (2010). *Counseling sexual and gender minorities.* Upper Saddle River, NJ: Pearson.

Cherlin, A. J. (2004). The deinstitutionalization of American marriage. *Journal of Marriage and Family, 66*, 848–861.

Chow, C. M., Buhrmester, D., & Tan, C. C. (2014). Interpersonal coping styles and couple relationship quality: Similarity versus complementarity hypotheses. *European Journal of Social Psychology, 44*, 175–186.

Christensen, A., Wheeler, J. G., Doss, B. D., & Jacobson, N. S. (2012). Couple distress. In D. Barlow (Ed.), *Clinical Handbook of Psychological Disorders* (pp. 703–731). New York: The Guilford Press.

Cunradi, C. B., Caetano, R., & Schafer, J. (2002). Socioeconomic predictors of intimate partner violence among White, Black, and Hispanic couples in the United States. *Journal of Family Violence, 17*(4), 377–389.

Dion, K. K., & Dion, K. L. (1993). Individualistic and collectivistic perspectives on gender and the cultural context of love and intimacy. *Journal of Social Issues, 49*(3), 53–69.

Eckholm, E. (2010). Recession raises poverty rate to a 15-year high. *New York Times, 16.*

Falconier, M. K. (2015). Together—A couples' program to improve communication, coping, and financial management skills: Development and initial pilot-testing. *Journal of Marital and Family Therapy, 41*(2), 236–250.

Falconier, M. K., Nussbeck, F., & Bodenmann, G. (2013). Dyadic coping in Latino couples: Validity of the Spanish version of the Dyadic Coping Inventory. *Anxiety, Stress, & Coping, 26*(4), 447–466.

Falconier, M. K., Nussbeck, F., Bodenmann, G., Schneider, H., & Bradbury, T. (2015). Stress from daily hassles in couples: Its effects on intradyadic stress, relationship satisfaction, and physical and psychological well-being. *Journal of Marital and Family Therapy, 41*(2), 221–235.

Feldman, B. N., & Broussard, C. A. (2005). The influence of relational factors on men's adjustment to their partners' newly-diagnosed breast cancer. *Journal of Psychosocial Oncology, 23*(2/3), 23–43.

Feldman, B. N., & Broussard, C. A. (2006). Men's adjustment to their partner's breast cancer: A dyadic coping perspective. *Health & Social Work, 31*(2), 117–127.

Finkel, E. J., Hui, C. M., Carswell, K. L., & Larson, G. M. (2014). The suffocation of marriage: Climbing Mount Maslow without enough oxygen. *Psychological Inquiry: An International Journal for the Advancement of Psychological Theory, 25*, 1–41.

Fuenfhausen, K. K., & Cashwell, C. S. (2013). Attachment, stress, dyadic coping, and marital satisfaction of counseling graduate students. *The Family Journal, 21*(4), 364–370.

Gottman, J. M. (1994). *What predicts divorce?: The relationship between marital processes and marital outcomes.* New York: Lawrence Erlbaum.

Harper, J. M., Schaalje, B. G., & Sandberg, J. G. (2000). Daily hassles, intimacy, and marital quality in later life marriages. *American Journal of Family Therapy, 28*, 1–18.

Hays, P. A. (1996). Cultural considerations in couples therapy. *Women & Therapy*, *19*(3), 13–23.

Hernandez, D. J. (1993). *America's children: Resources from family, government, and the economy.* New York: Russell Sage Foundation.

Hunter, S. (2012). *Lesbian and gay couples: Lives, issues, and practice.* Chicago, IL: Lyceum.

Ickes, W. (1993). Traditional gender roles: Do they make, and then break, our relationships? *Journal of Social Issues*, *49*(3), 71–85.

Johnson, M. D., Anderson, J. R., Walker, A., Wilcox, A., Lewis, V. L., & Robbins, D. C. (2013). Common dyadic coping is indirectly related to dietary and exercise adherence via patient and partner diabetes efficacy. *Journal of Family Psychology*, *27*(5), 722–730.

Karney, B. R., Story, L. B., & Bradbury, T. N. (2005). Marriages in context: Interactions between chronic and acute stress among newlyweds. In T. A. Revenson, K. Kayser, & G. Bodenmann (Eds.), *Couples coping with stress: Emerging perspectives on dyadic coping* (pp. 13–32). Washington DC: American Psychological Association.

Kayser, K. (1998). Skills training for breast cancer patients and their partners: An evaluation study. Proposal submitted to The Massachusetts Department of Public Health Breast Cancer Research Program.

Kayser, K., Watson, L. E., & Andrade, J. T. (2007). Cancer as a 'we-disease': Examining the process of coping from a relational perspective. *Families, Systems, & Health*, *25*(4), 404–418.

King, K. R. (2005). Why is discrimination stressful? The mediating role of cognitive appraisal. *Cultural Diversity and Ethnic Minority Psychology*, *11*(3), 202.

Lazarus, R. S., & Folkman, S. (1984). *Stress, appraisal, and coping.* New York: Springer.

Ledermann, T., Bodenmann, G., Gagliardi, S., Charvoz, L., Verardi, S., Rossier, J., . . . Iafrate, R. (2010). Psychometrics of the Dyadic Coping Inventory in three language groups. *Swiss Journal of Psychology*, *69*, 201–212.

Marini, I., Glover-Graf, N. M., & Millington, M. (2011). *Psychosocial aspects of disability: Insider perspectives and strategies for counselors.* New York: Springer.

Matjasko, J. L., Niolon, P. H., & Valle, L. A. (2013). The role of economic factors and economic support in preventing and escaping from intimate partner violence. *Journal of Policy Analysis and Management*, *32*(1), 122–128.

Meyer, I. H. (2003). Prejudice, social stress and mental health in lesbian, gay, and bisexual populations: Conceptual issues and research evidence. *Psychological Bulletin*, *129*, 674–697.

Mirowsky, J., & Ross, C. E. (1989). *Social causes of psychological distress.* NY: Aldine.

Mohr, J. J., & Daly, C. A. (2008). Sexual minority stress and changes in relationship quality in same-sex couples. *Journal of Social and Personal Relationships*, *25*(6), 989–1007.

Neff, L. A., & Karney, B. R. (2004). How does context affect intimate relationships? Linking external stress and cognitive processes within marriage. *Personality and Social Psychology Bulletin*, *30*(2), 134–148.

Neff, L. A., & Karney, B. R. (2009). Stress and reactivity to daily relationship experiences: How stress hinders adaptive processes in marriage. *Journal of Personality and Social Psychology*, *97*(3), 435–450.

NPR/Robert Wood Johnson Foundation/Harvard School (2014). *The burden of stress in America* [Data file]. Retrieved from www.rwjf.org/en/research-publications/find-rwjf-research/2014/07/the-burden-of-stress-in-america.html

Papp, L. M., & Witt, N. L. (2010). Romantic partner's individual coping strategies and dyadic coping: Implications for relationship functioning. *Journal of Family Psychology*, *24*(5), 551–559.

Randall, A. K., & Bodenmann, G. (2009). The role of stress on close relationships and marital satisfaction. *Clinical Psychology Review, 29*, 105–115.

Randall, A. K., Hilpert, P., Jiménez-Arista, L. E., Walsh, K. J., & Bodenmann, G. (2015). Dyadic coping in the U.S.: Psychometric properties and validity for use of the English version of the Dyadic Coping Inventory. *Current Psychology.* Advanced online publication.

Randall, A. K., Totenhagen, C. J., Walsh, K. J., Adams, C., & Tao, C. (in press). Coping with workplace minority stress: Associations between dyadic coping and anxiety in female same-sex couples. *Journal of Lesbian Studies, Special Issue on Contemporary Lesbian Relationships.*

Rodman Aronson, K. M., & Buchholz, E. S. (2001). The post-feminist era: Still striving for equality in relationships. *The American Journal of Family Therapy, 29*, 109–124.

Schulz, M. S., Cowan, P. A., Cowan, C. P., & Brennan, R. T. (2004). Coming home upset: Gender, marital satisfaction, and the daily spillover of workday experience into couple interactions. *Journal of Family Psychology, 18*, 250–263.

Schwartz, P. (1994). *Peer marriage: How long between equals really works.* New York: Free Press.

Story, L. B., & Repetti, R. (2006). Daily occupational stressors and marital behavior. *Journal of Family Psychology, 20*(4), 690–700.

Strong, B., & Cohen, T. F. (2014). *The marriage and family experience: Intimate relationships in a changing society* (12th ed.). Belmont, CA: Wadsworth.

Sue, D. W., & Sue, D. (2008). *Counseling the culturally diverse: Theory and practice.* Hoboken, NJ: John Wiley & Sons, Inc.

Totenhagen, C. J., Butler, E. A., & Ridley, C. A. (2012). Daily stress, closeness, and satisfaction in gay and lesbian couples. *Personal Relationships, 19*, 219–233.

United States Census Bureau. (2014). *State & county quickfacts.* Retrieved from www. quickfacts.census.gov/qfd/states/00000.html

Vedes, A., Nussbeck, F. W., Bodenmann, G., Lind, W., & Ferreira, A. (2013). Psychometric properties and validity of the Dyadic Coping Inventory in Portuguese. *Swiss Journal of Psychology, 72*(3), 149–157.

Weaver, K. M. (2014). An investigation of gay male, lesbian, and transgender dyadic coping in romantic relationships (Doctoral dissertation, Spalding University).

5

DYADIC COPING IN LATINO COUPLES IN THE U.S.

Mariana K. Falconier

Introduction

According to the U.S. Census Bureau (2014) in 2013 there were nearly 54 million Latinos, making up 17 percent of the total U.S. population. Latinos are the largest minority group and the fastest growing population in the U.S., accounting for almost half of the total population growth between 2012 and 2013 and projected to become 31 percent of the U.S. population by 2060.

The U.S. Census Bureau survey (2014) defines Latino as 'a person of Cuban, Mexican, Puerto Rican, South or Central American, or other Spanish culture or origin regardless of race.' This means that despite sharing the Spanish language (except for Brazil whose language is Portuguese) and some common cultural aspects (discussed later in this chapter), Latinos are not an homogeneous group as they may have origins in any of the twenty existing Latin American countries. These countries differ regarding their cultural traditions, geography, history, socio-economic-political situation, and relationships with the U.S. (García-Preto, 2005). These differences have played a significant role in the timing and reasons for Latinos to immigrate into the U.S. (e.g., civil war, political persecution and torture, poverty, reunification with family members in the U.S., educational and economic advancement). As a result of these factors, differences in population size, length of presence as well as resources and opportunities exist among the various Latino groups in the U.S. For example, Mexicans have the longest presence in the U.S. and markedly largest population (Falicov, 2005), Cubans are the most highly educated and have attained political power (Bernal & Shapiro, 2005), and Salvadorans are the newest but also youngest, poorest, and least educated group in the U.S. (Kusnir, 2005). These dissimilar realities in the U.S. pose a different set of challenges and stressors for each Latino group and their couple's relationships. Despite the varying realities of each of the Latino groups, Latinos share some commonalities in their history and cultural traditions and beliefs, which has been collectively described as the Latino culture. This chapter discusses the Latino cultural values that are relevant to understand couple relationships in this population, what we know about stress and coping processes in Latino couples living in the U.S., and the implications for clinical practice and future research derived from this knowledge.

Review of the Literature

Latino Couples' Relationships

Most Latin American countries have been deeply influenced by the Spanish culture and the Roman Catholic faith as a result of the Spanish colonization in the sixteenth century and the subsequent forced conversion to Catholicism. The way in which the Spanish and Catholic influences evolved in each country has been the result of various factors, including the presence and survival of indigenous cultures, the impact of large immigration waves, the availability of economic and natural resources, and the regular presence of military dictatorships during the twentieth century among other factors. The Spanish culture and Roman Catholicism shaped for decades the structure of Latino families, particularly regarding their family orientation, traditional gender roles and the preference for heterosexual unions. Despite a trend toward more liberal gender views and acceptance of same-sex partnerships both in Latin American countries and among Latinos living in the U.S., Latino couples and families are still influenced by long-held values and traditions (Bejarano, Manzano, & Montoya, 2011; Falicov, 2014).

The term *familismo* has been used to describe Latinos' strong family orientation, in which family well-being, ties, and loyalty are prioritized over individual ones. It is 'a core cultural value that requires the individual to submit to a more collective, family-based form of decision-making, and responsibility for, and obligation to ensuring the well-being of family members (both nuclear and extended)' (Smith-Morris, Morales-Campos, Castaneda Alvarez, & Turner, 2012, p. 37). Familismo entails the obligation to provide material and emotional support to other family members in the nuclear and extended family and an expectation that any family member can always count on such support (Sabogal, Marin, Otero-Sabogal, Marin, & Perez-Stable, 1987). The presence of multigenerational households among Latinos in the U.S. speaks to this sense of familismo (García-Preto, 2005). But besides providing a network of instrumental and emotional support, familismo has important implications for the couple's relationship. Caring for their children is the couple's primary goal, which means that the parent-child dyad is prioritized over the husband–wife relationship (Falicov, 2014). Familismo also means that boundaries are flexible between the spousal subsystem and the extended family and, as a result, the extended family becomes involved in childrearing, participates in disputes between the spouses (usually siding with their own blood relative) (Falicov, 2014), and provides open guidance and opinion on parental and spousal issues. In short, the involvement of the extended family may be a source of support as well as of intense conflict for the couple (Falicov, 2014).

Closely related to the value of familismo is the presence of traditional gender roles in Latino cultures. Families with traditional gender roles view the man as the ultimate authority in the household, who is responsible for providing financially for the family, whereas the woman is expected to be the caretaker of children and the elderly and the homemaker. These traditional gender roles have been linked to the Latinos' concepts of *machismo* in men and *marianismo* in women. Machismo has been associated with hypermasculinity and evokes the idea of men as controlling, unfaithful, authoritarian, and possessive (Arciniega, Anderson, Tovar-Blank, & Tracey, 2008; Falicov, 2014). Marianismo refers to the idealized characteristics of women, which should reflect the virtues of Virgin Mary: submissiveness, purity, humility, non-sexuality, devotion as a mother and wife, superior spiritualty (Castillo & Cano, 2007), but above all, capable of 'extreme sacrifices and suffering for the sake of the family' (Castillo, Pérez, Castillo, & Ghosheh, 2010, p. 164). Nonetheless, late reviews of traditional masculine and feminine identities among Latinos have differentiated between negative and positive dimensions of the concepts. The positive dimension of this hypermasculine identity has been referred to as *caballerismo* and it includes 'nurturance, protection of the family and its honor, dignity, wisdom, hard work, responsibility, spirituality, and emotional connectedness' (Arciniega et al., 2008, p. 20) whereas the negative dimensions of machismo include aggression, emotional restrictiveness, sexism, and chauvinism (Arciniega et al., 2008). Research has shown that machismo tends to be more prevalent among lower educated groups (Arciniega et al., 2008). Similar to machismo, the construct of marianismo has been criticized for promoting a characterization of Latino women as weak and submissive and for concealing positive aspects of Latino women such as their strength and their nurturing and proactive role in family life (Castillo et al., 2010).

Once in the U.S. many Latino immigrant couples are exposed to more liberal gender roles, the need for many women to work, and legal protections against domestic violence, all of which may lead one of the partners to seek changes in their marital relationship (Hirsch, 2003). In fact, research suggests that it is not a traditional gender role attitude that is linked to interpartner violence among Latinos in the U.S. (e.g., Neff et al., 1995) but rather partners' differences in gender role orientation that are associated with interpartner aggression and relationship satisfaction (Falconier, 2013; Falconier et al., 2013; Klevens et al., 2007).

Stress and Coping in Latino Couples

Despite the family orientation of Latinos, their divorce rates have been increasing in the U.S. and are similar to those for Whites and much lower than those for Asians. Between 2006 and 2010, 9.3 percent of Latino women and 5.4 percent of Latino men were divorced compared to 8.9 percent of White women,

5.6 percent of White men, 5.2 percent of Asian women, and 0.7 percent of Asian men (Copen, Kaniels, Vespa, & Mosher, 2012). Divorce rates among Latinos can be explained in part by the conflict between traditional and more liberal gender roles (see earlier discussion), but it can also be the result of the stressful conditions in which most Latino couples live, which threaten the stability and well-being of their relationships.

In addition to the psychosocial stressors that many families may face in the U.S. (e.g., juggling childcare and job responsibilities in dual income families, financial difficulties), Latino couples face a set of additional stressors (Padilla & Borrero, 2006) stemming from their educationally and economically disadvantaged situation in the U.S. Latinos are the least educated group in the U.S. with only 18 percent of the population 25 years and older in 2013 having a Bachelor's degree compared to 37 percent among Whites, 27 percent among Blacks or African Americans, and 59 percent among Asians (U.S. Bureau of Labor Statistics, 2014). Unsurprisingly, Latinos also tend to have the lowest paying jobs and unemployment rates are higher than the total population (U.S. Bureau of Labor Statistics, 2014) with 23.5 percent of Latino families still living in poverty compared to 14.5 percent nationally, 10.4 percent among Asians, and 9.6 percent among Whites. Consequently, Latinos in the U.S. tend to work multiple jobs and struggle to afford housing, childcare, education, and medical insurance (DeNavas-Walt, Proctor, & Smith, 2011; Trevelyan, Acosta, & De La Cruz, 2013).

In addition to the above-mentioned stressors, Latino couples who are first-generation immigrants (around 40 percent of the total Latino population) also deal with *immigration stress* (Aroian, Norris, Tran, & Schapper-Morris, 1998). Part of these couples' immigration stress relates to what is commonly known as *acculturative stress* which includes the stress related to adapting to a new culture and stemming from occupational challenges, language barriers, cultural differences in values and practices (e.g., authoritarian vs. authoritative parenting, individualism vs. familismo, liberal vs. traditional gender roles), and difficulties in navigating new legal, school, and labor systems. Other dimensions of immigration stress, which do not relate to acculturative stress include losing material and emotional support systems, missing family and children left behind in the home country, fearing for one's immigration status, and sometimes losing family members to deportation (Falconier, Nussbeck, & Bodenmann, 2013b).

Despite the large number of everyday stressors that Latino couples report, there has been limited research on the effects of such stressors on couples' relationships. In addition to the authors' studies on immigrant Latino couples (described later in this chapter) there have been only three studies on stress and relationship quality among Latino couples in the U.S., and all of them indicate that stress does take a toll on intimate relationships in this population. Two of those studies indicated that acculturative stress could be linked to increased interpartner violence (Caetano, Ramisetty-Mikler, Caetano Vaeth, & Harris, 2007) and decreased relationship satisfaction (Negy, Hammons, Reig-Ferrer, & Carper,

2010). The third study by Helms and colleagues (2014) with a sample of 120 first-generation Mexican immigrants indicated that economic pressure and stress from cultural adaptation affected marital satisfaction and negativity indirectly by increasing depressive symptoms.

Regarding the coping strategies that Latinos rely on to face stressors in the U.S., the anecdotal literature suggests that, consistent with familismo, social support from family is a valuable resource (Falicov, 2014; García-Preto, 2005). Nonetheless, Latinos also seek support from friends. A recent meta-analysis on coping strategies to deal with discrimination indicated that support from family and friends protected Latinos from the effects of discrimination on their physical and mental health and education and employment outcomes (Lee & Ahn, 2012).

Nonetheless, Latinos are also said to rely on spiritual resources to cope. Spirituality, either through organized religious institutions or folk practices, has been described as a significant dimension in the U.S. Latino population (Falicov, 2014). Ninety percent of Latinos in the U.S. identify with a specific religion (Pew Hispanic Center, 2007) and many of those also use *Espiritismo* (the belief in an invisible world of both good and evil spirits), and *Santeria* (the belief in priests and priestesses who heal and perform rituals; Falicov, 2009). Spiritual beliefs and practices can help many Latinos cope with stress and become part of religious communities, which can also provide instrumental and emotional support, particularly for first-generation immigrants. In addition and closely related to their spiritual orientation Latinos also cope through *fatalism*, the belief that most of what happens in our lives is beyond our control and that God is in charge of our destiny (Falicov, 2014). Research at the individual level seems to support the notion that spirituality does serve as a coping mechanism among Latinos. For example, Latina caregivers of family members with dementia have been found to rely more on religious coping (e.g., attendance of religious services, praying) than Caucasian caregivers (Mausbach & Thompson, 2003) and Latinas caring for partners recovering from a stroke also use religious coping (De Leon Arabit, 2008). Similarly, a study on 200 Latinos with arthritis found that religious coping contributed to psychological well-being (Abraído-Lanza, Vasquez, & Echeverria, 2004).

While social support and religion have been identified as effective coping mechanisms, Latinos have also been found to cope by drinking to deal with acculturative stress (Ehlers, Gilder, Críado, & Caetano, 2009; Gil, Wagner, & Vega, 2000; Lee, Colby, Rohsenow, López, Hernández, & Caetano, 2013). Among Latino men, drinking has been found to be used as a coping mechanism among those who adhere to the ideology of machismo (Arciniega et al., 2008) whereas caballerismo is more associated with problem-solving strategies.

First Study on Stress and Coping in Immigrant Latino Couples

Given the absence of research on Latino couples' coping processes, in 2009 the author of the present chapter collected cross-sectional data from 114 Latino immigrant couples living in the Washington, DC, metropolitan area in order to examine stress and coping processes from a systemic-transactional model (STM; Bodenmann, 1997). These data were initially used to validate the Spanish translation of the Dyadic Coping Inventory (DCI; Bodenmann, 2008) and assess the extent to which Latino couples rely on dyadic coping. Later on, the data were used to examine factors affecting dyadic coping, the effects of dyadic coping on relationship quality, and the moderating role of dyadic coping in the immigration stress–relationship satisfaction association. All of the findings resulting from the analyses of these data are unique in that it is the first study collecting dyadic quantitative data on immigration stress and dyadic coping in Latino couples and analyzing both partners' data within the same model, allowing for the examination and control for the interdependence of partners' data. The next sections describe these studies and discuss their results and implications.

Conceptual Framework: Applying the Systemic-Transactional Model to Latino Couples

The systemic-transaction model (Bodenmann, 1997) offers a conceptual framework to understand stress and coping processes in the context of couples' relationships and may be particularly useful to study stress and coping processes in immigrant and Latino couples. According to STM one partner's stress experience and coping efforts cannot be understood without considering the other partner's. This is particularly relevant for Latino couples in which both partners experience immigration related stressors, as each partner is not only coping individually with their own immigration stress but he or she is also affected by the other partner's immigration stress. Furthermore, STM dyadic coping involves not only how partners communicate stress to each other and assist the other partner to cope by providing emotion- and problem-focused support but also partners' conjoint efforts to cope together with common stressors (see Chapter 1). Common dyadic coping may be particularly important for Latino immigrant couples as both partners may be experiencing immigration stressors, and they may be coping with such stressors conjointly. In addition, STM emphasis on partners' mutual assistance to cope and their conjoint efforts to deal with common stressors is congruent with the cultural orientation of familismo in which family members are expected to be a source of support.

Sample and Procedure

The DCI validation study (Falconier et al., 2013a) included 114 community couples in which both partners identified themselves as Latino/a and had been living together or married at least for a year. However, the rest of the studies (Austin & Falconier, 2013; Falconier, 2013; Falconier et al., 2013b; Falconier, Huerta, & Hendrickson, 2015), excluded the ten couples in which at least one partner had been born in the U.S. or had arrived in the U.S. before the age of 10. First-generation immigrant participants had been born in El Salvador (32.7 percent), Peru (13.9 percent), Mexico (12 percent), Guatemala (11.1 percent), or other Latin American countries (30.3 percent). In terms of country of origin distribution, the sample is not representative of the Latino population in the U.S. (64.5 percent Mexican, 3.2 percent Salvadoran, 2.0 percent Guatemalan, 1.0 percent Peruvian; U.S. Census Bureau, 2009), but it may be of the Latino population in the Washington, DC, metropolitan area (e.g., Montgomery County: 9.4 percent Mexican, 32.2 percent Salvadoran, 7.2 percent Guatemalan, 6.3 percent Peruvian; U.S. Census Bureau, 2009). In the sample of 114 couples, women's mean age was 38.91 (SD: 8.11) and men's mean age was 39.81 (SD: 8.96). The average length of residence in the U.S. was 12.37 years (SD: 7.43) for women and 14.32 years (SD: 8.03) for men. Eighty-four couples (74.3 percent) were married and 28 (23 percent) couples were cohabiting. On average couples had been living together for 11.55 years (SD: 7.63) and had 1.93 children (Median: 2.00; SD: 1.25) 21 years old or younger living in the household. The majority of men (56.3 percent) and women (67.2 percent) held at least a high school diploma, 19.5 percent of women and 24.9 percent of men held at least a bachelor's degree but 10.6 and 6.6 percent had not completed elementary school. The majority of men (85 percent) and women (61.9 percent) were employed. The combined income for the couple was at least $50,000 for 47.7 percent of the sample (middle-class), between $20,000 and $49,999 (low-middle class or working class) for 32.7 percent, and below $20,000 (lower class) for 13.2 percent. The majority of participants reported being Catholic (69 percent) whereas 17.9 percent were of other Christian religions, 0.9 percent Jewish, 0.9 percent Buddhist, and 3.5 percent reported no religious affiliation.

Partners were mailed a dozen standardized self-report measures for them to complete separately. Upon receipt of completed questionnaires each partner received a $25 gift card. Back-translation methods were used for those instruments for which there was not a Spanish version available.

Validation of the Spanish Version of the DCI

The DCI was translated from Bodenmann's English translation of the original German version using back-translation methods. With the exclusion of two items from the stress communication subscale and one from the negative dyadic coping subscale (by oneself and by partner), results from confirmatory factor analysis (Men: χ_{AB} (356) = 443.70, $p = 0.001$, robust CFI= 0.956, SRMR= 0.065, robust RMSEA= 0.040 (0.021, 0.055); women: χ_{AB} (356) = 492.924, $p < 0.001$, robust CFI = 0.930, SRMR = 0.069, robust, RMSEA = 0.052 (0.037, 0.065) of this Spanish version of the DCI supported the factorial structure proposed in the original thirty-seven-item DCI, which included the following twelve subscales: Stress Communication by Oneself and by Partner, Emotion- and

Problem-Focused Supportive Dyadic Coping by Oneself and by Partner, Delegated Dyadic Coping by Oneself and by Partner, Negative Dyadic Coping by Oneself and by Partner, Emotion- and Problem-Focused Common Dyadic Coping, and Evaluation of Dyadic Coping. Factor loadings and internal consistencies for each of those twelve subscales and the aggregated scales of Positive Dyadic Coping, Dyadic Coping by Oneself, and Dyadic Coping by Partner were acceptable and comparable to previous studies (e.g., Bodenmann, 2008; Donato, Iafrate, Barni, Bertoni, Bodenmann, & Gagliardi, 2009).

The correlational analysis among subscales indicated that overall the DCI subscales of the Spanish version of the DCI also had good discriminant validity. The concurrent validity of this version was supported by (a) positive (and negative for the Negative Dyadic Coping subscale) correlations between each of the DCI subscales and relationship satisfaction as measured by the Dyadic Satisfaction subscale of the Dyadic Adjustment Satisfaction Scale (DAS; Spanier, 1976) and (b) positive correlations of the positive forms of dyadic coping subscales and aggregated dyadic coping by oneself and partner scales with each partner's report of partners' efforts for constructive conflict resolution as measured by the Negotiation subscale from the Conflict Tactics Scale-Revised (CTS-R; Strauss, Hamby, Boney-McCoy, & Sugarman, 1996). The criterion validity was supported by the positive associations of the positive dyadic forms of dyadic coping subscales and aggregated dyadic coping by oneself and partner scales with engagement coping strategies as measured by the Engagement aggregated scale (Problem-Solving, Cognitive Restructuring, Express Emotions, and Social Support subscales) from the Coping Strategies Inventory (CSI; Cano García, Rodríguez Franco, & García Martínez, 2007).

Frequency of Dyadic Coping Among Latino Couples

On average, both men and women communicated stress to their partner and engaged in emotion- and problem-focused supportive dyadic coping and delegated and common dyadic coping from *sometimes* to *frequently* and tended to engage less frequently in negative forms of dyadic coping from *rarely* to *sometimes* (Falconier et al., 2013a) (see Table 5.1). Latino couples' frequent engagement in positive forms of dyadic coping is consistent with their family and collectivistic orientation by which emotional and practical support is expected from family members and the family needs, well-being, and stability are prioritized over the individual. Nonetheless, in this sample both partners agreed that women tended to provide more emotion-focused supportive dyadic coping than men did, which is consistent with the Latino traditional gender-role orientation present in the values of machismo/caballerismo and marianismo. Latino women are expected to care for the emotional needs of their children, spouse, and extended family (Castillo & Cano, 2007), which might explain why they are more likely to provide emotional support to their male partners.

TABLE 5.1 DCI Subscales' Means and Standard Deviations

Subscales and		Men		Women	
		Mean	*SD*	*Mean*	*SD*
Stress communication	O	3.35	1.11	3.48	.97
	P	3.44	1.08	3.22	1.05
Emotion-Focused SDC	O	3.68	.87	3.85	.73
	P	3.75	.96	3.37	1.27
Problem-Focused SDC	O	3.48	.96	3.64	0.82
	P	3.46	1.03	3.14	1.15
Delegated DC	O	3.33	1.07	3.51	0.94
	P	3.46	.91	3.19	1.08
Negative DC	O	2.28	.86	2.29	.82
	P	2.44	.93	2.40	.88
DC total by Oneself		3.56	.65	3.72	.54
DC total by Partner		3.59	.74	3.29	.80
Emotion-Focused CDC		3.36	1.19	3.27	1.21
Problem-Focused CDC		3.57	1.13	3.78	.97
Evaluation of DC		3.74	1.13	3.51	1.17
Total DC		110.65	20.81	106.91	20.87

Note: CDC, common dyadic coping; DC, dyadic coping; O, Oneself; P, Partner; SDC, supportive dyadic coping.

★ Statistically significant differences between men and women at least at $p < .05$

Answer options: 1 = *very rarely*; 2 = *rarely*; 3 = *sometimes*; 4 = *frequently*; 5 = *very often*.

Factors Affecting Dyadic Coping: Gender Role Orientation and Spirituality

Structural equation modeling (SEM) was used to analyze the data from the 104 immigrant Latino couples and examined the contributions of spirituality in one model (Austin & Falconier, 2013) and traditional gender role orientation in two other models (Falconier, 2013) to both supportive and common dyadic. Spirituality, which was highly important in both partners' everyday life but significantly higher for women, was positively associated with partners' own supportive dyadic coping toward the other partner (Standardized Path Coefficients: Men: 0.19; Women: 0.25) and the couples' common dyadic coping (Standardized Path Coefficients: Men: 0.28; Women: 0.17). These findings were consistent with the highly spiritual orientation associated with the Latino population, particularly for women as a result of the ideals of marianismo. More importantly, however, the results suggested that spirituality promotes positive forms of dyadic coping.

SEM results for the models analyzing the influence of each partner's traditional gender role orientation (as measured by the Equalitarian Roles subscale of the ENRICH Marital Inventory; Olson, Fournier, & Druckman, 1983) on supportive and common dyadic coping (Falconier, 2013) indicated that men who were more traditionally gender role oriented tended to provide less supportive dyadic coping to their partners (Standardized Path Coefficient: −0.18) but that the women's traditional gender role views did not influence her levels of dyadic coping toward their male partner. Furthermore, results also indicated that couples in which the man reported stronger traditional gender role views tended to engage in common dyadic coping less frequently (Standardized Path Coefficient: −0.43). Interestingly, a further analysis of a different model that included the difference in partners' traditional gender role orientation showed that this difference had no significant effect on either supportive or common dyadic coping, highlighting again that the man's traditional gender role orientation negatively affects his supportive dyadic coping and the couple's common dyadic coping above and beyond the effects of the woman's gender role views and how different partners' views are from each other's. The finding suggests that the hypermasculine aspects, which are part of a traditional gender role orientation and, which make Latino men responsible for instrumental rather than emotional roles in the family, do not favor their involvement in coping strategies to assist the partner or to work together with the partner in facing common stressors. It is worth noting that this sample reported relatively high levels of traditional gender role orientation and those levels were significantly higher for men than for women.

Effects of Dyadic Coping on Psychological Aggression and Relationship Satisfaction

The models analyzed through SEM that included spirituality or traditional gender role orientation as predictors of dyadic coping also included psychological aggression (measured by the CTS-R Psychological Aggression subscale) or relationship satisfaction (measured by the DAS Dyadic Satisfaction subscale) as relational outcomes. SEM results indicated that neither partner's efforts to provide supportive dyadic coping to the other partner increased or decreased the likelihood of interpartner psychological aggression. By contrast, common dyadic coping was negatively associated with the man's (Standardized Path Coefficient: −0.32) and the woman's (Standardized Path Coefficient: −0.36) psychological aggression toward the other partner. Furthermore, in the model that included spirituality the protective effects of common dyadic coping on the likelihood of interpartner psychological aggression were present above and beyond the protective effects of spirituality. Unlike the spirituality model, in the model that included traditional gender role orientation, common dyadic coping mediated part of the association between the man's traditional gender role orientation and his psychologically aggressive behaviors toward the other partner. In other words, when a Latino male spouse had more traditional gender role views the couple is less likely to engage in conjoint efforts to manage common stressors (Standardized Path Coefficient: −0.22), which in turn increases the likelihood of their engagement in mutual psychological aggression (Standardized Path Coefficients: Men: 0.43; Women: −0.48).

Results from SEM models that included relationship satisfaction as a relational outcome were close to the results for psychological aggression models. Common dyadic coping was found to predict each partner's relationship satisfaction positively (Unstandardized Path Coefficients: Men: 0.64; Women: 0.29) whereas it was only the man's supportive dyadic coping efforts that was positively associated with the woman's relationship satisfaction (Unstandardized Path Coefficient: 0.43). The woman's supportive dyadic coping did not affect her partner's satisfaction with the relationship. This set of findings suggest that it is common dyadic coping rather than supportive dyadic coping that protects Latino couples from psychological aggression and relationship dissatisfaction in *both* partners and that it was only the woman's relationship satisfaction that was also dependent on the support provided by the partner to cope with stress.

Dyadic Coping as a Moderator

In another set of SEM analyses used to examine whether dyadic coping moderated the relationship between immigration stress and relationship satisfaction, common dyadic coping seemed to buffer the negative effects only of Latina women's immigration stress on both partners' relationship satisfaction. In these analyses the data on immigration stress had been collected through a modified version of the Demands of Immigration Scale (DIS; Aroian et al., 1998), which included the following subscales: Sense of Loss, Novelty, Occupational Challenges, Language Barriers, Discrimination, Not at Home Feeling, Missing Family, and Legal Issues. Men and women experienced similar levels of immigration stress.

Consistent with the findings from previous models, SEM unstandardized results indicated that common dyadic coping moderated the negative effects of the woman's overall immigration stress (0.75) and the dimensions of female novelty (0.96), not at home (0.48), occupation (0.88), discrimination (0.48), and loss (0.57) stress in particular on her relationship satisfaction and the negative effects of the female novelty (0.53), language (0.59), and loss (0.44) stress on the male relationship satisfaction. Also consistent with the previous analyses, SEM unstandardized results did indicate the supportive dyadic coping provided by the male partner buffered the effects of the woman's stress from missing her family (0.63) and experiencing stress from novelty (0.88), language challenges (0.62), a sense of loss (0.46), and discrimination (0.51) on her own satisfaction with the couple's relationship. Nevertheless, common dyadic coping seemed to *exacerbate* the potential negative effects of male novelty (Men: −0.70; Women: −0.87) and loss (Men: −0.38; Women: −0.32) on each partner's relationship satisfaction, of male language stress on his own relationship satisfaction (−0.66), and of the male occupation stress on the female relationship satisfaction (−0.71).

Taken together this set of findings suggests that common dyadic coping and the male supportive dyadic coping are associated with lower psychological aggression and increased relationship satisfaction in both partners. However, when it comes to immigration stress it seems that common dyadic coping only protects the couple's relationship from Latino women's immigration stress but not the men's, even exacerbating the negative effects of immigration stress on both partner's relationship satisfaction. These gender differences could be the result of the prevalence of traditional gender roles in the Latino culture, a prevalence that was also observed in this sample. It is possible that, given their orientation towards marianismo, Latinas may value and benefit more from interpersonal connectedness and support from others, explaining why common dyadic coping and supportive dyadic coping from their male partners may help them cope with stress. Unlike women, given their traditional gender role orientation, Latino men might not view such common and supportive dyadic coping as helpful but perhaps more as an indicator of their inability to cope with stressful situations independently. This could explain why they might feel comfortable in supporting their female partners in dealing with their immigration stress, but they might not experience supportive and common dyadic coping effective in dealing with their own immigration stress. However, given that this finding emerged in relation to immigration stress, it is unknown if common and supportive dyadic coping might be experienced in this way when dealing with other stressors.

Implications for Practice

Considering the various stressors that Latinos, and particularly immigrant Latinos, are likely to face in the U.S., clinicians working with this population should always assess for the sources and levels of stress that their Latino clients experience, the effect of such stress on their individual and relational well-being, and the effectiveness of their coping strategies. The validated Spanish version of the DCI could be used as part of this assessment. Clinicians should also be aware of the beneficial effects for the individual and the couple's relationship of both spirituality and family support as coping mechanisms since both strategies are consistent with Latino cultural values. Therapists should also focus on Latino couples' use of dyadic coping strategies as all of the positive dimensions of dyadic coping were found to be associated with relationship satisfaction and common dyadic coping seemed to protect the couple from mutual psychological aggression. Nevertheless, it is important that before encouraging any form of dyadic coping, therapists assess each partner's adherence to traditional gender role orientation as this may play a role in a couple's likelihood of using dyadic coping strategies and the effect that dyadic coping may have on men. Before further research is conducted and results are replicated, clinicians should also assess the relational effects of common dyadic coping to deal with men's stress given the exacerbating effects in relationship dissatisfaction that was found for the men's immigration stress.

Implications for Research

Since the study with immigrant couples presented in this chapter is the first one on dyadic coping in Latino couples in the U.S., further research is needed with larger, nationally representative Latino samples to replicate some of the findings of this first study and to continue expanding our knowledge about this population. This knowledge is necessary to develop culturally sensitive clinical and programmatic approaches to work with a population that has to cope with a significant amount of stressors. Future studies should include not only first-generation immigrant Latinos but also, second- and third-generation immigrants as there may be variation in dyadic stress and coping processes across generations. Even though the validation of the DCI provides a reliable and valid instrument with which to assess dyadic coping in Latino couples, future studies should try to incorporate observational data as well to reduce social desirability biases. Given the findings from our initial study on Latino couples, it is also important that future studies examine whether there are differences in the protective function of supportive and common dyadic coping depending on the type of stressor and the gender of the partner. Qualitative studies are also necessary to gain a more in-depth understanding about how each partner experiences stress communication and supportive and common dyadic coping.

Conclusion

Despite the large number of stressors that Latino couples living in the U.S. experience, little research has been conducted on how these couples cope with their stress. Findings from the first study on immigrant Latino couples indicate that partners do use the various positive dimensions of dyadic coping identified by the STM and that they tend to avoid negative dyadic coping strategies. Findings also indicate that Latino cultural aspects such as the importance of spirituality and traditional gender role orientation may affect the frequency with which dyadic coping strategies are used and probably its effects on relationship quality, all of which highlights the role of cultural factors in dyadic coping. Even though many of these preliminary findings suggest that supportive and common dyadic coping may protect the couple from dissatisfaction and psychological aggression, further research is warranted before full-scale programs and clinical interventions are developed.

References

Abraído-Lanza, A. F., Vasquez, E., & Echeverria, S. E. (2004). En las manos de dios [in God's hands]: Religious and other forms of coping among Latinos with arthritis. *Journal of Consulting & Clinical Psychology, 72*, 91–102.

Arciniega, G. M., Anderson, T. C., Tovar-Blank, Z. G., & Tracey, T. J. G. (2008). Toward a fuller conception of machismo: Development of a traditional machismo and caballerismo scale. *Journal of Counseling Psychology, 55*, 19–33.

Aroian, K. J., Norris, A. E., Tran, T. V., & Schappler-Morris, N. (1998). Development and psychometric evaluation of the demands of immigration scale. *Journal of Nursing Measurement, 6*, 175–194.

Austin, J., & Falconier, M. K. (2013). Spirituality and common dyadic coping: Protective factors from psychological aggression in Latino immigrant couples. *Journal of Family Issues, 34*, 323–346.

Bejarano, C. E., Manzano, S., & Montoya, C. (2011). Tracking the Latino gender gap: Gender attitudes across sex, borders, and generations. *Politics & Gender, 7*, 521–549.

Bernal, G., & Shapiro, E. (2005). Cuban families. In M. McGoldrick, J. Giordano, & N. García-Preto (Eds.), *Ethnicity and family therapy* (3rd ed.) (pp. 202–215). New York: The Guilford Press.

Bodenmann, G. (1997). Dyadic coping: A systemic-transactional view of stress and coping among couples: Theory and empirical findings. *European Review of Applied Psychology, 47*, 137–140.

Bodenmann, G. (2008). *Dyadisches Coping Inventar (DCI). Testmanual [Dyadic Coping Inventory (DCI). Test manual].* Bern, Göttingen: Huber & Hogrefe.

Caetano, R., Ramisetty-Mikler, S., Caetano Vaeth, P. A., & Harris, T. R. (2007). Acculturation stress, drinking, and intimate partner violence among Hispanic couples in the U.S. *Journal of Interpersonal Violence, 22*, 1431–1447.

Cano García, F., Rodríguez Franco, L., & García Martínez, J. (2007). Spanish version of the Coping Strategies Inventory. *Actas Españolas de Psiquiatría, 35*, 29–39.

Castillo, L. G., & Cano, M. A. (2007). Mexican American psychology: Theory and clinical application. *Cross-cultural psychotherapy: Toward a critical understanding of diverse client populations*, 85–102.

Castillo, L. G., Pérez, F. V., Castillo, R., & Ghosheh, M. R. (2010). Construction and initial validation of the Marianismo Beliefs Scale. *Counseling Psychology Quarterly, 23*, 163–175.

Copen, C. E., Daniels, K., Vespa, J., & Mosher, W. D. (2012). First marriages in the United States: Data from the 2006–2010 National Survey of Family Growth. *National Health Statistics Reports, 49.* Center for Disease Control and Prevention, National Center for Health Statistics: Hyattsville, MD.

De Leon Arabit, L. (2008). Coping strategies of Latino women caring for a spouse recovering from a stroke: A grounded theory. *Journal of Theory Construction & Testing, 12*, 42–49.

DeNavas-Walt, C., Proctor, B. D., & Smith, J. C. (2014). Income, poverty, and health insurance coverage in the United States: 2010. *Current Population Reports.* Washington DC: U.S. Department of Commerce, Economics and Statistics Administration, U.S. Census Bureau.

Donato, S., Iafrate, R., Barni, D., Bertoni, A., Bodenmann, G., & Gagliardi, S. (2009). Measuring dyadic coping: The factorial structure of Bodenmann's Dyadic Coping Questionnaire in an Italian sample. *Testing, Psychometrics, Methodology in Applied Psychology, 16*, 25–47.

Ehlers, C., Gilder, D. A., Críado, J. R., & Caetano, R. (2009). Acculturation stress, anxiety disorders, and alcohol dependence in a select population of young adult Mexican Americans. *Journal of Addiction Medicine, 3*, 227–233.

Falconier, M. K. (2013). Traditional gender role orientation and dyadic coping in immigrant Latino couples: Effects on couple functioning. *Family Relations, 62*, 269–283.

Falconier, M. K., Nussbeck, F., & Bodenmann, G. (2013a). Dyadic coping in Latino couples: Validity of the Spanish version of the Dyadic Coping Inventory. *Anxiety, Stress, & Coping, 26*, 446–466.

Falconier, M. K., Nussbeck, F., & Bodenmann, G. (2013b). Immigration stress and relationship satisfaction in Latino couples: The role of dyadic coping. *Journal of Social and Clinical Psychology, 32*, 813–843.

Falconier, M. K., Huerta, M., & Hendrickson, E. (2015). Immigration stress, exposure to traumatic life experiences, and problem drinking among first-generation immigrant Latino couples. *Journal of Social and Personal Relationships, 41*(2), 221–235.

Falconier, M. K., McCollum, E., Austin, J., Wainbarg, M., Hasbun, G., & Mora, S. (2013). IPV among Latinos: Community perceptions on help-seeking and needed programs. *Partner Abuse, 4*, 1–24.

Falicov, C. (2005). Mexican families. In M. McGoldrick, J. Giordano, & N. García-Preto (Eds.), *Ethnicity and family therapy* (3rd ed.) (pp. 229–241). New York: The Guilford Press.

Falicov, C. (2014). *Latino families in therapy* (2nd ed.). New York: The Guilford Press.

García-Preto, N. (2005). Latino families: An overview. In M. McGoldrick, J. Giordano, & N. García-Preto (Eds.), *Ethnicity and family therapy* (3rd ed.) (pp. 153–165). New York: The Guilford Press.

Gil, A. G., Wagner, E. F., & Vega, W. A. (2000). Acculturation, familism, and alcohol use among Latino adolescent males: Longitudinal relations. *Journal of Community Psychology, 28*(4), 443–458.

Helms, H. M., Supple, A. J., Su, J., Rodriguez, Y., Cavanaugh, A. M., & Hengstebeck, N. D. (2014). Economic pressure, cultural adaptation stress, and marital quality among Mexican-origin couples. *Journal of Family Psychology, 28*, 77–87.

Hirsch, J. S. (2003). *A courtship after marriage: Sexuality and love in Mexican transnational families.* Berkeley, CA: University of California Press.

Klevens, J., Shelley, G., Clavel-Arcas, C., Barney, D. D., Tobar, C., Duran, E. S., . . . Esparza, J. (2007). Latinos' perspectives and experiences with intimate partner violence. *Violence against Women, 13, 141–158.*

Kusnir, D. (2005). Salvadoran families. In M. McGoldrick, J. Giordano, & N. García-Preto (Eds.), *Ethnicity and family therapy* (3rd ed.) (pp. 256–265). New York: Guilford.

Lee, C. S., Colby, S. M., Rohsenow, D. J., López, S. R., Hernández, L., & Caetano, R. (2013). Acculturation stress and drinking problems among urban heavy drinking Latinos in the Northeast. *Journal of Ethnicity in Substance Abuse, 12*, 308–320.

Lee, D. L., & Ahn, S. (2012). Discrimination against Latina/os: A meta-analysis of individual-level resources and outcomes. *The Counseling Psychologist, 40*, 28–65.

Mausbach, B. T., & Thompson, L. W. (2003). Religious coping among Caucasian and Latina dementia caregivers. *Journal of Mental Health and Aging, 9*, 97–110.

Neff, J. A., Holamon, B., & Schluter, T. D. (1995). Spousal violence among Anglos, Blacks, and Mexican Americans: The role of demographic variables, psychosocial predictors, and alcohol consumption. *Journal of Family Violence, 10*(1), 1–21.

Negy, C., Hammons, M. E., Reig-Ferrer, A., & Carper, T. M. (2010). The importance of addressing acculturative stress in marital therapy with Hispanic immigrant women. *International Journal of Clinical and Health Psychology, 10*, 5–21.

Olson, D. H., Fournier, D. G., & Druckman, J. M. (1983). *PREPARE/ENRICH Counselor's Manual*. Minneapolis, MN: PREPARE/ENRICH, Inc.

Padilla, A. M., & Borrero, N. (2006). Effects of acculturative stress on the Hispanic family. In P. T. P. Wong & L. C. J. Wong (Eds.), *Handbook of multicultural perspectives on stress and coping* (pp. 299–318). New York: Springer.

Pew Hispanic Center (2007). Pew Forum on Religion and Public Life. *Changing Faiths: Latinos and the Transformation of American Religion*. Washington, DC (April 25, 2007).

Sabogal, F., Marin, G., Otero-Sabogal, R., Marin, B. V., & Perez-Stable, E. J. (1987). Hispanic familism and acculturation: What changes and what doesn't. *Hispanic Journal of Behavioral Sciences, 9*, 397–412.

Smith-Morris, C., Morales-Campos, D., Castaneda Alvarez, E. A., & Turner, M. (2012). An anthropology of *familismo*: On narratives and description of Mexican/immigrants. *Hispanic Journal of Behavioral Sciences, 35*, 35–60.

Spanier, G. B. (1976). Measuring dyadic adjustment: New scales for assessing the quality of marriage and similar dyads. *Journal of Marriage and the Family, 38*, 15–28.

Straus, M. A., Hamby, S. L., Boney-McCoy, S., & Sugarman, D. B. (1996). The Revised Conflict Tactics Scales (CTS2): Development and preliminary psychometric data. *Journal of Family Issues, 17*, 283–316.

Trevelyan, E. N., Acosta, Y. D., & De La Cruz, P. (2013). Homeownership among the foreign-born population: 2011. American Community Survey Briefs. Retrieved from www.census.gov/content/dam/Census/library/publications/2013/acs/acsbr11-15

U.S. Bureau of Labor Statistics (August, 2014). *Labor force characteristics by race and ethnicity, 2013*. Retrieved from www.bls.gov/cps/cpsrace2013.pdf

Walsh, F. (2006). *Strengthening family resilience* (2nd ed.). New York: The Guilford Press.

6

DYADIC COPING IN SWISS COUPLES

Rebekka Kuhn, Peter Hilpert, and Guy Bodenmann

Introduction

Switzerland is a small, but wealthy country with approximately 8 million inhabitants located in the middle of Europe. It shares three of the four national languages (German, French, Italian) with its neighboring countries. Switzerland benefits from a politically stable situation (direct democracy) and a good health-care system. In international comparisons, Switzerland ranks very high in income, social security, life satisfaction, and general well-being (Organisation for Economic Co-operation and Development [OECD], 2013). Switzerland's economic prosperity is characterized by the following: strong economic power, a very good education system, a high degree of modernization, a low rate of unemployment, a low level of corruption, and low rates of poverty (7.7 percent in 2012 with rates declining; Federal Statistical Office, 2014).

Many people are attracted by the prosperity, high living standards, and socio-political stability of the country. In 2013, about 25 percent of the Swiss population were foreigners (Bundesamt für Statistik [BFS], 2013). The cultural influence of the migrant population contributes to Switzerland's diversity. Indeed, this melting pot is renowned for its peaceful cohabitation of different cultures, languages, and religions (Rutherford et al., 2014).

Similar to other Western countries, the Swiss population is categorized as individualistic according to the individualism-collectivism continuum (Hofstede, Hofstede, & Minkov, 2010). As also described in Chapter 2, individual goals are thus valued more than the goals of the entire society (Hofstede et al., 2010; Triandis, Bontempo, Villareal, Asai, & Lucca, 1988). The importance of independence and autonomy (i.e., making life decisions individually and freely) implies that one should be able to master life well without others. Therefore, it is claimed that Swiss individuals often emphasize their own goals above a common group endeavor.

A corresponding characteristic of Switzerland's individualistic society is a deep respect for privacy and personal discretion (Katz, 2006). Business and private life are usually separated; as such, the Swiss tend to be quite cautious and reserved during social interaction until a certain level of trust has been established. Although Switzerland can be categorized as a low-context society in which communication is more direct and less oriented towards non-verbal behavior and contextual cues (Katz, 2006; see Chapter 2), Swiss people communicate less directly than Germans (Diehm, Pill, & Baumann, 2013; Katz, 2006). In addition, values such as politeness, harmony, and consensus allow Swiss people to avoid conflicts and strive for compromise (Diehm et al., 2013).

Despite economic prosperity and high living standards, Swiss people complain of high work and time pressure. Worryingly, reports about work stress show an upward trend. According to a stress study with Swiss employees, a third of the working population reports being stressed often to very often (State Secretariat for Economic Affairs [SECO], 2011), an increase of 30 percent from 2000. The more the respondents reported experiencing stress, the lower they estimated their coping competences ($r = -0.23$). In turn, the lower their appraisal of their coping competences, the more they felt emotionally exhausted ($r = -0.36$), which is closely associated with burnout. Employees reporting higher coping competences were more satisfied with their work conditions ($r = 0.17$) and were in better general health ($r = 0.25$). The most common stressors were frequent interruptions, continuous work with high speed and constant time pressure. Half of the respondents claimed to have worked while sick, a phenomenon called *presenteeism*, which is positively correlated with experiencing stress ($r = 0.27$).

We can conclude that stress in Switzerland usually refers to minor, everyday stress, for example at work (time pressure, high performance standards, professional competition). Major stressors such as poverty, unemployment, racial discrimination that threaten not only individual but familial well-being are not commonly experienced by the Swiss. However, because this minor stress experienced in Switzerland is often chronic and accumulates, it also influences well-being and social interactions including the intimate relationship.

Review of the Literature

Couples' Relationships in Switzerland

In international comparisons, Swiss couples are among the oldest couples when they first get married (average age 30–32 years; BFS, 2014), as well as when having their first child (average age of maternity 31.8 years; BFS, 2014). Furthermore, a decline in marriages over the last 30 years and divorce rates since 2010 has been observed, with the divorce rate reaching 40.3 percent in 2014 (BFS, 2014). Swiss attitudes towards marriage have changed during the last decades similarly to other Western countries (Bernardi, Ryser, & Le Goff, 2013). Before the 1960s, attitudes towards marriage were traditionally patriarchal in which men's and women's roles were defined with men being the providers and women being the caregivers (Höpflinger, 1987). With the political protests of 1968 and the introduction of women's voting rights at the federal level in 1971, attitudes towards marriage and family changed considerably (Höpflinger, 1987). The stronger focus on women's emancipation in upcoming generations led to relatively high gender equality and shared household roles as long as no children were present (Bernardi et al., 2013). An international survey by Kelso, Cahn, and Miller (2012) comparing opinions about gender equality across Switzerland and the U.S. showed that Switzerland was more supportive of gender equality than the U.S. but less gender egalitarian than other Western European countries.

When couples become parents, however, a shift towards more traditional roles is found with the woman typically holding feminine roles, assuming more relational, domestic, and nurturing functions within the family, whereas men hold more masculine roles, such as providing financial support for the family (Bernardi et al., 2013). This tendency is even more prevalent when couples have more than one child. Since childcare is seen as the main responsibility of the mother, a heavy work-family burden is placed on women, who often also try to keep a professional position while taking care of the household (Bernardi et al., 2013). Usually, women reduce their working hours during the child-rearing phase (Bernardi et al., 2013; Levy, Gauthier, & Widmer, 2006). Among Swiss women, 57 percent work part-time compared to 13 percent of Swiss men (Kelso, Cahn, & Miller, 2012). Although part-time work and job sharing are growing, these work patterns are still seen as being inconsistent with management positions, and women's vocational choices are therefore often based on more pragmatic issues (OECD, 2013). Statistics show that women also earn much less than men (OECD, 2013). The poor availability of childcare services in Switzerland (Branger et al., 2008) and the restriction of maternity leave to 14 weeks place a further constraint on Swiss families. These obstacles seem to be more prevalent than in other European countries, such as Germany or the Netherlands and especially Scandinavia (Brauchli, Bauer, & Hämmig, 2011). In conclusion, childbearing is a challenge for the couple and—given the background of an individualistic society—experienced as a threat to a woman's independence (Bernardi et al., 2013).

Many marriages (48 percent) are bi-national marriages, meaning that only 52 percent of marriages per year are between a Swiss woman and a Swiss man. Due to the increased immigration rate, the number of such marriages is very high in comparison to other European countries. One of the most common foreign nationalities is German (BFS, 2013)—it is therefore not uncommon that relationships are formed between a Swiss and a German. Given the differences in communication described above (direct vs. indirect, resolving conflicts vs. consensus, etc.), these bi-national couples might face difficulties in their communication.

An even stronger cultural influence on communication is observed when people from individualistic and collectivistic cultures form intimate relationships. Gagliardi, Bodenmann, and Bregy (2010) compared bi-national Swiss-Thai couples with mono-national Swiss couples. Swiss-Thai couples communicated differently about their stress, and displayed different supportive behaviors. In addition, bi-national couples often face a unique set of challenges in regard to cultural adaptation of the migrating partner. Adaptation to the new cultural environment, learning a new language, or the distance to the family of origin are sources of stress, which might lead to additional relationship conflicts.

The systemic-transactional model (STM; Bodenmann, 1995; see Chapter 1) does not only aim to define what kinds of stressors couples experience, and how this stress spills over and affects the relationship but also under which conditions they engage in coping when extra-dyadic stress spills over into the dyad. An overview of studies examining stress and its consequences in Swiss couples is presented in Table 6.1. Most of the studies have focused on different kinds of stress, but mainly on daily hassles (e.g., work stress) since the STM was originally developed in this context. In fact, results reveal that Swiss people are mainly suffering from work stress or other daily hassles. Bodenmann (2000) showed that high workload and other daily hassles were the most prominent stressors for couples from a community sample ($N = 600$ couples). This result is supported by findings of an ongoing longitudinal study with 368 Swiss couples.[1] Stress related to work is perceived as the highest stressor among both women and men. Swiss women report significantly more stress in general. Daily hassles are equally prevalent in all three age groups. Across all domains except for daily hassles, older couples experience less stress than either of the other two age groups participating in the study. Among the different external stressors, daily hassles are the best predictor of relationship satisfaction.

There is consistent evidence for detrimental long-term effects of chronic minor stress on relationship satisfaction in Swiss couples (e.g., Bodenmann, Meuwly, & Kayser, 2011; Bodenmann, Pihet, & Kayser, 2006). Furthermore, couples with high stress and low dyadic coping are more likely to end in divorce (Bodenmann & Cina, 2005). Research has identified one of the mechanisms of how stress is linked to negative relationship outcomes. Daily hassles have been found to spill over into the relationship, meaning that stress that originates outside of the relationship affects partners' behaviors and increases couple's conflicts by eroding partners' communication skills. Bodenmann, Ledermann, and Bradbury (2007) found evidence for this stress spillover in a sample of 396 Swiss couples. Higher levels of daily stress predicted higher levels of tension within the dyad, and in turn, lower levels of relationship satisfaction. This is in line with international findings on spillover (e.g., Neff & Karney, 2004; Repetti, 1989). Increased levels of stress have been found to be negatively associated with positive communication patterns (e.g., constructive problem solving) in couples (Hilpert, Bodenmann, Nussbeck, & Bradbury, 2013).

TABLE 6.1 Studies on stress in Swiss couples

Authors	Sample size	Study design	Main findings
(1) Bodenmann (1997), (2) Bodenmann and Cina (1999)★	70 couples	questionnaires, longitudinal (2 y. (1) and 4 y. (2)), behavioral observation data	(1) couples with a higher stress level experience greater reductions in relationship satisfaction and health; stress can be used as a predictive variable for dissolution after 2 years; (2) stress and coping play an important role for relationship stability even after 4 years
Bodenmann (2000)	different Swiss samples	questionnaires	work, daily hassles, and relationship conflicts are most common stressors; men report more work-related stress, whereas women report more stress with the family or household
Bodenmann and Cina (2005)★	62 couples	prospective longitudinal (5 y.), questionnaires	stable-satisfied couples were characterized by a lower level of stress, practiced less dysfunctional individual coping strategies, and relied more frequently on interpersonal (dyadic) coping when dealing with stress in comparison to stable-dissatisfied and divorced couples
Bodenmann et al. (2010)★	317 subjects	cross-sectional, questionnaires	individuals differed in verbal aggression when stress was low, but not when stress was high; effective individual coping and DC reduces the effects of stress on aggression
(1) Bodenmann et al. (2006); (2) Bodenmann et al. (2007b)	198 couples	cross-sectional, questionnaires	(1) primarily internal daily stress and in some cases critical life events rather than external daily stress are related to sexual problems; (2) relationship satisfaction and sexual activity are governed by hassles and problems experienced within the dyad that are in turn related to stress arising outside the dyad

Study	Sample	Method	Findings
Bodenmann et al. (2007a)★	663 subjects (Germany, Italy, Switzerland)	retrospective, questionnaires	accumulation of everyday stresses were perceived as a trigger for decision to divorce, and low commitment and deficits in interpersonal competencies (communication, problem solving, coping) were perceived as reasons for divorce
Bodenmann et al. (2010)	103 female students	longitudinal (3 m.), questionnaires and diaries	higher self-reported stress in daily life was associated with lower levels of sexual activity and satisfaction and a decrease in relationship satisfaction; dyadic coping was positively associated with sexual outcomes
Falconier et al. (2014)	110 couples	cross-sectional, questionnaires	daily hassles led to lower psychological and physical well-being and indirectly to lower relationship satisfaction through increased intradyadic stress; female extradyadic and intradyadic stress had partner effects on male intradyadic stress and male relationship satisfaction
Gabriel et al. (2006)★	83 pairs of parents	cross-sectional, questionnaires	parents of a child with inattention and conduct problems reported higher levels of stress and less competencies in DC
Ledermann et al. (2010)	345 couples	cross-sectional, questionnaires	intradyadic stress is more strongly related with one's own external stress than with the partner's external stress; importance of low relationship stress and a high level of positive communication

Note. DC = dyadic coping, y. = years, m. = months, ★ = coping variables also included.

As the STM proposes, contextual factors such as culture play an important role in the couples' coping process (see Chapter 2). The coping process is initiated by stress communication being followed by the support from the partner. Swiss people usually express their stress verbally and explicitly, as might be expected in a low-context individualistic society. Gender equality allows that both men and women can freely express their stress. Stress communication in bi-national couples might be different, especially when coming from very different cultural backgrounds. Close relationships in Switzerland are viewed as an exclusive unit where individuals are able to share difficulties and personal stress. In fact, the partner is the greatest source of support, and people usually turn to their partner first in times of stress (Bodenmann, 2000). Support, in turn, is expected to follow after explicit stress communication and is often more problem-focused than emotion-focused (Bodenmann, 2000). Gender equality facilitates reciprocal receiving and giving support or engaging in common dyadic coping, and it is expected that men and women solve their problems mutually.

Table 6.2 presents an overview of the main findings of studies investigating coping in Swiss couples. Studies have consistently shown that communication in the couple, and hence dyadic coping, can falter under conditions of stress (e.g., Hilpert et al., 2013; Hilpert, Kuhn, Anderegg, & Bodenmann, 2015). There is strong empirical evidence that dyadic coping is not only closely linked to marital outcomes such as relationship satisfaction (e.g., Bodenmann et al., 2006) and stability (e.g., Bodenmann & Cina, 2005), but does also play an important role for couples suffering from psychological disorders or health problems (e.g., Bodenmann et al., 2011; Bodenmann, Widmer, Charvoz, & Bradbury, 2004; Jenewein, Meier, & Bodenmann, 2011).

Two mechanisms explain the positive impact dyadic coping has on the relationship (Bodenmann, 2005). On the one hand, dyadic coping alleviates the impact of chronic external stress on chronic internal stress, thus helping to prevent spillover. For example, the buffering effect on stress reported by Bodenmann and colleagues (2007) was replicated by Merz, Meuwly, Randall, and Bodenmann (2014), which shows that dyadic coping is negatively associated with chronic internal stress, and positively associated with relationship satisfaction. On the other hand, dyadic coping strengthens feelings of we-ness, mutual understanding, trust, intimacy, and attachment.

In longitudinal studies, dyadic coping served to be an important predictor of relationship outcomes. In a five-year prospective longitudinal study (Bodenmann & Cina, 2005), higher levels of supportive and common dyadic coping were found among 'stable-satisfied couples,' whereas couples that were divorced after five years displayed less of these behaviors. It was possible to predict 62.1 percent of the relationship outcomes after two years correctly only by using the level of dyadic coping as a predictor. Even after ten years, dyadic coping of men served as a predictor for their relationship satisfaction (Ruffieux, Nussbeck, & Bodenmann, 2014).

TABLE 6.2 Studies on dyadic coping in Swiss couples

Authors	Sample size	Study design	Main findings
Bergstraesser et al. (2015)	46 married parents (23 couples)	interviews, questionnaires	DC played an important role in grief work and adjustment to bereavement, as aspects of common DC helped to work through grief individually and as a couple
Bodenmann (2008)	2399 subjects	validation study	Results provide empirical evidence for the quality of the Dyadic Coping Inventory (DCI)
Bodenmann and Widmer (2000)	242 couples	cross-sectional, questionnaires	In the comparison of three age-groups, the oldest couples had the lowest values in positive DC
Bodenmann et al. (2001)	39 clinically depressed patients and 21 former depressed subjects	cross-sectional, standardized questionnaires	Severely depressed patients have a severe lack of dyadic coping resources; remitted patients did not differ from controls in their coping, coping deficiencies do not represent a stable personality trait
Bodenmann et al. (2004)	106 depressed or formerly depressed patients and 106 matched controls	cross-sectional, questionnaires	Deficits in DC are highest in the highly depressed group, depressed women reported less stress communication and supportive DC whereas men reported marginally more negative DC towards their partner
Bodenmann et al. (2006)	90 couples	longitudinal (2 y.)	DC was significantly associated with marital quality over two years
Bodenmann et al. (2011)	443 couples	cross-sectional, questionnaires	Both DC measures (comparative approach and systemic model) were related to relationship quality and psychological well-being

continued . . .

TABLE 6.2 Continued

Authors	Sample size	Study design	Main findings
Gagliardi et al. (2010)	225 Thai-Swiss couples and 234 Swiss couples	cross-sectional, questionnaires	Bi-national couples showed less negative DC and stress communication than Swiss couples
Gagliardi et al. (2013)	304 couples (Swiss, German, Italian)	cross-sectional, questionnaires	Securely attached couples reported better relationship quality as well as more positive and less negative DC compared to fearful-avoidant couples and couples with different attachment styles
Gmelch and Bodenmann (2007)	443 couples	cross-sectional, questionnaires	Discrepancy indexes and equity index were related to relationship quality; women's appraisals of DC were slightly more relevant than the men's appraisal of DC
Hilpert et al. (2013)	1944 married individuals	cross-sectional, questionnaires	External stress is highly associated with an increase in negative interactions and a decrease in DC; being supported by the partner in times of need seemed to be particularly relevant for marital quality
Kramer et al. (2005)	18 persons having experienced a physical assault, 18 control persons	structural clinical interview, questionnaires	Participants having experienced a trauma, compared to controls, report a general lack of DC and decreased individual coping
Landis et al. (2013)	132 married couples (German, Swiss)	cross-sectional, questionnaires	Partner's subjective perception of their spouse's supportive behavior was more strongly linked to their relationship satisfaction than to their self-reported support
Landis et al. (2014)	201 couples	cross-sectional, questionnaires	Relationship satisfaction mediated the effects between commitment and DC; findings support the essentiality of commitment for consistency in long-term relationships

Study	Sample	Method	Findings
Ledermann et al. (2010)	216 German-, 378 Italian-, and 198 French-speaking participants (Swiss, Italy)	replication study, questionnaires	Previous findings could be replicated in all three language groups, showing that aspects of DC were more strongly related to marital quality than to dyadic communication
(1) Meier et al. (2011); (2) Meier et al. (2012)	43 couples with COPD and 138 healthy couples	cross-sectional, patient and partner questionnaires	(1) A higher imbalance in delegated DC was associated with a lower quality of life; more negative and less positive DC were associated with lower quality of life and higher psychological distress in couples with COPD (chronic obstructive pulmonary disease); (2) DC of couples with COPD is unbalanced and more negative compared to that of healthy couples
Merz et al. (2014)	131 couples	longitudinal (1 y.), questionnaires	DC was found to decrease the impact of chronic external stress on chronic internal stress (spillover), particularly in women
Meuwly et al. (2012)	123 couples	standardized public speaking task, questionnaires	Stressed individuals recovered faster from stress the more positive DC they received from the partner, with women high in attachment anxiety benefiting less from these behaviors
Meuwly et al. (2013)	82 Swiss women with either a male or a female partner	cross-sectional, questionnaires	Homosexual women reported receiving better support from and experiencing less conflict with their female partners compared to heterosexual couples; the lesbian couples also showed a trend toward being more satisfied in their relationship
Ruffieux et al. (2014)	162 couples	longitudinal (10 y.), questionnaires	Predictors of relationship satisfaction were relationship satisfaction in the beginning of measurement, and for men their dyadic coping competencies; predictors of relationship stability were relationship length and satisfaction, and women's positive communication

Note. DC = dyadic coping, y. = years.

Dyadic Coping Across the Lifespan

To our knowledge, Switzerland may be the only country where the impact of dyadic coping in older couples has been examined. Landis et al. (2013) studied older Swiss spouses (M age = 68 years) in long-term marriages to disentangle the secret of stable long-term relationships. Consistent with findings of studies with younger couples (e.g., Bodenmann, 2000), older spouses' dyadic coping is significantly associated with relationship satisfaction. One study by Bodenmann and Widmer (2000) showed that older couples (aged between 51 and 81) report higher stress communication but lower positive dyadic coping compared to younger couples. The lack of coping in older couples could be explained by a cohort effect. For example, relationships might be perceived as more functional by older couples while younger generations might see the partner as a source of emotional support. However, Landis et al. (2013) found that, although objective dyadic coping might be low, it is the subjective perception of the coping that is crucial for relationship satisfaction. How partners perceived spousal coping was a stronger predictor of relationship satisfaction than their self-reported coping. Therefore, dyadic coping might have a stabilizing function for long-term relationships.

Implications for Practice

Based on findings of stress and coping, Bodenmann developed the Couples Coping Enhancement Training (CCET; Bodenmann & Shantinath, 2004), an evidence-based and widely evaluated relationship education program. Its major aim is to improve stress-related self-disclosure and foster mutual dyadic coping in couples. Couples are taught these skills in a 15-hour workshop and are being prompted during exercises within the three-phase method (phase 1: one partner self-discloses about a stress experience, the other one listens empathically, phase 2: the former listener provides dyadic coping to the stressed partner, phase 3: the stressed partner gives a feedback to the supporting partner of how effective his/her support was). Different formats of the CCET have been developed in Switzerland over the last decade, such as a program focusing more on commitment, a program for couples in the transition to parenthood, and a program for couples dealing with work–life balance issues.

The enhancement of dyadic coping was also effective in couple therapy. In the coping-oriented couple therapy (COCT; Bodenmann, 2010), one core element is the strengthening of couples' coping by means of the three-phase method (Bodenmann, 2010). In a study with 60 couples in which one partner was diagnosed with medium to severe depression, coping-oriented couple therapy performed comparably in reducing depressive symptoms to cognitive behavioral therapy or interpersonal therapy, but was more effective in reducing relapse in patients who were treated by COCT (Bodenmann et al., 2008). Table 6.3 presents findings on the effectiveness of CCET and COCT with Swiss couples. Research

TABLE 6.3 Intervention studies with Swiss couples

Authors	Sample size	Study design	Main findings
Bodenmann et al. (2001)	143 couples	longitudinal (1 y.), questionnaires	CCET leads to significant increase in marital quality, couples appraise their relationship even after one year in other domains (communication, intimacy)
Bodenmann et al. (2002)	146 subjects (intervention), 140 subjects (controls)	longitudinal (2 y.), questionnaires	Subjects participating in the program displayed better individual coping skills after the Coping Enhancement Training (CET); they relied upon dysfunctional coping strategies less often even after two years
(1) Bodenmann et al. (2008); (2) Gabriel et al. (2008)	60 (1) and 57 (2) couples with a depressed partner	longitudinal (1.5 y.), questionnaires, observational data	(1) COCT is as effective in improving depressive symptomatology as are the well-established, evidence-based CBT and IPT approaches; (2) from pre- to post-therapy, all three treatments (CBT, IPT, COCT) produced similar improvements in depression and observed DC of patients
Bodenmann et al. (2009)	109 couples	longitudinal (2 y.), questionnaires	Over the course of the CCET, couples improved their problem-solving behaviors; wives and husbands increased their positive DC
Bodenmann et al. (2014)	330 couples	longitudinal (6 months), questionnaires	Intimate relationships could, within limits, be positively influenced by a self-directed approach using a DVD based on the CCET
Bodenmann et al. (2006)	59 couples (intervention), 59 couples (control)	longitudinal (2 y.), questionnaires	Short-term interventions with the CCET could improve marital quality, however, effects decreased after two years

continued . . .

TABLE 6.3 Continued

Authors	Sample size	Study design	Main findings
Hilpert et al. (in press)	220 couples	longitudinal (1 y.), questionnaires	Personal happiness could be increased through the CCET; change in personal happiness was predicted by an increase in skills and relationship satisfaction through the intervention; the least happy participants benefitted most from the intervention
Ledermann et al. (2007)	100 couples	longitudinal (1 y.), questionnaires	Previous findings on the efficacy of the CCET were supported; positive effects of the program were noted among both women and men immediately after the training, with stronger effects noted among women
Pihet et al. (2007)	59 couples (intervention), 59 couples (control)	longitudinal (1 y.), questionnaires	The CCET is able to improve psychological well-being among both genders and life satisfaction among women
Schaer et al. (2008)	157 couples	longitudinal (1 y.), questionnaires	The CCET outperformed both the ICT (individual coping training) and the waiting-list control group; CCET participants scored higher in relationship and individual variables after the training
Widmer et al. (2005)	70 couples who received intervention	longitudinal (2 y.), questionnaires, observational data	Couples who received the CCET reported a greater change in marital satisfaction, dyadic communication, and coping; the improvement was also observed in the videotapes; women showed a higher increase in positive DC and a greater decline in negative DC

Note. CCET = Couples Coping Enhancement Training, COCT = Coping-Oriented Couple Therapy, CBT = Cognitive-Behavioral Therapy, IPT = Interpersonal Therapy, DC = dyadic coping, y. = years.

on CCET and COCT has found a significant improvement of relationship functioning after participation in either program (also see for an overview Halford & Bodenmann, 2013). A recently published study shows that also a self-directed form during which couples train with a DVD of the CCET is effective (Bodenmann, Hilpert, Nussbeck, & Bradbury, 2014). The dyadic coping-oriented interventions (CCET and COCT) prove to be effective, possibly because of their correspondence with Swiss values, attitudes, and behaviors within the culture and specifically the intimate relationship. However, more specialized training programs could be implemented for sub-groups of couples, e.g., homosexual or bi-national couples, and thereby practitioners could take into account that stress communication or supportive behavior might be different.

Implications for Research

Although a great deal of research on dyadic coping has been conducted in Switzerland, results are mostly generalizable to Swiss heterosexual middle-class couples and not aforementioned subgroups. Therefore, studies should start to focus more on different groups of couples in order find out whether these subgroups are benefiting from different intervention trainings. For example, one study currently examines dyadic coping in young couples (aged 16–21 years), and the STM is thus tested in adolescent couples for the first time. Furthermore, research has started to investigate the effectiveness of intervention trainings for Swiss couples who are expecting their first child. In addition, new measurement methods (e.g., face recognition, voice intonation, implicit diagnostics) in combination with sophisticated statistical models (e.g., latent differential equation modeling) might broaden the current knowledge on dyadic coping research. This would allow us to facilitate large-scale analyses where we could also examine dyadic coping over time.

Conclusion

Couples in Switzerland mainly undergo stressors such as work stress or daily hassles. The STM suggests that such stressors can spill over into the relationship and impede couples' communication skills. In the last decades, Bodenmann and his team extensively studied these spillover and coping mechanisms in Switzerland. The results show that dyadic coping is effective in reducing the negative consequences of stress spillover and therefore relevant for relationship maintenance. One reason for the beneficial effects of dyadic coping might be the Swiss cultural background characterized by individualism and egalitarian relationships.

Given this relevance of dyadic coping in stabilizing the couple, the CCET was developed in order to prevent couples from faltering under high conditions of stress. The implementation of the CCET and the COCT proves to be effective for Swiss couples. Future research, however, should (i) use new technological developments to study how coping processes unfold over time as a dynamical process within couples, and (ii) focus on different subgroups (e.g., couples with low financial or educational resources), as it is reasonable to assume that they might not only face more or different stressors but also have a different conceptualization of dyadic coping.

Note

1 Data presented here are unpublished results from an ongoing study funded by the Swiss National Fond (SNF: CRSI11_133004/1). In this five-year longitudinal study, 368 Swiss heterosexual couples (three age cohorts: cohort 1 = 20–35 years; cohort 2 = 40 – 55 years; cohort 3 = 65–80 years) provide self-reports and videotaped observations each year.

References

Bergstraesser, E., Inglin, S., Hornung, R., & Landolt, M. A. (2015). Dyadic coping of parents after the death of a child. *Death Studies*, *39*(3), 128–138.

Bernardi, L., Ryser, V.-A., Le Goff, J.-M. (2013). Gender role-set, family orientations, and women's fertility intentions in Switzerland. *Swiss Journal of Sociology*, *39*(1), 9–31.

Bodenmann, G. (1995). A systemic-transactional conceptualization of stress and coping in couples. *Swiss Journal of Psychology*, *54*(1), 34–49.

Bodenmann, G. (1997). The influence of stress and coping on close relationships: A two-year longitudinal study. *Swiss Journal of Psychology*, *56*(3), 156–164.

Bodenmann, G. (2000). *Stress und Coping bei Paaren* [*Stress and coping in couples*]. Göttingen, Germany: Hogrefe.

Bodenmann, G. (2005). Dyadic coping and its significance for marital functioning. In T. A. Revenson, K. Kayser, & G. Bodenmann (Eds.) (2005), *Couples coping with stress: Emerging perspectives on dyadic coping* (pp. 33–50). Washington DC: American Psychological Association.

Bodenmann, G. (2008). *Dyadisches Coping Inventar (DCI)* [*Dyadic Coping Inventory*]. Manual. Bern: Huber Testverlag.

Bodenmann, G. (2010). New themes in couple therapy: The role of stress, coping and social support. In K. Hahlweg, M. Grawe, & D. H. Baucom (Eds.), *Enhancing couples. The shape of couple therapy to come* (pp. 142–156). Cambridge, MA: Hogrefe Publishing.

Bodenmann, G., & Cina, A. (1999). Der Einfluß von Streß, individueller Belastungs-bewältigung und dyadischen Coping auf die Partnerschaftsstabilität: Eine 4-Jahres-Längschnittstudie. [The influence of stress and individual and dyadic coping on the stability of partnerships: A 4-year longitudinal study]. *Zeitschrift für Klinische Psychologie*, *28*(2), 130–139.

Bodenmann, G., & Cina, A. (2005). Stress and coping among stable-satisfied, stable-distressed and separated/divorced Swiss couples: A 5-year prospective longitudinal study. *Journal of Divorce and Remarriage*, *44*, 71–89.

Bodenmann, G., & Shantinath, S. D. (2004). The Couples Coping Enhancement Training (CCET): A new approach to prevention of marital distress based upon stress and coping. *Family Relations*, *53*(5), 477–484.

Bodenmann, G., & Widmer, K. (2000). Stressbewältigung im Alter: Ein Vergleich von Paaren jüngeren, mittleren und höheren Alters. [Coping in elderly couples: A comparison with young and middle-aged couples]. *Zeitschrift für Gerontologie und Geriatrie, 33*, 217–228.

Bodenmann, G., Atkins, D. C., Schär, M., & Poffet, V. (2010). The association between daily stress and sexual activity. *Journal of Family Psychology, 24*, 271–279.

Bodenmann, G., Bradbury, T. N., & Pihet, S. (2009). Relative contributions of treatment-related changes in communication skills and dyadic coping skills to the longitudinal course of marriage in the framework of marital distress prevention. *Journal of Divorce and Remarriage, 50*(1), 1–21.

Bodenmann, G., Charvoz, L., Bradbury, T. N., Bertoni, A., Iafrate, R., Giuliani, C., . . . Behling, J. (2007(a)). The role of stress in divorce: A three-nation retrospective study. *Journal of Social and Personal Relationships, 24*(5), 707–728.

Bodenmann, G., Charvoz, L., Cina, A., & Widmer, K. (2001). Prevention of marital distress by enhancing the coping skills of couples: 1-year follow-up-study. *Swiss Journal of Psychology, 60*(1), 3–10.

Bodenmann, G., Charvoz, L., Widmer, K., & Bradbury, T. N. (2004). Differences in individual and dyadic coping among low and high depressed, partially remitted, and nondepressed persons. *Journal of Psychopathology and Behavioral Assessment, 26*(2), 75–85.

Bodenmann, G., Cina, A., & Schwerzmann, S. (2001). Individuelle und dyadische Copingressourcen bei Depressiven. [Individual and dyadic coping resources in depressives]. *Zeitschrift für Klinische Psychologie und Psychotherapie: Forschung und Praxis, 30*(3), 194–203.

Bodenmann, G., Hilpert, P., Nussbeck, F. W., & Bradbury, T. N. (2014). Enhancement of couples' communication and dyadic coping by a self-directed approach: A randomized controlled trial. *Journal of Consulting and Clinical Psychology, 82*(4), 580–591.

Bodenmann, G., Ledermann, T., & Bradbury, T. N. (2007(b)). Stress, sex, and satisfaction in marriage. *Personal Relationships, 14*, 407–425.

Bodenmann, G., Ledermann, T., Blattner-Bolliger, D., & Galluzzo, C. (2006). Associations between everyday stress, critical life events and sexual dysfunction. *Journal of Nervous and Mental Disease, 194*, 494–501.

Bodenmann, G., Meuwly, N., & Kayser, K. (2011). Two conceptualizations of dyadic coping and their potential for predicting relationship quality and individual well-being. *European Psychologist, 16*, 255–266.

Bodenmann, G., Meuwly, N., Bradbury, T., Gmelch, S., & Ledermann, T. (2010). Stress, anger and verbal aggression in intimate relationships: Moderating effects of trait anger and dyadic coping. *Journal of Social and Personal Relationships, 27*, 408–424.

Bodenmann, G., Perrez, M., Cina, A., & Widmer, K. (2002). The effectiveness of a coping-focused prevention approach: A two-year longitudinal study. *Swiss Journal of Psychology, 61*(4), 195–202.

Bodenmann, G., Pihet, S., & Kayser, K. (2006). The relationship between dyadic coping, marital quality and well-being: A 2-year longitudinal study. *Journal of Family Psychology, 20*, 485–493.

Bodenmann, G., Pihet, S., Shantinath, S. D., Cina, A., & Widmer, K. (2006). Improving dyadic coping in couples with a stress-oriented approach: A 2-year longitudinal study. *Behavior Modification, 30*(5), 571–597.

Bodenmann, G., Plancherel, B., Beach, S. R. H., Widmer, K., Gabriel, B., Meuwly, N., . . . Schramm, E. (2008). Effects of coping-oriented couples therapy on depression: A randomized clinical trial. *Journal of Consulting and Clinical Psychology, 76*, 944–954.

Bodenmann, G., Widmer, K., Charvoz, L., & Bradbury, T. N. (2004). Differences in individual and dyadic coping in depressed, non-depressed and remitted persons. *Journal of Psychopathology and Behavioral Assessment, 26*, 75–85.

Branger, K., Crettaz, E., Oetliker, U., Robatti Mancini, V., Rochat, S., Roulet, F., . . . Zoder, I. (2008). *Les familles en Suisse [Families in Switzerland]*. Neuchâtel: Office fédéral de la statistique.

Brauchli, R., Bauer, G. F., & Hämmig, O. (2011). Relationship between time-based work-life conflict and burnout: A cross-sectional study among employees in four large Swiss enterprises. *Swiss Journal of Psychology, 70*(3), 165–173.

Bundesamt für Statistik [BFS] (2013). *Migration and integration*. Neuchâtel: Author. Retrieved from www.bfs.admin.ch/bfs/portal/en/index/themen/01/07/blank/key/01/01.html

Bundesamt für Statistik [BFS] (2014). *Components of population change*. Neuchâtel. Retrieved from www.bfs.admin.ch/bfs/portal/en/index/themen/01/06/blank/key/01.html

Diehm, N., Pill, I., & Baumann, F. (2013). Der kleine Unterschied: Interkulturelle Kommunikation zwischen Schweizern und Deutschen in der Medizin [The small difference: Intercultural communication between Swiss and Germans in medicine]. *Schweizerische Ärztezeitung, 94*, 31–33.

Falconier, M. K., Nussbeck, F., Bodenmann, G., Schneider, H., & Bradbury, T. (2014). Stress from daily hassles in couples: Its effects on intradyadic stress, relationship satisfaction, and physical and psychological well-being. *Journal of Marital and Family Therapy, 41*(2), 221–235.

Federal Statistical Office (2014). Poverty in Switzerland: Results from 2007 to 2012 (Order number 1379–1200). Retrieved from www.bfs.admin.ch/bfs/portal/en/index/news/publikationen.html?publicationID=5650

Gabriel, B., & Bodenmann, G. (2006). Stress und Coping bei Paaren mit einem verhaltensauffälligen Kind [Stress and coping in couples with a child with behavioral problems]. *Zeitschrift für Klinische Psychologie und Psychotherapie, 35*(1), 59–64.

Gabriel, B., Bodenmann, G., Widmer, K., Charvoz, L., Schramm, E., & Hautzinger, M. (2008). Auswirkungen der kognitiven Verhaltenstherapie, der interpersonellen Psychotherapie sowie der bewältigungsorientierten Paartherapie zur Behandlung von Depressionen auf das beobachtete dyadische Copingverhalten [Effects of cognitive behavioral therapy, interpersonal psychotherapy and coping oriented couple therapy to treat depression in the observed dyadic coping behavior]. *Zeitschrift für Klinische Psychologie und Psychotherapie, 37*(3), 179–189.

Gagliardi, S., Bodenmann, G., & Bregy, M. (2010). Coping bei binationalen Paaren: Ein Vergleich zwischen thailändisch-schweizerischen und mononationalen Schweizer Paaren [Coping with binational couples: A comparison between Thai-Swiss and mononational Swiss pairs]. *Zeitschrift für Klinische Psychologie und Psychotherapie, 39*(3), 141–150.

Gagliardi, S., Bodenmann, G., Heinrichs, N., Maria Bertoni, A., Iafrate, R., & Donato, S. (2013). Unterschiede in der Partnerschaftsqualität und im dyadischen Coping bei verschiedenen bindungsbezogenen Paartypen [Differences in the quality and partnership in dyadic coping in different binding pair related types]. *PPmP—Psychotherapie · Psychosomatik · Medizinische Psychologie, 63*(5), 185–192.

Gmelch, S., & Bodenmann, G. (2007). Dyadisches Coping in Selbst- und Fremd-wahrnehmung als Prädiktor für Partnerschaftsqualität und Befinden [Dyadic coping in self-perception as a predictor of quality and partnership-being]. *Zeitschrift für Gesundheitspsychologie, 15*(4), 177–186.

Halford, K., & Bodenmann, G. (2013). Effects of relationship education on maintenance of couple relationship satisfaction. *Clinical Psychology Review, 33,* 512–525.

Hilpert, P., Bodenmann, G., Nussbeck, F. W., & Bradbury, T. N. (2013). Predicting relationship satisfaction in distressed and non-distressed couples based on a stratified sample: A matter of conflict, positivity, or support? *Family Science, 4*(1), 110–120.

Hilpert, P., Kuhn, R., Anderegg, V., & Bodenmann, G. (2015). Comparing simultaneously the effects of extra-dyadic and intra-dyadic experiences on relationship outcomes. *Family Science, 6,* 129–142. doi: 10.1080/19424620.2015.1082018.

Hofstede, G., Hofstede, G. J., & Minkov, M. (2010). *Cultures and organizations: Software of the mind* (3rd ed.). New York: McGraw-Hill.

Höpflinger, F. (1987). *Wandel der Familienbildung in Westeuropa* [*Changes in family formation in Western Europe*]. Frankfurt: Campus.

Jenewein, J., Meier, C., Mörgeli, H., & Bodenmann, G. (2011). Dyadic coping, quality of life, and psychological distress among COPD patients and their partners. *Journal of Psychosomatic Research, 70,* 597–597.

Katz, L. (2006). *Negotiating international business: The negotiator's reference guide to 50 countries around the world.* Charleston, SC: Booksurge.

Kelso, M., Cahn, N., & Miller, B. (2012). *Gender equality in employment—Policies and practices in Switzerland and the U.S.* George Washington University, Washington DC. Retrieved from www.gwu.edu/~igis/assets/docs/report-gender-equality-switzerland2012.pdf

Kramer, U., Ceschi, G., Van der Linden, M., & Bodenmann, G. (2005). Individual and dyadic coping strategies in the aftermath of a traumatic experience. *Swiss Journal of Psychology, 64*(4), 241–248.

Landis, M., Bodenmann, G., Bradbury, T. N., Brandstätter, V., Peter-Wight, M., Backes, S., . . .Nussbeck, F. W. (2014). Commitment and dyadic coping in long-term relationships. *The Journal of Gerontopsychology and Geriatric Psychiatry, 27*(4), 139–149.

Landis, M., Peter-Wight, M., Martin, M., & Bodenmann, G. (2013). Dyadic coping and marital satisfaction of older spouses in long-term marriage. *The Journal of Gerontopsychology and Geriatric Psychiatry, 26*(1), 39–47.

Ledermann, T., Bodenmann, G., & Cina, A. (2007). The efficacy of the Couples Coping Enhancement Training (CCET) in improving relationship quality. *Journal of Social and Clinical Psychology, 26*(8), 940–959.

Ledermann, T., Bodenmann, G., Gagliardi, S., Charvoz, L., Verardi, S., Rossier, J., . . . Iafrate, R. (2010). Psychometrics of the dyadic coping inventory in three language groups. *Swiss Journal of Psychology, 69*(4), 201–212.

Ledermann, T., Bodenmann, G., Rudaz, M., & Bradbury, T. N. (2010). Stress, communication, and marital quality in couples. *Family Relations, 59,* 195–206.

Levy, R., Gauthier, J.-A., & Widmer, E. (2006). Entre contraintes institutionnelles et domestiques: Les parcours de vie masculins et féminins en Suisse [Between institutional and domestic constraints: Male and female life courses in Switzerland]. *Canadian Journal of Sociology, 2006, 31*(4), 461–489.

Meier, C., Bodenmann, G., Moergeli, H., Peter-Wight, M., Martin, M., Buechi, S., & Jenewein, J. (2012). Dyadic coping among couples with COPD: A pilot study. *Journal of Clinical Psychology in Medical Settings, 19*(3), 243–254.

Meier, C., Bodenmann, G., Mörgeli, H., & Jenewein, J. (2011). Dyadic coping, quality of life, and psychological distress among chronic obstructive pulmonary disease patients and their partners. *International Journal of Chronic Obstructive Pulmonal Disorders, 6,* 583–596.

Merz, C. A., Meuwly, N., Randall, A. K., & Bodenmann, G. (2014). Engaging in dyadic coping: Buffering the impact of everyday stress on prospective relationship satisfaction. *Family Science, 5*(1), 30–37.

Meuwly, N., Bodenmann, G., Germann, J., Bradbury, T. N., Ditzen, B., & Heinrichs, M. (2012). Dyadic coping, insecure attachment, and cortisol stress recovery following experimentally induced stress. *Journal of Family Psychology, 26*, 937–947.

Meuwly, N., Feinstein, B. A., Davila, J., Nuñez, D. G., & Bodenmann, G. (2013). Relationship quality among Swiss women in opposite-sex versus same-sex romantic relationships. *Swiss Journal of Psychology, 72*(4), 229–233.

Neff, L. A., & Karney, B. R. (2004). How does context affect intimate relationships? Linking external stress and cognitive processes within marriage. *Personality and Social Psychology Bulletin, 30*(2), 134–148.

Organisation for Economic Co-Operation and Development [OECD]. (2013). *OECD Economic Surveys: Switzerland 2013*, OECD Publishing.

Pihet, S., Bodenmann, G., Cina, A., Widmer, K., & Shantinath, S. (2007). Can prevention of marital distress improve well-being? A 1 year longitudinal study. *Clinical Psychology & Psychotherapy, 14*(2), 79–88.

Repetti, R. L. (1989). Effects of daily workload on subsequent behavior during marital interaction: The roles of social withdrawal and spouse support. *Journal of Personality and Social Psychology, 57*(4), 651–659.

Ruffieux, M., Nussbeck, F. W., & Bodenmann, G. (2014). Long-term prediction of relationship satisfaction and stability by stress, coping, communication, and well-being. *Journal of Divorce & Remarriage, 55*(6), 485–501.

Rutherford, A., Harmon, D., Werfel, J., Gard-Murray, A. S., Bar-Yam, S., Gros, A., . . . Bar-Yam, Y. (2014). Good Fences: The importance of setting boundaries for peaceful coexistence. *PLoS ONE, 9*(5), e95660.

Schaer, M., Bodenmann, G., & Klink, T. (2008). Balancing work and relationship: Couples Coping Enhancement Training (CCET) in the workplace. *Applied Psychology, 57*, 71–89.

State Secretariat for Economic Affairs [SECO] (2011). Stresstudie 2010. Stress bei Schweizer Erwerbstätigen—Zusammenhänge zwischen Arbeitsbedingungen, Personenmerkmalen, Befinden und Gesundheit [Stress-study 2010. Stress in Swiss employees—Associations of working conditions, personal traits, well-being and health]. Bern: Staatssekretariat für Wirtschaft. Retrieved from www.seco.admin.ch/dokumentation/publikation/00008/00022/04731/index.html

Triandis, H. C., Bontempo, R., Villareal, M. J., Asai, M., & Lucca, N. (1988). Individualism and collectivism: Cross-cultural perspectives on self-ingroup relationships. *Journal of Personality and Social Psychology, 54*(2), 323–338.

Widmer, K., Cina, A., Charvoz, L., Shantinath, S., & Bodenmann, G. (2005). A model dyadic coping intervention. In T. A. Revenson, K. Kayser, & G. Bodenmann (Eds.) (2005), *Couples coping with stress: Emerging perspectives on dyadic coping* (1st ed.). Washington DC: American Psychological Association.

7

DYADIC COPING IN PORTUGUESE COUPLES

*Ana M. Vedes, Marta Figueiredo Pedro,
Ivone Martins Patrão, Sara Magalhães
Albuquerque, Susana Costa Ramalho,
Marco Daniel Pereira, Isabel Narciso Davide,
Alexandra Marques Pinto, and
Maria Teresa Ribeiro*

Introduction

Portugal is located in the very southwest of Europe with approximately 11 million inhabitants, of which only 4 percent are foreigners. The average household has 2.6 persons, and the most common family types are couples with children (43 percent) followed by couples without children (21 percent) (PORDATA, 2015a), clearly revealing the centrality of the couple's system. Portugal can be considered very homogeneous with respect to language (Portuguese), religion (Roman Catholic), and culture. In general, Portugal has been classified as a collectivist (in-group) country since people value close familiar and organizational bonds, as well as strong interpersonal relationships (Geert-Hofstede, 2015; Schoebi, Wang, Ababkov, & Perrez, 2010). Portuguese culture can be characterized by endorsing a *familialism* and *maternalism* model. For most Portuguese, marrying and having children is highly valued and viewed as a source of happiness, personal fulfillment, and support, wherein women play a crucial role as mothers and caregivers (Aboim, 2007).

Despite this homogeneity, meanings associated with family have changed dramatically in Portugal (Aboim, 2013) in the last four decades. Nowadays, couples' relationships are more egalitarian and partners share more decision making concerning family functioning than in former times. Nevertheless, both men and women frequently have contradictory family attitudes, oscillating between modern values and traditional values (Aboim, 2007). These contradictions are due to Portugal's particular historical and cultural pathway over the last century.

For nearly fifty years, Portugal had a right-wing dictatorship that ended with the April Revolution in 1974 (Wall, Cunha, & Marinho, 2013). This revolution catalyzed and implemented fast ideological-socio-economic-political changes, which are still transforming mentalities and behaviors. Furthermore, the economic crisis of 2008 deeply hampered life conditions, making Portugal a difficult milieu for relationships to endure due to high levels of stress and a scarcity of resources. Accordingly, the increased number of divorces in 2013 (70 percent of marriages ended in divorce; PORDATA, 2015b) highlights Portuguese couples' vulnerability. They not only have to deal with challenges within the relationship (e.g., conflicts) but also need to manage numerous daily external stressors (work-family balance, financial difficulties), as well as major long-term adversities (e.g., unemployment, economic pressure) and unexpected life events (e.g., oncological disease, death of a child). Therefore, dyadic coping (DC), by acknowledging both partners' interdependence and comprising partners' coping efforts to communicate their stress, mutually support each other, and their joint coping strategies to deal with adversities (e.g., Bodenmann, 2005, see Chapter 1), is paramount to investigate and foster in the Portuguese context. Thus, this chapter aims to illustrate and discuss the role of DC in Portugal based on the systemic transaction model (STM; see Chapter 1) of stress and coping.

Review of the Literature

Couples' Relationships in Portugal

Based on the STM perspective (Bodenmann, 2005), it is crucial to consider the evolution of the Portuguese culture because it sets the stage for understanding the interplay between the environment and the couples' stressors and coping behaviors. Therefore, in the following subsections, we address: (1) the contrast in work and family policies before and after the Revolution of 1974; (2) the 'dominant culture' of Portuguese couples; (3) the major stressors affecting couples; and (4) the lack of resources Portuguese couples may face.

From Dictatorship to Democracy: Work and Family Policies

During the right-wing Salazar dictatorship (1928–1974), pro-traditional family policies fostered a male breadwinner model emphasizing women's subordination to the patriarch authority and men's role as head of family and provider (Wall et al., 2013). Nevertheless, during this period, the mobilization of men to the colonial war along with high levels of emigration caused significant labor shortages. This forced Portuguese women to enter the labor market significantly earlier and at higher levels than in the other southern European countries (Tavora & Rubery, 2013). The changes that occurred after the revolution, in terms of the legislation regarding family and gender equality policies, further encouraged women to enter into the labor force, promoting the model of a dual-earner couple (Amâncio, 2007). As a result, Portugal has a considerably higher female employment rate (over 60 percent) compared to the European Union [EU] average, and the highest among southern European countries (Aboim, 2010a; Tavora & Rubery, 2013). Dual-earner couples with young children, both working full-time, have been a prevailing reality in the Portuguese society (Wall et al., 2013).

Changes in both the attitudes to family life and the economic behavior of women have led to a continuing decline of the male breadwinner model (Aboim, 2010a). Family policies after the transition to democracy rejected earlier gender cultural models and promoted state responsibilities to support full-time working men and women, causing a slow but steady increase in parents' entitlements to leave schemes and in publicly subsidized services to support dual-earner couples with children. Altogether, these changes led to a combination of old and new trends in family forms and gender roles (Wallet al., 2013).

Dominant Relationship Culture

Unfortunately, the growth of female employment and the expansion of a universal breadwinner model are not associated with significant changes in gender role attitudes in Portugal. The dominant informal gender culture still emphasizes the primacy of women as nurturers and child-rearers (Aboim, 2010a). In addition, research indicates that the division of domestic and care work in Portugal is among the most gender unequal in Europe (Aboim, 2010b). In the context of couples with a pre-school child, Portugal is the only European country showing an increase in the pattern of dual earner/highly unequal practices (Aboim, 2010a). These statistics clearly highlight a resilience of a traditional femininity in Portugal and that women still have a 'second shift' when they arrive home from their paid work (Aboim, 2010a; Aboim & Vasconcelos, 2012).

More importantly, empirical evidence indicates a strong ambivalence in the Portuguese population, combining high support for traditional gender roles and motherhood-centered values, with a strong desire for greater participation of men in domestic and childcare responsibilities (Aboim, 2010a). Qualitative studies reveal a generalized consensus around the ideal of a caregiving father, and most men value the norm of the father who is involved in parenting and interacts with his children (Aboim & Vasconcelos, 2012). However, a male breadwinner culture seems to persist in Portugal, and masculinity still appears to be equated with the ideal of men as family providers, despite the high rates of female full-time employment (Aboim, 2010a). The movement of women into the labor force has not resulted in an equivalent movement of men into the sharing of unpaid domestic and caregiving work (Aboim & Vasconcelos, 2012) and attitudinal emphasis on the equal sharing of both paid and unpaid labor is not entirely reflected in actual practices (Aboim, 2010a).

Given the factors noted above, Portugal seems to be a country divided between values. On one hand, there is a system of values related to a traditional conception of family (including the vision of women as mothers or the idea that children suffer when mothers work) that is still supported by a significant part of the Portuguese population. On the other hand, modern values emphasizing gender equality, the importance of women's participation in the labor market, or the acceptance of divorce are also common (Aboim, 2013; Amâncio, 2007). In fact, recent data shows that in terms of attitudes and values related to family life, Portuguese opinion is close to Scandinavian countries in some dimensions (e.g., being less conservative in terms of the notion that children can only be happy in a traditional two-parent family, and refusing the idea that being a housewife is rewarding for women), yet similar to southern European countries in other aspects (e.g., regarding the fact that maternal employment has a negative impact on children's development) (Aboim, 2013).

Multiple Stressors

The influence of the Portuguese cultural context as explained above on couples' relationships, is reflected in statistics regarding stress. Compared with other countries of the EU, Portugal has the highest levels of family stress (including the amount of domestic tasks and the lack of time to perform them, and feelings of tension while at home) and of work-family stress (related to work-family conflict, such as returning from work so tired that they cannot perform domestic tasks or having concentration problems at work due to family responsibilities) (Guerreiro & Carvalho, 2007). This is particularly the case for Portuguese women, whose stress is significantly above the average of European women, presenting the highest levels of family and work-family stress (Guerreiro & Carvalho, 2007).

As a result of the economic crisis, which originated cuts in wages and increased the unemployment rate and low-paid precarious work contracts (PORDATA, 2015c), couples' stress increased exponentially. Indeed, Portugal is one of the European countries with the lowest yearly disposable income per household, the highest risk of poverty, and the highest inequality of income distribution (EUROSTAT, 2014). A recent study conducted with a random sample of 2,230 Portuguese families revealed important findings on how the severe economic problems are affecting individuals' mental health and family functioning. In particular, the study showed that: (1) 1 in 10 families lived in 'real poverty,' being unable to pay the house rent, water and electricity bills, and essential medical treatments; (2) since 2012, in a quarter of these households, at least one of the family members had lost his/her job; (3) 30 percent of individuals were pessimistic about the future and afraid that another family member would lose his/her job; (4) 50 percent of participants lived with daily anxiety, 21 percent had depressive symptoms, 17 percent had sleep problems, and 1 in 10 individuals eventually considered suicide; and (5) more than 50 percent of participants stated that the crisis was causing family functioning problems (Defesa do Consumidor [DECO], 2013). More recently, empirical evidence revealed that Portuguese couples experience considerable levels of economic pressure, which was linked to higher levels of emotional stress (depression, anxiety, and hostility), decreasing marital satisfaction, and increasing inter-partner conflict (Ferreira, Pedro, & Francisco, 2015).

Lack of Resources

Portuguese families struggle not only with multiple stressors (i.e., contradictory values, gender inequalities, work–life management, unemployment, and low income), but also with a significant lack of resources that may hamper how the families could cope with the various stressors they may face. Specifically, families may experience an absence of: (1) economic resources due to the economic crisis; (2) weak welfare policies supporting women in work as well as couples in which one or both partners are unemployed; (3) overall lack of employment, and, interestingly, (4) family support (Tavora & Rubery, 2013). In fact, results from a representative national survey exploring the social networks of support of families with children, showed that support was not always as extended and systematic as was thought for a country with a supposedly strong 'family' tradition. In this study, nearly half of the Portuguese families reported a weak level of support (Aboim, Vasconcelos, & Wall, 2013). Another national survey showed that most individuals selected partners as the most important person in their lives (Aboim et al., 2013). Similarly, a recent daily diary study examining the support experiences of dual-earner parents across different cultural contexts, showed that Portuguese couples mainly expected and received support from their partners, and that couples' interdependence was very high (Schoebi et al., 2010).

Summary

Given the evidence abovementioned, it is plausible to assume that most Portuguese couples face multiple and chronic (i.e., long lasting) stressors, which have serious implications at the individual, dyadic, familiar, and societal level. More precisely, couples have to deal with different types of stressors at the same time, while struggling with limited resources. Frequently, the main resource is confined to the support received from the partner since support from extended networks (e.g., family and friends) is not as strong as it would be expected. Moreover, research has remained mostly focused on the individual's perception and non-dyadic data analyses of couple's data. Only recently, scholars (Vedes, Lind, & Lourenço, 2011) have started to proclaim that an STM approach to coping within couples was paramount to understand and help Portuguese couples cope more effectively with stress.

Couples Coping with Stress

The relevance of dyadic coping (DC) in the Portuguese context is clearly supported by several studies. These studies were conducted with seven independent samples of heterosexual couples or individuals in a committed relationship coping with different types of stressors. In the following section we present and discuss the main empirical findings by attending to diverse types of stress: External stress (stress from outside of the relationship), internal stress (stress from inside of the relationship), and major stressors (normative and non-normative critical life events), given the numerous stressors that Portuguese couples face.

External Stress, Dyadic Coping, and Couples' Functioning

Consistent with several international studies (see Chapter 1), when facing overall external stress,[1] positive DC behaviors by Portuguese partners are related to better relational outcomes, while negative supportive behaviors are associated with worse outcomes for both men and women. More specifically, in one study with 605 heterosexual individuals in a committed relationship (76 percent female), positive DC was associated with partners' better quality of sex, romance, and passion; more constructive and less destructive conflict processes; high shared meaning and relationship satisfaction (Vedes, Nussbeck, Bodenmann, Lind, & Ferreira, 2013). In another study, with a sample of 427 heterosexual individuals in a committed relationship (66 percent females), positive DC was associated with partners' dyadic adjustment dimensions. Specifically, positive DC was associated with high consensus (the degree of agreement on a number of issues or matters of importance to the relationship), cohesion (frequency of positive interactions, closeness, and shared activities), satisfaction, and affectional expression (the degree of agreement on how affection is expressed) (Ramalho, Ribeiro, & Pinto, 2015) between partners. Additionally, in two studies with different Portuguese samples (605 heterosexual committed individuals and 72 heterosexual couples), positive DC behaviors were associated with high relationship satisfaction by increasing we-ness (i.e., partners' perception of being more an interdependent unit, rather than two independent units) (Vedes, Bodenmann, Nussbeck, Randall, & Lind, 2015). Finally, in another study with 212 Portuguese couples with at least one adolescent child, positive DC was associated with less negative styles of family communication (e.g., family members blame each other when things go wrong) and with more family resources (i.e., strengths and adaptability to deal with things that are difficult for the family members) (Pedro & Francisco, 2015a).

The previous results are particularly noteworthy as they may underline Portuguese cultural characteristics. First, in the study of Vedes and colleagues (2013), a strong pattern of association was mostly found between perceived emotion-focused supportive DC by the partner, partners' joint DC, and relational qualities. These findings are consistent with studies showing that collectivistic-oriented cultures show more emotion-focused coping and common DC than cultures with a more individualistic orientation (see Chapter 2). Second, in the study of Vedes and colleagues (2015), the findings showed that in general, common DC was the most important form of DC, being positively associated with we-ness for both genders and we-ness strongly covaried with high relationship satisfaction. In addition, wives' outcomes were more strongly associated with their husbands' DC and we-ness than the opposite. From a cultural perspective, this study is particularly relevant given the role that interdependence plays in Portuguese couples (Aboim, 2006; Schoebi et al., 2010). Moreover, the differential findings for husbands and wives are in line with cultural research on intimate relationships showing that even in collectivistic cultures women tend to have a stronger interdependent self than men (Kuo, 2010), given their role as caregivers. This should be particularly true in the Portuguese context given the maternalism values that characterize Portuguese society.

In addition, Ramalho and colleagues (2015) not only replicated the influence of perceived support from the partner and common DC on dyadic adjustment above other DC behaviors, but also found further interesting findings. First, positive DC by oneself was not associated with women's dyadic adjustment dimensions but it was associated with men's high consensus, satisfaction, and affective expression. Considering Portuguese gender roles attitudes, these findings seem to suggest that when women support their partners, they may feel they are merely doing what is socially expected from them as family keepers. Therefore, women's positive DC does not affect their perception of dyadic adjustment facets. On the other hand, for men, supporting their partner may signify that they are meeting their partner's needs, thus perceiving more dyadic adjustment. Second, negative DC by the partner had a stronger effect on women's dyadic adjustment than for men. This suggests that women are more sensitive to their partner's negative supportive behaviors compared to men. One plausible explanation for this difference can be due to the high family and work-family stress that Portuguese women face, making them more susceptible to their partners' support. Finally, the study of Pedro and Francisco (2015a) expanded the role of DC from the couple system to the family system, which is line with Portuguese familism model.

Gender and Socio-Demographic Differences

Gender differences were found in some studies. Overall, women perceived themselves as communicating more stress, providing more positive DC (delegated and emotion-focused) than their partners, while men perceived their partners as communicating more stress and themselves as using more negative DC (Ramalho et al., 2015; Vedes et al., 2013; Vedes et al., 2015). These differences between men and women are consistent with the Portuguese collectivistic orientation, high-context communication style (see Chapter 2), and gender role attitudes. In partnerships oscillating between equal and traditional gender roles, open communication of stress may occur less often among men because they may feel uncomfortable with seeking support, as they may still appraise it as 'not being strong enough.' In addition, given women's role as caregivers, support should be to a certain extent dependent on women's capacity to decode their partners' non-verbal behaviors, as well as on their own provision of support. Moreover, the fact that men provided more negative DC than women and communicate less stress can also be explained by men's socialization in Portugal. Men are still commonly seen as the 'providers,' which could make them feel that they should solve problems by themselves, therefore communicating less stress to their partners. For the same reasons, it could be hypothesized that men may also be less likely to offer support and even to minimize women's complaints, by thinking they should be better at solving and dealing with their own stressors.

Regarding socio-demographic differences, one study (Pires, 2011) revealed that couples with higher levels of education (master or Ph.D.) living in urban areas, endorsed higher levels of positive DC (by oneself, partner, and common). On the other hand, partners with lower levels of education (i.e., secondary school), presented higher scores on negative DC behaviors. These findings align with sociology studies, which have shown that despite Portuguese cultural homogeneity, the social context and education matters (Aboim, 2006).

Internal Stress, Dyadic Coping, and Family Functioning

Empirical evidence indicating high levels of family stress in Portuguese families, as well as the fact that both couplehood and parenthood are paramount for Portuguese couples, highlights the need to understand the role of DC in the association between couple and parent-child relationships in the Portuguese society. Accordingly, one national (Pedro, Ribeiro, & Shelton, 2012) and several international studies have shown the impact of the couple relationship (e.g., satisfaction, conflict) on parent-child interaction (for a review, see Krishnakumar & Buehler, 2000). Moreover, in a qualitative study conducted with twelve married Portuguese couples with pre-adolescent children, DC was reported as one of the main resources for parents to avoid the spillover of stress from the couple relationship into the parent-child subsystems (Pedro, 2012). In another study, Pedro and Francisco (2015b) showed that DC had a mediating role in the association between open marital conflict (to which the adolescents were exposed), parental emotional support, and adolescents' adjustment. The findings indicated that couples' conflict was associated with less parental emotional support, by decreasing the capacity of providing and perceiving positive support, preventing partners' efforts to deal with stress, and especially, by increasing one's provision of ambivalent, superficial, and hostile support. Furthermore, direct effects were also found between DC and adolescents' emotional adjustment (externalization and internalization behavior), such that higher positive DC by oneself and the partner, as well as common DC, were associated with higher levels of an adolescent's adjustment. Altogether, these findings clearly suggest the negative impact of internal stress on couples' resources to perform as parents, highlighting the role of DC as an important protective factor that decreases the impact of couple conflict on parent–child interaction and adolescents' emotional adjustment.

Major Stressors, Dyadic Coping, and Couples' Functioning

Economic Pressure

Economic pressure represents the painful experiences created by hardship conditions such as being unable to purchase basic goods or pay monthly bills (Conger, Rueter, & Elder, 1999; Conger et al., 2002). The impact of economic pressure on couples' conflict and psychological distress is well established in the literature of family studies (e.g., Conger & Donnellan, 2007; Conger et al., 1999). Moreover, as explained above, economic pressure is particularly high in the Portuguese context, especially since the economic crisis of 2008, having negative effects on couple and family functioning (Ferreira et al., 2015). Considering the lack of studies in Portugal using the STM approach to economic stress, Pedro and Francisco (2015c) investigated the mediating role of DC between economic pressure, couples' conflict, and partners' psychological distress (depressed mood, anxiety, and angry or hostile feelings). Findings revealed that higher economic pressure was associated with higher levels of couples' conflict and psychological distress, by increasing both self and partner negative DC. These results are in line with the cascade model of Bodenmann (see Chapter 1) showing that high external chronic stress decreases couples' individual and dyadic resources. Interestingly, gender differences were not found between men and women in what concerns economic pressure, suggesting that in a country marked by dual-earner couples this type of stressor may be appraised as shared. Considering the financial crisis affecting Portugal, these findings may also indicate that the economic pressure experienced by both partners is so severe that it prevents them to support one another in an effective way, and cope with stress in a conjoint manner. Therefore, couples may resort to using negative forms of DC, which in turn contribute to increase conflict in the couple's relationship. Moreover, although previous studies with Portuguese couples indicate that women tend to provide more support to partners than men (Ramalho et al., 2015; Vedes et al., 2013; Vedes et al., 2015), this does not seem to be the case for financial stress. We may speculate that the high levels of economic pressure experienced by women makes them unable to provide the positive DC support consistent with their role of nurturers and family caregivers in the Portuguese culture.

Death of a Child

The death of a child is perhaps the most traumatic event a parent could go through (Wheeler, 2001) and the negative impact in several dimensions of parents' lives and relationship domains is well established. In Portugal, 295 children under one year old and 334 children and adolescents died in 2012 (World

Health Organization [WHO], 2015). Although these numbers are relatively lower than those reported in the year 2000 (deaths of children under one year old = 567; death of children and adolescents 1–19 years old=726) (WHO, 2015), they remain, nevertheless, high. The death of a child is often a shared stressor for both parents, as they must address not only the impact of the death as individuals, but also the changes to their relationship as a couple (Rando, 2000). After the death of an offspring, the spouse is commonly the primary source of support of the father/mother in grief, and there is sound evidence attesting the importance of the couple relationship to parents' individual adjustment (e.g., Lang, Gottlieb, & Ansel, 1996; Song, Floyd, Seltzer, Greenberg, & Hong, 2010). Nevertheless, existing research has traditionally examined how parents adjust to the death of a child from an individual perspective and the interpersonal context in which parental grieving occurs has been only scarcely considered (Stroebe, Schut, & Finkenauer, 2013).

In a country with a familial and maternalism cultural background, such as Portugal, the STM approach to understand coping with the death of a child as a joint endeavor should be particularly relevant. In accordance, Albuquerque, Pereira, and Narciso (2015) examined the mediating role of DC between grief and individual and dyadic adjustment in a sample of 152 parents with a deceased child (58.6 percent male). Findings showed that lower levels of grief were significantly associated with higher joint DC, which in turn was associated with better dyadic adjustment. Although marginally significant, parents' grief response was also significantly associated with lower depression, better quality of life, and dyadic adjustment, through higher positive DC by the partner. These findings suggest that common DC may be a potential mechanism through which the grief response of parents facing the shared loss of a child affects dyadic adjustment, and have important implications for interventions with these parents because after the death of a child parents are often deprived of their individual resources (Rosenblatt, 2000). In agreement with a cultural background marked by a fusion between women's identity and motherhood (Amâncio, 2007), mothers scored higher on grief, depressive, and anxiety symptoms, and lower on quality of life than fathers. In addition, mothers' individual adjustment was more strongly associated with DC behaviors, than for fathers' (Albuquerque et al., 2015).

Breast Cancer

Breast cancer is the most common oncological disease in the female population and the medical condition with the highest number of survivors worldwide. In Portugal, with a female population of five million, there are 4,500 new cases of breast cancer per year, i.e., eleven new cases per day, and four women dying daily because of this disease (Bastos, Barros, & Lunet, 2007; Direcção-Geral de Saúde [DGS], 2013b). Although most women diagnosed with breast cancer (stages I–III) survive their disease (Bastos et al., 2007; DGS, 2013b), the cancer experience embodies considerable intra- and interpersonal challenges. Given the interdependence that characterizes an intimate relationship, breast cancer is considered a dyadic stressor that can affect both partners individually and collectively as a couple. Research shows the importance of couples dealing with cancer as a 'we-disease' (Kayser, Watson, & Andrade, 2007), particularly in cultures in which interdependence is valued (Kayser et al., 2014), as well as DC being a key process involved in the adjustment of both partners facing breast cancer (e.g., Heinrichs et al., 2012). Unfortunately, an individual approach to this disease prevails in the Portuguese context; being cross-cutting to all the involved systems, such as the National Health System and couples themselves (Patrão, Neves, Paul, & Santos Rita, 2014a). Moreover, in a country where women have the role of caregivers it can be particularly difficult for women to be cared for, even when they are ill, and for men to adapt to the change of roles.

Aiming to provide the first steps for Portuguese BC couples cope with the disease as a unit, Patrão and colleagues (2014b) conducted a qualitative study using focus group methodology with eight couples' BC survivors (N = 16 participants; 50–55 years old), in order to adapt the *Couples Coping Enhancement Training* (CCET; Bodenmann & Shantinath, 2004) to Portuguese couples' BC survivors needs. Results revealed the necessity to include in the CCET training the cancer-related survivorship worries: (1) physical function and daily home activities; (2) cancer-related communication; (3) body image related to sexuality and intimacy; (4) instrumental support related to children care; and (5) management of stress related to employees and financial changes (Patrão et al, 2014b). This study provides a first step for the adaptation of a survival care plan to Portuguese couples with breast cancer.

Implications for Practice

Grounded in all the research conducted in Portugal, using an STM approach to stress and coping, we *again* (cf. Vedes et al., 2011) reiterate that positive DC skills should be promoted with Portuguese couples and families, while attending to its contextual and stress specificities. Interventions based on the STM approach, such as the CCET, the Coping-Oriented Couples Therapy (COCT; Bodenmann, 2007), and TOGETHER, for couples coping with financial strain (Falconier, 2014), have great potential to fit both Portuguese couples' and clinicians' needs as well as future program and policy markers' measures.

STM-derived interventions have high potential because they focus on stress and coping issues that can unite partners against a common enemy outside of their relationship (Bodenmann & Shantinath, 2004). This factor is crucial as Portuguese attitudes on looking for help are often skeptical and, specifically, regarding couples' relationships, the famous Portuguese proverb 'Entre marido e mulher ninguém mete a colher' (between husband and wife, no one puts the spoon) is a hallmark. Second, the CCET further addresses coping at the individual level, a long with issues related to mutual fairness, equity, and respect, as well as to dyadic communication. These facets can be particularly important for Portuguese couples. On the one hand, better individual coping could help reduce both partners' negative DC behaviors when dealing with different types of stressors (e.g., conflict and economic pressure) and their negative effect on children. On the other hand, fostering equal relationships along with dyadic communication skills is important because Portuguese couples often struggle with gender roles, division of care, and housework contradictions and/or inequalities. Third, the CCET, in particular, exists in a DVD format. If adapted to the Portuguese context, it could afford efficient low cost self-direct approaches (see Bodenmann, Hilpert, Nussbeck, & Bradbury, 2014) and respect flexibility within the 'culture' of each couple. Moreover, its adaptation for couples facing financial stress (TOGETHER; Falconier, 2014) is particularly relevant given the high number of Portuguese families facing economic challenges and pressure. TOGETHER not only decreases financial strain and its harmful effects on the individual (reducing anxiety and depression) and the couples' relationship (decreasing negative communication and fostering relationship satisfaction), but it also promotes couples' financial management skills (Falconier, 2014). In addition, interventions aimed to foster DC at the workplace should be implemented given the high levels of work-family stress in Portugal. Fourth, all STM-derived approaches aimed to foster not only better coping but also couples' we-ness. Fostering partners' we-ness seems therefore vital in the Portuguese context, since the partner is the main source of support and interdependence is dominant in Portuguese couples (Aboim, 2006; Schoebi et al., 2010). Fifth, as our findings suggest, supportive behaviors are crucial for couples' and partners' adjustment when facing more general stressors, but also major stressors, such as economic pressure, the death of a child, and breast cancer. Thus, clinicians and healthcare workers could integrate in their work measures of stress and DC (see Dyadic Coping Inventory in Portuguese, Vedes et al., 2013) and progressively foster couples' DC behaviors. Importantly, evidence-based principles and methods are available, and therefore could be easily adapted (e.g., CCET; Bodenmann, 2007). Based on the national and international empirical evidence of the STM, we suggest that program and policy makers may consider funding research to attest the validity of the STM-derived interventions in Portugal in DVD format and/or on-line platform. The media and key 'actors' in the Portuguese cultural context could divulge and publicize it, such as, family doctors, hospitals, and the centers of the Institute of Employment.

Implications for Research

Considering the Portuguese studies and the cultural specificities previously mentioned, four main lines for further research seem paramount. First, given the prevalence of economic stressors in Portugal and the contradictory gender findings in the literature, future studies should extend research regarding the role of DC in the spillover of economic stress to partners' well-being and relational outcomes, by considering gender roles. More specifically, cross-cultural studies comparing gender-equal countries (e.g., Scandinavian countries) and countries with more traditional gender roles (e.g., South European countries) could provide important clues to understand the patterns between these variables. Moreover, economic pressure studies in Portugal should control for work-family stress, division of domestic and care labor, as well as parenting variables. This research will help to disentangle the impact of gender role characteristics, on the one hand, and the impact of different stressors that seem to affect a culture with unequal gender role values such as the one in Portugal, on the other hand. Second, research could explore the role of DC behaviors in comparison with other variables (e.g., co-parenting) known to mediate the spillover of couple stress to parent-child interaction. This would inform if DC is a stronger buffer for this type of mechanism, as national research showing direct effects of couple's DC on adolescent's adjustment suggested. Third, the above-mentioned lines of research should further explore actor and partner effects to better understand crossover mechanisms between partners. Finally, future research should expand the study of the DC to other relevant family contexts/stressors in Portugal, such as, homosexual couples and couples coping with HIV.

Conclusion

In this chapter, we addressed the role of an STM approach to DC in the Portuguese cultural context. Overall, Portugal is a country with a collectivistic orientation characterized by (1) a strong familialism and maternalism focus; (2) contradictory values on gender roles and work-life management as well as on child and house care; (3) predominance of dual-earner couples; (4) multiple stressors; and (5) high levels of external and internal stress. Therefore, in Portugal, dyadic coping behaviors play a crucial role not only for couples' functioning, but also for family functioning in general and at the parent-child level, as well as for adolescents' adjustment. Furthermore, dyadic coping is relevant for couples when dealing with overall external stressors, with intra-dyadic stressors as well as with major stressors, such as, economic pressure, death of a child, and breast cancer. Since interdependence within Portuguese couples is valued, and the partner is the most important source of support, interventions aimed to foster DC can be paramount, because they promote couples' dyadic coping behaviors and we-ness against a common enemy: stress.

Note

1   It is important to mention that none of these studies measured stress independently. Thus, overall external stress means partner's global perception of stress with which they were trying to cope.

References

Aboim, S. (2006). *Conjugalidades em Mudança [Conjugalities Changing]*. Lisboa: ICS.

Aboim, S. (2007). Clivagens e continuidades de género face aos valores da vida familiar (em Portugal e noutros países europeus) [Gender cleavages and continuities towards family in Portugal and in other European countries]. In K. Wall & L. Amâncio (Eds.), *Família e género em Portugal e na Europa [Family and gender in Portugal and Europe]* (pp. 35–91). Lisboa: ICS.

Aboim, S. (2010a). Gender cultures and the division of labour in contemporary Europe: A cross-national perspective. *The Sociological Review, 58*(2), 171–196.

Aboim, S. (2010b). Family and gender values in contemporary Europe: The attitudinal gender gap from a cross-national perspective. *Portuguese Journal of Social Science, 9*(1), 33–58.

Aboim, S. (2013). Família e atitudes sociais: Portugal no contexto europeu [Family and social attitudes: Portugal in the European Context]. In A. Ramos, C. R., Pereira, J. Barreto, J. Tavares, M. J. Chambel, P. Magalhães, & S. Aboim (Eds.), *20 anos de opinião pública em Portugal e na Europa [20 years of public opinion in Portugal and Europe]* Lisboa: Fundação Francisco Manuel dos Santos.

Aboim, S., & Vasconcelos, P. (2012). Study on the role of men in gender equality in Portugal. *ICS Studies & Reports, ER3–2012*, 1–32.

Aboim, S., Vasconcelos, P., & Wall, K. (2013). Support, social networks and the family in Portugal: Two decades of research. *International Review of Sociology: Revue Internationale de Sociologie, 23*(1), 47–67.

Albuquerque, S., Pereira, M., & Narciso, I. (2015). Grief response and parents' individual and dyadic adjustment after the death of a child: The mediating role of dyadic coping. Manuscript in preparation.

Amâncio, L. (2007). Género e divisão do trabalho doméstico—O caso português em perspectiva [Gender and the division of domestic work—The Portuguese case in perspective]. In K. Wall & L. Amâncio (Eds.), *Família e género em Portugal e na Europa [Family and gender in Portugal and Europe]* (pp. 181–209). Lisboa: ICS.

Bastos, J., Barros, H., & Lunet, N. (2007). Evolução da mortalidade por cancro da mama em Portugal [Evolution of breast cancer mortality in Portugal] (1955–2002). *Acta Médica Portuguesa, 20*(2), 139–144.

Bodenmann, G. (2005). Dyadic coping and its significance for marital functioning. In T. Revenson, K. Kayser, & G. Bodenmann (Eds.) (2005), *Couples coping with stress: Emerging perspectives on dyadic coping* (pp. 33–50). Washington DC: American Psychological Association.

Bodenmann, G. (2007). Dyadic coping and the 3-phase-method in working with couples. In L. VandeCreek (Ed.), *Innovations in clinical practice: Focus on group and family therapy* (pp. 235–252). Sarasota: Professional Resources Press.

Bodenmann, G., Hilpert, P., Nussbeck, F. W., & Bradbury, T. N. (2014). Enhancement of couples' communication and dyadic coping by a self-directed approach: A randomized controlled trial. *Journal of Consulting and Clinical Psychology, 82*, 580–591.

Bodenmann, G., & Shantinath, S. D. (2004). The Couples Coping Enhancement Training (CCET): A new approach to prevention of marital distress based upon stress and coping. *Family Relations, 53*(5), 477–484.

Conger, R. D., & Donnellan, M. B. (2007). An interactionist perspective on the socioeconomic context of human development. *Annual Review of Psychology, 58*, 175–199.

Conger, R. D., Rueter, M. A., & Elder, G. H. (1999). Couple resilience to economic pressure. *Journal of Personality and Social Psychology, 76*(1), 54–71.

Conger, R. D., Wallace, L., Sun, Y., Simons, R., McLoyd, V., & Brody, G. (2002). Economic pressure in African American families: A replication and extension of the family stress model. *Developmental Psychology, 38*(2), 179–193.

Defesa do Consumidor (2013). Famílias cada vez mais pobres: 500 mil vivem em situação grave [Poorer families: 500.000 live in serious condition]. Retrieved from www.deco. proteste.pt/dinheiro/orcamento-familiar/noticia/familias-cada-vez-mais-pobres

Direcção Geral da Saúde (2013a). *Portugal—Saúde mental em números* [*Portugal—Mental health in numbers*]. Lisboa: DGS.

Direcção Geral da Saúde (2013b). *Doenças Oncológicas em números* [*Oncologic diseases in numbers*]. Lisboa: DGS.

EUROSTAT (2014). Quality of life indicators—material living conditions. Retrieved from www.epp.eurostat.ec.europa.eu/statistics_explained/

Falconier, M. K. (2015). TOGETHER—A couples' program to improve communication, coping, and financial management skills: Development and initial pilot-testing. *Journal of Marital and Family Therapy*, 1–15, Advanced online publication.

Ferreira, S. I., Pedro, M. F., & Francisco, R. (2015). 'Entre marido e mulher, a crise mete a colher': A relação entre pressão económica, conflito e satisfação conjugal. [Economic crisis and marital quality: The relationship between economic pressure and marital conflict and satisfaction]. *Psicologia, 29*(1), 11–22.

Geert-Hofstede (2015). *Portugal*. Retrieved from www.geert-hofstede.com/portugal.html

Guerreiro, M. D., & Carvalho, H. (2007). O stress na relação trabalho-família: Uma análise comparativa [The work-family stress: A comparative analysis]. In K. Wall & L. Amâncio (Eds.), *Família e género em Portugal e na Europa* [*Family and gender in Portugal and Europe*]. Lisboa: ICS.

Heinrichs, N., Zimmermann, T., Huber, B., Herschbach, P., Russell, D. W., & Baucom, D. H. (2012). Cancer distress reduction with a couple-based skills training: A randomized controlled trial. *Annals of Behavioral Medicine, 43*, 239–252.

Kayser, K., Cheung, P., Rao, N., Chan, Y. C., Chan, Y., & Lo, P. H. (2014). The influence of culture on couples coping with breast cancer: A comparative analysis of couples from China, India, and the United States. *Journal of Psychosocial Oncology, 32*(3), 264–288.

Kayser, K., Watson, L. E., & Andrade, J. T. (2007). Cancer as a 'we-disease': Examining the process of coping from a relational perspective. *Families, Systems and Health, 25*, 404–418.

Krishnakumar, A., & Buehler, C. (2000). Interparental conflict and parenting behaviors: A meta-analytic review. *Family Relations, 49*(1), 25–44.

Kuo, B. (2010). Culture's consequences on coping: Theories, evidences, and dimensionalities. *Journal of Cross-Cultural Psychology, 42*(6), 1084–1110.

Lang, A., Gottlieb, L., & Ansel, R. (1996). Predictors of husbands' and wives' grief reactions following infant death: The role of marital intimacy. *Death Studies, 20*, 33–57.

Patrão, I., Neves, C., Paul, V., & Santos Rita, J. (2014a, October). *Using emotional experiences to promote clinical knowledge: A qualitative study on breast cancer.* Poster session presented at the meeting of the IPOS 16th World Congress of Psycho-Oncology and Psychosocial Academy, Lisbon, Portugal.

Patrão, I., Bodenmann, G., Vedes, A., Carvalheira, A., Moura, M., Tapadinhas, R., . . . Leal, I. (2014b, October). *Breast cancer survivorship: A couples-focused group protocol to improve dyadic coping and we-ness.* Poster session presented at the meeting of the IPOS 16th World Congress of Psycho-Oncology and Psychosocial Academy, Lisbon, Portugal.

Pedro, M. F. (2012). *Relação conjugal e relação pais-filhos: Estudo de variáveis mediadoras e moderadoras* [*Marital and parental-child relationships: A study of mediators and moderators*]. Unpublished doctoral dissertation, University of Lisbon, Portugal.

Pedro, M. F., & Francisco, R. (2015a). *Associations between dyadic coping and family functioning.* Manuscript in preparation.

Pedro, M. F., & Francisco, R. (2015b). Marital conflict, parental support and adolescents' adjustment: The mediating role of dyadic coping. Manuscript in preparation.

Pedro, M. F., & Francisco, R. (2015c). Couples' conflict and partners' psychological distress in the context of economic pressure: The mediating role of dyadic coping. Manuscript in preparation.

Pedro, M., Ribeiro, M. T., & Shelton, K. H. (2012). Marital satisfaction and partner's parenting practices: The mediating role of coparenting behavior. *Journal of Family Psychology, 26*(4), 509–522.

Pires, A. (2011). *Coping diádico e satisfação conjugal: Um estudo com casais Portugueses* [*Dyadic coping and conjugal satisfaction: A study with Portuguese couples*]. Unpublished master thesis presented to the University of Lisbon, Portugal.

PORDATA (2015a). *Private households: total and by household type.* Retrieved from www.pordata.pt/en/Subtheme/Portugal/Households-29

PORDATA (2015b). *Number of divorces per 100 marriages.* Retrieved from www.pordata.pt/en/Portugal/Number+of+divorces+per+100+marriages-531

PORDATA (2015c). *Employment and labour market.* Retrieved from www.pordata.pt/en/Theme/Portugal/Employment+and+Labour+Market-3

Ramalho, C. S., Marques-Pinto, A., & Ribeiro, M. T. (2015). *Dyadic coping and adjustment on the first ten years of couple relationship.* Manuscript in preparation.

Rando, T. A. (2000). *Clinical dimensions of anticipatory mourning: Theory and practice in working with the dying, their loved ones, and their caregivers.* Champaign, IL: Research Press.

Rosenblatt, P. C. (2000). *Parent grief: Narratives of loss and relationship.* Philadelphia, PA: Taylor & Francis.

Schoebi, D., Wang, Z., Ababkov, V., & Perrez, M. (2010). Daily support across cultural contexts: A comparison of daily support experiences of young families in four cultural contexts. In K. Sullivan & J. Davilla (Eds.), *Social support processes in intimate relationships* (pp. 335–359). New York: Oxford University Press.

Song, J., Floyd, F. J., Seltzer, M. M., Greenberg, J. S., & Hong, J. (2010). Long-term effects of child death on parents' health-related quality of life: A dyadic analysis. *Family Relations, 59*, 269–282.

Stroebe, M., Schut, H., & Finkenauer, C. (2013). Parents coping with the death of their child: From individual to interpersonal to interactive perspectives, *Family Science, 4*, 28–36.

Tavora, I., & Rubery, J. (2013). Female employment, labour market institutions and gender culture in Portugal. *European Journal of Industrial Relations, 19*(3), 221–237.

Vedes, A., Bodenmann, G., Nussbeck, F. W., Randall, A. K., & Lind, W. (2015). The role of we-ness in mediating the association between dyadic coping and relationship satisfaction. *Family Science.* Submitted.

Vedes, A., Nussbeck, F. W., Bodenmann, G., Lind, W., & Ferreira, A. (2013). Psychometric properties and validity of the Dyadic Coping Inventory in Portuguese. *Swiss Journal of Psychology, 72*, 149–157.

Vedes, A. M., Lind, W., & Lourenço, M. (2011). Grounds for the design of prevention strategies for the promotion of couples' satisfaction and resilience. *Psicologia, 25*, 91–112.

Wall, K., Cunha, V., & Marinho, S. (2013). Negotiating gender equality in conjugal life and parenthood in Portugal: A case study. Working papers: ICS. Retrieved from www. repositorio.ul.pt/bitstream/10451/8958/1/ICS_KWall_VCunha_SMarinho_Negotiating_ WORN.pdf

Wheeler, I. (2001). Parental bereavement: The crisis of meaning. *Death Studies, 25,* 51–66.

World Health Organization (2015). Global Health Observatory Data Repository. Retrieved from www.apps.who.int/gho/data/?theme=main&vid=61310

8

DYADIC COPING IN GERMAN COUPLES

Philipp Y. Herzberg and Susan Sierau

Introduction

The present chapter covers the nature of dyadic coping in German couples. Dyadic coping can be briefly described as the interplay between the stress signals of people in intimate relationships (Revenson, Kayser, & Bodenmann, 2005). First, we present demographic data on family forms and intimate relationships in Germany to introduce the sociocultural background of German couples. Second, we summarize research on differences between coping on an individual and on a dyadic level, as well as on determinants of dyadic coping (e.g., marital standards, adult attachment) and dyadic coping in specific samples (couples after retirement, couples with a chronic disease of one partner). Finally, implications for practice and research will be given.

The German society is a truly individualistic one (Band & Müller, 2001). In individualistic cultures, people are independently oriented with a focus on themselves, not on a group of people, and these individuals follow mainly personal goals and values in life (Rothwell, 2010). People in individualistic societies value personal achievements and individual rights. This influences how these individuals act in their personal relationships. In an individualistic country, like Germany, people tend to have more relationships with less commitment (e.g., cohabiting instead of married couples) as well as various forms of intimate relationships (e.g., long-distance relationships, living apart together), compared to countries where there is collectivism orientation, with more traditional relationship forms (e.g., heterosexual married couples). According to the microcensus (2013), the largest annual household survey in Europe, individual family forms (e.g., single parents) have increased since 1996 in Germany, while there has been a decrease in numbers of traditional families (i.e., heterosexual married couples). Despite this trend towards 'non-traditional' families, married couples with minor children still are the most frequent family form (70 percent). Non-married or same-sex cohabiting couples with children under 18 years account for 10 percent of the families, while 20 percent were single parent families. In 1996, the proportion of married couples was higher (81 percent), while the percentage of single parents (14 percent) or cohabiting couples (5 percent) was lower. In more than half of the German households (60 percent), people live together as families with or without children. One-child families (1.4 children per women in one household on average) with a focus on the parent-children relationship are most common.

Review of the Literature

Couples' Relationships in Germany

The Federal Institute for Population Research (2014) interviewed people between 20 and 39 years of age in a survey about attitudes toward relationship and family. The love for one's partner and the allowance of personal freedom are reported as key components of a fulfilling partnership by 98 percent of the individuals, followed by a fulfilled sex life (93 percent), and good financial security (86 percent). In contrast, the presence of shared children was less important for a satisfying relationship; yet, parents (72 percent) and men (67 percent) rated this attitude as more important compared to childless people (56 percent), or women (58 percent). The higher importance of personal values compared to the lower significance of common family factors such as having one's own children, indicates a trend towards an increasing individualization within couples. As a result, the individual success of intimate relationships is based on the individual needs and goals of the partners, which may change over time, and could also result in conflicts within the couple.

Germans are increasingly oriented toward equality of gender roles (Cooke, 2006). One example of this can be found in the accessibility to paternal parental leave, which can be taken for a minimum of two and a maximum of twelve months in Germany. When the couple shares the parental leave, another two months can be granted. In 2010, 76 percent of the fathers took the two months concurrently with the mothers. Only 6 percent of the fathers took one full year of the parental leave. Likewise, in more than half (52 percent) of the married couples with at least one child, both partners were employed, while only 31 percent of the couples followed the traditional role model of a working father and a non-working mother. The reverse situation—the mother working and the father staying home—was present in only 6 percent of the couples.

Although 90 percent of Germans consider a fulfilling intimate relationship as the most important goal in their lives, a divorce rate of approximately 36 percent of all marriages registered per year can be assumed within the next twenty-five years (Federal Institute for Population Research, 2014). According to the microcensus (2013), there were 169,800 married couples who had divorced in Germany, representing a decrease of 5.2 percent compared to 2012. The relationship duration of these couples was on average 14 years and 8 months, which implies a trend towards long-term relationships before divorce. Nearly half of the divorced couples had children under the age of 18. In a study of 662 divorced individuals from Germany, Italy, and Switzerland, a low commitment level and deficits in interpersonal competencies such as communication, problem solving, and coping were main reasons for the decision to divorce with the accumulation of everyday stresses as a main trigger (Bodenmann et al., 2007). Thus, couple communication and dyadic coping seem to be important factors for German couple's relationship stability.

Beyond everyday stressors, health may also be an important factor for couples' relationship satisfaction. In Germany, chronic diseases, such as diabetes, cancer, or heart disease, are among the leading causes for death with high lifetime prevalence. According to the microcensus (2012), chronic ischaemic heart disease (women: 8.1 percent, men: 8.4 percent) and cancer (5.1 percent) were the most frequent chronic diseases causing death. For women, the most frequent forms of cancer were breast cancer (3.9 percent) or lung cancer (3.3 percent), while men suffered from lung cancer (7.1 percent) or prostate cancer (3.1 percent). Germany provides patients with universal healthcare that usually covers necessary medical treatment and psychotherapy when needed (Altenstetter, 2003). For Germans, health insurance is obligatory with most people utilizing the compulsory public insurance, which is calculated on the financial income of each person. The health insurance premium paid is based on joint employer-employee contributions. In 2012, total spending on healthcare amounted to € 300.4 million (€ 3740 per capita) which was an increase of 2.3 percent compared to 2011. Therefore, a diagnosis of a chronic illness is likely to be associated with less of a financial burden on patients in Germany than in other countries where different healthcare systems are utilized (Moran, 1999).

Given the above reported characteristics of the German society as an individualistic culture (Band & Müller, 2001) and the trend towards an increasing individualization of values (Rothwell, 2010), how does the concept of dyadic coping fit in? It was deemed necessary to pursue the question of how individual and dyadic coping efforts are related in the context of relationships. Only a few studies have examined individual and dyadic coping conjointly. Results indicated that individual and dyadic coping strategies may be perceived and employed distinctly (e.g., Bodenmann, Widmer, Charvoz, & Bradbury, 2004). According to the stress-coping cascade model (Bodenmann, 2005), adults in individualistic societies like Germany are likely to start with individual coping when confronted with stress. Bodenmann (2000) reported that 97 percent of couples tackle daily hassles initially individualistically, and emotion-focused stress is initially approached individualistically by 73 percent of couples. However, analyses were performed with couple-aggregated data, and not on the dyadic level. Consequently, the next step in examining the interplay between individuals' coping strategies and dyadic coping required an approach in which the dyad, rather than the individual, is the unit of analysis.

Individual Versus Dyadic Coping

Focusing on the dyad rather than the individual was the intention of a study by Herzberg (2013). Based on a sample of 240 German heterosexual couples (480 participants) with a mean relationship duration of 14.5 years (SD = 13.6), three hypotheses were tested: First, it was expected that dyadic coping would be more powerful in predicting relationship satisfaction than individual coping. Second, according to the partial evidence of the sequential order of individual and dyadic coping (that couples tackle daily hassles and stress initially individualistically) provided by Bodenmann (2000), and the process of feedback of partners' dyadic coping efforts, it was hypothesized that dyadic coping mediates the influence of individual coping. Third, it was hypothesized that the interdependence between partners' dyadic coping occurs as a mutual influence in which females exert a stronger influence on males than vice versa (Bodenmann et al., 2004). These hypotheses were complemented by exploratory investigations of a) whether actor or partner-effects exerts stronger influence of dyadic coping on relationship satisfaction (Kenny & Cook, 1999), and b) whether sex differences for problem-focused and emotion-focused dyadic coping exist (e.g., Ptacek, Smith, & Dodge, 1994).

In this study, individual coping was measured with the Coping Inventory for Stressful Situations (CISS; Endler & Parker, 1990) and dyadic coping with the common dyadic coping subscale of the Dyadic Coping Inventory (DCI; Bodenmann, 2008). The association of individual and dyadic coping with relationship satisfaction was investigated using two Actor-Partner-Interdependence Models (Kenny, 1996): one for task-oriented and one for emotion-oriented coping.

Results indicated that for both partners the association of problem-focused dyadic coping on relationship satisfaction were large in terms of effect-size, whereas individual coping was not related to relationship satisfaction. The importance of dyadic coping for relationship satisfaction was also supported for emotional dyadic coping, although this association was inverse, suggesting that emotion-oriented individual coping efforts may deteriorate relationship quality.

Furthermore, sex differences in partner effects were tested. The dyadic coping efforts of males were unrelated to females' relationship satisfaction. These observed sex differences in partner effects match the results from Bodenmann, Pihet, and Kayser (2006) in Swiss couples. Unequal benefits of dyadic coping are parallel with the notion that relationships are more central to women's lives than to men's; that women report greater commitment in relationships and engage in more relationship-maintenance behaviors (Impett & Peplau, 1996). These findings align with the literature on the demand/withdraw pattern (e.g., Christensen & Heavey,

1993) among couples, which is a frequent pattern of low-context communication (see Chapter 2). Furthermore, results lend support to a mutual influence of partners' problem-focused dyadic coping, suggesting that females' dyadic coping may exert a stronger influence on males' dyadic coping than vice versa. In contrast, the mutual-influence hypotheses had to be rejected for emotional dyadic coping.

For both sexes, problem-focused dyadic coping fully mediates the association between individual task-oriented coping and relationship satisfaction. This finding extends results derived from hypothesis 1 by showing that task-oriented individual coping is indirectly related to relationship satisfaction via problem-focused dyadic coping. Furthermore, preliminary support for partner mediation was established. Stated differently, females' perception of the couple's common dyadic coping completely mediated the relationship between female individual coping and male relationship satisfaction. The positive influence of females' dyadic coping on males' relationship satisfaction is supported by a positive influence of females' individual coping, which is carried through their dyadic coping efforts. Beyond the stronger association of dyadic coping discussed above, this result emphasizes the importance of dyadic coping for relationships by clarifying the interplay of individual and dyadic coping. It also stresses the two-fold role of problem-focused dyadic coping as an important predictor (direct effects) and mediating variable (indirect effects).

Findings also indicated that, contrary to prediction, dyadic emotional coping was not a mediator of the association between one's own individual emotional coping and relationship quality. On the other hand, partial actor-partner mediation for emotional dyadic coping was observed, meaning that males' individual emotional dyadic coping predicts females' dyadic coping, which in turn predicts female relationship satisfaction. Finally, partner effects were found for males only. Males' individual emotion-oriented coping lowers not only their partner's relationship satisfaction, but also reduces their partner's emotional dyadic coping efforts. Although the partner effects in accordance with prior studies on actor and partner effects (Kenny & Cook, 1999) are weaker than the corresponding actor-effects, they do deserve attention. A potential explanation is the importance of the female's perception of her partner's coping. The significance of females' perceptions of the relationship satisfaction of both couple members has been demonstrated by Huston and Vangelisti (1991), who found that the female's satisfaction was more strongly related to her perceptions of her partner's behavior than with her partner's perception of her own behavior, which correlates with the described gender role orientation in European couples (see Chapter 2).

Overall, results indicate that there is a complex interplay between individual and dyadic coping, including mutual influence and several kinds of mediation such as actor–actor as well as actor–partner mediation (Herzberg, 2013). Given the steady rise of economic stressors and strains in the German society and the observation that resources become less available in the larger society, Revenson et al. (2005) concluded that '. . . more pressure is placed on intimate partners and family members to deal with the stresses of daily life' (p. 4). In addition, research on emotional transmission between partners (Larson & Almeida, 1999) as well as stress spill-over models (Edwards & Rothbard, 2000) argue that what happens to one partner outside of the relationship may affect how the other partner thinks and behaves inside the relationship. Thus, daily and chronic stressors severely challenge a couple's ability to maintain their relationship (e.g., Bodenmann, 1997). The importance of dyadic coping then becomes obvious. In contrast to most previous research, where individual coping was conceptualized as independent, theoretical, and empirical, considerations in this study point to the synergistic relationship of individual and dyadic coping and their determination of relationship satisfaction.

Determinants of Dyadic Coping

The systemic-transactional model (STM) of dyadic coping (see Chapter 1) postulates that dyadic coping is influenced not only by individual and dyadic appraisals, but also by intra- and interpersonal factors (e.g., individual coping, personal dispositions, attributions), motivational factors (intrinsic, e.g., attitudes about relationships; or extrinsic, e.g., relationship standards), and contextual factors (e.g., current level of stress). We present the research on determinants of dyadic coping from a German perspective.

Marital Standards

Using a sample of 663 married individuals, Wunderer and Schneewind (2008) investigated the association between relationship-focused standards (i.e., partners expecting little boundaries and high levels of sharing inside their relationship, equal decision-making, and great instrumental and emotional investment in the relationship), supportive dyadic coping (see Chapter 3), and relationship satisfaction. Relationship-focused standards predicted dyadic coping; thus relationship-focused standards can be seen as motivational factors for dyadic coping. Furthermore, dyadic coping had a significant mediating effect on the relationship between marital standards and marital satisfaction for both genders (Wunderer & Schneewind, 2008). Unfortunately, the authors conducted analyses on the individual and not the couple level, thereby omitting the analyses of partner effects. Notwithstanding their separate analyses, the authors reported gender differences: For husbands, the correlation between standards and their own dyadic coping was higher than for wives. For wives, marital satisfaction depends to a higher degree on the support experienced through their partner than for husbands. Thus, marital standards of husbands are of central importance for the relationship: Husbands with high standards supported their wives, who, in turn, felt that they were being supported. As a consequence, wives reported higher satisfaction in their relationship. Dyadic support is also more frequently provided in relationships with a positive relationship climate as indexed by high commitment and activity, and low independence (Wunderer, Schneewind, Grandegger, & Schmid, 2001). When partners differ from each other in their relationship experience (e.g., committed wife and distancing husband or vice versa), dyadic coping was reported less frequently.

Adult Attachment

A potentially influential intra- and inter-personal determinant of dyadic coping is attachment. Gagliardi, Bodenmann, Heinrichs, Bertoni, Iafrate, and Donato (2013) examined this assumption in a mixed sample of couples from Switzerland, Italy, and Germany. Using both partners' scores of attachment dimensions (anxiety and avoidance), a cluster analysis was conducted to examine whether attachment-related couple-clusters differ in self-reported relationship quality and dyadic coping. Three clusters were derived: *secure couples*, where both partners reported low scores on anxiety and avoidance, *fearful-avoidant couples*, where both partners display higher scores on both attachment dimensions than secure couples, and a third cluster, named *mixed couples* cluster, where men reported higher anxiety scores than women. Secure couples reported more inherent dyadic coping than mixed couples, but did not differ from fearful-avoidant couples. For supportive coping of partners, secure couples reported higher values than fearful-avoidant and mixed couples. Negative coping was lowest among secure couples compared to fearful-avoidant and mixed couples. No differences for the remaining dimensions of dyadic coping were reported. The mean-level differences from this study were supported from correlation data from 192 individuals (Dinkel, 2006). Secure attachment showed a medium negative relationship to negative dyadic coping, and a positive relationship of the same magnitude to positive dyadic coping. An independent attachment style showed a smaller negative relationship to negative dyadic coping, and a positive relationship to positive dyadic coping.

Although both studies used a cross-sectional design, they give a first clue that attachment may influence the way couples engage in dyadic coping. Given the continuity of attachment across the lifespan (e.g., Lewis, Feiring, & Rosenthal, 2000) and importance in a variety of relationship contexts (Campbell & Marshall, 2011; Grossmann, Grossmann, Winter, & Zimmermann, 2002; Holmberg, Lomore, Takacs, & Price, 2011), it can be assumed that attachment representations influence the way couples jointly deal with stress and hassles. This has to be investigated by future longitudinal studies.

Dyadic Coping in Older Couples

Although Germany faces the challenges of an aging population (Naegele & Tews, 2013), research on dyadic coping in older couples is rather scarce in Germany. This holds true for couples after retirement. We are aware of one study addressing the role of dyadic coping in German retired couples. Baas and Schmitt (2004) interviewed 99 couples where both partners were retired. Two findings are worth mentioning. First, former male counterparts of a 'dual earners' relationship were more satisfied when compared with former male 'breadwinners,' while female marital satisfaction depended more upon dyadic coping and environmental mastery. This could reflect the trend towards an equal distribution of gender roles in Germany (Cooke, 2006). Second, for males, income distribution was significantly related with problem-focused common dyadic coping, which in turn, was significantly predictive of male relationship satisfaction. Emotion-focused common dyadic coping was not influenced by income distribution but was more strongly associated with male relationship satisfaction than problem-focused common dyadic coping. For females, emotion-focused common dyadic coping was only predictive of female relationship satisfaction. Income distribution exerts no influence on either form of common dyadic coping. The above-mentioned stronger orientation towards personal needs and values in German partnerships might foster emotion-focused common dyadic coping as a strategy in long-term partnerships. These interesting results point out the necessity to also focus on long-term marriages in order to gain deeper insights into the antecedents and dynamics of dyadic coping.

Beyond convenience and community samples or samples with non-chronic diseases, there is accumulating evidence that dyadic coping is much more crucial when coping with a chronic disease like diabetes, cancer, or coronary heart diseases.

Dyadic Coping with Chronic Illness

There is a growing interest to understand the role of dyadic coping and to utilize this knowledge for patients and their partners during counseling, as well as for therapy and rehabilitation. Beginning with the notion that partners are typically a patient's most important caregiver and are most often looked to for support (Coyne & Fiske, 1992), and that the quality of support from partners plays a crucial role in patients' ability to cope with their disease (Coyne & Fiske, 1992), a deeper search into the association between dyadic coping and coping with diseases has been recently examined. For instance, Körner and colleagues (2013) investigated parental dyadic coping in families of children and adolescents with Type 1 diabetes. Based on a cluster analysis from forty-four parental dyads of children/adolescents with Type 1 diabetes, three parental coping clusters were identified. Clusters differed according to their dyadic coping and stress communication. Although not reaching statistical significance, the glucose level (HbA1c) of adolescents with parents characterized by high levels of stress communication and common dyadic coping were consistently lower than the glucose levels of adolescents with parents with low levels of stress communication accompanied by low levels of common dyadic coping or parents characterized by comparatively low stress communication combined with high dyadic and common coping efforts. Despite the failed statistical significance, results suggest that parental dyads with suboptimal coping patterns (i.e., employing avoidant coping and problematic communication strategies) may benefit from minimal psychosocial intervention. This suggestion correlates with studies from Switzerland (e.g., Gabriel & Bodenmann, 2006), which have shown the promotion of dyadic coping may be very important for parents with a child with behavioral problems in dealing effectively with family stress. Both studies lend to the conclusion that elevated levels of family stress and strain originating from children who either suffer from a chronic disease or are afflicted with behavioral problems, may be reduced through dyadic coping strategies adopted by their parents. Psychosocial interventions may not only benefit parents caring for ill children but also couples facing severe illness.

'Side-by-Side' A Couple-Based Psycho-Oncological Intervention Program for Women Diagnosed with Breast Cancer

An example of a psychosocial intervention program is the 'Side-by-Side' program (Heinrichs & Zimmermann, 2008). The program is built on the assumption that communication and dyadic coping skills are crucial for couples coping with chronic illness (see Berg & Upchurch, 2007; Bodenmann, 1997, see Chapter 6). 'Side-by-Side' informs couples in five sessions about the disease and its medical treatment, individual and dyadic coping skills, and provides support in areas of communication, dealing with children, and sexual problems. The intervention is aimed toward enhancing these skills, thereby increasing the couples' competencies in addressing and sharing cancer-related issues, which in turn will reduce cancer-related distress. Zimmermann (2011) provides a case report for women diagnosed with breast cancer, which also gives an overview of the five sessions.

Heinrichs, Zimmermann, Huber, Herschbach, Russell, and Baucom (2012) investigated the utility of the 'Side-by-Side' program. Their study results, based on data from seventy-two couples, suggest that females assigned to the intervention showed larger reductions in fear of progression, and couples reported less avoidance in dealing with the cancer, more post-traumatic growth, and better relationship skills relative to the females assigned to the control program. Furthermore, couples who joined the intervention maintained a high level of dyadic coping, whereas couples in the control program showed a decline in a 10-month period of time. However, all differences favoring the intervention disappeared by 16 months after the diagnosis.

It is interesting to note that changes in the intervention among women seemed more pronounced than changes among men. The intervention may, therefore, be more helpful to women than to men; although men did show significant changes in relationship variables and benefit finding. One explanation for the greater benefit of women could be based on the type of cancer, as breast cancer is one of the most frequent forms of cancer in women (microcensus, 2012).

Another configuration is in parent couples where one parent is ill and the impact of the disease on the offspring is the focus of investigation. Heinrichs, Zimmermann, and Herschbach (2010) investigated nineteen couples where the mothers were diagnosed with gynecological cancer, and fathers were healthy. They concluded that common dyadic coping (measured with the GDC scale from the DCI) among parents reduces child distress. This pilot study found that those mothers who were more distressed at T1 reported more psychological problems in their children at T2. This prospective association was completely mediated through the level of common dyadic coping at T1. Thus, it seems that the 'spill-over' effect of inter-parental stress on children can be compensated by the use of dyadic coping.

Chronic diseases are frequently accompanied by fear of progression, which may impact the coping process. From the STM-perspective, fear of progression is not limited to the patient alone, but may also be prevalent in partners of chronically ill patients. In a sample of 332 partners of lung cancer, colon cancer, migraine, and rheumatism patients, Zimmermann, Alsleben, and Heinrichs (2012) investigated the association between fear of progression and one's own and partner dyadic coping. Univariate correlation analyses revealed that partner dyadic coping was negatively associated only in partners of rheumatism patients with fear of progression. For the remaining groups there was no such association. One's own dyadic coping was related with fear of progression only for partners of lung cancer patients but not for the remaining groups. A multivariate path analysis showed that dyadic coping of the partner was not related to fear of progression, but one's own dyadic coping was.

To summarize results from studies conducted in Germany, the importance of dyadic coping in dealing with chronic illness becomes more and more recognized in clinical practice and treatment in a wide spectrum of chronic diseases. This adjudication is mirrored in recommendations for staff nurses in psycho-oncology and rehabilitation (e.g., Ernst & Weißflog, 2013). An example for the role of emotion-focused supportive dyadic coping in relationships with one partner impaired by chronic tinnitus is given by Stürz et al. (2008).

Implications for Practice

Given the positive evaluation of couples-based intervention programs in other countries and in part in Germany (Heinrichs et al., 2012), we conclude by claiming two issues for further research in Germany. First, considering the efforts and costs required to provide such interventions, future research should evaluate whether there are specific couples (e.g., same-sex couples, intercultural couples, old couples) who would benefit most from such intervention programs. Second, physicians, hospitals, treatment staff, and National Health Services should acknowledge the role of the partners in coping with diseases by involving them in participated decision making, compliance issues, as well as in further relevant issues and stages of therapy and prevention. Stated differently, the role of partners as a resource of inestimable value should be recognized by stakeholders in the medical and psychological realm.

Implications for Research

Finally, considering previous research on the role of dyadic coping in couples' relationship satisfaction and the determinants of dyadic coping in individualistic societies such as Germany, it seems necessary to capture gender differences in dyadic coping styles and their links to relationship functioning. Moreover, more complex models such as dyadic data analysis (Kenny, Kashy, & Cook, 2006) seem to be beneficial compared to individualistic approaches to tap interpersonal appraisals within the complex nature of dyadic coping. Future studies could broaden these dyadic models by integrating intra- (e.g., personality traits like optimism, personal values), interpersonal (e.g., attachment, fidelity), and contextual factors (e.g., unemployment of one partner) of the couple.

Conclusion

Given the individualistic culture of the German society, which provides a lens for the individual's view and interpretation of the environment and the relative wealth and security in our culture, it is interesting to observe the importance of dyadic coping. Results from studies conducted in Germany revealed that dyadic coping is crucial for relationship functioning above and beyond a partner's individual coping (Herzberg, 2013). It is noteworthy to mention that dyadic coping seems to be somewhat more important for women's relational outcomes, and that wives were more affected by their husbands' dyadic coping than vice versa (Herzberg, 2013; Wunderer & Schneewind, 2008). This is congruent with the notion that in most German couples, especially in the older ones, females are more concerned about relationship issues and put higher emphasis on dyadic coping compared to men (e.g., Bodenmann, 2008; Baas & Schmitt, 2004). Concerning dyadic coping styles, problem-focused dyadic coping seems to play a crucial role in German couples' relationship functioning, whereas individual coping—more specifically emotion-oriented coping—seems to be detrimental for couples' relationship satisfaction (Herzberg, 2013). Problem-focused dyadic coping could be a functional strategy for couples to deal with accumulated everyday life stressors, which are a main trigger for communication problems and divorces in Germany (e.g., Bodenmann et al., 2007; Revenson et al., 2005).

In the context of chronic illness, the importance of dyadic coping was illustrated for couples coping with disease of one partner or with disease of their children. Dyadic coping is positively associated with high relational and psychological adjustment, and to a lesser degree, may even influence relevant parameters of diseases, e.g., the glucose level of children and adolescents with

Type 1 diabetes (Körner et al., 2013). Given the fact that couples in which a partner suffers from a mental disorder (e.g., depression) or a physical illness (e.g., cancer) do not exhibit the same dyadic coping pattern (see Bodenmann, 2000) and given the distinct contribution of dyadic coping in dealing with major stressors or chronic illness, it becomes apparent that fostering skills, which in turn enhance couple communication and positive forms of dyadic coping, are indispensable for therapy and relapse prevention. Several such trainings have been developed and evaluated (see Chapter 1).

Thus, dyadic coping in an individualistic culture such as Germany seems to play not only an important role in terms of intimate partnership functioning, but also in terms of the family system when one or more family members are facing major life stressors. Therefore, we emphatically plead that dyadic coping will find its place in clinical and psychosocial practice and prevention as well as in longitudinal research on its effects on family functioning.

References

Altenstetter, C. (2003). Insights from health care in Germany. *American Journal of Public Health, 93*, 38–44.

Baas, S., & Schmitt, M. (2004). Die Bedeutung der Einkommensverteilung für die Ehezufriedenheit langjährig verheirateter Ehepaare. [The impact of income distribution on marital satisfaction in long-term marriages]. *Zeitschrift für Familienforschung, 15,* 268–288.

Band, H., & Müller, H. P. (2001). Lebensbedingungen, Lebensformen und Lebensstile. [Living conditions, living forms, and lifestyles]. In *Handwörterbuch zur Gesellschaft Deutschlands* (pp. 427–435). Wiesbaden: VS Verlag für Sozialwissenschaften.

Berg, C. A., & Upchurch, R. (2007). A developmental-contextual model of couples coping with chronic illness across the adult life span. *Psychological Bulletin, 133*, 920–954.

Bodenmann, G. (1997). The influence of stress and coping on close relationships: A two year longitudinal study. *Swiss Journal of Psychology, 56*, 156–164.

Bodenmann, G. (2000). *Stress und Coping bei Paaren* [Stress and coping in couples]. Göttingen: Hogrefe.

Bodenmann, G. (2005). Dyadic coping and its significance for marital functioning. In T. A. Revenson, K. Kayser, & G. Bodenmann (Eds.) (2005), *Couples coping with stress: Emerging perspectives on dyadic coping* (pp. 33–50). Washington DC: American Psychological Association.

Bodenmann, G. (2008). *Dyadisches Coping Inventar (DCI).* In S. G. in Zusammenarbeit mit [in cooperation with] T. Ledermann, L. Charvoz, & N. Meuwly (Eds.), *[Dyadic Coping Inventory].* Test manual. Bern: Huber.

Bodenmann, G., Charvoz, L., Bradbury, T. N., Bertoni, A., Iafrate, R., Giuliani, C., . . . Behling, J. (2007). The role of stress in divorce: A three-nation retrospective study. *Journal of Social and Personal Relationships, 24*, 707–728.

Bodenmann, G., Pihet, S., & Kayser, K. (2006). The relationship between dyadic coping and marital quality: A 2-year longitudinal study. *Journal of Family Psychology, 20,* 485–493.

Bodenmann, G., Widmer, K., Charvoz, L., & Bradbury, T. N. (2004). Differences in individual and dyadic coping among low and high depressed, partially remitted, and nondepressed persons. *Journal of Psychopathology and Behavioral Assessment, 26,* 75–85.

Campbell, L., & Marshall, T. (2011). Anxious attachment and relationship processes: An interactionist perspective. *Journal of Personality, 79,* 917–947.

Christensen, A., & Heavey, C. L. (1993). Gender differences in marital conflict: The demand/withdraw interaction pattern. In S. Oskamp & M. Costanzo (Eds.), *Gender issues in contemporary society* (pp. 113–141). Newbury Park, CA: Sage.

Cooke, L. P. (2006). 'Doing' gender in context: Household bargaining and risk of divorce in Germany and the United States. *American Journal of Sociology, 112,* 442–472.

Coyne, J. C., & Fiske, V. (1992). Couples coping with chronic illness. In T. J. Akamatsu, J. C. Crowther, S. C. Hobfoll, & M. A. P. Stevens (Eds.), *Family health psychology* (pp. 129–149). Washington DC: Hemisphere.

Dinkel, A. (2006). Der Einfluss von Bindungsstil und dyadischem Coping auf die partnerschaftliche Beziehungsqualität. Eine Analyse moderierter Mediationseffekte [The effect of attachment style and dyadic coping on the partnership relationship quality. An analysis of moderated mediation effects]. (Unpublished doctoral thesis). Technische Universität Dresden.

Edwards, J. R., & Rothbard, N. P. (2000). Mechanism linking work and family: Specifying the relationship between work and family constructs. *Academy of Management Review, 25,* 178–199.

Endler, N. S., & Parker, J. D. A. (1990). *Coping Inventory for Stressful Situations (CISS): Manual.* Toronto: Multi-Health Systems.

Endler, N. S., & Parker, J. D. A. (1994). Assessment of multidimensional coping: Task, emotion, and avoidance strategies. *Psychological Assessment, 6,* 50–60.

Ernst, J., & Weißflog, G. (2013). Gemeinsam stark—Angehörige als Unterstützung [Strong united—member of the family as support]. *Heilberufe, das Pflegemagazin, 65,* 56–59.

Gabriel, B., & Bodenmann, G. (2006). Stress und Coping bei Paaren mit einem verhaltensauffälligen Kind [Stress and coping in parents of a child with behavioral problems]. *Zeitschrift für Klinische Psychologie und Psychotherapie, 35,* 59–64.

Gagliardi, S., Bodenmann, G., Heinrichs, N., Bertoni, A., Iafrate, R., & Donato, S. (2013). Unterschiede in der Partnerschaftsqualität und im dyadischen Coping bei verschiedenen bindungsbezogenen Paartypen [Differences in relationship quality and dyadic coping for attachment-related couple types]. *Psychotherapie, Psychosomatik, Medizinische Psychologie, 63,* 185–192.

Grossmann, K. E., Grossmann, K., Winter, M., & Zimmermann, P. (2002). Attachment relationships and appraisal of partnership: From early experience of sensitive support to later relationship representation. In L. C. Pulkkinen & A. Caspi (Eds.), *Paths to successful development: Personality in the life course* (pp. 73–105). Cambridge: Cambridge University Press.

Heinrichs, N., & Zimmermann, T. (2008). *Bewältigung einer gynäkologischen Krebserkrankung in der Partnerschaft: Ein psycho-onkologisches Behandlungsprogramm für Paare. [Coping of gynecological cancer in a relationship: A psycho-oncological treatment for couples].* Göttingen: Hogrefe.

Heinrichs, N., Zimmermann, T., & Herschbach, P. (2010). Welche Stärken und Schwächen sehen Mütter mit einer gynäkologischen Krebserkrankung und gesunde Väter bei ihren Kindern? [What strengths and difficulties do mothers with gynecological cancer and healthy fathers report in their children?]. *Verhaltenstherapie, 20,* 248–257.

Heinrichs, N., Zimmermann, T., Huber, B., Herschbach, P., Russell, D. W., & Baucom, D. H. (2012). Cancer distress reduction with a couple-based skills training: A randomized controlled trial. *Annals of Behavioral Medicine, 43*, 239–252.

Herzberg, P. Y. (2013). Coping in relationships: The interplay between individual and dyadic coping and their effects on relationship satisfaction. *Anxiety, Stress, & Coping, 26*, 136–153.

Holmberg, D., Lomore, C. D., Takacs, T. A., & Price, E. L. (2011). Adult attachment styles and stressor severity as moderators of the coping sequence. *Personal Relationships, 18*(3), 502–517.

Huston, T. L., & Vangelisti, A. L. (1991). Socioemotional behavior and satisfaction in marital relationships: A longitudinal study. *Journal of Personality and Social Psychology, 61*, 721–733.

Impett, E. A., & Peplau, L. A. (1996). 'His' and 'her' relationships? A review of the empirical evidence. In A. L. Vangelisti & D. Pearlman (Eds.), *The Cambridge handbook of personal relationships* (pp. 273–291). New York: Cambridge University Press.

Kenny, D. A. (1996). Models of nonindependence in dyadic research. *Social and Personal Relationships, 13*, 279–294.

Kenny, D. A., & Cook, W. (1999). Partner effects in relationship research: Conceptual issues, analytic difficulties, and illustrations. *Personal Relationships, 6*, 433–448.

Kenny, D. A., Kashy, D. A., & Cook, W. L. (2006). *Dyadic data analysis.* New York: The Guilford Press.

Körner, A., Würz, J., Brosseau, D. C., Brähler, E., Kapellen, T., & Kiess, W. (2013). Parental dyadic coping in families of children and adolescents with type 1 diabetes. *Journal of Pediatric Endocrinology Metabolism, 26*, 867–875.

Larson, R. W., & Almeida, D. M. (1999). Emotional transmission in the daily lives of families: A new paradigm for studying family process. *Journal of Marriage and the Family, 61*, 5–20.

Lewis, M., Feiring, C., & Rosenthal, S. (2000). Attachment over time. *Child Development, 71*, 707–720.

Lussier, Y., Sabourin, S., & Turgeon, C. (1997). Coping strategies as moderators of the relationship between attachment and marital adjustment. *Journal of Social and Personal Relationships, 14*, 777–791.

Moran, M. (1999). *Governing the health care state: A comparative study of the United Kingdom, the United States, and Germany.* Manchester University Press.

Naegele, G., & Tews, H. P. (2013). *Lebenslagen im Strukturwandel des Alters: Alternde Gesellschaft—Folgen für die Politik.* [*Circumstances in structural changes through aging—older societies—consequences for politics*]. Berlin: Springer-Verlag.

Papp, L. M., & Witt, N. L. (2010). Romantic partners' individual coping strategies and dyadic coping: Implications for relationship functioning. *Journal of Family Psychology, 24*, 551–559.

Ptacek, J. T., & Dodge, K. L. (1995). Coping strategies and relationship satisfaction in couples. *Personality and Social Psychological Bulletin, 21*, 76–84.

Ptacek, J. T., Smith, R. E., & Dodge, K. L. (1994). Gender differences in coping with stress: When stressor and appraisals do not differ. *Personality and Social Psychological Bulletin, 20*, 421–430.

Revenson, T. A., Kayser, K., & Bodenmann, G. (2005). Introduction. In T. A. Revenson, K. Kayser, & G. Bodenmann (Eds.) (2005), *Couples coping with stress: Emerging perspectives on dyadic coping* (pp. 3–10). Washington DC: American Psychological Association.

Rothwell, J. D. (2010). *In the company of others: An introduction to communication* (pp. 65–84). New York: Oxford University Press.

Stürz, K., Viertler, H. P., Kopp, M., Pfaffenberger, N., & Günther, V. (2008). Die Qualität der Partnerschaft von Tinnituspatienten. [Quality of partnerships in patients with tinnitus]. *HNO, 56,* 701–716.

Wunderer, E., & Schneewind, K. A. (2008). The relationship between marital standards, dyadic coping and marital satisfaction. *European Journal of Social Psychology, 38,* 462–476.

Wunderer, E., Schneewind, K. A., Grandegger, C., & Schmid, G. (2001). Ehebeziehungen. eine Typologie auf Basis von Paarklima-Skalen. [Marital relationships: A typology based on the 'Partnership-Climate Scale']. *Zeitschrift für Familienforschung, 13,* 74–95.

Zimmermann, T. (2011). «Seite an Seite»: Ein Fallbericht über partnerschaftliche Unterstützung im Rahmen einer Brustkrebserkrankung. ['Side by side': Couple-Based Psycho-Oncological Intervention Program for women diagnosed with breast cancer: A case report]. *Verhaltenstherapie, 21,* 171–177.

Zimmermann, T., Alsleben, M., & Heinrichs, N. (2012). Progredienzangst gesunder Lebenspartner von chronisch erkrankten Patienten. [Fear of progression in partners of chronically ill patients]. *Psychotherapie, Psychosomatik, Medizinische Psychologie, 62,* 344–351.

9

DYADIC COPING IN ITALIAN COUPLES

Silvia Donato

Introduction

Forming and maintaining a satisfying romantic relationship are important life goals for Italians (Monzani, Greco, & Steca, 2011). Accomplishing such goals, however, is subject to specific challenges in the Italian context. While the number of marriages in Italy showed a significant decrease over the past years, divorce rates have been gradually increasing (Istituto Nazionale di Statistica, 2014). Indeed, these signs of a general weakening of the marital bond in Italy reflect a cultural shift in values as well as the many stressful circumstances that partners have to face in their everyday life. Partners' ability to manage stressful circumstances together has proved to have relevant repercussions on partners' well-being (e.g., Bertoni et al., 2007; Donato & Parise, 2012). Nonetheless, studies on couples' stress and coping are scarce in Italy and have only recently received attention by the Italian scientific community (Donato, 2014).

The goals of the present chapter are as follows: First, it highlights the specific characteristics of the Italian culture and background that render some features of couples' coping particularly relevant in this context. Second, it presents the available evidence on Italian partners' dyadic coping. The section includes Italian studies regarding a) the assessment of dyadic coping in the Italian context; b) the impact of different forms of dyadic coping responses to partners' personal and relational well-being, and the buffering role of dyadic coping in the link between partners' stress and well-being; c) the congruence of partners' perceptions in the process of dyadic coping; as well as d) the intergenerational transmission of dyadic coping competences. Finally, the chapter will conclude with the implications for programs aiming at improving couples' stress management and for dyadic coping research.

Review of the Literature

Couples' Relationships in Italy

Contextual and Cultural Aspects

While some features of Italian couple relationships are in line with other European and international trends, others are specific characteristics of the Italian and Mediterranean context. In line with the European trend, Italy has shown a progressive weakening of the marital bond, as indexed by the steady decrease in the number of marriages and increase in the divorce rates over the past forty years, with accelerations in recent years (Eurostat, 2013). Furthermore, Italy is among those European countries showing the lowest marriage rate (i.e., marriages per 1000 inhabitants), which was 3.4 in 2011 (Eurostat, 2013). A typical feature of the Italian context, however, is the relatively low (though increasing) rate of marital dissolution. Retrospective research on the facilitators and barriers to divorce across three European countries (Italy, Germany, and Switzerland; Bodenmann et al., 2006) has shown, moreover, that the most important motives reported by Italian partners for divorce were relational difficulties (i.e., loss of love), while the most relevant barriers involved contextual constraints (i.e., social pressures, the presence of children, and financial strain).

Italy is also different from other European countries in the age that partners enter marriage. On average Italian women marry at the age of 31 and men at the age of 34, which are among the oldest ages in Europe, where the minimum age for women is 26 (Latvia) and for men is 28 (Lithuania) while the maximum is 32 for women and 35 for men (Sweden) (Eurostat, 2012). Italians are also known for living with their families of origin until marriage, a phenomenon that is typical of the Mediterranean model[1] of transition to adulthood (Galland, 1995; Lanz & Tagliabue, 2007). Among the main structural factors contributing to this delayed transition, we can list the high costs of the Italian real estate market, the absence or scarcity of social policies supporting young couples and families, the rate of youth unemployment (26 percent in 2009; De Rose, Racioppi, & Zanatta, 2008), the lower salaries as compared to other European countries (Rosina, Billari, & Livi Bacci, 2006), and the persistence of a 'strong' familistic cultural model (Dalla Zuanna, 2001) in which young-adult children are often financially supported by parents even after they have left their parents' home.

The role of the family of origin in Italy is, in fact, particularly important, especially when partners have children. Italian grandparents, in fact, are invaluable resources for children's daily care in Italy. Among the Italian grandparents taking care of at least one grandchild, about 50 percent do it on a daily basis, which is the highest percentage when compared to other European countries (Bordone, Arpino, & Aasve, 2012). The Italian welfare system, in fact, provides only minimal childcare assistance that could absorb family caring responsibilities and allow easier participation of women in the labor market. Such a system contributes to a traditional, not egalitarian division of housework within Italian couples. Italy appears to be a country where gender segregation of household tasks persists. In particular, as compared with twelve industrialized countries around the world, Italian men's unpaid work time was shorter in Italy than in other countries (Gershuny & Kan, 2012).

In addition to contextual factors, Italy presents cultural characteristics featuring contrasting and tensional forces (e.g., between individual and group needs, private and social views of marriage, traditional gender role orientation and egalitarian expectations), which can make Italian partners' daily lives particularly challenging and stressful. Italians, in fact, score relatively high in individualism, though the prevalence of such an orientation in Italy is not homogeneous. Today's Italian culture presents aspects of individualism (e.g., the relevance of individual goals; the value of independence; etc.) together with features of collectivism (e.g., the centrality of Italian families of origin; the relatively stable social and community networks; etc.) (Hofstede, Hofstede, & Minkov, 2010). Italian partners, for example, have been found to construe their couple identity in concert with their belonging to their families of origin (Manzi, Parise, Iafrate, Sedikides, & Vignoles, *in press*; Parise, 2013; Parise, Manzi, Donato, & Iafrate, 2015). This combination of individualistic and collectivistic features creates a tension between individual, couple, and group needs that requires continuous negotiation for Italian partners (e.g., between each partner's career development and nuclear and extended family demands).

In Italy, similarly to Western and individualistic countries, partners share a relatively private view of their couple relationship, defining the couple as a private matter that pertains only to the two partners (e.g., Bertoni, Parise, & Iafrate, 2012; Iafrate, Donato, & Bertoni, 2010). As already observed, however, Italian couples are also deeply connected to social and family ties that contribute to defining Italian partners' couple identity (Parise, 2013). Furthermore, it has been found that when partners report a positive heritage (in terms of values, norms, and models), they tend to be more satisfied with their lives and their relationship (Iafrate, Donato, & Bertoni, 2013). Similarly, Italian partners' relationship satisfaction was found to be positively associated to partners' trust in their family and social networks (Bertoni et al., 2012).

Role orientation within the couple relationship also presents some contrasting features in the Italian context. Although Italian couples were found to be quite traditional in their division of housework labor (e.g., Gershuny & Kan, 2012), fairness in such a division was found to be highly valued by Italian partners (Carriero, 2011), thereby creating potential ground for conflicts and tensions within the couple. The contextual features described above (e.g., increasing cost of living and unemployment, relatively low salaries, and inefficient welfare services) and the cultural aspects highlighted (e.g., individualistic and collectivistic motives, egalitarian expectations, and traditional role orientations) show how Italian partners are faced with both external and internal stressful circumstances that can put their relationship at risk. Stress, in fact, was found to significantly erode Italian partners' personal and relational well-being (Roggero, Vacirca, Mauri, & Ciairano, 2012).

Couple Relationship Research in Italy

Although the ways Italian couples cope with stressful circumstances call for scientific attention, couple relationship research has been fairly overlooked in Italian psychological studies till relatively recent times. Particularly lacking is basic research devoted to the study of how non-distressed couples function and to the examination of factors that can foster community couples' relationship quality and stability (cfr. Bradbury, Karney, Iafrate, & Donato, 2010). In Italy the relational-symbolic model (RSM; see Cigoli & Scabini, 2006) has been among the first and most influential models to devote specific theoretical and empirical attention to the study of non-distressed family relationships. The attention of Italian family researchers has been attracted to partners' dyadic coping processes thanks to the interconnections between the RSM and the systemic-transactional model (STM).

The RSM describes family relationships both in terms of their defining dimensions, and in terms of the ways they change when faced with critical events. With regard to the defining dimensions of family relationships, the RSM highlights the affective, ethical, intergenerational, and social dimensions. With regard to the couple relationship, the affective dimension refers to partners' reciprocal attraction and satisfaction of emotional needs, while the ethical dimension refers to partners' commitment and responsibility. The RSM, moreover, posits that the couple is inherently embedded in a broader context that represents a complex set of both constraints and resources. In particular, this broader context refers to the intergenerational and social ties. The couple is the 'mechanism' through which the intergenerational heritage passes on, filtered and inevitably changed, to the next generation (Donato, Iafrate, & Barni, 2013). The couple, moreover, plays a fundamental role of 'mediator' also in the relations between what is inside and what is outside the family, such as the social and cultural context in which it is embedded.

With regard to the ways they develop, the RSM recognizes the role of critical events as well as minor stressors for families' daily lives and transitions and regards STM as a fundamental reference point for couples' functioning in times of stress. The construct of dyadic coping, as defined within the STM, which emphasizes the complex, dynamic, and relational nature of the stress and coping process in couples, is particularly suited to integrate the analysis of important interactive processes with a relational approach characteristic of the RSM. In particular, the study of partners' interpersonal perceptions of dyadic coping especially represents the relational approach to dyadic coping research in Italy. Finally, the RSM emphasizes the intergenerational dimension of couple relationships and this focus was translated into a specific line of dyadic coping research in the Italian context.

Measuring Dyadic Coping in Italian Partners

One of the first steps in research on dyadic coping in Italy was the adaptation and validation of an existing measure of the construct to the Italian context. In particular, the structure and psychometrics of the Dyadic Coping Questionnaire, a precursor of the current Dyadic Coping Inventory (Bodenmann, 2008; see Chapter 3), were analyzed in a sample of Italian partners. The Dyadic Coping Questionnaire is a forty-one-item scale that intends to measure partners' stress communication, positive and negative dyadic coping reactions to the other's stress signals (both self-perceptions and perceptions of the other), and partners' common dyadic coping.

As the study by Donato and colleagues (2009) showed, the original four-factor model (stress communication, supportive, delegated, and negative dyadic coping) previously tested in a Swiss sample (Bodenmann, 2000) was only marginally appropriate in the Italian sample ($N = 389$ heterosexual couples). Moving from the four-factor solution to a five-factor one (by adding a problem-focused supportive dyadic coping factor), significantly improved women's self-perception model, while both solutions fit the data equally well for men. In this regard, it appears that providing emotional rather than instrumental support to the partner carries a different value in Italian men and women's view, in that women need to distinguish among these forms of coping more clearly than men do. This finding is consistent with other international research highlighting that in the U. S., women value emotion-oriented supportive skills as more important than men do (Burleson, Kunkel, Samter, & Werking, 1996). This may be especially true in Italy, where gender differences are proven to be more pronounced than in other northern European countries.

Consequences of Dyadic Coping for Italian Partners' Well-Being

Given that dyadic coping has shown to foster partners' well-being in other cultural contexts (see, for reviews, Donato, 2014; Iafrate & Donato, 2012), some Italian studies examined the role that different forms of dyadic coping play for Italian couples' functioning. In particular, Bertoni and colleagues (Bertoni et al., 2007) explored the impact of stress communication and different dyadic coping styles (i.e., positive dyadic coping, negative dyadic coping, common dyadic coping) on partners' relationship satisfaction in 141 Italian and 208 Swiss couples with a wide range of relationship duration (6 months to 35 years). The authors found generally no major differences in dyadic coping styles between Italian and Swiss couples, with the exception of common dyadic coping responses, which were more frequently enacted by Swiss couples than Italian ones. We can hypothesize that Swiss couples may be more egalitarian than Italian partners in the definition of roles within the relationship, expecting both partners to contribute equally to the coping process, and that such an orientation may facilitate Swiss couples' common dyadic coping responses. Nonetheless, the study highlighted that, after controlling for relationship duration, partner's stress communication, positive and common dyadic coping were all positively associated to both Swiss and Italian partners' satisfaction. Among these aspects of dyadic coping, common dyadic coping showed the strongest positive effect on partners' satisfaction, thereby showing the relevance of partners' joint efforts in coping with everyday stressors (Bertoni et al., 2007). The same study also found that negative dyadic coping, on the other hand, had a negative impact on partners' couple satisfaction, showing the potential risks inherent in unskillful or superficial dyadic coping responses (Bertoni et al., 2007). Such findings were also confirmed on more specific aspects of Italian couples' functioning. In particular, in a sample of 448 Italian couples (relationship duration: $M = 13.00$ years; $SD = 11.00$ years), positive dyadic coping and common dyadic coping responses were associated with higher partners' affection and sexual satisfaction as well as with lower indices of tensions, while the opposite pattern was found for negative dyadic coping styles (Donato, Canzi, Parise, & Ferrari, 2014).

A recent study showed how good dyadic coping skills, together with partners' communication, represent also a relevant moderator of partners' responses to stress in a community sample of 119 heterosexual, married couples in Italy (Gasbarrini et al., 2015). In particular, the study examined the moderating effects of communication skills and dyadic coping on relationship satisfaction in the context of existing common stressors[2] (i.e., child-related and sexual dissatisfaction). Results indicated that dyadic coping moderated the effects of sexual dissatisfaction on relationship satisfaction for both husbands and wives. In particular, the adverse impact of wives' sexual dissatisfaction on their own relationship satisfaction was greatest among wives who concurrently reported poor dyadic coping. Moreover, also the deleterious effect of wives' sexual dissatisfaction on their husbands' relationship satisfaction was greatest when the husband concurrently reported poor dyadic coping.

Finally, the critical role of dyadic coping styles was also revealed in a study examining couples with a partner suffering from cardiac illness (Bertoni, Donato, Graffigna, Barello, & Parise, 2015). Findings showed that the partner's negative dyadic coping behaviors were associated with the patient's engagement in the treatment, that is, patients' ability to take responsibility and action in their disease management. Unexpectedly, patients whose partners were involved in more negative dyadic coping responses were also more engaged in their disease management, exhibiting higher levels of patient engagement. It is possible that in the acute phase of the illness (patients were interviewed a few days after an acute cardiac event, like infarction or angina), in which patients are particularly dependent and disoriented, partners exhibiting less sympathy for the patient and less indulgence may provoke his/her own active involvement in his/her treatment. Further studies will explore whether in the longer run these benefits may backfire, in case the partner may continue to engage in negative dyadic coping with the patient. In sum, the findings reported above showed that positive forms of dyadic coping are beneficial for Italian couples' relationship. Some inconsistencies were revealed with regard to negative dyadic coping responses, which can be a liability for Italian partners' couple satisfaction, but can also motivate treatment engagement when enacted by partners of cardiac patients.

Italian Partners' Perceptions in the Process of Dyadic Coping

An original line of research on dyadic coping in the Italian context refers to the investigation of how interpersonal perceptions of dyadic coping (i.e., the degree of congruence between partners' perceptions) are linked to partners' relationship functioning. Indeed, the STM ascribes a critical role to partners' perceptions of dyadic coping responses and stress signals for the success of the dyadic coping process (see Chapter 1). The first study examined the role of partners' perceived similarity (i.e., how each partner perceived himself/herself to be similar to the other in dyadic coping), actual similarity (i.e., how partners reported similar dyadic coping styles), and understanding (i.e., the congruence between one partner's coping responses and the other partner's perceptions of such responses) for partners' satisfaction (Iafrate, Bertoni, Barni, & Donato, 2009). The study involved 124 Italian couples (relationship duration: $M = 13.90$ $SD = 11.20$) and findings showed that perceived similarity was higher than actual similarity in dyadic coping, suggesting that partners' perceptions of the other's dyadic coping were subject to bias, in terms of a perception of similarity that did not correspond to the actual level of it. As for the understanding of the partner's dyadic coping responses, men's understanding was higher when referred to negative dyadic coping styles than to positive ones. While in this study only Italian women's perceived similarity in negative dyadic coping predicted their relationship satisfaction, another study showed positive associations between Italian partners' perceived similarity in positive dyadic coping and satisfaction (Iafrate, Bertoni, Margola, Cigoli, & Acitelli, 2012). In these two studies partners' understanding, however, did not predict relationship satisfaction.

To further explore the role of perceived similarity and understanding of dyadic coping for Italian couples, a study involved 197 young premarital heterosexual couples ($M_{age} = 29.32$, $SD = 4.47$ for women; $M_{age} = 31.39$, $SD = 4.82$ for men) and 192 mature couples, composed of young partners' parents ($M_{age} = 57.41$, $SD = 6.56$ for women; $M_{age} = 60.34$, $SD = 6.73$ for men), and aimed at considering how relationship duration may moderate the association between interpersonal perceptions of dyadic coping and partners' satisfaction (Iafrate, Bertoni, Donato,

& Finkenauer, 2012).[3] In this study the authors refined the measures of interpersonal perceptions and computed two components of perceptual congruence: Unique and stereotypical. The unique component reflects partners' specific similarity, idiosyncratic to their own relationship. Stereotypical responding reflects partners' shared knowledge and expectations about how couples cope with stress together in their specific cultural context. It means, for example, that partners may understand the others' coping responses not only because he/she recognizes the specific ways the other behaves in times of stress, but also because he/she knows how couples in his/her culture normally respond (or are expected to respond) to stress together. Findings highlighted that partners' perceived stereotypical similarity in dyadic coping responses was higher in young Italian couples than in mature couples and that stereotypical and unique understanding of their dyadic coping responses were higher in mature couples than in younger partners (Iafrate et al., 2012). Stereotypical understanding was also positively related to relationship quality, but only among mature Italian couples. Moreover, unique understanding was not associated with relationship quality in mature couples, and it was negatively associated with relationship quality in young Italian couples, probably because for young, less committed partners understanding of partner-specific ways of dyadic coping may contrast their need for idealization and therefore be experienced as relationship threatening.

Finally, using a subsample from the above study ($N = 114$ young Italian couples in transition to marriage, relationship duration before marriage: $M = 5.7$ years, $SD = 3.4$ years), Donato and colleagues (2015) investigated the mediating role of partners' perceptions in the association between Italian partners' reported dyadic coping responses and their satisfaction. Findings showed evidence for both understanding and perceived similarity in Italian partners' perceptions of dyadic coping. Moreover, partners' perceptions mediated the association between change in reported dyadic coping responses and change in relationship satisfaction. In particular, the study showed that increases in partners' positive dyadic coping behaviors corresponded to increases in the other partner's satisfaction with the relationship, (partly for men) because he/she noticed his/her partner's change in behaviors. Finally, the study also highlighted that partners' dyadic coping responses predicted increases in their own satisfaction, partially because they were associated with increases in their own perceptions of the other's dyadic coping behaviors.

In sum, these findings highlight the key role of partners' perceptions of dyadic coping responses, and the fact that such perceptions are both accurate and biased. Given that in individualistic societies, such as Italy in some respects, relationships are viewed as places where partners can express and fulfill their personal needs; in such cultural contexts partners' dyadic coping responses may be considered as particularly diagnostic of how well the partner responds to one's need for support, trust, and security. Thus, especially within this context, partners have reasons to be both accurate and biased in their dyadic coping perceptions. Accurate perceptions of the partners' dyadic coping responses, in fact, would allow the other to test partners' regard and responsiveness and to react accordingly (by reciprocating the responses or by expressing their needs for different partners' behaviors), while positively biased perceptions of the partner's dyadic coping efforts would protect the partners from potentially threatening information (e.g., the partner's low levels of regard and dedication).

Intergenerational Continuity and Discontinuity in Dyadic Coping Competences of Young Italian Couples

A particularly innovative line of research on dyadic coping in Italian couples was the one exploring potential determinants of dyadic coping and isolating those factors that can foster or, on the contrary, impede the use of positive dyadic coping strategies. Given the role that the family of origin plays for Italian young adult children and the specific attention devoted to intergenerational ties by the RSM in Italy, the study of dyadic coping determinants in Italy has considered the role of intergenerational sources of dyadic coping acquisition. In particular, one study explored whether and how the internalization of parental models of dyadic coping and the reciprocity between partners influenced Italian partners' dyadic coping acquisition (Donato, Iafrate, Bradbury, & Scabini, 2012). Internalization of parental models means that partners may internalize and conform to the ways their mothers and fathers typically support each other in times of stress. Reciprocity, on the other hand, refers to the fact that the partner's typical positive or negative dyadic coping responses may determine the other's propensity to respond similarly in return. In particular, the study analyzed similarities in positive and negative dyadic coping styles between Italian young-adult partners as well as between partners and their parents. It was also investigated whether parent–child similarities were moderated by child's gender and by the type of dyadic coping model (positive vs. negative) parents embodied. This study also distinguished between unique and stereotypical components of dyadic similarity.

Findings showed evidence for both internalization of parental models and partner's reciprocation of dyadic coping responses. In positive dyadic coping only stereotypical parent-child similarities, but both unique and stereotypical partners' similarities were found significant. In negative dyadic coping, instead, Italian children internalized and reciprocated their parents' and partners' specific (i.e., unique) responses. Similarities in negative dyadic coping were actually higher than those in positive dyadic coping. Daughters in particular were more similar to their parents in negative dyadic coping than sons were. In addition, Italian children's ability to distinguish between positive and negative parental models influenced their internalization. Daughters, in fact, were more similar to their parents the less parents engaged in negative dyadic coping. The authors argued that daughters may be more sensitive to the parental models than sons and more prone to reproduce them as long as they are less negative and more socially acceptable.

In sum, these findings emphasize the role of the family of origin in the acquisition of Italian partners' dyadic coping styles. Similarly to other relational competences (see Donato, Iafrate, & Barni, 2013), dyadic coping is likely to be modeled by the experiences partners have lived within their families of origin. This intergenerational determinant of dyadic coping could be particularly evident in Italian partners, given the critical and long-lasting role of Italian families of origin in Italy. At the same time, however, the findings highlight that partners are able to filter their parental models and to exert an influence on each other's dyadic coping responses. We may hypothesize that the combination between individualistic and collectivistic forces in the Italian culture makes the tension between intergenerational (i.e., parental models) and relational (i.e., partners' reciprocal influence) sources of dyadic coping acquisition especially evident. Notably, this same tension allows for both intergenerational continuity and discontinuity in Italian couples.

Implications for Practice

Given the cultural challenges (e.g., tensions between individual and group needs, private and social views of marriage, traditional gender role orientation, and egalitarian expectations) and stressors (e.g., financial difficulties, the lack of effective family social policies, etc.) Italian couples are facing, as well as the findings of dyadic coping studies on Italian partners, Italian scholars and policy makers should devote specific attention to interventions aimed to support partners' ability to cope with the stressors and challenges of family life in Italy. Some efforts have been made by Italian scholars toward integrating the notion of dyadic coping in couples' therapy and in the context of illness (Margola & Costa, 2014; Randall, Bodenmann, Molgora, & Margola, 2010), but in Italy scarce attention has been devoted so far to this form of intervention. Among the rare exceptions to this trend was the application in the Italian context of the CCET (cfr. Chapter 5; Bodenmann & Bertoni, 2004).

Findings from the studies presented in this chapter, as well as the research tradition inspired by the relational-symbolic model (see Cigoli & Scabini, 2006), also revealed some specific foci of attention that could complement Italian partners' training of dyadic coping skills. Studies have highlighted how specific attention should be devoted to foster Italian partners' common dyadic coping responses, as they were revealed particularly important for their satisfaction. Moreover, the role of perceptions in Italian partners' dyadic coping attests the importance to consider partners' needs to negotiate a shared reality (as expressed by partners' understanding in perceiving their dyadic coping responses) as well as to perceive that their dyadic coping transactions are based on equal exchanges (as expressed by partners' assumed similarity in dyadic coping responses). This aspect could be especially important in Italian interventions, if we consider that such needs for understanding and equality are expressed by partners living in a context of mostly traditional and not egalitarian gender role orientations. The attention to partners' shared reality and perceptions of equality in dyadic coping invites Italian professionals to complement the training of adaptive dyadic coping responses with aspects related to the meaning and symbolic dimensions underlying dyadic coping exchanges. The need to include such aspects in the intervention has already been considered within the CCET, which incorporates a module dedicated to justice and equity in the relationship, but could be further developed in Italian interventions. In addition, relationships and exchanges that partners maintain with their families of origin have been shown to discriminate between satisfied and dissatisfied Italian partners (e.g., Bertoni & Bodenmann, 2010), who were found to build their couple identity integrating their reciprocal belongings to those families (Parise, 2013). Preventive interventions for couples in Italy should also consider the role of intergenerational and social ties for couples' dyadic coping acquisition and functioning. While intergenerational relationships could be evoked when helping partners reflect on their typical responses to stress, one interesting way to implement a focus on the social dimension of couples in dyadic coping interventions could be through the use of the group of participants as a specific tool of intervention (the group of couples in the intervention is the first social context in which to experience different relational modes) and through the promotion of couples' networking.

In Italy, a prevention program for couples has been designed (*Percorsi di enrichment familiare* Groups for Family Enrichment—Couple version; Bertoni, Donato, Morgano, Iafrate, & Rosnati, *in press*; Iafrate, Rosnati, & Bertoni, 2007) with the aim of combining couples' information and training on relational competencies with activities devoted to help partners reflect on the dimensions of the couple identity as defined by the RSM (i.e., partners' intimacy and affection, the value they place on their relationship and the other, their connection with the partners' family histories and lineages, and the connection with the social context). Although not specifically devoted to train partners' dyadic coping abilities, drawing from the STM and Italian research findings on dyadic coping, the program emphasizes communication and dyadic coping skills among partners' relational competences and seems a good candidate to complement dyadic coping interventions in Italy.

Implications for Research

Future paths of research should be devoted to the refinement of the assessment of dyadic coping. While the most recent version of the questionnaire (i.e., DCI–Bodenmann, 2008) is currently being validated in Italy, another step for dyadic coping measurement could be to implement observational measures of dyadic coping behaviors as well as newer self-report methods such as daily diary (e.g., Pagani, 2014). Diary measures would help distinguish between the effects of typical dyadic coping responses (and perceptions of such responses) from the ones of specific behaviors (and perceptions) shown in everyday interactions. Larger, representative samples could also be used for the purpose of validating such measures.

With regard to the consequences of dyadic coping for partners' relational well-being, Italian studies confirm that positive dyadic coping responses promote partners' satisfaction, while negative ones put partners at risk for dissatisfaction. Moreover, Italian studies confirm the pivotal role of common dyadic coping, that is partners' joint efforts to cope together against stress, but also reveal that (at least as compared to Swiss couples) Italian partners report engaging less in this form of coping (Bertoni et al., 2007), which could be therefore particularly important to facilitate and train. Common dyadic coping was found to be particularly important in Latino couples, such as U.S. Latin American immigrants (e.g., Falconier, 2013). Comparing Italian and Latino couples may allow researchers to carefully examine the cultural nuances within the same Latin tradition. While both Italians and Latinos share a familistic background and a traditional gender-role orientation, they may differ in terms of the levels of collectivism and individualism that partners express. In general, the role of individualism and collectivism in dyadic coping should be further explored. In particular, future research should explore the specific Italians' dilemma between modern individualism, traditional collectivism, and intergenerational norms in different age cohorts of Italian partners as well as in northern versus southern Italy.

Research conducted in the Italian context highlight how partners' perceptions are particularly relevant in dyadic coping and that both accuracy and perceived similarity in partners' perceptions play a role in the process of dyadic coping, especially in the Italian culture. Italian studies also showed the need for considering the different components (stereotype vs. uniqueness) of interpersonal perceptions of dyadic coping and the importance of a contextual approach to these issues, as interpersonal perceptions may differ and have different effects for different couples (e.g., young vs. mature). Both aspects emphasize the role of cultural influences on dyadic coping. Future research should compare the role of stereo-typical responding as well as relationship duration for dyadic coping behaviors and perceptions in other cultural contexts.

Finally, Italian studies were the first to investigate the intergenerational transmission of dyadic coping competences, revealing that partners' acquisition of dyadic coping competences present some intergenerational continuity. The family of origin has been shown, in fact, to play an important role for young couples in Italy (e.g., Parise et al., *in press*), where the frequency of contacts between partners and parents may maintain modeling processes for a long time. The findings presented here, however, highlight how Italian young couples have room for innovation, expressed in children's capacity for distinguishing between positive and negative parental models (i.e., showing lower vs. higher levels of negative dyadic coping). Physical distance and frequency of contacts between Italian young adults and their parents have been shown, in fact, to be a less crucial marker for Italian children's autonomous functioning than for UK young adult children (Manzi, Vignoles, Regalia, & Scabini, 2006). Future studies should examine such processes in other cultures. In addition, dyadic coping research in Italy would benefit from implementing longitudinal studies, which could test the validity of cross-sectional findings as well as examine how the processes highlighted in them may unfold over time.

Conclusion

In light of the demanding tasks couples are faced with in the Italian context and the specific attention of Italian family researchers to relational and dyadic constructs, this chapter presented a review of Italian studies aimed at tapping different aspects of dyadic coping in Italian partners, and specifically the measure of dyadic coping responses within the Italian context; the impact of Italian partners' different forms of dyadic coping responses for their well-being; the buffering role of dyadic coping in the link between Italian partners' stress and well-being; the congruence of partners' perceptions in the process of dyadic coping; and the intergenerational continuity in dyadic coping competences. In conclusion, research on dyadic coping in Italian couples has shown the pivotal role of such a process for Italian partners' relational well-being and highlighted innovative paths for preventive intervention aiming at fostering partners' dyadic coping and relational well-being as well as for future dyadic coping research in this and other cultural contexts.

Notes

1 Galland (1995) identified three European models of the transition to adulthood: a Mediterranean model, where the youth stays longer within their family of origin and leaves home mostly to enter marriage or cohabitation; a 'northern'and French model, characterized by a prolonged time of living away from home not immediately followed by starting a new family; and a British model whereby young adults enter into the job market quite early and/or live for a long time with a partner, but without children.
2 Common stressors are the ones partners perceive the problem pertains to both of them and they both have resources to manage the stressful circumstances (see Chapter 1).
3 This study as well as the ones by Donato et al. (2012) and by Donato, Iafrate, Bradbury, and Scabini (2014) were part of a broader research project on partners in transition to marriage and their families of origin.

References

Bertoni, A., Barni, D., Bodenmann, G., Charvoz, L., Gagliardi, S., Iafrate, R., & Rosnati, R. (2007). Comunicazione dello stress, coping diadico e benessere della coppia: Uno studio cross-sectional e cross-nazionale [Stress communication, dyadic coping, and couple well-being: A cross-sectional and cross-national study]. *Età Evolutiva, 86*, 58–66.

Bertoni, A., & Bodenmann, G. (2010). Satisfied and dissatisfied couples: Positive and negative dimensions, conflict styles, and relationships with family of origin. *European Psychologist, 15,* 175–184.

Bertoni, A., Donato, S., Graffigna, G., Barello, S., & Parise, M. (2015). Engaged patients, engaged partnerships: Singles and partners dealing with an acute cardiac event. *Psychology, Health, and Medicine, 20,* 505–517.

Bertoni, A., Donato, S., Morgano, A., Iafrate, R., & Rosnati, R. (in press). A qualitative evaluation of a preventive intervention for parents: The Groups for Family Enrichment_ Parent Version (GFE_P). *Journal of Prevention and Intervention in the Community.*

Bertoni, A., Parise, M., & Iafrate, R. (2012). Beyond satisfaction: Generativity as a new outcome of couple functioning. In P. E. Esposito & C. I. Lombardi, *Marriage: Psychological implications, social expectations, and role of sexuality* (pp. 115–132). Hauppauge: Nova Science Publishers.

Bodenmann, G. (2000). *Stress und Coping bei Paaren* [*Stress and coping in couples*]. Göttingen: Hogrefe.

Bodenmann, G. (2008). *Dyadisches Coping Inventar (DCI)* [*Dyadic Coping Inventory*]. Manual. Bern: Huber Testverlag.

Bodenmann, G., & Bertoni, A. (2004). *Promuovere le competenze della coppia. Il Couples Coping Enhancement Training* [*Promoting the couple's competence: The Couples Coping Enhancement Training*]. Roma: Carocci Editore.

Bodenmann, G., Charvoz, L., Bradbury, T. N., Bertoni, A., Iafrate, R., Giuliani, C., . . . Behling, J. (2006). Attractors and barriers to divorce: A Retrospective study in three European countries. *Journal of Divorce and Remarriage, 45,* 1–23.

Bordone, V., Arpino, B., & Aasve, A. (2012). Policy perspectives of grand parenting in Europe. *Dondena Working Paper, 51.* Retrieved from www.dondena.unibocconi.it/wp51

Bradbury, T. N., Karney, B., Iafrate, R., & Donato, S. (2010). Building better intimate relationships: Advances in linking basic research and preventive interventions. In V. Cigoli & M. L. Gennari (Eds.), *Close relationships and community psychology: An International perspective* (pp. 224–240). Milano: Franco Angeli.

Burleson, B. R., Kunkel, A. W., Samter, W., & Werking, K. J. (1996). Men's and women's evaluations of communication skills in personal relationships: When sex differences make a difference and when they don't. *Journal of Social and Personal Relationships, 13,* 201–224.

Carriero, R. (2011). Perceived fairness and satisfaction with the division of housework among dual-earner couples in Italy. *Marriage & Family Review, 47,* 436–458.

Cigoli, V., & Scabini, E. (2006). *Family identity: Ties, symbols, and transitions.* New York: Lawrence Erlbaum Associates Publishers.

Dalla Zuanna, G. (2001). The banquet of Aeolus: A familistic interpretation of Italy's lowest low fertility. *Demographic Research, 4,* 133–161.

De Rose, A., Racioppi, F., & Zanatta, A. L. (2008). Italy: Delayed adaptation of social institutions to changes in family behaviour. *Demographic Research, 19,* 161–183.

Donato, S. (2014). Il coping diadico, ovvero far fronte allo stress insieme: Una rassegna della letteratura [Dyadic coping, that is managing stress together: A review of the literature]. *Giornale Italiano di Psicologia, 36,* 471–499.

Donato, S., & Parise, M. (2012). The role of enacted and perceived dyadic coping for young couples' satisfaction. In B. Molinelli & V. Grimaldo (Eds.), *Handbook of the psychology of coping: New research* (pp. 261–278). Hauppauge: Nova Science Publishers.

Donato, S., Iafrate, R., & Barni, D. (2013). Parents as models for partners' relational competences: Theoretical bases and empirical findings. In P. Barberis & S. Petrakis (Eds.), *Parenting: Challenges, practices, and cultural influences* (pp. 83–102) Hauppauge: Nova Science Publishers.

Donato, S., Iafrate, R., Bradbury, T. N., & Scabini, E. (2012). Acquiring dyadic coping: Parents and partners as models. *Personal Relationships, 19*, 386–400.

Donato, S., Canzi, E., Parise, M., & Ferrari, L., (2014). Partnership Questionnaire: Factorial structure, gender invariance, and concurrent validity. *TPM-Testing, Psychometrics, Methodology in Applied Psychology, 21*, 161–180.

Donato, S., Iafrate, R., Barni, D., Bertoni, A., Bodenmann, G., & Gagliardi, S. (2009). Measuring dyadic coping: The factorial structure of Bodenmann's 'Dyadic Coping Questionaire' in an Italian sample. *TPM -Testing, Psychometrics, Methodology in Applied Psychology, 9*, 25–47.

Donato, S., Parise, M., Iafrate, R., Bertoni, A., Finkenauer, C., & Bodenmann, G. (2015). Dyadic Coping Responses and Partners' Perceptions for Couple Satisfaction: An Actor-Partner Interdependence Analysis. *Journal of Social and Personal Relationships, 32*, 580-600. doi: 10.1177/0265407514541071

Eurostat (2012). Demographic outlooks: National reports of the demographic developments in 2010. *European Union Methodologies and Working Papers.*

Eurostat (2013). European social statistics. *European Union Pocketbooks.*

Falconier, M. K. (2013). Traditional gender role orientation and dyadic coping in immigrant Latino couples: Effects on couple functioning. *Family Relations, 62*, 269–283.

Galland, O. (1995). What is youth? In A. Cavalli & O. Galland (Eds.), *Youth in Europe.* London: Pinter.

Gasbarrini, M. F., Snyder, D. K., Iafrate, R., Bertoni, A., Donato, S., & Margola, D. (2015). Investigating the relation between stress and marital satisfaction: The moderating effects of dyadic coping and communication. *Family Science, 6*, 143–149.

Gershuny, J., & Kan, M. Y. (2012). Halfway to gender equality in paid and unpaid work? Evidence from the time-use study. In J. Scott, S. Dex, & A. Plagnol (Eds.), *Gendered lives: Gender inequalities in production and reproduction* (pp. 74–94). Northampton: Edward Elgar Publishing.

Hofstede, G., Hofstede, G. J., & Minkov, M. (2010). *Cultures and organizations: Software of the mind*, 3rd ed. New York: McGraw-Hill.

Iafrate, R., Bertoni, A., Barni, D., & Donato, S. (2009). Congruenza percettiva nella coppia e stili di coping diadico [Perceptual congruence in the couple and dyadic coping styles]. *Psicologia Sociale, 1*, 95–114.

Iafrate, R., Bertoni, A., Donato, S., & Finkenauer, C. (2012). Perceived similarity and understanding in dyadic coping among young and mature couples. *Personal Relationships, 19*, 401–419.

Iafrate, R., Bertoni, A., Margola, D., Cigoli, V., & Acitelli, L. K. (2012). The link between perceptual congruence and couple relationship satisfaction in dyadic coping. *European Psychologist, 17*, 73–82.

Iafrate, R., & Donato, S. (2012). Coping in a relational context: The case of dyadic coping. In B. Molinelli & V. Grimaldo (Eds.), *Handbook of the psychology of coping: New research* (pp. 111–132). Hauppauge: Nova Science Publishers.

Iafrate, R., Donato, S., & Bertoni, A. (2010). Knowing and promoting the couple bond: Research findings and suggestions for preventive interventions. *INTAMS Journal for the Study of Marriage & Spirituality, 16*, 65–82.

Iafrate, R., Donato, S., & Bertoni, A. (2013). Family heritage, individual well-being and relationship satisfaction in young couples. In P. Barberis & S. Petrakis (Eds.), *Parenting: Challenges, practices, and cultural influences* (pp. 201–212), Hauppauge: Nova Science Publishers.

Iafrate, R., Rosnati, R., & Bertoni, A. (2007). Percorsi di Promozione e arricchimento dei Legami Familiari [Groups for Family Enrichment]. In E. Scabini & G. Rossi (Eds.), *Promuovere famiglia nella comunità* [*Promoting the family in the community*] (pp.113–140). Milano: Vita e Pensiero.

Istituto Nazionale di Statistica (2014). *Il matrimonio in Italia. Anno 2013* [*Marriage in Italy—Year 2013*]. Retrieved from www.istat.it

Lanz, M., & Tagliabue, S. (2007). Do I really need someone in order to become an adult? Romantic relationships during emerging adulthood in Italy. *Journal of Adolescent Research, 22*, 531–549.

Ledermann, T., Bodenmann, G., Gagliardi, S., Charvoz, L., Verardi, S., Rossier, J., . . . Iafrate, R. (2010). Psychometrics of the dyadic coping inventory in three language groups. *Swiss Journal of Psychology, 69*, 201–212.

Manzi, C., Parise, M., Iafrate, R., Vignoles, V. L., & Sedikides, C. (2015). Insofar as you can be part of me: The influence of intrusive parenting on young adult children's couple identity. *Self and Identity, 14*, 570–582.

Manzi, C., Vignoles, V. L., Regalia, C., & Scabini, E. (2006). Cohesion and enmeshment revisited: Differentiation, identity, and well-being in two European cultures. *Journal of Marriage and Family, 68*, 673–689.

Margola, D., & Costa, G. (2014). Il trauma della malattia fisica: Quando la speranza è il legame [The trauma of physical illness: When hope is the bond]. In V. Cigoli, D. Margola, M. Gennari, & D. K. Snyder (Eds.), *Terapie di coppia. L'approccio integrativo e l'approccio relazionale-simbolico* [*Couple therapy. The integrated approach and the relational symbolic approach*] (pp. 289–309). Milano: FrancoAngeli.

Monzani, D., Greco, A., & Steca, P. (2011). Obiettivi e soddisfazione di vita [Life goals and satisfaction]. *Rassegna di Psicologia, 28*, 9–23.

Pagani, A. F. (2014). *Nella buona sorte: Il processo di capitalizzazione nella relazione di coppia* [*In the good luck: Capitalization process in the couple relationship*] (Unpublished Doctoral dissertation). Università Cattolica del Sacro Cuore, Milano, Italia.

Parise, M. (2013). *Molto più di due. Costruzione dell'identità di coppia e relazioni familiari* [*Much more than two. Construction of couple identity and family relationships*]. Milano: Vita e Pensiero.

Parise, M., Manzi, C., Donato, S., & Iafrate, R. (in press). Free to love? The role of intrusive parenting for young adult children's romantic relationship quality. *Journal of Prevention and Intervention in the Community.*

Randall, A. K., Bodenmann, G., Molgora, S., & Margola, D. (2010). The benefit of 'stress and coping' research in couples for couple therapy. In V. Cigoli & M. L. Gennari (Eds.), *Close relationship and community psychology: An international perspective* (pp. 169–186). Milano: Franco Angeli.

Roggero, A., Vacirca, M. F., Mauri, A., & Ciairano, S. (2012). The transition to cohabitation: The mediating role of self-efficacy between stress management and couple satisfaction. *Journal of Alternative Medicine Research, 4*, 325–339.

Rosina, A., Billari, F., & Livi Bacci, M. L. (2006). Famiglia e figli [Family and children]. In F. G. Agnelli & GCD-SIS (Eds.), *Generazioni, famiglie, migrazioni. Pensando all'Italia di domani* [*Generations, families, migrations. Thinking about Italy's future*]. Torino: Edizioni Fondazione Giovanni Agnelli.

10

DYADIC COPING IN GREEK COUPLES

Pagona Roussi and Evangelos C. Karademas

Introduction

Although stress has been traditionally defined at the individual level, it is increasingly recognized that stress in couples is almost always a dyadic process (Coyne & Smith, 1991), as the 'individual processes' in each member of the couple are not isolated, but mutually affected and inter-connected (Bodenmann, 2005). Thus, a stressful condition affects both partners, either directly (i.e., the same condition affects either both partners or it originates from within the couple) or indirectly (i.e., a 'crossover' effect). Provided that partners live in a close relationship, a stressful condition initiates a dyadic coping process: 'a process on the dyadic level in which the coping reactions of one partner take into account the stress signals of the other partner' (Bodenmann, Pihet, & Kayser, 2006a, p. 486).

This process is important for the well-being of both partners and for the quality of the relationship. For instance, positive dyadic coping has been associated with a higher level of relationship quality and stability, physical and psychological well-being, as well as with lower levels of stress (e.g., Badr, Carmack, Kashy, Cristofanilli, & Revenson, 2010; Bodenmann, Meuwly, & Kayser, 2011; Bodenmann et al., 2006a). Thus, the conceptualization of stress and coping at a dyadic level is important in order to better understand how stress affects couples and how to help partners deal with it. This conceptualization may be especially important for Greek families and couples.

Family has a central role in the Greek culture. Greeks tend to feel emotionally closer to family members and to live in closer distance to their parents and siblings when compared to Western European countries (Georgas et al., 2001). They have frequent contact with their close and extended family, especially with parents and siblings, and use the family as a primary source of support and help, especially during hard times (Georgas et al., 2001; Georgas, Berry, van de Vijver, Kagitcibasi, & Poortinga, 2006). Yet, there is surprisingly little in terms of research on dyadic coping with stress in Greece; possible reasons for that may be the lack of appropriate instruments and the fact that questions about intra-family interactions are more likely to be regarded with suspicion in Greece (Georgas et al., 2006; Helmes & Gallou, 2014). Even so, it is important that this gap in the extant literature be addressed for the following reasons: 1. dyadic coping, positive and negative, may be very important, given the central role of the Greek family in everyday life. 2. Greece has been changing rapidly and some of these changes have had a negative impact on the family institution. For example, although the Greek divorce rate is one of the lowest in Europe (about 25 percent), it has doubled between 1990 and 2010 (Eurostat, 2014).

According to the Hellenic Statistical Authority (HSA, 2015), about half of the marriages are religious. About half (52 percent) of Greek families include both parents and at least one child, about 30 percent of Greek families have no children, and 15 percent are single-parent families. The vast majority of couples with a child are married, with only 3 percent cohabitating (HSA, 2015, April). Same-sex unions were not recognized in Greece until very recently; therefore, formal statistical data are not available.

In this chapter, we will first discuss characteristics of the Greek culture that might be of relevance to the study of dyadic coping. Second, we will discuss the types of stressors Greek couples face and will review studies examining how Greek couples cope with stress. Finally, we will review studies employing a dyadic perspective in researching how Greek couples cope with stress. In this section, we will present preliminary findings from a study that examined dyadic coping and how it is related to relationship satisfaction and psychological distress among Greek couples. Finally, we will discuss the implications of the reviewed material for clinical practice and future research.

Characteristics of the Greek Culture

First, Greece has been described as being in the middle position between individualistic and collectivist cultures (Oyserman, Coon, & Kemmelmeier, 2002; Triandis, 1995). Recent studies comparing Greek and UK students on issues of self-construal and social support suggest that Greece continues to be characterized by collectivist values when compared to Western European countries (Kafetsios & Nezlek, 2012; Pouliasi & Verkuyten, 2007). For example, in a study that examined children's spontaneous social self-representations in Greece and in a more individualistic society (the Netherlands), it was found that in both populations a perception of social self in relation to nuclear family, close friends, and significant others was the most important aspect of social self (Pouliasi & Verkuyten, 2007). However, Greek children were more likely to understand their social self in a group-wise manner that is as part of a unit; whereas Dutch children were more likely to understand their social self in a pair-wise mode that is as part of dyadic bonds.

Second, it has been proposed that the Greek culture is relatively high on masculinity (Hofstede, 1980) and has been described as traditional with clearly differentiated gender roles. In such societies, men are supposed to be 'assertive' and 'tough,' and women are supposed to be 'tender.' Greece has undergone major changes in the past thirty-five years, including high urbanization, joining the European Union, and a significant expansion of the higher education system (Statista, 2013). Even so, there is evidence that, in comparison to Western European societies, the Greek society is still characterized by higher level of gender-role stereotyping and that Greeks score lower on gender empowerment measures and on egalitarian attitudes as far as fathers' and mothers' participation in household tasks and child care is concerned (Apparala, Reifman, & Munsch, 2003; Maridaki-Kassotaki, 2000). These non-egalitarian attitudes appear to be stronger among males and in rural areas (Maridaki-Kassotaki, 2000).

The importance attached to family (Georgas et al., 2001) and the traditional gender roles (Hofstede, 1980) have implications for the broader family dynamics and possibly for how couples cope with stress. For example, collectivism implies that the welfare of the in-group, such as the family, and the communal concerns and mutual goals (e.g., about the family financial status, issues related to children's welfare, relations with the broader family) are priorities for partners. Therefore, dyadic coping may very well be high among Greeks and may play an important role in relationship satisfaction and well-being. At the same time a number of factors may hinder dyadic coping. Families of origin in Greece expect that they will keep close contact with the couple, which may result in the weakening of the spousal dyad and friction (Georgas et al., 2001). In addition, in collectivist societies, roles are less likely to be negotiated and more likely to be prescribed based on gender. In such cultures, the important subsystem is more likely to be the parent-child dyad and not the spousal dyad, thus limiting the opportunity for dyadic coping (Katakis, 1998; see also Chapter 2), which assumes equity and reciprocity between the partners.

Review of the Literature

Couples' Relationships in Greece

Although Greece is more collectivist when compared to Western European countries, there are signs that this is changing (Georgas, 1991; van den Heuvel & Poortinga, 1999), with some researchers claiming that Greece is a country in transition because of the urbanization of the Greek society and the concomitant increase in individualistic values (Georgas et al., 2001). Thus, in urban areas one is more likely to find multiple value systems, which vary across generations with young people more likely to be characterized by both collectivist and individualistic values. This has led researchers to suggest that there are three different types of family organizations functioning simultaneously in Greece (Katakis, 1998). The first type is the traditional closely-knit extended family, wherein male and female identities are embedded in a broader social network with clearly defined roles, duties, and obligations. The emphasis is on one's obligations toward the group as a whole and not on the quality of the couple's relationship. This family prototype is more likely to be found in small, rural communities, characterized by collectivist values. The second type is based on the nuclear family. It is more likely to be found in urban areas, but again the emphasis is not on the spousal relationship and its quality. In this family, the parent-child dyad is of the utmost importance, and more specifically it is the mother-child relationship that is particularly strong. In such a family organization, the male partner is more likely to have the role of the provider and to be rather isolated, whereas the mother has strong bonds with her children. The third type of family is closer to the Western European family organization wherein the spousal dyad is central. In this modern family type, the partners are strongly motivated by a desire to maintain the quality of their relationship and one's sense of obligation toward the partner is strongly connected to the quality of the relationship. Katakis (1998) suggests that as Greece becomes more and more urbanized, newer generations may move away from the traditional type of family organization toward the other two, the nuclear and the modern. The co-existence of the three family types across generations inevitably leads to conflicting goals and potentially to familial friction. Although Katakis' observations are based on interviews with a limited number of participants and on clinical observations, more systematic research indirectly provides support for her theses (Georgas, 1991; Georgas et al., 2006; Thorpe, Dragonas, & Golding, 1992; Tsamparli-Kitsara & Kounenou, 2004). As a result, Greek couples may be facing chronic internal and external stressors, the type of stressors typically associated with a deleterious effect on the relationship in the international literature (Randall & Bodenmann, 2009), due to family conflict.

In addition, for the past six years, Greek couples face common external stressors due to unemployment and financial stress (Economou, Madianos, Peppou, Patelakis, & Stefanis, 2013). The austerity measures that followed the ongoing fiscal crisis, which began in 2010, have impoverished the population and became the source of great burden. Unemployment rose from 6.6 percent in 2008 to 27.6 percent in 2013, affecting mostly women and young adults who were prevented from leaving their parental home; poverty levels have increased, especially among families with children, the elderly, and women (Matsaganis, 2013). As a result, there has been a rise in mental and physical health problems, while at the same time, public healthcare services were substantially reduced (Economou et al., 2013; Ifanti, Argyriou, Kalofonou, & Kalofonos, 2013). However, there are some indications that families in Greece have been instrumental in helping their members to survive the crisis (e.g., Christodoulou & Christodoulou, 2013). Thus, families seem to be facing significant stressors in Greece. Nevertheless, very limited research has been conducted in Greece regarding dyadic stress and how partners cope or what partners do to help each other cope with stress, as the Systemic-Transactional Model (STM) proposes (Bodenmann et al., 2011).

Studies on the Stress Process in Greek Couples

In this section, we review research examining how Greek couples cope with a variety of stressors, including health and economic stressors, at the individual level. In a study with cancer patients who had a stable relationship, Karademas and Giannousi (2013) examined how each partner's illness representations affected the other partner. The STM proposes that one partner's appraisal of a stressor that 'concerns only him/her' will also involve his/her evaluation of the partner's appraisal as well as the degree to which there is congruence or discrepancy between his/her appraisal and his/her partner's (see Chapter 1). Consistent with the STM predictions, partners' individual representations of personal and treatment control were related to patients' anxiety and depressive symptoms, respectively. In a study with patients with cardiovascular disease, Karademas, Zarogiannos, and Karamvakalis (2010) examined the extent to which discrepancies in illness representations between the two partners were related to adherence to medical advice. Indeed, discrepancy in perceived cyclicality of illness and treatment control were negatively related to adherence. These studies provide support for the conceptualization of stress as a social phenomenon where one partner's appraisals exert influence on the well-being of the other partner (Bodenmman, 2005). However, they are based on individual reactions to stress, in that they fail to address the degree to which the stressor is appraised as a common stressor and the actual partner interactions in the formation of those appraisals.

Pateraki and Roussi (2013) conducted a study with couples, half of whom lived in an urban setting and the other half in rural areas, which are characterized by more collectivist values than urban areas (Georgas et al., 1991). The study explored the impact of the quality of the interaction between the two partners on mental health and showed that spouses who felt satisfied by their marriage and spouses who believed that they were supported by their partner, experienced fewer depressive symptoms. Consistent with the assumption that the positive impact of social support is greater in collectivist societies (Kafetsios & Nezlek, 2012), the relationship between perceived partner support and depressive symptoms was stronger for couples living in rural areas.

The high reliance on the family unit for support may also have negative side-effects, in that it may hinder the couple's ability to ascertain receipt of the necessary resources to cope with a common stressor (Georgas et al., 2006; Helmes & Gallou, 2014). In a descriptive study with the parents of children diagnosed with cancer, parents used dyadic coping by turning to each other for help and considered their partner the most important source of emotional and practical support (Patistea, Makrodimitri, & Panteli, 2000). At the same time, they were unlikely to turn to non-family for help and particularly to individuals outside their in-group, such as other parents with children diagnosed with cancer. The Patistea et al. (2000) study also underscores the distinct role that Greek men and women play in dyadic coping. Although women were more likely to communicate stress (e.g., anxiety), the fathers were more likely to convey an image of strength and competence. In addition, women were more likely to engage in supportive dyadic coping by assuming responsibility for maintaining communication in the dyad, a role consistent with a culture high in masculinity and collectivism (Hofstede, 1980).

Differences between women and men have been reported by other studies too. The current economic crisis exerts heavy pressure on Greek families, but seems to strain Greek men and women in different ways. For example, Kostouli (2014) examined the impact of the economic crisis on well-being, marital satisfaction, and parental self-efficacy. Perceived inability to cover the material needs of the family had a negative impact on both men and women, as well as on their partner. In addition, there were gender differences in that *women's* perceptions that the family income could not cover the family's material needs affected *men's* parental self-efficacy. The author speculates that how spouses perceive men's ability to fulfill their traditional role as providers may affect men's sense of self-efficacy as parents. Men's parental self-efficacy was also related to family income, a relationship not observed among women. However, not all findings with Greek couples are consistent in that some studies do not show interdependence between partner's appraisals, actions, and well-being when coping with stress (Panagopoulou, Triantafyllou, Mitziori, & Benos, 2009; Thorpe et al., 1992).

Overall, these studies indicate interdependence between partners' coping processes and highlight the need to focus on dyadic coping, which are the partner interactions when coping with stress. In the next section, we briefly present two studies, conducted by our research groups, which examine dyadic coping and its relationship to two types of outcomes, relationship quality, and psychological symptoms. The studies utilize two ways of measuring dyadic coping, the coping-congruence method (Pakenham, 1998; Revenson, 2003) and the STM (Bodenmann, 2005).

Studies on Coping in Greek Couples

In the first study, Hatzianastasiou and Roussi (2013) collected data from ninety-two Greek couples undergoing fertility treatment and examined the degree to which congruence or discrepancy in coping between the two partners was related to marital satisfaction and depressed mood. Most couples were childless (93 percent) and about 45 percent had at least one in-vitro fertilization. Hierarchical cluster analysis indicated a four-cluster solution based on the following coping variables: planning, active coping, positive reinterpretation, venting of emotions, and mental disengagement for both partners. The four clusters differed on all ten coping strategies, five for each partner.

In a highly *congruent* group in which both men and women relied primarily on active coping, planning, and positive reinterpretation, couples reported high overall marital satisfaction and low levels of depressed mood. Relatively high levels of marital satisfaction and low levels of depressed mood were also reported by couples in one of the two *discrepant* groups, where women used exclusively emotion-focused coping (venting of emotions) and men relied on both problem- and emotion-focused coping (planning, mental disengagement, and positive reinterpretation); a pattern consistent with traditional gender roles. In contrast, the lowest levels of marital satisfaction and the highest levels of depressed mood were reported by spouses in the second *discrepant* group where participants exhibited a pattern reverse to the one expected based on traditional gender roles: women reported high active coping, moderate planning, moderate positive reinterpretation, and high mental disengagement; whereas men used venting of emotions and mental disengagement. In this case, men may perceive women's assertiveness as undermining their role, whereas men in the highly congruent group may not feel threatened as they too used problem-focused coping.

The last group was moderately *congruent*, in that men used a combination of problem- and emotion-focused coping (active coping, positive reinterpretation, and venting of emotions) and were moderately satisfied by their marriage, but women, who used primarily positive reinterpretation to cope, reported low levels of marital satisfaction. Both men and women in this group reported moderate levels of depressed mood. These findings indicate that the degree of congruence and discrepancy in coping may not be the main determining factor for marital quality and well-being and that specific combinations of coping between the two partners, given the cultural context, may be most relevant (see also Chapter 2).

Even though the congruence in coping approach yields useful information (Bodenmann et al., 2011), it has been criticized, because it does not really examine the interaction between the two partners in coping with stress but rather focuses on the degree to which two *individual* types of coping match or complement each other (Bodenmann et al., 2011). That is, the unit of study remains the individual and not the dyad. A better approach to studying dyadic coping is to capture the actual interaction between the partners and to view couples' coping as a truly dyadic phenomenon (Bodenmann, 2005; Coyne & Smith, 1991). Among these approaches, the STM provides a framework to understand dyadic coping as something distinct from individual coping in that it emphasizes: (a) the communication that takes place between the two partners, such as the stress communication experienced by one of the partners; (b) the interactive processes between the two partners, both positive and negative; and (c) the common-coping taking place at the unit level. In the next section, we present a study with Greek couples who used the Dyadic Coping Inventory (Bodenmann, 2008), a self-report questionnaire based on the STM.

Psychometric Properties of the Dyadic Coping Inventory in Greece

Aiming at promoting dyadic coping research in Greece, we adapted the Dyadic Coping Inventory (DCI; Bodenmann, 2008; see also Chapter 3) to a Greek population, consisting of heterosexual couples. Our study was based on a convenience community sample of 144 Greek couples, being in a relationship for at least two years. Women's mean age was 37.1 years (*SD* = 10.8), and men's mean age was 40.3 (*SD* = 11.8). The majority were married (70.1 percent) with a mean duration of relationship of 14.10 years (*SD* = 9.39). Sixty-nine percent had at least one child. Participants completed the Greek version of the DCI, the General Health Questionnaire—12 (GHQ; Goldberg, 1978; see Moutzoukis, Adamopoulou, Garyfallos, & Karastergiou, 1990, for the Greek adaptation), and the Relationship Assessment Scale (RAS; Hendrick, Dicke, & Hendrick, 1998). The DCI and the RAS were translated into Greek for the purposes of this study employing standard procedures (i.e., forward and backward translation by independent bilingual psychologists).

Separate confirmatory factor analyses (CFA) for men and women using maximum likelihood estimation, using LISREL 8.80 (Joreskog & Sorbom, 2006), were employed in order to confirm the typical five-factorial structure of the dyadic coping by oneself and by partner aggregated subscales (i.e., stress communication, emotion-focused, problem-focused, delegated, and negative dyadic coping), as well as the two-factor dimension of the joint dyadic coping, found in previous studies with other populations (e.g., Falconier, Nussbeck, & Bodenmann, 2013; Vedes, Nussbeck, Bodenmann, Lind, & Ferreira, 2013; see also Chapter 3). Model fit was assessed using the indices recommended by Hu and Bentler (1999).

Regarding dyadic coping by oneself and by partner, the results of the fit indices indicate a rather acceptable fit of the hypothesized five-factor model to the data (see Table 10.1), with one exception. The model did not fit the data for men's coping by oneself. Inspection of the results indicated that three items (items 2 and 3 of the stress communication factor, and item 22 of the negative dyadic coping factor) had low factor loadings (<0.40). The same was true for women's coping by oneself. In addition, the corresponding items for men's and women's dyadic coping by partner (i.e., items 17, 18 and 7) had relatively low factor loadings. Therefore, we excluded these items from the analyses as in previous adaptations of the DCI (e.g., Falconier et al., 2013). As shown in Table 10.1, the test of this model showed a much better fit for both men's and women's coping by oneself and by partner. Regarding joint dyadic coping, the two-factor structure (problem-focused and emotion-focused joint coping) provided a good fit to the data for both men and women (Table 10.1).

The items loading on each factor were high. They ranged from 0.46 to 0.96, and the majority were higher than 0.60. In addition, all subscales showed adequate internal consistency (Cronbach's *a* ranged from 0.60 to 0.93; Table 10.2). Overall, the structure of the Greek DCI appears to be similar to the structure found in

TABLE 10.1 Goodness of fit indices for the confirmatory factor analysis of dyadic coping (DC) by oneself and by partner for men's and women's reports

Model	χ^2 (p)	df	CFI	RMSEA	SRMR	χ^2 difference (df; p-value)
Self DC—men's report; 1st model	191.31 (<0.001)	80	0.90	0.10	0.09	
Self DC—men's report; 2nd model	94.84 (<0.001)	44	0.95	0.08	0.07	96.47 (36; p<0.001)
Self DC—women's report; 1st model	132.95 (<0.001)	80	0.95	0.07	0.07	
Self DC—women's report; 2nd model	62.76 (<0.05)	44	0.98	0.05	0.06	70.19 (36; p<0.001)
Partner DC—men's report; 1st model	125.98 (<0.001)	80	0.97	0.06	0.07	
Partner DC—men's report; 2nd model	55.87 (>0.10)	44	0.99	0.04	0.04	70.01 (36; p<0.001)
Partner DC—women's report; 1st model	132.62 (<0.001)	80	0.97	0.08	0.07	
Partner DC—women's report; 2nd model	58.22 (>0.05)	44	0.99	0.05	0.05	74.40 (36; p<0.001)
Joint DC—men's report (2 factors)	9.90 (<0.05)	4	0.98	0.10	0.03	
Joint DC—women's report (2 factors)	7.98 (>0.05)	4	0.99	0.08	0.03	

Notes: 1st model: Five factor structure—all items included; 2nd model: Five factor structure—items 2, 3, and 22 for Oneself DC, and items 17, 18, and 7 for Partner DC excluded.

CFI = comparative fit index; RMSEA = standardized root mean square error of approximation; SRMR = standardized root mean square residual.

TABLE 10.2 Descriptive statistics, reliabilities (Cronbach's α) and gender differences (Wilcoxon Signed Rank Test) for the DC subscales

DC Subscale	Men Mean (SD)	a	Women Mean (SD)	a	p
Stress communication—by oneself	3.45 (0.88)	0.65	3.58 (0.91)	0.69	0.095
Stress communication—by partner	3.64 (0.90)	0.65	3.40 (1.05)	0.79	0.001
Emotion-focused DC—by oneself	4.09 (0.72)	0.81	4.25 (0.74)	0.86	0.004
Emotion-focused DC—by partner	4.12 (0.83)	0.86	3.95 (0.91)	0.84	0.010
Problem-focused DC—by oneself	3.85 (0.78)	0.62	3.81 (0.82)	0.60	0.548
Problem-focused DC—by partner	3.63 (0.95)	0.74	3.50 (1.00)	0.78	0.269
Delegated DC—by oneself	3.68 (0.86)	0.68	3.82 (0.90)	0.79	0.195
Delegated DC—by partner	3.56 (0.90)	0.67	3.45 (0.98)	0.82	0.314
Negative DC—by oneself	2.20 (0.87)	0.70	1.86 (0.78)	0.68	0.001
Negative DC—by partner	2.08 (0.86)	0.69	2.25 (0.79)	0.62	0.012
Problem-focused joint DC	3.95 (0.88)	0.88	3.94 (0.87)	0.88	0.553
Emotion-focused joint DC	3.49 (1.02)	0.77	3.45 (1.03)	0.69	0.479
DC evaluation	3.89 (0.88)	0.93	3.73 (1.02)	0.93	0.091

Notes: DC = dyadic coping.

other languages and cultures (e.g., Falconier et al., 2013; Vedes et al., 2013). Furthermore, bivariate correlations among all dyadic coping subscales were in the expected direction for both genders, and their magnitude indicated that the subscales are related but at the same time they reflect distinct dyadic coping aspects.

Table 10.2 presents the means for the DCI subscales for men and women separately. Women reported higher emotion-focused dyadic coping by oneself, an observation also made among Latino couples (Falconier et al., 2013), and negative dyadic coping by partner. Men also reported higher emotion-focused dyadic coping by partner, negative dyadic coping by oneself, and stress communication by partner (see Table 10.2). The higher level of emotion-focused dyadic coping by women and higher negative dyadic coping by men are consistent with the traditional gender role characteristic of the Greek society, in that women are more likely to be compassionate and supportive, and men more likely to adopt a role of being 'tough' (Hofstede, 1980). The latter may lead men to perceive their partner's call for help as 'weakness' and thus devalue their partner when she seeks help. An alternative explanation for the high level of negative dyadic coping among men may be that because of the traditional gender role adopted by men and women, men may be more likely to perceive women's stressors as less important and thus be dismissive of their concerns. Our findings do not allow us to differentiate between the different explanations. However, it is important to note that the level of negative dyadic coping reported by Greek men is lower than the level of positive forms of dyadic coping, such as emotion-focused.

Additional support for construct validity of the DCI was provided by the associations between the DCI subscales and relationship satisfaction. The data for the subscales were not normally distributed; and therefore, non-parametric tests were used. Men's relationship satisfaction was associated with their reports of dyadic coping by oneself and by partner (Spearman's ρ ranged from 0.23 to 0.62 for all subscales, $p < 0.01$, except for the negative dyadic coping subscale which ranged from −0.45 to −0.43, $p < 0.01$), as well as with their partners' reports about dyadic coping (ρ ranged from 0.26 to 0.56 for all subscales, $p < 0.01$, except for the negative dyadic coping subscale which ranged from −0.19 to −0.34, $p < 0.01$). The same pattern was observed among the correlations between women's relationship satisfaction and their reports of dyadic coping by oneself and by partner. We used Fisher's z-transformation in order to test for differences between the correlation coefficients for men and women. There was a tendency for the correlation coefficients between women's relationship satisfaction and dyadic coping to be somewhat stronger, than the corresponding coefficients between men's relationship satisfaction and dyadic coping. Specifically, correlations were higher for stress communication by oneself, emotion-focused dyadic coping by other, delegated dyadic coping by other, negative dyadic coping by oneself, emotion-focused joint dyadic coping, and dyadic coping evaluation. Women tend to construe themselves in relational terms, and thus it is more likely that women's marital satisfaction will be affected by the quality of dyadic coping (Helgeson, 1994).

Finally, we examined the relationship between dyadic coping and psychological distress symptoms. The results were consistent with the STM and the existing international literature (e.g., Bodenmann et al., 2011). Among women, psychological symptoms were related to eight dyadic coping subscales (ρ ranged from −0.18 to −0.24, for the dyadic coping subscales, $p < 0.05$, except for the negative dyadic coping subscale which ranged from 0.19 to 0.23, $p < 0.05$); whereas among men, psychological symptoms were related to eighteen out of the twenty dyadic coping subscales, with ρ ranging from −0.18 to −0.34, for the dyadic coping subscales, $p < 0.05$, except for the negative dyadic coping subscale which ranged from 0.18 to 0.30, $p < 0.05$. The pattern of the correlation coefficients indicates that men's psychological symptoms were related to men's and women's reports of dyadic coping alike, whereas women's symptoms were related mostly to their own reports of dyadic coping. Men are more likely to rely on their partner for support (Pateraki & Roussi, 2013) and presumably on their partner's coping efforts for their well-being.

Overall, research on Greek couples' dyadic coping with stress is scarce. In fact, the only study focused on dyadic coping in Greek couples is the one presented above. This study confirmed that the DCI is a reliable and valid instrument to study dyadic coping with Greek couples and adds to the existing literature suggesting that dyadic coping is a valid and sound construct across cultures (Falconier et al., 2013; Ledermann et al., 2010). The associations observed between dyadic coping, relationship satisfaction, and psychological symptoms provide support to the notion that dyadic coping is important for both the quality of the relationship and the well-being of the partners.

Implications for Practice

The presented findings have implications for couples' counseling and prevention programs for marital distress. First, the high degree of interdependence between the two partners, observed in the broader stress and coping literature on Greek couples (e.g., Karademas & Giannousi, 2013; Pateraki & Roussi, 2013) and in the DCI study presented here indicate that preventive stress management programs for couples may be particularly beneficial. Further, the findings suggest that gender is an important variable to take into account when designing interventions for Greek couples in that females are more likely to be supportive of their partner, whereas males are more likely to be dismissive of their partner's concerns and to devalue them (this chapter). These differences may have a cost on the quality of the relationship and particularly on women who tend to report higher levels of perceived stress (Andreou et al., 2011).

Therefore, preventive stress management programs need to address, in a culturally sensitive manner, the lack of equity between Greek partners, to enhance egalitarian attitudes, and to facilitate, particularly among Greek men, greater consideration and empathy for one's partner. For example, the counselor could help partners detect inequality and educate them about the costs of unfairness and the advantages of fairness in couples' coping with stress (Bodenmann & Shantinath, 2004). In addition, partners, especially men, could be trained to become more considerate, empathic, and supportive of their partner. The beneficial effects of greater equity and supportive behaviors in the quality of the relationship are evident in the high correlations between perceived relationship quality by women on the one hand and assumption of additional responsibilities and emotion-focused coping by the male partner on the other hand, observed in the study presented in this chapter. As mentioned earlier, families of origin in Greece expect that they will keep close contact with the members of the couple (Georgas et al., 2001). Therefore, it may be important to teach the partners how to establish boundaries not only within the couple but also with respect to other groups, such as members of the extended family.

A program that includes specific components addressing these issues is the Couples Coping Enhancement Training [CCET; Bodenmann & Shantinath (2004)]. The CCET was developed to help couples who face difficulties and includes interventions designed to increase empathy and understanding between partners, fairness in the relationship, and boundaries. Studies have shown that the CCET is effective in increasing positive dyadic coping and in decreasing negative dyadic coping (Bodenmann, Pihet, Shantinath, Cina, & Widmer, 2006b). However, Greek couples may be reluctant to engage in interventions, as they tend to keep problems within the family and are less willing to discuss private matters with 'strangers,' including professionals (Georgas et al., 2006). Therefore, interventions should be designed in such a way as to be acceptable, particularly by men who are expected to be 'tough.' One advantage of the CCET is that it is designed to help couples cope with stress and thus may be more appealing to Greek couples who tend to view help from outsiders with suspicion (Georgas et al., 2006). Recently, the CCET has been adapted to a DVD-based, self-directed approach with some success among Swiss couples (Bodenmann, Hilpert, Nussbeck, & Bradbury, 2014). Even though the impact of the intervention was stronger on women, Swiss men who received the intervention were more likely to use positive communication, and both men and women were more satisfied with their relationship six months after the intervention. This technology-based approach may be even more compatible with Greek couples as it is self-directed, in that the partners can log on together or alone and use the DVD as they wish. Thus, there are no 'strangers' involved in the delivery of the intervention, making it potentially less threatening to Greek couples (Helmes & Gallou, 2014).

Implications for Research

Future research should first focus on replicating the DCI findings with larger, diverse samples on a number of demographic variables (e.g., age, SES, sexual orientation, and area of Greece) and on type of stressor (e.g., health stressors), as different stressors pose different challenges. As reported earlier, differences have been found in collectivist values between urban and rural areas, and Greece is believed to be shifting to more individualistic values (Georgas et al., 1991). Therefore, the comparison of dyadic coping in urban and rural couples may provide useful information in that it may facilitate the mapping of the ways that dyadic coping changes during this transition. Prospective studies will provide information regarding the predictive validity and the test-retest reliability of the DCI, as well as more definitive answers regarding the role of dyadic coping on relationship quality and well-being. A worrisome finding that needs to be researched further is why Greek men self-report a higher level of negative dyadic coping, a behavior confirmed by their partner (this chapter). This type of research would better inform the designing of culture-sensitive interventions in order to address this issue.

Conclusion

In conclusion, the reviewed literature and the presented research suggest that the systemic-transactional model (Bodenmann et al., 2011) is useful for the study of coping with stress at the couple level in Greece, and that the dyadic coping inventory (DCI; Bodenmann, 2008), translated into Greek (this chapter), is a valid instrument for assessing dyadic coping behaviors in Greek couples. Based on the systemic-transactional model, our research confirmed the interdependence between the two partners, observed in earlier studies (e.g., Karademas & Giannousi, 2013), but also clearly demonstrated the importance of studying the interactions between the two partners when coping with stress, both positive and negative (this chapter). Dyadic coping in Greek couples shares common features with dyadic coping in other cultures (Falconier et al., 2013; Vedes et al., 2013), such as Portugal and Germany, but also conveys some unique characteristics, such as high use of negative dyadic coping by men, when compared to women (this chapter). These results underline the importance of developing interventions, which facilitate dyadic coping and enhance egalitarian attitudes, and empathy, particularly so among men. Thus, further use of the systemic transactional model and the DCI in local studies will promote not only a better understanding of the Greek couples' dyadic coping characteristics, but also the development of suitable and effective intervention programs.

References

Andreou, E., Alexopoulos, E. C., Lionis, C., Varvogli, L., Gnardellis, C., Chrousos, G. P., . . . Darviri, C. (2011). Perceived Stress Scale: Reliability and validity study in Greece. *International Journal of Environmental Research and Public Health, 8*, 3287–3298.

Apparala, M. L., Reifman, A., & Munsch, J. (2003). Cross-national comparison of attitudes toward fathers' and mothers' participation in household tasks and childcare. *Sex Roles, 48*, 189–203.

Badr, H., Carmack, C. L., Kashy, D. A., Cristofanilli, M., & Revenson, T. A. (2010). Dyadic coping in metastatic breast cancer. *Health Psychology, 29*, 169–180.

Bodenmann, G. (2005). Dyadic coping and its significance for marital functioning. In T. A. Revenson, K. Kayser, & G. Bodenmann (Eds.) (2005), *Couples coping with stress: Emerging perspectives on dyadic coping* (pp. 33–50). Washington DC: American Psychological Association.

Bodenmann, G. (2008). *Dyadic Coping Inventory. Test manual.* Bern, Switzerland: Huber [in German].

Bodenmann, G., Hilpert, P., Nussbeck, F. W., & Bradbury, T. N. (2014). Enhancement of couples' communication and dyadic coping by a self-directed approach: A randomized control trial. *Journal of Consulting and Clinical Psychology, 82*, 580–591.

Bodenmann, G., Meuwly, N., & Kayser, K. (2011). Two conceptualizations of dyadic coping and their potential for predicting relationship quality and individual well-being: A comparison. *European Psychologist, 16*, 255–266.

Bodenmann, G., Pihet, S., & Kayser, K. (2006a). The relationship between dyadic coping, marital quality and well-being: A two year longitudinal study. *Journal of Family Psychology, 20*, 485–493.

Bodenmann, G., Pihet, S., Shantinath, S., Cina, A., & Widmer, K. (2006b). Improving dyadic coping in couples with a stress-oriented approach. *Behavior Modification, 30*, 571–597.

Bodenmann, G., & Shantinath, S. (2004). The Couple's Coping Enhancement Training (CCET): A new approach to prevention of marital distress based upon stress and coping. *Family Relations, 53*, 477–484.

Christodoulou, N. G., & Christodoulou, G. N. (2013). Financial crisis: Impact on mental health and suggested responses. *Psychotherapy and Psychosomatics, 82*, 279–284.

Coyne, J. C., & Smith, D. A. F. (1991). Couples coping with a myocardial infarction: A contextual perspective on wives' distress. *Journal of Personality and Social Psychology, 61*, 404–412.

Economou, M., Madianos, M., Peppou, L. E., Patelakis, A., & Stefanis, C. N. (2013). Major depression in the era of economic crisis: A replication of a cross-sectional study across Greece. *Journal of Affective Disorders, 145*, 308–314.

Eurostat (2014). *Marriage and divorce statistics.* Brussels: Eurostat. Retrieved from www.epp. eurostat.ec.europa.eu/statistics_explained/index.php/

Falconier, M. K., Nussbeck, F., & Bodenmann, G. (2013). Dyadic coping in Latino couples: Validity of the Spanish version of the Dyadic Coping Inventory. *Anxiety, Stress, & Coping, 26*, 447–466.

Georgas, J. (1991). Intrafamily acculturation of values in Greece. *Journal of Cross-Cultural Psychology, 22*, 445–457.

Georgas, J., Berry, J. W., van de Vijver, F. J. R., Kagitcibasi, C., & Poortinga, Y. H. (2006). *Families across cultures: A 30-nation psychological study.* Cambridge, UK: Cambridge University Press.

Georgas, J., Mylonas, K., Bafiti, T., Poortinga, Y.H., Christakopoulou, S., Kagitcibasi, C., Kodic, Y. (2001). Functional relationships in the nuclear and extended family: A 16-culture study. *International Journal of Psychology, 36*, 289–300.

Goldberg, D. (1978). *Manual of the General Health Questionnaire.* Windsor, UK: NFER-NELSON.

Hatzianastasiou, R., & Roussi, P. (2013). [Coping with infertility among Greek couples: A dyadic approach]. Unpublished raw data.

Helgeson, V. S. (1994). Relation of agency and communion to well-being: Evidence and potential explanations. *Psychological Bulletin, 116,* 412–428.

Hellenic Statistical Authority (2015, April). *Living conditions in Greece.* Athens: Hellenic Statistical Authority.

Helmes, E., & Gallou, L. (2014). Culture and attitudes toward psychological help seeking influence clients' self-disclosure. *European Journal of Psychotherapy and Counselling, 16,* 173–186.

Hendrick, S. S., Dicke, A., & Hendrick, C. (1998). The Relationship Assessment Scale. *Journal of Social and Personal Relationships, 15,* 137–142.

Hofstede, G. (1980). *Culture's consequences: International differences in work-related values.* Beverly Hills, CA: Sage.

Hu, L. T., & Bentler, P. M. (1999). Cut-off criteria for fit indexes in covariance structure analysis: Conventional criteria versus new alternatives. *Structural Equation Modelling, 6,* 1–55.

Ifanti, A. A., Argyriou, A. A., Kalofonou, F. H., & Kalofonos, H. P. (2013). Financial crisis and austerity measures in Greece: Their impact on health promotion policies and public health care. *Health Policy, 113,* 8–12.

Joreskog, K. G., & Sorbom, D. (2006). *LISREL 8.8 for Windows.* Skokie, IL: Scientific Software International, Inc.

Kafetsios, K., & Nezlek, J. B. (2012). Emotion and support perceptions in everyday social interaction: Testing the 'less is more' hypothesis in two cultures. *Journal of Social and Personal Relationships, 29,* 165–184.

Karademas, E. C., & Giannousi, Z. (2013). Representations of control and psychological symptoms in couples dealing with cancer: A dyadic-regulation approach. *Psychology and Health, 28,* 67–83.

Karademas, E. C., Zarogiannos, A., & Karamvakalis, N. (2010). Cardiac patient-spouse dissimilarities in illness perception: Associations with patient self-rated health and coping strategies. *Psychology and Health, 25,* 451–463.

Katakis, C. (1998). *The three identities of the Greek family.* Athens, Greece: Ellinika Grammata.

Kostouli, M. (2014). *Financial strain and subjective well-being: A dyadic approach to married couples with children.* Unpublished Master's thesis, Aristotle University of Thessaloniki, Thessaloniki, Greece.

Ledermann, T., Bodenmann, G., Gagliardi, S., Charvoz, L., Verandi, S., Rossier, J., . . . Iafrate, R. (2010). Psychometrics of the Dyadic Coping Inventory in three language groups. *Swiss Journal of Psychology, 69,* 201–212.

Maridaki-Kassotaki, K. (2000). Understanding fatherhood in Greece: Father's involvement in child care. *Psicologia: Teoria e Pesquisa, 16,* 213–219.

Matsaganis, N. (2013). *The Greek crisis: Social impact and policy responses.* Berlin: Friedrich-Ebert-Stiftung.

Moutzoukis, C., Adamopoulou, A., Garyfallos, G., & Karastergiou, A. (1990). *Manual of the General Health Questionnaire (GHQ).* Thesalloniki: Thessaloniki Psychiatric Hospital [in Greek].

Oyserman, D., Coon, H., & Kemmelmeier, M. (2002). Rethinking individualism and collectivism: Evaluation of theoretical assumptions and meta-analyses. *Psychological Bulletin, 128,* 3–72.

Pakenham, K. I. (1998). Couple coping and adjustment to multiple sclerosis in care receiver-carer dyads. *Family Relations, 47,* 269–277.

Panagopoulou, E., Triantafyllou, A., Mitziori, G., & Benos, A. (2009). Dyadic benefit finding after myocardial infarction: A qualitative investigation. *Heart & Lung, 38,* 292–297.

Pateraki, E., & Roussi, P. (2013). Marital quality and well-being: The role of gender, marital duration, social support and cultural context. In A. Efklides & D. Moraitou (Eds.), *A positive psychology perspective on quality of life* (pp. 125–145). Dordrecht, The Netherlands: Springer.

Patistea, E., Makrodimitri, P., & Panteli, V. (2000). Greek parents' reactions, difficulties and resources in childhood at the time of diagnosis. *European Journal of Cancer Care, 9,* 86–96.

Pouliasi, K., & Verkuyten, M. (2007). Networks of meaning and the bicultural mind: A structural equation modeling approach. *Journal of Experimental Social Psychology, 40,* 955–963.

Randall, A. K., & Bodenmann, G. (2009). The role of stress on close relationships and marital satisfaction. *Clinical Psychology Review, 29,* 105–115.

Revenson, T. A. (2003). Scenes from a marriage: Examining support, coping, and gender within the context of chronic illness. In J. Suls & K. A. Wallston (Eds.), *Social psychological foundations of health and illness* (pp. 530–559). Malden, MA: Blackwell Publishing.

Statista (2013). *Statistics and Market Data on Greece.* The Statistics portal. Retrieved from www.statista.com/markets/422/topic/507/greece/

Thorpe, K. J., Dragonas, T., & Golding, J. (1992). The effects of psychosocial factors on the emotional well-being of women during pregnancy: A cross-cultural study of Britain and Greece. *Journal of Reproductive and Infant Psychology, 10,* 191–204.

Triandis, H. C. (1995). *Individualism and collectivism.* Boulder, CO: Westview Press.

Tsamparli-Kitsara, A., & Kounenou, K. (2004). Parent-child interaction in the context of a chronic disease. *Australian and New Zealand Journal of Family Therapy, 25,* 74–83.

van den Heuvel, K., & Poortinga, Y. H. (1999). Resource allocation by Greek and Dutch students: A test of three models. *International Journal of Psychology, 34,* 1–13.

Vedes, A., Nussbeck, F. W., Bodenmann, G., Lind, W., & Ferreira, A. (2013). Psychometric properties and validity of the Dyadic Coping Inventory in Portuguese. *Swiss Journal of Psychology, 72,* 149–157.

11

DYADIC COPING IN HUNGARIAN COUPLES

Tamás Martos, Viola Sallay, and Rita Tóth-Vajna

Introduction

Hungary is sometimes referred to as a society in transition or changing society (e.g., Eiro Orosa, 2013; Kopp, Skrabski, & Szedmák, 2000); one that has faced several societal level challenges after the rapid political and economic changes around 1990, from a totalitarian economic and political system (governed by the communist party) to a more democratic one (free market and institutions of a liberal democracy, along with increasing social inequality and insecurity, and cultural diversity). Kopp and Réthelyi (2004) hypothesized that this socio-economic and cultural transition process and the resulting subjective experience of relative disadvantage and social challenges caused chronic stress in several levels of society. Potential effects of this social level of chronic stress can be seen in Hungary's health and demographic statistics: Life expectancy and death rate are better than in Russia but lower than the average in the European Community or in the United States; however, the birth rate, marriage rate, or growth rate of the population show lower scores than any of the other regions (KSH, 2003; see Table 11.1 for selected data).

Along with growing social insecurity and challenges, decreasing trust in other people (in general) and in social institutions has been detected. In the 2005 wave of the European Social Survey, Hungary ranked twentieth among twenty-five European countries in the domain of trust in people outside of close relationships; thus, close-others (that is, friends and especially family members) may increasingly become the primary source of support (Dupcsik & Tóth, 2008). The increased reliance on close relationships may be both a protective factor for the individual but also a risk factor in two interrelated ways. First, those whose social network is smaller and less supporting are much more vulnerable when facing social challenges (e.g., loss of work, health problems). Second, without appropriate social

TABLE 11.1 Main demographic characteristic of Hungary and reference societies

Country	Population 1,000,000 inhabitants	Marriage Rate 1000 inhabitants	Divorce Rate 1000 inhabitants	Live Birth Rate 1000 inhabitants	Death Rate 1000 inhabitants	Growth Rate 1000 inhabitants	Life exp. Men years	Life exp. Women years
Hungary	9.89	3.7	2.0	9.0	12.8	-3.9	71.6	78.7
European Community (excl. Hungary)	498.92	4.6	2.0	10.2	10.0	0.0	76.3	82.4
United States	316.13	6.8	3.4	12.6	8.1	4.6	76.3	81.1
Russia	143.20	9.2	4.7	13.3	13.3	0.0	64.6	75.9

level mechanisms of care and self-care (e.g., mental health promotion services, community based self-help groups, civil engagement) close relationships may be overladen by the higher demands and challenges and thus become more stressed. This may lead to mental health issues.

Moreover, along with increased reliance on close relationships there is also a culturally coded ambivalence toward them. Family is the most highly ranked value in Hungarian society according to the European Values Study (EVS, 2010). Moreover, valuing the family is accompanied by a relatively non-democratic/closed thinking style as well as high masculinity, which implies an acceptance of relatively fixed and traditional gender roles for both genders in Hungarian society (Inglehart, 1997). But on the other hand, these traditional views sharply contradict everyday practice in most families; for example, traditional single earner families are the exception rather than the rule (Dupcsik & Tóth, 2008). The resulting tension between culturally held traditional views on family and everyday practice may lead to feelings of incongruence and stress in the relationships of many couples.

Therefore, in this chapter we first review findings on the associations between chronic stress, mental health, and the role of close relationships in Hungarian society. We then discuss important themes of dyadic stress in Hungarian couples and review them with regard to the systemic transactional model (STM) of dyadic coping (Bodenmann, 1995; see also Chapter 1 for more information) and the first empirical evidence with the Dyadic Coping Inventory (DCI; Bodenmann, 2008) in Hungary. Subsequently, we provide new data on dyadic coping patterns and relationship satisfaction in a sample of Hungarian couples. Finally, we outline the most important suggestions that can be derived from the literature and our results.

Review of the Literature

Couples' Relationships in Hungary

The above presented socio-economic transition process and the resulting social level experience of chronic stress in Hungarian society has had a profound and far reaching impact both on individuals and couples. Epidemiology of mental health problems (high prevalence of depression and anxiety disorders, high suicide rate) has been one of the major concerns of Hungarian behavioral sciences in the last twenty years (Kopp et al., 2000; Kopp, Skrabski, Székely, Stauder, & Williams, 2007). Moreover, mortality rate has increased dramatically in the last decades of the twentieth century, especially among men: between 1960 and 2005, the mortality rate increased by 33 percent (from 12 to 16 per thousand) for men ages 40–69 years old, while it decreased by 4 percent in the same age group among women.

Social bonds and social capital in general, especially close relationships, were hypothesized to give extra significance in transitory states of society (Kopp & Réthelyi, 2004; Kopp et al., 2007). Corresponding research showed that the negative consequences of chronic stress can be alleviated by a series of social factors, among them married status and better spousal support (Kopp et al., 2007). Lack of partner support and chronic stress were also found in the background of depressive symptomatology, a major mental health problem in Hungarian society (point prevalence of severe depression episodes is around 8 percent, e.g., Szádóczky, Rózsa, Zámbori, & Füredi, 2004). Finally, results of a longitudinal study showed that there was a cumulative deleterious effect of previous marital stress and depressive symptomatology on both later marital functioning and mental health (Balog, 2008). As a conclusion, Kopp and colleagues (2007) suggested that two levels of interventions are equally of vital importance in stress reduction and health promotion, that is, interventions on societal-political and on personal-relational level. The latter should include training sessions for individuals on specific skills that would enable them to cope better with stressful conditions.

We may conclude that mainstream research on stress and coping was concerned primarily with individual aspects of stress processes; however, it does recognize the importance of social support and the couples' relationship as well. On a general level, relationship quality and support has been studied as vital ingredients of individual coping with stress (Balog, 2008; Kopp et al., 2007). Furthermore, the focus on individuals can be organically extended with a more systemic view of stress and coping. The systemic transactional model (STM) of dyadic stress and coping may give a theoretical framework to understand the strength and weaknesses of Hungarian couples when coping with dyadic stress. Now we turn to specific relationship challenges and the applications of the STM.

Couple Relationship Research on Sources of Dyadic Stress

Although specific empirical evidence is still sparse, there are certain lines of research in Hungarian psychological science that represents culturally relevant challenges for couple's relationships. For example, ways of conflict resolution in couples, and the stress experienced by couples who face infertility problems represent major stress situations in many couples' relationships in Hungary. We shall shortly review the relevant research and refer to the applicability of the systemic transactional model of dyadic stress and coping.

Dyadic stress often provokes conflict between partners, but it may evoke cooperation as well (e.g., Cserepes, Kollár, Sápy, Wischmann, & Bugán, 2013). Therefore, study of conflict and conflict resolution is regarded as fundamental for many researchers in Hungary (e.g., Pilinszki, 2013). For example, Bajor (2012) found associations between the coping resources of the couples (e.g., problem solving capacity, communication quality, intimacy, and flexibility) and the level of conflict in their communication patterns: less resourceful couples showed more negative communication patterns, where women exerted more criticism and blaming while men were more likely to withdraw from the situation and become absent. Spiritual orientation may be also a relational resource for conflict resolution; while shared belief and regular participation in spiritual activities do not make the couples less stressful, they do feel themselves more balanced and resourceful and can cope with stressful situations better. However, research also showed that spirituality may be a double-edged sword that belief differences caused increased stress in couples (Kisgyörgyné, Mirnics, & Bagdy, 2008). We suggest that the systemic conceptualization of STM helps to see the couple as a unit, and thus it may help disentangle individual conflict resolution strategies and processes in the couple.

Another relationship burden couples may face is infertility. Since the birth rate is rather low in Hungary (see Table 11.1), fertility issues receive considerable attention in research as well. It is well known that infertility, whether it is a temporary or a chronic experience, may cause serious stress for the couple. Cserepes and colleagues (2013) note in their study on infertility related stress and marital adjustment that, 'infertility as a common experience can strengthen the relationship, but on the other hand, the failure in fulfilling child wish, gender roles, and burdens of reproductive interventions can generate conflicts and communication problems between the members' (pp. 925–926). Even if infertility is a common experience for the couple, women and men may perceive it differently. Emotional and social aspects of fertility related quality of life was found lower in women partners of infertile couples than in men; however, relationship satisfaction was equally high in both partners (Cserepes et al., 2014).

Adjustment of women in coping with infertility may be connected to individual level but also to dyadic level factors. Infertility related distress in seventy-two women in fertility treatment was positively predicted by active avoidant coping and negative affectivity, as well as negatively by relationship satisfaction and perceived communication quality with the partner (Pápay, Rigó, & Nagybányai Nagy, 2013). Mata, Boga, and Bakonyi (2001) found that almost every couple in fertility treatment thought that they needed psychological help during the treatment. As the authors put it, these couples need to acquire new ways to cope with a problem that is in most cases rather permanent. Therefore, they suggest a series of couple oriented coping techniques, which resemble elements of the systemic transactional model of dyadic coping; for example, the suggested upright stress communication is a vital part of the STM model and its practical applications (e.g., Couples Coping Enhancement Training; Bodenmann & Shantinath, 2004) as well. Another suggestion is, that the sharing of the burdens and joy during the treatment process can be seen as delegated coping and common dyadic coping techniques.

STM Research in Hungary

Extending the previous work on individual and marital stress, couple functioning, and well-being, Martos and colleagues (Martos, Sallay, Nistor, & Józsa, 2012) presented the first validation study on the Hungarian version of the Dyadic Coping Inventory (DCI; Bodenmann, 2008, Hungarian version will be referred to as DCI-H). Using DCI-H in a cross-sectional design, the authors assessed the dyadic coping strategies of 472 adults living in committed relationships (176 male and 296 female). Along with the Hungarian version of the DCI, they also measured satisfaction with life (SWLS; Diener, Emmons, Larsen, & Griffin, 1985) and marital satisfaction (Balog, Székely, Szabó, & Kopp, 2006).

Scale reliability estimates were satisfactorily high for all of the subscales and aggregate scales (α coefficients between 0.67 and 0.90). Predictive validity of the measure was tested through a series of hierarchical linear regression analyses where dyadic coping subscale scores were used to predict relationship satisfaction and life satisfaction, separately for male and female respondents. Forms of dyadic coping explained a significant amount of variance in life satisfaction (31.8 percent and 27.7 percent for male and female respondents respectively) and marital satisfaction (48.5 percent for female respondents). Moreover, authors reported gender differences in the predictive power of the DCI-H subscales. Marital satisfaction of women was negatively predicted both by negative coping of oneself and the partner (βs = –0.174 and –0.152), and positively by the support of the partner and the evaluation of the common dyadic coping (βs = 0.255 and 0.187); whereas there was only one significant link in male respondents with one's own supportive coping (β = 0.320). Martos and colleagues (2012) concluded that the Hungarian version of the DCI was a reliable and valid measure, and also suggested that there might be specific gender differences in dyadic coping, which have to be considered when planning further research, training programs, and therapeutic interventions for couples.

Building on the work of Martos and colleagues (2012), Topolánszky-Zsindely and Hadházi (2014) presented data on dyadic coping of parents who raise disabled children in a recent annual meeting of the Hungarian Family Therapy Association. Raising a disabled child is another situation that has been found to be a great burden on the couple, both practically (due to low community support) and psychologically (e.g., through the processes of marginalization and stigmatization; e.g., Radványi, 2013). The authors used DCI-H with sixty-three adults, who had at least one child and who attended an early development service for disabled children in a Children's Hospital in Budapest. Comparing the parents' dyadic coping scores with the results of Martos and colleagues (Martos et al., 2012) as a reference sample, they found that they reported lower use of supportive coping and more frequent reliance on negative coping. Moreover, parents raising at least one disabled child were less satisfied with the quality of their common dyadic coping as well. Authors concluded that these parents are in an extremely stressful situation and this kind of chronic stress makes it more difficult for them to maintain constructive forms of dyadic coping in the long run.

Relationship Patterns in Hungarian Couples in STM Perspective

The above presented research shows that although dyadic stress and couple dynamics is an important topic in psychological research in Hungary, direct data on dyadic coping, and especially on specific relationship patterns of dyadic coping, are still sparse. In order to broaden this picture, we present here new empirical research evidence on dyadic coping patterns of Hungarian couples.[1] The rationale behind a pattern-oriented approach is twofold. First, these patterns may mirror qualitatively different ways how the partners may be involved in the coping process. These different ways may lead to specific outcomes, may bear with special vulnerabilities, etc. Second, dyadic coping patterns may reveal through their complexity something about the deep structure of the relationships, the so-called 'relational contract' (c.f., Sager, 1976).

To this end, we decided to use here a variant of the 'person-centered approach' for data analysis, which is in fact a systemic approach taking into account a system level's attributes and the most typical ways of the relationships between these attributes inside the system as a unit of analysis (Bergman, Magnusson, & El-Khouri, 2003). As in our case, the unit of the analysis is the couple, and we well refer henceforth to this approach as 'relationship-centered analysis.' Relationship-centered analysis—in contrast to a variable-centered approach—makes it possible to identify complex patterns in a set of individual characteristics, and thus it may contribute to better disentangle those groups of couples who have common characteristics or experiences.

Overview of the Sample and Procedure

We used data from a cross sectional questionnaire study with 162 heterosexual couples from the central region of Hungary.[2] Couples did the assessment separately and anonymous data assessment and processing were secured. For assessing the preferred dyadic coping processes in the couples, the standard thirty-seven-item DCI-H form (Martos et al., 2012) was used.[3] Relationship satisfaction was measured with the same fourteen-item Marital Stress Scale[4] that was used as in the original DCI-H article (Martos et al., 2012).

Dyadic Coping Patterns

We identified patterns of dyadic coping strategies via exploratory cluster analysis. Variables entered into the analysis were the basic elements of the dyadic coping process: 1) one's own stress communication and, 2) partner's perceived stress communication, 3) one's own positive reaction index, that is, the weighted sum of the supportive and delegated coping scores and the reversed negative coping scores, and 4) the partner's perceived positive reaction index to stress communication, and 5) the joint dyadic coping with stress. Both partners' five coping variables were included; thus, the relationship-centered cluster analysis was based on ten variables.

The cluster analysis was performed with SPSS using Ward's method that differentiates clusters by minimizing within-cluster and maximizes between-cluster variance (see Bergman et al., 2003). Thus, five clusters were retained, and we assigned all couples to one of the five groups. In order to better visualize the different dyadic coping patterns, we present the z-scored clusters' means as radar charts (see Figure 11.1).

The five dyadic coping clusters included three groups, which could be characterized by congruent (symmetric) patterns of scores reported by the partners: (1) 'all inclusive coping' (N = 27), high levels of every coping dimension referring to the self as well as referring to the partner; (2) 'restrained coping' (N = 36), average level of stress communication and lower levels of one's own and the

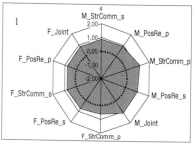
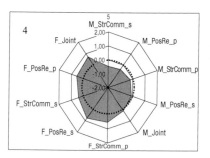
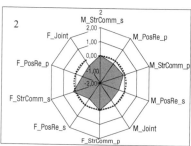
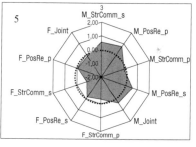
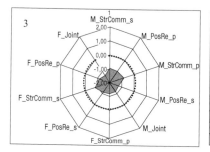

Labels of the axes	Coping dimension	Agent	Respondent
M_StrComm_s	Stress communication	Self	Male
M_PosRe_p	Positive reactivity	Partner	Male
M_StrComm_p	Stress communication	Partner	Male
M_PosRe_s	Positive reactivity	Self	Male
M_Joint	Joint dyadic coping	Couple	Male
F_StrComm_p	Stress communication	Partner	Female
F_PosRe_s	Positive reactivity	Self	Female
F_StrComm_s	Stress communication	Self	Female
F_PosRe_p	Positive reactivity	Partner	Female
F_Joint	Joint dyadic coping	Couple	Female

FIGURE 11.1 Graphic representation of the five clusters of dyadic coping strategies. Clusters are: 1 = "All inclusive", 2 = "Restrained", 3 = "Missing", 4 = "Woman's positive perception", 5 = "Man's positive perception"; for a more detailed description of the clusters see the text

partner's perceived positive reactions as well as lower level of joint dyadic coping; and (3) 'missing coping' (N = 22), low levels of all coping dimensions referring to the self as well as referring to the partner. Further, two groups could be characterized by incongruent (asymmetric) patterns: (4) 'women's positive perception' (N = 43), with women reporting higher levels of their own and their partner's stress communication and positive reactions than their partners, as well as higher level of joint dyadic coping; (5) 'men's positive perception' (N = 33), with men reporting higher levels of their own positive reactions and stress communication than their partners.

Symmetric patterns are congruent in two ways: first, partners report similar levels of each dyadic coping dimension, and second, their perception of the partner's level of stress communication and positive reactions is consistent with the partner's own rating. Similarly, incongruence in asymmetric patterns is twofold as well. Partners report different levels of several dyadic coping dimensions (e.g., stress communication), and even more strikingly, perceptions of the partner's levels of stress communication and positive reactions differ consistently from the partner's own rating. Seemingly, 'women's positive perception' and 'men's positive perception' groups differ in the way partners see and evaluate themselves and each other with regard to the couple's competence in dyadic coping.

What may these variations in dyadic coping mean for other characteristics of the couples? We found significant differences between the five groups in the age of the respondents, duration of the relationship, appraisal of the dyadic coping, and relationship satisfaction (see Table 11.2). Respondents in Cluster 1 ('all inclusive coping' couples) are younger and live in their relationships for a shorter time than in other groups. Moreover, 'all inclusive coping' couples are the most satisfied with both their dyadic coping in particular and their relationship in general. In contrast, 'missing coping' couples are the less satisfied in both dimensions. Interestingly, couples with an asymmetric division of coping competencies (groups 4 and 5) are just a little bit behind 'all inclusive' couples. This may be interpreted as a certain amount of asymmetry being still relatively adaptive for some couples whose 'relational contract' includes one of the partners taking the responsibility for a more active role in the coping process. In spite of the incongruent pattern, the partners in these clusters are almost equally satisfied with their relationships. However, it is unsure whether these asymmetric relationship patterns represent transitory states or they are stable over a longer period/time in the relationship.

Cross-Evaluation of the Results: Case Analysis of Couple A

Based on the results presented above, the 'missing coping' group clearly consists of at-risk couples, where partners are lacking elementary coping skills, and in the space of the relationship there is a diminishing forum for expressing stressful feelings and asking for support. From a family therapist's point of view, it is especially important to gain deeper insight into the relational processes behind the pattern

TABLE 11.2 Descriptive statistics of the five clusters in male and female partners: basic socio-demographic characteristic, appraisal of dyadic coping, and relationship satisfaction

Cluster	1		2		3		4		5		F_{ANOVA}
N	27		36		22		43		33		
	m	SD	m	SD	m	SD	m	SD	m	SD	
Relationship duration (y's)	6.66	5.26	13.31	8.90	10.95	6.38	11.78	10.95	9.13	7.65	2.45★
Male partner											
Age (y's)	30.81	7.09	39.33	8.78	39.55	6.86	36.63	10.69	35.18	8.77	4.52★★
Appraisal of dyadic coping	9.33	1.07	6.75	1.54	5.95	1.29	7.88	1.64	8.64	1.34	24.70★★★
Relationship satisfaction	0.32	1.10	−0.29	1.11	−0.80	0.97	0.13	1.00	0.17	1.05	4.51★★
Female partner											
Age (y's)	31.04	7.62	36.81	8.69	35.68	4.95	34.72	10.02	34.00	8.36	1.95
Appraisal of dyadic coping	9.15	1.20	7.50	1.66	6.18	1.56	8.86	1.34	8.52	1.18	19.61★★★
Relationship satisfaction	0.34	1.07	−0.26	1.19	−0.68	0.85	0.16	1.11	0.08	1.04	3.36★

★★★ $p < 0.001$, ★★ $p < 0.01$, ★ $p < 0.05$

Clusters are: 1 = "All inclusive", 2 = "Restrained", 3 = "Missing", 4 = "Woman's positive perception", 5 = "Man's positive perception"; for a more detailed description of the clusters see the text.

of missing dyadic coping. For this end, we choose the case of Couple A, a young married couple, from the 'missing coping' group. This couple also participated in an extension of the presented study where couples were interviewed through the Personal Project Assessment for Couples (PPA-C) procedure. In PPA-C, each partner lists his/her most relevant personal projects (i.e., personally relevant goals, which direct everyday thoughts and actions) and evaluates them according to a series of relationship relevant aspects: how much support they receive from their partner in terms of providing competence, and autonomy, how much their partner reacts to the project with positive and negative affections. Thus, comparison of the results with the two methods may also mutually validate each other and help to interpret the results.

Couple A was a young married couple with one child (2 years old) and could be characterized as a 'missing coping' couple since both partners scored far below the sample average on every DCI dimension. Obviously, they faced a hard period with financial concerns (they lived off the salary of Mr. A) and the emotional struggles of Ms. A, who felt stuck at home with their toddler. Correspondingly, Mr. A, a 24-year-old teacher had an important personal project, 'I would like to supervise my students as well as possible.' However, Ms. A, a 27-year-old student 'wanted to travel.' When they evaluated their relationship experience with regard to their projects, both spouses reported high felt rejection from the partner. They highly endorsed statements like 'My partner believes that I won't be able to do my project' and 'In my project, my partner criticizes me and knows everything better than me.' Mr. A also declared very low 'autonomy support' from his spouse, which means that he felt 'My partner takes over the lead in the project.' In turn, Ms. A criticized her partner because of his negative affective reactions to her journey intentions.

Taken together, these accounts on personal projects show how the partners in this young, married couple struggle with the lack of missing dyadic coping skills. But even worse, they have developed attitude patterns toward each other's projects that are mutually invalidating, that is, are infiltrated with criticism and rejection. This attitude may be further reinforced through missing and negative dyadic coping strategies where lack of adaptive dyadic coping skills may not allow them to engage in each other's challenges during their pursuit of important personal projects. Not surprisingly, both partners indicated low levels of life satisfaction. Through a family therapist's eyes, these parents, who are caring for a little child, would certainly need systemic support to improve their dyadic coping skills and to create a more positive emotional atmosphere in the family. Systemic development in their coping skills would not just allow them to be more effective in their own projects but also be more supportive to their partners as well. From a cultural point of view, we may interpret the case of Couple A that their struggle represents the stress that many couples may experience because of the incongruence between traditional role expectations and individualized ways of family functioning.

Implications for Practice

The above presented review of the literature on dyadic stress and coping as well as the evidence with DCI-H shows that the systemic transactional model of dyadic coping (Bodenmann, 1995) with stress may contribute to providing both a theoretical framework for conceptualization, scientific research, and practice-based interventions for couples in Hungary. STM-based interventions may be especially useful and feasibly implementable in professional praxis.

While there is stress management training in Hungary for individuals (e.g., employees, teachers, etc., Stauder et al., 2010), no programs are provided that would directly aim to improve the dyadic coping capacity of couples. Modules of dyadic coping could also be easily incorporated into marriage preparation programs, which are provided by many church communities[5] (Kolonits & Tárkányi, 2010). We are convinced that behavioral skills like giving and receiving stress communication and constructive ways of coping responses to one's partner's stress are manageable pieces of knowledge for most people with average psychological sensitivity and culture in Hungary. Culturally sensitive adaptations of STM based training programs such as Couples Coping Enhancement Training (CCET; Bodenmann, & Shantinath, 2004) and TOGETHER (Falconier, 2015) may help couples to improve their individual and dyadic coping strategies, even in special situations, such as under financial strain, a frequent latent stressor for many couples in Hungary.

Moreover, knowing the different kinds of relationship patterns in dyadic coping, as presented in our results, couple therapists may identify how specific relationship patterns in dyadic coping (e.g., 'missing coping' style of couple stress management) may lead to lacking support in significant life pursuits, and may be reinforced by mutual behavioral patterns in couples. Mindful attention to couples with less advantageous dyadic coping patterns holds the chance that their functioning may be significantly improved by a systemic relationship-centered approach. There are some relevant domains where STM-based programs could be implemented.

Infertility Clinics

Research shows that fertility treatment patients and their partners are in especially high need of support (e.g., Mata et al., 2001). Couple training or couple therapy may help them to restructure their communication and reaction patterns around fertility problems and the stress caused by the treatment itself. Research with Hungarian couples and individuals are in concordance with the international literature, and point to the importance of individual and dyadic stress management for improving well-being and potentially also to help couples overcome their fertility problems. Despite this, in their extensive review on psychological aspects of infertility, Szigeti and Konkolÿ Thege (2012) conclude that 'while the medical technology [used in infertility care in Hungary] is almost up to date, even in comparison to the methods applied in more developed countries, psychological care lags long behind it' (p. 576).

Parents with a Disabled Child

As Topolánszky-Zsindely and Hádhazi (2014) and also others (e.g., Radványi, 2013) showed, parents of a disabled child struggle with their tasks and experience a lot of individual and relational stress. These couples need support to prevent the kind of erosion of their original coping capacity, which may affect their relationship as well. Therefore, Topolánszky-Zsindely and Hadhazi (2014) also presented preliminary plans, which their early development service center would offer parents couple therapy together with the child's development and, which DCI-H might be an important measure to screen for potentially vulnerable couples.

Implications for Research

Scientific psychological research on close relationships, and especially on couples, may take advantage of a more systemic view of dyadic coping processes. While systemic practice and teaching is firmly incorporated in the training programs of the Hungarian Family Therapy Association (MCSE, 2014), the review of the research indicates that relational constructs are often treated as individual variables (e.g., Balog, 2008; Cserepes et al., 2014; Pápay et al., 2013) even in research with couples. There is a definite lack of a more refined systemic assessment, which would include circular questioning on mutual perceptions of the partners. The publication of the DCI in Hungarian may be a first step toward this goal (Martos et al., 2012), because it uses an inherently systemic, circular perspective on dyadic processes (see also Chapter 1). DCI-H could be easily included into mental health and infertility-oriented research agendas as well. Moreover, other research topics, for example, coping with chronic illness and rehabilitation, the consequences of economic crises in families or dyadic adjustment in restructured families could make use of this new way of systemic assessment. Finally, parallel use of the DCI-H and other methodological approaches that aim at the couples' relationship and coping potential seems very promising. For example, the above presented case study of couple A used personal project analysis and dyadic coping pattern, and it showed that such comparisons can mutually complete the conclusions of the different methods.

To elaborate this methodological point of view further, there are two branches of relationship research methods in Hungary, which may be directly used for the simulation of the couples coping with stressful situations: the so called Consensus Rorschach Test (CRT; Bagdy & Mirnics, 2002) and the Drawing Together Method (DTM; Vass & Vass, 2011). Both methods are based on relatively unstructured projective tasks, which are intended to expose the couple together to a 'mild' stress situation and thus provoke their communications skills, cooperation, power balance, and constructive management of challenges. In sum, these methods may evoke the couple's dyadic coping responses similarly to real life challenges. Moreover, these projective tests may be combined with DCI-H in clinical practice as well, as they might allow clinicians to validate their impression gained by the projective tests by means of the DCI-H and get clues for specific areas of intervention (e.g., helping stress communication).

Conclusion

In sum, we may conclude with a paraphrase of Ebbinghaus' statement that STM-based dyadic coping research and practice has a long past, but only a short history in Hungary. That is, while there are many relevant research topics and corresponding findings with regard to dyadic stress and coping, as outlined above, STM-based research is still new. However, as researchers and family therapists, we believe that this systemic approach has also a great potential to be applied in many ways both for scientific research and clinical and programmatic interventions. As noted before, despite several socio-economic changes, Hungarian culture still holds a relatively traditional stance toward couples' relationships. As we might see also in the case of couple A, this constellation may cause relationship struggles that are accompanied by a set of poorly functioning dyadic coping skills. Therefore, many relational implications of an STM-oriented approach may be challenging, but at the same time also enriching for Hungarian couples, such as mutual and equal responsibility for the partners and active competence-based coping with dyadic stress and relationship issues.

Notes

1   This research was partly supported by the Hungarian Scientific Research Fund (OTKA) under the grant number PD 105685. The authors express their special thanks to Johanna Rezsöfi for her contribution in collecting the dyadic data.
2   Age ranged from 19 to 63 for men (m= 36.35, SD = 9.22) and from 20 to 57 for women (m= 34.54, SD = 8.52). Most of the couples were married (N = 111, 68.5 percent) the others lived in a committed relationship lasting from 0.5 to 40 years (m= 10.65, SD = 8.665). 31.5 percent of the couples had no children, 24.1 percent had one child, 32.1 percent had two children, and 12.3 percent had three children or more.
3   Subscales of the measure showed adequate internal consistency, with alpha coefficients ranging between 0.59 and 0.88 for men and 0.59 and 0.84 for women.
4   Higher scores indicate higher satisfaction with the relationship. Internal consistency was high (alpha = 0.89 and 0.90 for men and women, respectively).
5   Although church attendance is decreasing in Hungary, many couples still seek a religious wedding ceremony. Most of the church communities link this service to the attendance of a marriage preparation course that is held by priests and/or lay helpers.

References

Bagdy, E., & T. Mirnics, Zs. (2002). A Közös Rorschach Vizsgálat hazai alkalmazása [Application of the Consensus Rorschach Test in Hungary]. In E. Bagdy (Ed.), *Párkapcsolatok dinamikája: Interakciódinamikai vizsgálatok a Közös Rorschach teszttel*

[*Dynamics of couple relationship: Investigations of interaction dynamics with the Consensus Rorschach Test*] (pp. 69–87). Budapest, Animula.

Bajor, A. (2012). A kapcsolati erőforrások szerepe a párkapcsolati kommunikációban [The role of relation resources in the communication between couples]. *Alkalmazott Pszichológia, 14*(4), 31–49.

Balog, P. (2008). A házastársi/élettársi kapcsolat szerepe az esélyteremtésben [The role of relationship with spouse/partner in creating chance]. In M. Kopp (Ed.), *Magyar lelkiállapot 2008. Esélyerősítés és életminőség a mai magyar társadalomban [Hungarian state of mind 2008. Opportunity enhancement and quality of life in the society of today's Hungary]* (pp. 240–253). Budapest, Hungary: Semmelweis Kiadó.

Balog, P., Székely, A., Szabó, G., & Kopp, M. (2006). A Rövidített Házastársi Stressz Skála pszichometriai jellemzői [Psychometric properties of the Brief Marital Stress Scale]. *Mentálhigiéné és Pszichoszomatika, 3*, 193–202.

Bergman, L., Magnusson, D., & El-Khouri, B. (2003). *Studying individual development in an inter-individual context: A person-oriented approach*. Mahwah: Lawrence Erlbaum.

Bodenmann, G. (1995). A systemic-transactional conceptualization of stress and coping in couples. *Swiss Journal of Psychology, 54*, 34–49.

Bodenmann, G. (2008). *Dyadisches Coping Inventar. Test Manual [Dyadic Coping Inventory. Test Manual]*. Bern, Huber.

Bodenmann, G., & Shantinath, S. D. (2004). The Couples Coping Enhancement Training (CCET): A new approach to prevention of marital distress based upon stress and coping. *Family Relations, 53*(5), 477–484.

Cserepes, R. E., Kollár, J., Sápy, T., Wischmann, T., & Bugán, A. (2013). Effects of gender roles, child wish motives, subjective well-being, and marital adjustment on infertility-related stress: a preliminary study with a Hungarian sample of involuntary childless men and women. *Archives of Gynecology and Obstetrics, 288*(4), 925–932.

Cserepes, R. E., Kőrösi, T., & Bugán, A. (2014). A meddőséggel összefüggő életminőség jellemzői magyar pároknál. [Characteristics of infertility specific quality of life in Hungarian couples]. *Orvosi Hetilap, 155*(20), 783–788.

Diener, E., Emmons, R. A., Larsen, R. J., & Griffin, S. (1985). The Satisfaction with Life Scale. *Journal of Personality Assessment, 49*, 71–75.

Dupcsik, Cs., & Tóth, O. (2008). Feminizmus helyett familizmus. [Familism instead of feminism]. *Demográfia, 51*(4), 307–328.

Eiro Orosa, F. J. (2013). Psychosocial wellbeing in the Central and Eastern European transition: An overview and systematic bibliographic review. *International Journal of Psychology, 48*(4), 481–491.

EVS. (2010). European values study 2008: Hungary. 2010/47. Cologne, GESIS Data Archive.

Falconier, M. K. (2015). TOGETHER—A couples' program to improve communication, coping, and financial management skills: Development and initial pilot-testing. *Journal of Marital and Family Therapy, 41*(1), 1–15.

Inglehart, R. (1997). *Modernization and postmodernization: cultural, economic and political change in 43 societies*, Princeton: Princeton University Press.

Kisgyörgyné Pongrácz, D., Mirnics, Zs., & Bagdy, E. (2008). A spirituális orientáció hatásai: családi funkcionalitás és megküzdés [The effects of spiritual orientation: Family functionality and coping]. In E. Bagdy, Zs. Mirnics, & A. Vargha (Eds.), *Egyén—Pár—Család. Tanulmányok a pszichodiagnosztikai tesztadaptációs és tesztfejlesztő kutatások köréből*

[*Individual—Couple—Family. Studies about adaptation and development of psychodiagnostic test research*] (pp. 445–461). Budapest, Animula.

Kolonits, K., & Tárkányi, Á. (2010). Párkapcsolatra és házasságra nevelés Magyarországon és az USA-ban. Elmélet és gyakorlat rövid összefoglalása. [Relationship and marriage education in Hungary and in the USA. A theoretical and practical syllabus]. *Mester és Tanítvány, 27*, 29–50.

Kopp, M. S., & Réthelyi, J. (2004). Where psychology meets physiology: Chronic stress and premature mortality—the Central-Eastern European health paradox. *Brain Research Bulletin, 62*(5), 351–367.

Kopp, M. S., Skrabski, Á., & Szedmák, S. (2000). Psychosocial risk factors, inequality and self-rated morbidity in a changing society. *Social Sciences and Medicine, 51*, 1350–1361.

Kopp, M. S., Skrabski, Á., Székely, A., Stauder, A., & Williams, R. (2007). Chronic stress and social changes: Socioeconomic determination of chronic stress. *Annals of the New York Academy of Sciences, 1113*(1), 325–338.

KSH (2003). *Demográfiai Évkönyv.* [*Demographic Yearbook of the Central Statistical Office*]. Budapest.

Martos, T., Sallay, V., Nistor, M., & Józsa, P. (2012). Párkapcsolati megküzdés és jóllét —a Páros megküzdés Kérdőív magyar változata [Dyadic coping and well-being— Hungarian version of the Dyadic Coping Inventory]. *Psychiatria Hungarica, 27*(6), 446–458.

Mata, Zs., Boga, P., & Bakonyi, T. (2001). Meddő párok pszichés és szociális küzdelmének vizsgálata ápolói szemmel [Investigation of infertile couples' psychological and social struggle from a nurse's point of view]. *Nővér, 14*(5), 3–17.

MCSE (2015, June 23). A Magyar Családterápiás Egyesület Képzési Rendje. [Training Protocol of the Hungarian Family Therapy Association]. Retrieved from www.csaladterapia.hu/doc/MCSE_uj_%20kepzesi_rend_2014_09_10.pdf

Pápay, N., Rigó, A., & Nagybányai Nagy, O. (2013). A meddőségspecifikus distressz alakulása a megküzdési stratégiák és egyéb pszichoszociális változók függvényében [The formation of infertility specific distress as a function of coping strategies and other psychosocial variables]. *Magyar Pszichológiai Szemle, 68*(3), 399–418.

Pilinszki, A. (2013). Konfliktusok hatása a párkapcsolati instabilitásra [The effect of conflicts on partnership instability]. *Demográfia, 56*(2–3), 44–170.

Radványi, K. (2013). *Legbelső kör: A család: Eltérő fejlődésű vagy krónikus beteg gyermek a családban* [*Innermost circle: The family: Differently developed or chronically ill children in the family*]. Budapest: ELTE Eötvös Kiadó.

Sager, C. J. (1976). *Marriage contracts and couple therapy.* New York: Bruner/Mazel.

Stauder, A., Konkoly Thege, B., Kovács, M. E., Balog, P., Williams, V. P., & Williams R. B. (2010). Worldwide stress: Different problems, similar solutions? Cultural adaptation and evaluation of a standardized stress management program in Hungary. *International Journal of Behavioral Medicine, 17*, 25–32.

Szádóczky, E., Rózsa, S., Zámbori, J., & Füredi, J. (2004). Anxiety and mood disorders in primary care practice. *International Journal of Psychiatry in Clinical Practice, 8*, 77–84.

Szigeti, F. J., & Konkolÿ Thege, B. (2012). A meddőség pszichológiai aspektusai: szakirodalmi áttekintés [The psychological aspects of infertility: A review of the literature]. *Magyar Pszichológiai Szemle, 67*(3), 561–580.

Topolánszky-Zsindely, K., & Hadházi, É. (2014). *A párkapcsolati elégedettség összefüggése a páros megküzdéssel korai fejlesztésre szoruló gyermeket (is) nevelő szülőknél [Correlation between relationship satisfaction and dyadic coping in couples raising children with special needs in their early development*]. XXVIII. Conference of the Hungarian Family Therapy Association, Eger, April 25–27. 2014.

Vass, Z., & Vass, V. (2011). A közös rajzvizsgálat viselkedéses, kommunikációelemzési és interakciódinamikai kiértékelése [The evaluation of the Drawing Together Method's behavior, communication analysis and interaction-dynamics]. *Pszichológia*, *31*(2), 125–143.

12

DYADIC COPING IN ROMANIAN COUPLES

Petruţa P. Rusu

Introduction

The purpose of this book chapter is to increase understanding of stress and dyadic coping (DC) within married couples from Romania. Research on stress and coping in couples and families has received increasing empirical attention in North America and Western Europe (Falconier, Jackson, Hilpert, & Bodenmann, 2015). The generalizability of these findings may be limited due to the lack of variation in the contextual factors (such as culture and socio-economic status) of the samples. Romania, similar to other Eastern European countries, has been confronted with difficulties stemming from a post-communist transition, including the transformation of society with psychological consequences. The current chapter presents family functioning and DC within the specific cultural and socio-economic background of Romania by analyzing how DC is related to specific contextual factors (daily stress, economic status), individual variables (education, sanctification of marriage, positive emotions, individual coping), and dyadic variables (marriage duration, marital satisfaction). Based on these findings, policies and interventions to strengthen marriages and to improve DC in Romanian couples are presented.

Review of the Literature

Couples' Relationships in Romania

Romania is the largest Balkan country, located in the southeastern part of Europe and has a population of approximately 20 million (INS, 2014). Romanian society remains traditional, with a mix of collectivistic and individualistic values and goals (Friedlmeier & Gavreliuc, 2013). Compared to other life domains, family life offers the highest source of satisfaction for Romanians (Popescu, 2010), despite the fact that throughout time couples' relationships have been affected by socio-historic and economic changes. The communist period (1948–1989) negatively affected peoples' lives, both socially and economically, and resulted in vast implications at the family level. During communism, family autonomy was restricted; access to information and education were very limited, and family planning was not available. The communist pronatalist policy was associated with the interdiction of contraception and severe punishment for those performing abortions or receiving family planning. This was related to feelings of stress, anxiety, and helplessness among women, and had a negative influence on intimate relationships (David & Băban, 1996). In the communist period, the social sciences departments in universities were closed, and psychological research was constrained, resulting in a dearth of studies on family stress and coping in that period and a lack of educational and counseling resources for families.

The post-communist transition did not result in the expected positive effects, but instead engendered a multitude of other problems, including increasing poverty, corruption, and social inequalities (Robilă, 2004). Thus, the socio-economic conditions increased the emigration rate of Romanians, and currently more than 3.5 million people work in EU countries (SAR, 2014). Despite its positive aspects (increasing the family economic status and offering opportunities for professional development), migration has a considerable negative effect on both couples' and parent-child relationships. In many cases, only one partner works abroad, while in others, emigrant parents leave their children in Romania with relatives. Over 8 percent of Romanian children live without one or both of their parents, and parental migration is associated with children's depression, anxiety, and school problems (Tomşa, 2010).

Romanians' life satisfaction increased over time, with 63 percent of people reporting satisfaction with their lives in 2012 (Vasile, 2013). According to this survey, the variables that influenced life satisfaction in 2012 were health, freedom of choice, being involved in a stable relationship, and having a job. However, compared to other countries, life satisfaction of Romanian people is still low; Romania is situated below the average of EU countries on life satisfaction (Vasile, 2013).

Despite life satisfaction being relatively low, Romanians' satisfaction with family life is high. A national survey (Mărginean et al., 2010) indicated that 82 percent of people are satisfied with their family lives. Another study (Barometrul de Opinie Publică, BOP, 2007) of issues related to couple life revealed that of the 62 percent of Romanians involved in long-term relationships, 56 percent of them are married, and only 6 percent live in cohabitation (most of them being 25–34 years old). In general, Romanian families have few children (1.32 children born/woman according to CIA World Factbook, 2014). Economic problems cause 22 percent of couples to live with their parents or other relatives; only 78 percent of couples live in a separate house (BOP, 2007).

In Romania, the divorce rate (1.6 per thousand) is below the European average; yet 28 percent of marriages end in divorce (Eurostat, 2012). The reasons for divorce reported by couples in Romania were infidelity (3.3 percent), alcohol problems (2.5 percent), domestic violence (2.3 percent), combined reasons (3.5 percent), common agreement (65 percent), and other reasons (23.9 percent) (INS, 2013). The divorce rate below the European average could be explained by Romanians' high level of religiosity, but also by their low economic status and limited resources preventing couples from living apart.

In order to understand Romanian couples' relationships, it is important to clarify the male and female roles in the family. Moreover, due to the strong religious values among Romanians, we will also discuss the role of religion in family life.

Gender Roles

The attitudes on relationships and gender roles were influenced by the communist ideology, with women being expected to find their satisfaction primarily in family and to manage the household tasks (Robilă, 2004). Yet, at the same time, they were forced to work outside the home and often in low-status jobs (Friedlmeier & Gavreliuc, 2013). Nowadays, in general, Romanians report egalitarian attitudes on gender roles, but stereotypes on traditional gender roles still exist. In a national survey, both partners reported that women spent a significantly higher number of hours per week performing household tasks (twenty-nine hours) compared to men (nineteen hours), but both partners reported that they decide together on family issues (BOP, 2007). These attitudes were influenced by gender and education, with women and people with higher education reporting more egalitarian gender roles (BOP, 2008; Vanc & White, 2011).

Religion

Romanians are very religious; the majority of the Romanian population (86 percent) is Christian Orthodox, and a small proportion is represented by other religious affiliations (4.6 percent Roman Catholic, 6 percent Protestant) (INS, 2011). Ninety-six percent of respondents in a national survey indicated that they believe in God, 48 percent reported that they attend church several times per month, while 72 percent reported that they pray every day (INS, 2011). The Church has the highest level of credibility among public Romanian institutions, with 67 percent of people indicating trusting the Church greatly and very greatly (BOP, 2013). Many family practices and rituals have a religious basis. Fifty percent of Romanians consider religious similarity as one of the most important factors of marital satisfaction (BOP, 2007). In one study on Romanian families conducted by the author, 78 percent of participants indicated that religious faith is very important to the family; 75 percent reported that their families follow the teachings of religious faith; 80 percent reported that they celebrate religious holidays with the family; and 75 percent indicated that they assign a great importance to the religious education of their children (Rusu, 2012).

Stress in Romanian Couples

In general, Romanians experience a high amount of stress, and Romania was one of the lowest ranked countries from the EU in regards to income and time spent participating in enjoyable life activities (Randall & Corp, 2014). In a national survey, the most important variable in generating family conflicts reported by both men and women was economic strain, followed by household tasks, child behavior, and alcohol problems (BOP, 2007). The main explanatory variables of marital satisfaction were love, mutual support, financial situation, and social similarity (religion, education, and social position similarity). For Romanians, the most important reasons to worry were also related to economic circumstances: rising prices, job loss, and salary decreases (BOP, 2014).

These results were confirmed by one research study conducted on married Romanian individuals in which the strongest stressors outside the relationship were related to job situation (high demands, lacking of acknowledgments, and career opportunities), finances, and management of free time (too many activities, unsatisfactory recreational activities, too little time for oneself) (Rusu, 2012). The main daily stressors inside the relationship reported by both male and female partners were related to differences of opinion with the partner, different attitudes concerning relationship and life, and difficult personality of the partner (Rusu, 2012). The findings showed gender differences in terms of daily stress; women reported higher levels of long-term stress (e.g., external stress, such as financial stress or stress with children and internal stress, such as different goals and views or unsatisfactory distribution of duties and responsibilities). Higher stress reported by women is consistent with the results of a national survey, where women reported a lower life satisfaction compared to men (Mărginean et al., 2010). The question remains, however, of why Romanian women experience a higher level of stress compared to men. One possible explanation involves traditional gender roles and differences in the Romanian men and women socialization process. Women are taught to perform housework and to take care of children, which might result in a higher level of stress compared to men. A second explanation involves possible gender differences in the support that men and women receive from each other. We found significant differences between men and women on DC by partner (one spouse's perception of the support received from the partner), with husbands reporting higher levels than wives (Rusu, 2012). Therefore, husbands' lower stress levels could be explained by the higher levels of support they receive from their partners in times of stress. This result is comparable to findings reported in a previous study on American couples, which indicated that when partners experience work stress; wives offer a higher level of support to their spouse than husbands do to wives (Bolger, DeLongis, Kessler, & Wethington, 1989).

According to the Systemic Transactional Model (STM; Bodenmann, 2005, see Chapter 1), stress within a couple is an interpersonal process and influences both partners. In response to stressful situations, couples adopt different behaviors and attitudes for supporting the partner through a process defined as dyadic coping (DC; Bodenmann, 2005). A recent meta-analysis (Falconier et al., 2015) on more than 15,000 participants indicated that DC strongly predicts relationship satisfaction for both men and women regardless of gender, age, relationship length, education level, and nationality. The following section focuses specifically on DC in Romania.

Dyadic Coping in Romanian Couples

Given the absence of research on DC in Romania and the absence of a validated measure to assess such coping, the author conducted two studies on Romanian married couples. The first study was conducted in 2012, and collected data from 215 married couples ($N = 430$ individuals). The second study was conducted in 2013, with data from 295 married couples ($N = 590$ individuals). These data were analyzed by the author and colleagues in order to validate the Dyadic Coping Inventory (DCI; Bodenmann, 2008) as well as to identify the determinants and outcomes of DC.

In the studies conducted on Romanian samples, the author and colleagues found that DC is related to contextual, relational, and individual factors (Figure 12.1). First, we found that specific contextual factors (such as daily stress and economic strain) have a negative influence on a spouse's ability to provide support to the partner and to cope with stress together (Rusu, Hilpert, Falconier, & Bodenmann, submitted). Second, DC was associated with relational variables, which were analyzed as DC determinants (relationship stress, marriage duration), as well as DC outcomes (marital satisfaction). Third, our findings showed that DC is influenced by individual factors, such as demographics (i.e., education and gender), individual cognitions (i.e., sanctification of marriage), and individual coping strategies. Moreover, DC has a positive influence on individual outcomes such as a partner's well-being. The following section will present in detail the DCI validation, as well as contextual, relational, and individual variables related to Romanians' DC.

Measuring DC: Romanian version of the Dyadic Coping Inventory

The Dyadic Coping Inventory (DCI; Bodenmann, 2008) evaluates the frequency with which partners engage in different behaviors to cope with stress together as a couple (see Chapter 3). The study of DC in Romania started with the validation of the measure developed by Bodenmann (2008) based on his ST approach (Rusu, Hilpert, Turliuc, & Bodenmann, 2016). The DCI validation study analyzed

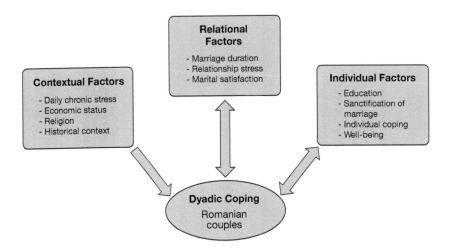

FIGURE 12.1 Contextual, relational, and individual factors as determinants and outcomes of dyadic coping

data from the two combined samples described above. The final sample was comprised of 510 Romanian married couples ($N = 1020$ individuals between 19 and 64 years old, who had been married an average of 13 years). The results confirmed the theoretical assumed factorial structure of the DCI for both partners. First, a five-factor structure was confirmed (stress communication, emotion-focused supportive DC, problem-focused supportive DC, delegated DC, and negative DC) for couple behavior if one member of the couple experienced external stress (e.g., stress at work). This remained consistent in the context of self-assessment (i.e., own behavior) as well as partner assessment (i.e., perception of partner's behavior). Second, a two-factor structure for couple behavior was confirmed (problem- and emotion-focused common DC) if both members of the couple endured the same stressor (e.g., financial burden, problems with child education). A particular strength of the Romanian validation study was the examination of the DCI measurement invariance across gender and across culture, comparing the Romanian sample with an existing Swiss sample of 368 couples. Results showed that the DCI measures the same construct across gender and cultures, allowing future cross-cultural studies to be planned in order to analyze the associations between DCI scales and other individual and marital outcomes.

Contextual Factors Influencing Romanians' Dyadic Coping

There are many contextual factors, which must be considered when analyzing stress and coping in Romanian couples, including the history of communism, religiosity, cultural values, chronic daily stress, and socio-economic status.

Communism influenced people's trust in others, affected individual and family autonomy, and led to a decline in optimism (Friedlmeier & Gavreliuc, 2013). In addition, traditional values and religiosity shape people's attitudes regarding family life and support they should provide to their partners (Rusu et al., 2015). Moreover, even if Romanian people have positive attitudes about marriage, the daily chronic stress on one hand and socio-economic status on the other hand have a negative influence on various aspects of couple interaction (Rusu, 2012; Rusu et al., submitted). Considering these findings, the following section focuses on contextual variables that may help us understand DC in Romanian couples.

Daily Chronic Stress

According to the stress-divorce model proposed by Bodenmann et al. (2007), external stress spills over into couple relationships. This negatively influences the time that partners spend together, communication, and DC, which in turn might lead to marital dissatisfaction and divorce. The results from one study on Romanian couples (Rusu, 2012) provided support for Bodenmann's model. These findings showed that external daily chronic stress (stress related to job, social contacts, children, daily hassles) influenced couple interactions by being negatively associated with positive forms of DC (supportive DC and common DC), and positively associated with negative DC. Moreover, this study indicated that only female external stress was negatively associated with her own and her partner's marital satisfaction. Therefore, higher female stress results in a higher stress spillover in the marital relationship. These results are a consequence of the higher amount of stress experienced by Romanian women compared to men. A possible explanation could be that women experiencing chronic external stress (e.g., daily hassles, stress with children and finances) might attribute their stress to their partners due to a lack of help, which will affect both partners' positive coping behaviors and marital satisfaction. Neff and Karney (2004) showed that as wives' external stress increased, so did their tendency to attribute the problems to their partners (e.g., blaming the partners for their negative behaviors). Therefore, in Romanian couples, women's daily stress seems to be more important for relationship quality than men's, and it influences both partners' DC and marital satisfaction.

Economic Stress

Bearing in mind that the economy is one of the main stressors for Romanians (BOP, 2014), two of the studies conducted by the author and colleagues focused particularly on measuring stress derived from economic circumstances. In the first study, data from 215 Romanian couples found that approximately 50 percent of participants reported medium and high levels of financial stress during the past twelve months (Rusu, 2012). The results of the second study (Rusu et al., submitted) revealed a negative association between economic strain and DC. Specifically, both spouses' chronic financial stress was associated with a decrease in both self and partner positive DC, and an increase in both self and partner negative DC. These results suggest that when spouses experience financial problems, they do not have personal resources to support their partners and to cope with stress together; and moreover, they use negative strategies of DC incuding hostile, ambivalent, and superficial DC. Our findings are consistent with past research conducted with Romanian (Robilă & Krishnakumar, 2005), Argentinian (Falconier, 2010), and American (Vinokur, Price, & Caplan, 1996) samples in which economic strain has been negatively related to relationship satisfaction and relationship stability.

The influence of economic strain on DC corroborates prior theory and research on this topic. First, Bradbury and Karney (2014) suggest low socioeconomic status brings additional challenges, such as health problems, substance abuse, and less time for the family; and these problems could negatively influence the way partners cope with stress together. Second, economic difficulties affect cognitive, emotional, and social resources. For example, in a series of experiments on American samples, Shah, Mullainathan, and Shafir (2012) demonstrated that poverty reduces cognitive resources by making people increase their focus on problems involving scarcity (such as daily basic expenses) and neglect other important problems. In addition to the cognitive effects of poverty, economic strain affects partners' emotional and social resources, by decreasing daily positive emotions (joy, contentment, and pride) and support provided to the partner (Rusu et al., submitted) in Romanian couples. Third, according to the Vulnerability-Stress-Adaptation-Model (VSA; Karney & Bradbury, 1995), demanding circumstances such as economic stress might activate personal vulnerabilities of the partners and negatively affect couples' interactions such as dyadic coping, by increasing the probability of experiencing distress.

Relational Variables Associated with Dyadic Coping

Marriage Duration

Research on Romanian married couples indicates that as marriage duration increases, positive DC decreases and negative DC increases (Rusu, 2013). These results are consistent with other American studies suggesting a negative association between marriage duration and relationship quality (Neff & Karney, 2004). However, more studies are needed in order to examine the association between DC and marriage duration. Despite the fact that couples in their first years of marriage seem better able to cope with stress together, marriage duration could be also a consequence of DC. Couples who cope well with stress together have longer marriages compared to those with lower levels of DC.

Marital Satisfaction

DC was strongly positively associated with marital satisfaction in Romanian couples (Buliga, 2014; Rusu et al., 2015; Rusu, Hilpert, Beach, Turliuc, & Bodenmann, 2015). Moreover, a recent cross-cultural study on family relations indicated that DC is a stronger predictor of marital satisfaction for Eastern European couples, including Romanians, than for Western ones (Hilpert et al., in preparation). The correlations between DC and marital satisfaction found in existing studies on the Romanian population are depicted in Table 12.1. The high correlations could be explained by the centrality of family for Romanian people, as family was rated the most important source of satisfaction for Romanians compared to other life areas (Mărginean et al., 2010), and a high proportion of people married and involved in long-term relationships (BOP, 2007). Another possible explanation for these results might be that external threats foster family commitment; high levels of stress outside the relationship (low income, low involvement in leisure activities, and low support received in society in general), may lead Romanians to focus on family to a greater extent than Western couples. Also, the Romanians' high level of religiosity could contribute to a higher level of DC and satisfaction through more investment of time and effort into the family.

Individual Factors Related to Dyadic Coping

Education

Education plays an important role in different behaviors and attitudes regarding family life for Romanians. Approximately 44 percent of the population has a low

TABLE 12.1 Correlations between dyadic coping and relationship satisfaction in Romanian couples

Measurement of Relationship Satisfaction	Number of participants	Correlation with DC
Couple Satisfaction Index (CSI 32; Funk & Rogge, 2007)	430 individuals (215 married couples)	0.65**
Couple Satisfaction Index (CSI 32; Funk & Rogge, 2007)	590 individuals (295 married couples)	0.68**
Quality of Relationship Inventory (QRI; Pierce, Sarason, Solky-Butzel, Nagle, 1997)	160 individuals (80 married couples)	0.69**
Marriage and Relationships Questionnaire (MARQ; Russell and Wells, 1986)	56 individuals	0.61**

**p<0.01

educational level (primary school and secondary school), 41.4 percent have a medium educational level (high-school, post-high-school education, or vocational education), and 14.4 percent have a high educational level (bachelor's degree) (INS, 2011). A national survey indicated that education increases family satisfaction in general, and that people with high levels of education reported to be three times more satisfied with family life compared to those with low levels of education (Mărginean et al., 2010). Consistent with these findings, we found that DC varies across education as well; individuals who completed university studies had a significantly higher score on DC than those who completed gymnasium (a lower form of secondary education), or high school (Rusu et al., 2016). The positive association between education and DC may be explained by the results of a national survey, which indicate that a higher level of education is associated with more egalitarian attitudes toward gender roles, less time spent performing household activities, and more cooperation in family decision making (BOP, 2007). Higher levels of education also correlate positively with greater disapproval of family violence, alcohol consumption, and infidelity, which are considered reasons for divorce (BOP, 2007).

Gender

There are significant gender differences in DC for Romanian men and women (Rusu et al., 2016). Women reported higher scores than men on their own stress communication and dyadic coping by oneself (total score), and likewise, men reported that their wives communicate their stress more frequently and that reported higher scores on dyadic coping by partner (total score) (Rusu et al., 2016). These results highlight the traditional role of Romanian women, who are more concerned with family care compared to their husbands. In addition, the higher levels of stress communication reported by wives could be explained by the higher amount of stress reported by women, due to the greater time they spend performing household tasks and taking care of the children (BOP, 2007).

Sanctification of Marriage

Evidence suggests that religiosity is related to marital satisfaction, a low risk of divorce, and positive behaviors in couples (problem-solving, positive communication, expressing positivity) (Mahoney, 2010; Stafford, 2013). However, past research did not investigate if religiosity influences the way partners cope with stress. The results of a study on Romanian couples showed that positive DC was positively associated with religious faith, religious cognitions (sanctification of marriage), and positive religious coping (Rusu, 2012). Moreover, we found that DC mediates the influence of sanctification on partners' marital satisfaction and well-being (Rusu et al., 2015). Our findings showed that at the dyadic level, sanctification motivates both partners to be more supportive toward each other, which in turn positively influences both marital satisfaction and well-being. Thus, for Romanian families, sanctification of marriage plays an important role in understanding family relationships.

Individual Cognitive Coping

The existing studies on couples coping with stress have focused either on the individual coping strategies of each partner (Pakenham, 1998) or on dyadic coping strategies (Bodenmann, Pihet, & Kayser, 2006) used by partners. Considering the few existing studies on the association between the individual and DC, and only one study using dyadic data analyses (Herzberg, 2013), we analyzed the association between the individual and DC in one of our research studies on Romanian couples (Rusu, 2013). The results showed positive correlations between functional individual cognitive coping (e.g., putting into perspective, positive refocusing, positive reappraisal, planning) and positive DC and between dysfunctional individual coping (e.g., catastrophizing, other-blame, self-blame) and negative DC. In addition, male and female positive DC mediated the association between adaptive individual coping and marital satisfaction. These findings support the importance of addressing the partner's individual cognitive strategies in couple therapy, given that individual cognitions about stressful events affect the way partners cope, which in turn, influences marital satisfaction.

Well-being

In two studies on Romanian couples, Rusu and colleagues found that male and female DC are related to personal and partner existential well-being (2015) and to personal and partner autonomy, environmental mastery, personal growth, positive relations, purpose in life, and self-acceptance (Rusu, 2013; see Table 12.2). In one of our studies, we conceptualized DC as a predictor of well-being, and we found that DC mediates the association between sanctification and existential well-being (Rusu et al., 2015). Considering the cross-sectional nature of these data, more longitudinal or daily diary studies are necessary to establish if well-being is a consequence of DC, a determinant of DC, or both. We could hypothesize not only that DC makes partners happier, but also that happier people could be more supportive with their partners and have better abilities to cope with stress in the couple dyad.

Summarizing the findings presented above, DC has a protective influence on relationship quality, stability, and partners' well-being. The association of dyadic coping with contextual, relational, and individual variables has important implications for both practice and research.

TABLE 12.2 Correlations between dyadic coping and psychological well-being
($N = 295$ couples)

Well-being	Positive Dyadic Coping		Negative Dyadic Coping	
	Men	Women	Men	Women
Autonomy				
Men	0.31★★	0.32★★	−0.35★★	−0.32★★
Women	0.18★★	0.28★★	−0.17★★	−0.27★★
Environmental mastery				
Men	0.40★★	0.37★★	−0.44★★	−0.39★★
Women	0.31★★	0.46★★	−0.38★★	−0.45★★
Personal growth				
Men	0.36★★	0.35★★	−0.49★★	−0.37★★
Women	0.28★★	0.39★★	−0.38★★	−0.49★★
Positive relations				
Men	0.40★★	0.29★★	−0.48★★	−0.40★★
Women	0.27★★	0.35★★	−0.39★★	−0.46★★
Purpose in Life				
Men	0.37★★	0.38★★	−0.49★★	−0.40★★
Women	0.28★★	0.37★★	−0.36★★	−0.48★★
Self acceptance				
Men	0.40★★	0.32★★	−0.36★★	−0.35★★
Women	0.19★★	0.36★★	−0.31★★	−0.42★★

★★$p<0.01$

Implications for Practice

There is a need for programs to support families and a need to change attitudes regarding couple and family counseling. Most of the Romanian people do not search for specialized help when they are confronting family problems; only 2 percent of the participants in a national survey reported that they referred to couple counseling (BOP, 2007). Negative attitudes toward counseling due to a lack of information, the lack of availability of couple and family counseling, and financial problems are all possible reasons for low rates of counseling attendance. Therefore, the first recommendation based on the research presented earlier in this chapter would be to help clinicians and researchers find efficient ways to inform couples about the benefits of psychological interventions, and to make the research on couples and families available to the public. Based on this research, interventions such as educational programs, as well as trainings and policies centered on individual, dyadic, and contextual variables, are needed in order to support Romanian families. A specific intervention that might be effective in working with Romanian couples is the psycho-educational program TOGETHER developed and tested by Falconier (2015) on American couples. This program is based on the Couples Coping Enhancement Training (CCET; Bodenmann & Shantinath, 2004) and is group therapy designed for couples under financial strain. TOGETHER focuses on both improving financial management skills, as well as on improving partners' psychological resources (individual and dyadic coping strategies, and communication). However, in addition to psycho-educational programs, as Karney (2009) suggests, highly vulnerable couples might need policies and interventions that address their problems directly (such as financial support). Therefore, governmental policies should consider specific couple and family stressors.

Implications for Research

Further systematic research on family stress and coping in Romania needs to be conducted in order to provide knowledge on dyadic processes in couple and family relationships, and must consider different age cohorts and socio-economic conditions. The cross-sectional nature of the existing data on DC in Romania increases the probability of other causal relations between the variables, and restricts the possibility of examining DC as a determinant or consequence of other variables over a longer period of time. Future longitudinal and daily diary studies on Romanian couples should analyze different variables related to DC over time. Additional studies might offer important insight about how contextual variables (daily stress or economic strain) and individual characteristics (religiosity or individual coping) could affect couple relationships on a day-by-day basis and over the long term. Moreover, considering that most of the studies from Romania were conducted on married couples and that many of these couples showcased relatively high levels of marital satisfaction, additional research is needed in order to examine dyadic coping in clinical samples of highly distressed Romanian couples.

Conclusion

The present chapter provided an overview on Romanian couples' stress and dyadic coping. The results of the studies presented in this chapter provide evidence that STM (Bodenmann, 2005) is a valid model for Romanian couples and helps us analyze how stress affects couples' interactions. Studies on Romanian couples have showed that stress outside of the relationship has a negative influence on couple interaction, marital satisfaction, and well-being (Rusu, 2012; Rusu et al., 2015). In these associations we found gender differences, with Romanian women experiencing higher amounts of stress, higher levels of stress spillover into their relationships, and less support from their partners compared to men (Rusu, 2012). However, couples' interactions in Romania can be fully understood only by analyzing the relationships in context. Specific contextual factors (socio-economic status, religion, cultural values) need to be considered in order to explain why DC is related to individual and relational variables in Romanian couples. To date, the studies show that specific contextual stressors, such as daily chronic stress and economic strain, could have a negative influence on spouses' abilities to provide support to their partners and to cope with stress together. As such, the demands and resources of the context, as well as the vulnerabilities and resources of individuals and relationships, shape the way couples cope with stress, which has important implications for understanding dyadic interactions in a specific culture.

References

Barometrul de Opinie Publica (BOP) [Barometer for Public Opinion] (2007, 2008). Bucharest, Romania, SOROS Foundation.

Barometrul de Opinie Publica (BOP) [Barometer for Public Opinion] (2013, 2014). Bucharest, Romania, INSCOP Research.

Bodenmann, G. (2005). Dyadic coping and its significance for marital functionning. In T. A. Revenson, K. Kayser, & G. Bodenmann, (Eds.) (2005), *Couples coping with stress: Emerging perspectives on dyadic coping. Decade of behavior* (pp. 33–50). Washington DC: American Psychological Association.

Bodenmann, G. (2008). *Dyadisches Coping Inventar (DCI). Testmanual [Dyadic Coping Inventory (DCI). Test manual]*. Bern, Göttingen: Huber & Hogrefe.

Bodenmann, G., Charvoz, L., Bradbury, T. N., Bertoni, A., Iafrate, R., Giuliani, G., . . . Behling, J. (2007). The role of stress in divorce: A retrospective study in three nations. *Journal of Social and Personal Relationships, 24,* 707–728.

Bodenmann, G., Pihet, S., & Kayser, K. (2006). The relationship between dyadic coping and marital quality: A 2-year longitudinal study. *Journal of Family Psychology, 20,* 485–493.

Bodenmann, G., & Shantinath, S. D. (2004). The Couples Coping Enhancement Training (CCET): A new approach to prevention of marital distress based upon stress and coping. *Family Relations, 53*(5), 477–484.

Bolger, N., DeLongis, A., Kessler, R. C., & Wethington, E. (1989). The contagion of stress across multiple roles. *Journal of Marriage and the Family, 51*(1), 175–183.

Bradbury, T. N., & Karney, B. R. (2014). Intimate relationships (Second ed.). New York: W. W. Norton.

Buliga, D. (2014). Family-work interface: From conflict and positive interaction perspective to integrative models. Unpublished doctoral dissertation, 'Al. I. Cuza' University of Iasi, Romania.

CIA World Factbook (2014). Country comparison: Total fertility rate. Retrieved from www.cia.gov/library/publications/the-world-factbook/rankorder/2127rank.html

David, H. P., & Băban, A. (1996). Women's health and reproductive rights: Romanian experience. *Patient Education and Counseling, 28*(3), 235–245.

Eurostat (2012). Divorce rate. Retrieved from www.ec.europa.eu/eurostat/statistics-explained/index.php/File:Crude_divorce_rate,_selected_years,_1960%E2%80%932012_%281%29_%28per_1_000_inhabitants%29_YB14.png

Falconier, M. K. (2010). Female anxiety and male depression: Links between economic strain and psychological aggression in Argentinean couples. *Family Relations, 59*(4), 424–438.

Falconier, M. K. (2015). TOGETHER–A couples' program to improve communication, coping, and financial management skills: Development and initial pilot testing. *Journal of Marital and Family Therapy, 41*(2), 236–250.

Falconier, M. K., Jackson, J., Hilpert, J., & Bodenmann, G. (2015). Dyadic coping and relationship satisfaction: A meta-analysis. *Clinical Psychology Review, 42*, 28–46.

Friedlmeier, M., & Gavreliuc, A. (2013). Value orientations and perception of social change in post-communist Romania. *Intergenerational Relations. European Perspective on Family and Society*, 119–130. Policy Press: University of Bristol.

Herzberg, P. Y. (2013). Coping in relationships: The interplay between individual and dyadic coping and their effects on relationship satisfaction. *Anxiety, Stress, & Coping, 26*(2), 136–153.

Hilpert, P., Sorokowski, P., Randall, A. K., DeLongis, A., Sorokowska, A., Paluszak, A., . . . Bodenmann, G. (in preparation). Comparing the association between dyadic coping and relationship satisfaction in couples around the world: A cross-cultural comparison of 45 nations.

Institutul National de Statistica (INS) (2011, 2013, 2014). (National Institute of Statistics). Bucharest, Romania.

Karney, B. (2009). Vulnerability-stress-adaptation model. In H. Reis & S. Sprecher (Eds.), *Encyclopedia of human relationships* (pp. 1675–1678). Thousand Oaks, CA: Sage.

Karney, B. R., & Bradbury, T. N. (1995). The longitudinal course of marital quality and stability: A review of theory, methods, and research. *Psychological Bulletin, 118*(1), 3–34.

Mahoney, A. (2010). Religion in families, 1999–2009: A relational spirituality framework. *Journal of Marriage & Family, 72*(4), 805–827.

Mărginean, I., Precupeţu, I., Dumitru, M., Mihalache, F., Mihăilescu, A., Neagu, G., . . . Vasile, M. (2010). Calitatea vieţii în România/Quality of life in Romania. Bucharest: Expert Publishing House.

Neff, L. A., & Karney, B. R. (2004). How does context affect intimate relationships? Linking external stress and cognitive processes within marriage. *Personality and Social Psychology Bulletin, 30*(2), 134–148.

Pakenham, K. I. (1998). Couple coping and adjustment to multiple sclerosis in care receiver-carer dyads. *Family Relations, 47*(3), 269–277.

Popescu, R. (2010). Profilul familiei româneşti contemporane [The profile of the contemporary Romanian family]. *Calitatea vieţii/Quality of life*, (1–2), 5–28.

Randall, C. & Corp, A. (2014). Measuring national well-being: European comparisons. Office for National Statistics. Retrieved from www.ons.gov.uk/ons/dcp171766_363 811.pdf

Robilă, M. (2004). Child development and family functioning within Romanian context. In M. Robila (Ed.), *Families in Eastern Europe* (pp. 141–154). Elsevier.

Robilă, M., & Krishnakumar, A. (2005). Effects of economic pressure on marital conflict in Romania. *Journal of Family Psychology, 19*(2), 246–251.

Rusu, P. P. (2012). Religiosity and religious coping in couple and family relations: Therapeutical implications. Unpublished doctoral dissertation, 'Al. I. Cuza' University of Iasi, Romania.

Rusu, P. P. (2013) [Family Stress: Contextual, Individual and Dyadic Factors]. Unpublished raw data.

Rusu, P. P., Hilpert, P., Beach, S., Turliuc, M. N., Bodenmann, G. (2015). Dyadic coping mediates the association of sanctification with marital satisfaction and well-being. *Journal of Family Psychology, 29*(6), 843.

Rusu, P. P., Hilpert, P., Falconier, M., & Bodenmann, G. (submitted). Economic Strain Affects Support in Couples: The Mediating Role of Positive Emotions.

Rusu, P. P., Hilpert, P., Turliuc, M. N., Bodenmann, G. (2016). Dyadic coping in an Eastern European context: Validity and measurement invariance of the Romanian version of Dyadic Coping Inventory. *Measurement and Evaluation in Counselling and Development, 49*(4).

Societatea Academică din România (SAR) [Romanian Academic Society]. Raport Anual. România 2014 [Annual Report, Romania, 2014]. Retrieved from www.sar.org.ro/wp-content/uploads/2014/04/RAPORT-SAR-2014-FINAL.pdf

Shah, A. K., Mullainathan, S., & Shafir, E. (2012). Some consequences of having too little. *Science, 338*(6107), 682–685.

Stafford, L. (2013). Marital sanctity, relationship maintenance, and marital quality. *Journal of Family Issues, 37*(1), 119–131.

Tomşa, R. (2010). Efectele psihologice ale migraţiei economice a părinţilor aspura pre-adolescenţilor [Psychological effects of parents' economic migration on preadolescents]. University of Bucharest. Unpublished dissertation.

Vanc, A., & White, C. (2011). Cultural perceptions of public relations gender roles in Romania. *Public Relations Review, 37*(1), 103–105.

Vasile, M. (2013). Sănătatea percepută, calitatea serviciilor publice şi satisfacţia faţă de viaţă [Perceived health, quality of public services and life satisfaction]. *Quality of Life (1018–0389)/Calitatea Vieţii, 24*(4).

Vinokur, A. D., Price, R. H., & Caplan, R. D. (1996). Hard times and hurtful partners: How financial strain affects depression and relationship satisfaction of unemployed persons and their spouses. *Journal of Personality and Social Psychology, 71*(1), 166–179.

13

DYADIC COPING IN PAKISTANI COUPLES

Zara Arshad and Nazia Iqbal

Introduction

Pakistan, located in the subcontinent of South Asia, has been an unstable country both politically and financially. Its economy has been severely affected by historical hostilities, conflicts, wars, and several armed skirmishes with India (Blood, 1995). Additionally, the wars in Afghanistan have had a devastating impact on Pakistan, leading to the infiltration of militant extremist Islamic forces and wreaking havoc in all the major cities in the country, such as terrorist attacks, kidnappings for ransom, and organized criminal activities. These circumstances have led to religious extremism and overall social intolerance, as well as breakdown of infrastructure and lack of resources for health, education, and women's empowerment (Blood, 1995). With such a political and economic backdrop, living conditions in Pakistan have become more challenging.

Even though Pakistan gained independence from British India in 1947, it still does not seem to have a national identity. Pakistanis identify themselves on the grounds of their culture, religion, or ethnicity, more than just as 'Pakistanis.' In terms of religion, Pakistan is a Muslim country in which the influence of religion and culture is strongly intertwined among its people. Over 96 percent of the population follows Islam as their religion (Pakistan Bureau of Statistics, 2015), with Sunni Muslims making up 81 percent of the population and Shiite Muslims making up 15 percent of the population. Minorities include Christians, Hindus, Sikhs, Ahmadiyya, and others.

Ethnicity is another strong unifier in Pakistan. Each of the four provinces, Punjab, Sindh, Balochistan, and Khyber Pakhtunkhwa, are carved out geographically reflecting the four dominant ethnicities in Pakistan (Blood, 1995). Each province has its own culture and language, or dialects. There are about 44 percent Punjabis, 14 percent Sindhis, 4 percent Balochis, and 15 percent Pathans in Pakistan

(Pakistan Bureau of Statistics, 2015). Urdu is the national language of Pakistan and one of the two official languages of the country, English being the other. While only spoken by a small minority (8 percent) of immigrants of Indian heritage, Urdu is widely understood and spoken as a second language by the vast majority.

In the predominant Muslim culture in Pakistan, the parents' position is sacred; disobeying them is sacrilegious (Obeid, 1988). Besides parents, the family, including extended family, is central to the life of a Pakistani (Blood, 1995). Even among the most Westernized elite individuals, the significance of the family is retained (Blood, 1995). Typically, and traditionally, the household includes a married couple, their unmarried children, and married sons with their families (Blood, 1995). Pakistani nuclear families are usually large, with four children being an average in the country (Population Council, 2014), although the national average may not be reflective of the number of children in urban families.

Pakistan is a patriarchal society where men are largely favored for making all major decisions and women are socialized to be passive, dependent, and subordinate to their male counterparts (Ayyub, 2000). Generally, men are primarily responsible for being the providers and protectors of the family whereas the women are responsible for care and service of their family (Ali, Krantz, Gul, Asad, Johansson, & Mogren, 2011). However, it is extremely difficult to generalize the cultural and social norms of the Pakistani society as a whole, due to differences among families. For instance, male domination flourishes under the patriarchal feudal and tribal systems, especially in the rural areas, which are home to 68 percent of the country's population (Pakistan Bureau of Statistics, 2015), and where the literacy rate is extremely low. In these rural areas, men exercise absolute control over women's lives by making all major and minor decisions for them (Naheed & Gah, 1997). This would be in sharp contrast to the population residing in urban cities with less patriarchal orientation. Even within the rural and urban populations, attitudes, beliefs, and practices vary to a great degree depending on the provincial region, socio-economic status, education level, religiosity, and how liberal or conservative a family is.

There is also a great gender disparity in terms of education in Pakistan (Quayes & Ramsey, 2015). Traditionally, men are expected to obtain advanced education as they are considered breadwinners of the family and care-takers of their parents in their old age. Women, on the other hand, are expected to get married soon after reaching puberty and focus on bearing children, raising a family, and taking care of their husband's elderly parents and unmarried siblings. Where parents are reasonably enlightened and can afford to do so, girls may be allowed to attend school up to elementary or secondary level, enabling them to acquire basic literacy. However, girls from educated and affluent families in urban areas have the opportunity of acquiring professional education and pursuing a successful career (Ali et al., 2011).

Marriage in Pakistan is considered a social and moral obligation (Critelli, 2012), where a person must be married in order to participate fully in the Pakistani society.

Marriage extends beyond the exchange of vows between the man and the wife, to socially unite the two families for all future joys and sorrows (Zainab, 2003). A Pakistani Muslim marriage is defined as a legal, social, and religious contract in which a man and woman are declared husband and wife after the religious ritual, nikah, is performed.

There is a strong social support system available to Pakistani couples to help them develop and sustain a sound marital relationship (Qadir, Khalid, Haqqani, Zill-e-Huma, & Medhin, 2013). The sheer strength of human bonding in the Pakistani society provides valuable support and a sense of belonging to all people living in it. The most important social resource available to a couple is the family system, which includes parents, siblings, grandparents, aunts, uncles, and cousins. The mother-daughter bond is very strong in Pakistani society, where mothers play an important part in grooming their daughters and providing them consistent support, both before and after marriage. Sisters, female cousins, and aunts are reliable confidants for a woman before and after marriage and fathers, brothers, and uncles are seen as a woman's strength in society as they provide her with a sense of security. Men's sources of support are usually their immediate family, including parents, grandparents, siblings, wife, and children.

In most Pakistani families, both the paternal and maternal grandparents play a prominent role in the upbringing of grandchildren by nurturing and grooming them, both in the presence and absence of the parents. Grandparents are highly respected and are considered a blessing in Pakistani households. They may also contribute financially if they have the resources, such as savings or pensions. Grandparents are a source of tremendous emotional, moral, social, and above all, spiritual support, as their prayers are supposed to bring blessings and ward off misfortunes. They also provide valuable guidance based on their experience and wisdom, and pass on the sound management skills they have developed over time.

In-laws are also supposed to provide a woman with the same social support and sense of security as her family-of-origin. Traditionally, women may have closer ties with their in-laws than their own families, as they marry young and get to spend more of their lives with their in-laws. Men also get valuable social support from the woman's family, and as male members of the family are highly valued in patriarchal societies, male members of the woman's family are considered a proud addition to the man's family.

Culturally, neighbors are no less than extended family and can be a great resource in times of need. Older neighbors consider themselves in place of parents for young couples living away from their families. However, young couples in urban cities do not seem to be as connected with their neighbors, as both partners are usually working and do not have time to socialize with them. These social ties, like all others, are developed more by women; and with more and more women working in professional careers, living in nuclear families, and raising their children, there is little time for them to spare for these relationships.

Most Pakistanis have strong religious beliefs that provide them inner strength in times of stress. Communal religious practices provide further social support within the community. Their faith also teaches them to be stoic and forbearing in times of distress. Here too, parents are a great source of comfort as, according to Islam, their prayers and good wishes are likely to be fulfilled by God. Furthermore, religious couples feel obligated by their faith to build a strong and stable marriage, and to strive for harmony in their marital relationship, even in times of distress.

Review of the Literature

Couples' Relationships in Pakistan

As in many other Asian countries, arranged marriages are an ancient practice in Pakistan (Critelli, 2012). The purpose of marriage in Pakistan, as in other collectivist societies, is to follow the communal norms and fulfill familial obligations rather than individual desires (Stewart, Bond, Zaman, Dar, & Anwar, 2000); in this sense, love follows marriage (Qadir et al., 2013). The selection of the partner and other marriage related decisions are made by the man's and the woman's families, generally with neither the man nor woman having much say in the matter; this is based on the assumption that the elders in the family have better wisdom and experience in the matter and they have a right to make decisions for their offspring (Critelli, 2012). In fact, children are generally satisfied with their parents choosing their spouse, as they trust their parents' decision (Qadir, De Silva, Prince, & Khan, 2005).

When selecting a partner, families consider the compatibility in various domains, such as religion, ethnicity, age, education, and profession (Mir, 2013). Commonalities and differences are carefully considered in the selection process. The social status and economic background is also taken into consideration as a strong socio-economic background ensures a successful marital life, free from financial tensions and the myriad stresses that come with it. Ethnically dissimilar marriages are not preferred because certain attitudes and perceptions are held of other ethnicities (Mullick & Hraba, 2001). Marriages where both partners belong to the same religious sect and ethnicity are most common, as there is a better chance of compatibility between the couple as well as their families.

Despite Islamic teachings and civil law in Pakistan, where an adult man and woman must give their approval and consent to marrying their partner, couples have often been forced into marriage against their will, especially women (Critelli, 2012). Women are culturally conditioned to suppress their desires as a mark of womanhood and to forgo their basic rights in order to uphold the traditions and honor of their family. A well-bred woman is to please her parents and not disapprove the partner selected for her (Qadir et al., 2005).

The decline of arranged marriages in the past few decades shows a change of attitude among the people. Educated women, particularly belonging to affluent urban families, as well as some from the working classes, are increasingly asserting their rights by either choosing their partner themselves or having a say in their families' selection (Naheed & Gah, 1997). Nonetheless, desire to choose one's partner is considered a Western concept, prominent only among urban people. Moreover, Pakistani children, regardless of their background, still feel strongly about their parents' opinion and seek their approval even when exercising their right to choose their partner. This stems from respect of their parents' wisdom and trust in their judgment to be in the children's best interest (Mir, 2013; Qadir et al., 2005). A natural consequence is the growing trend of 'semi-arranged marriages,' where a suitable man and woman are introduced to each other in a social setting, so that they may choose a partner who also meets their parents' approval (Mir, 2013).

In Pakistan, marriage is considered a sacred and social contract between the man and woman, both from the religious and cultural point of view, and expected to be a lifelong commitment. Pakistani couples are generally very loyal to their spouse and show a great deal of sincerity and respect for their partner (Qadir et al., 2005); their marriages thrive on loyalty and respect more than on love for each other. Divorce is generally not considered an option, especially by women, as it carries a stigma which mars a woman for life, bringing with it dishonor and shame to her family (Qadir et al., 2005). However, this is a cultural concept with no basis in the religion, as Islam allows couples to seek divorce, albeit as a last resort, if they are not able to live in peace and harmony.

Internal Stress

There are several sources of stress that are caused by factors within the couple system, which is referred to as *internal stress* (see Chapter 1). Pakistani wives value love, respect, and care from their husbands and their husbands' families, and some level of egalitarianism between husband and wife (Qadir et al., 2005). Wives who belong to higher socio-economic status place emphasis on friendship and companionship as well. It can be inferred that in the absence of certain marital values, namely respect and care between couples and between their families, Pakistani couples experience dissatisfaction and distress in their marriages. Pakistani couples can often cope with lack of love in the marriage, as most marriages are not a result of the couple falling in love. However, there is an expectation of respect and care. Lack of either of these can lead to emotional and physical abuse as well as financial deprivation. Moreover, in a society where men are expected to take care of their elderly parents, as well as unmarried siblings, along with their own wives and children, the weight of such responsibility can lead to marital discord and discontent in the relationship.

In the case of couples belonging to dissimilar social backgrounds, significant stress is created when their differences, especially ethnic and religious, become a point of contention between the couple and/or their families. Mir (2013) argues that despite the affection, love, respect, and personality compatibility found in love marriages, ethnic, religious, and regional differences between such couples may still create conflict for the families involved. Ethnic and religious dissimilarities are particularly avoided as the impact of the differences often deepens with time, especially if there is disagreement about whose culture the children should follow.

Pakistani women often feel insecure in their marital relationship until they bear a child. They become confident in their positions after becoming mothers, particularly after bearing a male child (Blood, 1995). This is more so among the uneducated and rural people, where girls are considered a liability and boys are considered an asset to the family. It can be particularly difficult for women living in joint families, as a woman who has not yet borne a male child is not given the same status as one who has, and suffers great insecurity and stress (Ali et al., 2011). A strong understanding and support from the husband is very important for her sense of security in this case. However, the husband's support is usually not forthcoming, particularly in the uneducated families and in the rural areas. The main reason for the woman's sense of insecurity is that in the Pakistani culture, a man finds it difficult to leave a woman who is the mother of his children. Thus, children ensure the long-term stability and strength of the marital relationship. Childless Pakistani couples are less satisfied with their marital life when compared to those couples with children (Sultan, 2010), and childless marriages often lead to either divorce, or in some cases, the husband's second marriage.

Domestic Violence

Cultural norms in Pakistan have given the husband absolute control over his wife, particularly among the less educated and those living in rural areas, giving him the right to take punitive action as he sees fit if she errs in her social or domestic duties (Ayyub, 2000). This has led to justifying domestic violence. Domestic violence against women in Pakistan is becoming an endemic concern (World Human Rights, 2009). Within a marriage, women have experienced violence at the hands of their husbands and at times, their in-laws. Often times, husbands try to misuse their authority through abuse, and wives become submissive and compromising in order to keep the family intact. The incidents of domestic violence are likely to be higher among couples who are less educated, economically disadvantaged, and live in rural areas, which makes up the majority of the population in Pakistan (Pakistan Bureau of Statistics, 2015). At this point, with hardly any government support and lack of mental health awareness, accessibility, and feasibility, many Pakistani women are silently suffering abuse in their marriages, causing them significant physical, emotional, and psychological distress (Fikree & Bhatti, 1999).

Mental Health

Low marital satisfaction and marital conflict among Pakistani couples are associated with common mental health problems in women, such as depression (Khan, 1998;

Niaz & Hassan, 2005; Qadir et al., 2013), and problems related to husband and in-laws have been associated with attempted suicide (Niaz, 2004). In a study by Fikree and Bhatti (1999), 42 percent of a sample of women belonging to low and middle socio-economic status were found to be anxiously depressed, with significant associations between anxious depression and physical abuse, lack of education, low monthly income, and younger than 15 years of age at the time of marriage. Nuclear and joint family systems have both been found to be risk factors for depression and anxiety (Mirza & Jenkins, 2004; Mumford, Minhas, Akhtar, Akhter, & Mubbashar, 2000), which suggests that family support can be a risk factor or a protective factor. Less is known about the impact of marital stressors on men.

External Stressors

In addition to internal stressors, there are several factors outside of the couple system that cause stress between a couple in Pakistan.

Fertility

Issues around infertility may become a major stress factor for Pakistani couples, particularly for the women (Ali et al., 2011). Families are very involved, especially in the early years of a couple's married life. Delays in starting a family put a lot of pressure on the woman. This is more the case in arranged marriages where parents feel the couple's familial progress is also the parent's responsibility; though the expectation may be there to a lesser degree in love marriages too. Both the pressure and expectation is less in educated families, especially where the woman is well educated and career-oriented. Nevertheless, the pressure may build if there is substantial delay in starting a family. In the less educated classes it becomes almost everybody's business to question the couple, including friends and neighbors. This puts extreme pressure on the marital relationship, especially if the couple is not intentionally delaying starting the family. This situation also results in feelings of guilt in the woman, as she is perceived to be infertile and incapable of bearing a child.

Large Families

On the other hand, having a greater number of children has also been found to lead to lower marital adjustment in Pakistani couples (Batool & Khalid, 2012). Since Pakistani nuclear families are usually large, it comes as no surprise that children are cited as one of the most common reasons for marital conflicts by Pakistani women (Fikree & Bhatti, 1999). Stress may be much lower in a family that can afford to hire domestic help for household chores and assistance with taking care of children, but much higher in economically disadvantaged couples as they do not have the resources to hire help for their daily chores and other domestic responsibilities.

Relationships With the In-Laws

Whereas in-laws can serve as a strong support system for couples, many in-laws in Pakistan also tend to be interfering in a couple's life and become a huge source of conflict (Fikree & Bhatti, 1999). In particular, a woman's life can be difficult during the first years of marriage. A newly married woman is expected 'to be subservient to her mother-in-law and must negotiate relations with her sister-in-laws' (Blood, 1995, p. 102). Pakistani wives are generally possessive of their home and family, and do not want others to interfere in their marital life. The husband usually is unable to provide proper emotional or moral support as he tends to avoid getting involved in these family dynamics, and if he does, he feels duty bound to favor his family of origin. These stressors on a woman can be lessened if she marries within her own extended family, as then she already has a relationship with her in-laws, and there is a better understanding of personalities and expectations from both sides.

Misunderstandings created between the spouses by the in-laws, especially the mother-in-law, are often found to be the case for causing stress among couples in Pakistan. A Pakistani mother and her son typically share a close relationship and the mother tends to retain a great influence over her son, at times more than the son's wife (Blood, 1995). When the son's time and affection is shared by the wife, the mother can become consumed in her effort to cope with this situation, at times resorting to create misunderstandings between her son and daughter-in-law, in an effort to win back their sons. Also, the perceived failure of the daughter-in-law to meet the expectations of the in-laws can create a situation of discontent in the family.

Finances

The unfortunate political and economical circumstances presently facing Pakistan's society also cause immense stress among couples. Financial constraints are cited as a common reason for marital conflicts in Pakistani couples (Fikree & Bhatti, 1999). Although work related stress is universal (Liu et al., 2007), people living in developing countries, such as Pakistan, can experience greater work related stress and financial instability due to the social and economic structure of the country. As a result of the strict gender role orientations (Gallup Pakistan, 2009), men are generally working long hours in stressful environments to provide for their families most of the week, which leads to family-life imbalance (Sarwar & Aftab, 2011). On the other hand, women in rural areas and those from less affluent families, work hard in the domestic sphere in terms of tending to the household, looking after children, and taking care of the husband and in-laws without much help. Generally, the reality for many Pakistani couples is working hard to provide for their families within their own gender ascriptions, with little emphasis placed on the quality of the marital relationship. This is especially true of a majority of the population that belongs to either a low socio-economic status or poverty. In couples belonging to the middle and upper class families, women generally experience much lower levels of stress as they can afford to hire domestic help.

In sum, there are several sources of stress for Pakistani couples, internal as well as external. Internal stressors may be especially prevalent in arranged marriages where spouses either do not know each other, or know very little of each other at the time of marriage. Such stressors include lack of love, respect, care, and understanding between the couple (Qadir et al., 2005). Other internal stressors include domestic violence (Ayyub, 2000), inability to have children (Sultan, 2010), and having no male child (Ali et al., 2011). External stressors include presence and interference of in-laws (Fikree & Bhatti, 1999), financial constraints (Fikree & Bhatti, 1999), and marital issues related to children (Batool & Khalid, 2012).

Pakistani couples engage in different types of individual and relational coping strategies depending on the type of stressor. Relational coping includes non-spousal social support and dyadic coping. Dyadic coping in response to stress varies greatly, depending on whether a couple is from a rural or urban area, the couple's socio-economic status, and their level of education. However, despite variations in coping styles, relying on religion and on family for support cuts across all classes of people in Pakistan.

Although there is a strong support system for Pakistanis, in several matters, particularly marital problems and financial issues, men and women are socialized to cope individually by bearing the burden alone, either to protect the other spouse or to protect their own honor. Men are trained to be stoic when facing stressors, especially financial difficulties, and try not to confide in others. This is a cultural value, with roots in Islamic teachings of relying on one's faith and forbearing difficulties, as they are a test of one's faith and resilience. However, when they do confide in family, or the stress becomes apparent, the family usually comes to their support. Similar to men, women are also socialized to bear their suffering as it speaks to their honor and dignity as a woman (Ali et al., 2011). An ideal Pakistani wife sacrifices her personal desires, minimizes conflicts, hides problems, and bears suffering for the sake of her husband and children (Abraham, 1998).

Having faith in God and their religion also contributes to Pakistani couples' reliance on individual coping. For most Pakistani men and women residing in both rural and urban settings, practicing their religion is the most important thing in their lives (Gallup Pakistan, 2009). Individuals in Pakistan rely on faith as a great source of strength in difficult times as it trains them to have patience and 'restrain' from worries, to have 'trust' in God, or Allah, to accept their circumstances as His will, and to be grateful to Allah under all circumstances (Khan, 2007). Couples frequently turn to faith and prayers along with other religious practices, seeking solace and resilience from Allah rather than each other.

Another reason for Pakistani couples often managing their stressors individually is the cultural lack of open communication between spouses, which is consistent with research on South Asian couples where less verbal and non-verbal communication has been found in couples who were arranged when compared to couples who married for love (Yelsma & Athappilly, 1998). Nevertheless, there is a high level of sharing spousal support, especially from the wife. If one spouse gets distressed, the other, usually the woman, tries to provide moral and emotional support through increased expression of love, care, and encouragement. Unlike in arranged marriages where couples build a relationship and understand each other after marriage, there is more openness in communication among Pakistani couples who marry for love as a result of their comfort and understanding of each other prior to marriage.

Non-Spousal Social Support

Couples frequently engage in relational coping, including family and extended family, in-laws, neighbors, and the community at large. Boundaries between couples and their sets of parents are often blurred within the Pakistani context (Qadir et al., 2013). Therefore, couples may turn to their parents rather than to their spouse for support to manage stress, more so due to lack of open communication with their spouses. This is truer for the women, as the man's pride in his manhood may keep him from seeking any form of help.

Families of couples generally play a positive and supportive role in helping them overcome marital stress and improving their relationships (Qadir et al., 2013), be it caused by internal conflict between the couple or some external stress. Nearly every kind of stressor among Pakistani couples, such as issues with in-laws, childcare, economic stress, etc., is likely to be coped with to some degree with a family member outside of the couple system, especially by the wife, regardless of whether it is coped with within the couple system or not. For example, it is frequent for wives to seek their mothers for support. In the case of financial support in particular, parents almost always provide financial aid if they can afford it, and siblings too may help if they can afford to. Quite often affluent members from the extended family system may also provide financial support as it is a religious duty in Islam to provide for kin, which is based strongly on the concept of charity beginning from home.

In the case of domestic violence, a Pakistani wife will likely conceal her stress due to both shame and feelings of helplessness (Babar, 2012). This is more so among educated women who may be victims of abuse, as they are acutely aware of their social image, which entails the assumption that a strong and resourceful educated woman cannot be subjected to such abuse. Furthermore, upholding the family honor, social and financial constraints, and the social stigma attached to divorce, keep women from standing up for themselves.

With fertility issues being a major stress factor for Pakistani couples, religious couples and families resort to their religious beliefs and accept not having a child as Allah's will. The less educated and the illiterate will resort to seeking help from often fraudulent holy men and women, who thrive on these couples' simplicity and ignorance, providing them with amulets and special rituals for fertility, which have no basis in Islam.

Dyadic Coping

Despite the internal and external sources of stress for couples living in Pakistan, no studies had examined their dyadic coping strategies. Given this lack of studies, one of the authors and colleagues conducted the first study on dyadic coping among Pakistani couples from a systemic transactional model (STM; Bodenmann, 1995, see Chapter 1) (Iqbal & Safdar, 2014). The study collected data from 100 married couples (N = 200 individuals). Forty-three percent of the sample ranged from 20–31 years of age, 43 percent received post-graduate education, 42 percent was married from 1 to 5 years, 63 percent had one to two children, 74 percent had arranged marriages, and 55 percent lived in a joint family system. The English version of the Dyadic Coping Inventory (DCI; Bodenmann, 2008) and the Evaluation and Nurturing Relationship Issues, Communication, and Happiness (ENRICH) Marital Satisfaction Scale (EMS; Fowers & Olson, 1993) were used to examine the relationship between dyadic coping and marital satisfaction in Pakistani couples. Dyadic coping was found to be positively associated with marital satisfaction ($r = 0.71$, $p < 0.01$). Pakistani couples who engaged in more positive dyadic coping to deal with stressors experienced greater marital satisfaction, whereas couples who used more negative dyadic coping experienced lesser marital satisfaction (see Table 13.1). Furthermore, wives (65 percent) were more likely than husbands to engage in positive dyadic coping to deal with stress whereas husbands (78 percent) were more likely to engage in negative dyadic coping. In particular, wives were more likely than husbands to engage in emotional-focused supportive dyadic coping and delegated dyadic coping. Both women and men engaged in problem-focused dyadic coping more than any other form of dyadic coping. However, these findings may not be generalizable to the population of

TABLE 13.1 Correlation between positive dyadic coping, negative dyadic coping, and marital satisfaction

	Dyadic Coping			
	Positive Dyadic Coping		*Negative Dyadic Coping*	
Marital satisfaction	*Men*	*Women*	*Men*	*Women*
Men	−.20★★	−.22★★	.23★★	.20★★
Women	−.27★★	−.28★★	.33★★	.31★★

Note. ★★ p <.01

Pakistan as they are based on a sample of mostly educated urban couples with sound socio-economic backgrounds.

The traditional gender roles typically observed among Pakistani couples can help explain the results of this research. Pakistani women, generally responsible for the care-taking of their families, may be more likely to engage in positive dyadic coping strategies in times of stress in an effort to comfort their husbands and retain harmony in the family. On the other hand, Pakistani men, raised in a patriarchal society, may be more likely to engage in negative dyadic coping as they do not generally view their role to be of providing emotional support or comfort to their families. Given the responsibility of providing for their wives, children, and often their families-of-origin too, husbands may have less tolerance and patience to support their partners in times of stress, especially after spending long hours working outside of their homes in stressful environments. Where stress is related to issues between wives and their in-laws, husbands may engage in negative coping strategies as they often find themselves in a difficult position between their wives and the husbands' families. The use of problem-focused dyadic coping more than any other form of dyadic coping could be explained by the nature of marriages in Pakistan, where most marriages are not based on the notion of love. In such marriages, emotion-focused dyadic coping may be less likely to occur. Within the social context of Pakistan where maintaining harmony within the family is important, and within the context of a politically and economically unstable country where resources are limited, couples may tend to use problem-focused dyadic coping in order to tackle their stresses and minimize them as much as possible.

Implications for Practice

Seeking help from a mental health professional is not a common practice among Pakistanis due to lack of awareness and shortage of mental health providers (Ali, 2014). However, since preliminary association has been found between dyadic coping and marital satisfaction (Iqbal & Safdar, 2014), Pakistani couples may benefit from seeking help from a professional to assist in developing and implementing positive dyadic coping skills to manage internal and external stressors and increase marital satisfaction. Understanding couples' dyadic coping processes within the context of their marital relationship (arranged, semi-arranged, or love) and within the larger context of the Pakistani society will assist mental health professionals in working with Pakistani couples. It is vital to understand the ethnic, religious, educational, socio-economic, and regional backgrounds of each partner in understanding the nature, degree, and impact of a stressor. Once a professional is able to fully appreciate the context of a stressor and the coping method used to manage it, they will be better equipped to assist the couple in exploring other forms of dyadic coping, which may be more effective.

Implications for Research

There is virtually no research on the STM approach, and coping in general, dyadic or otherwise, among couples in Pakistan. The lack of research on this topic could be attributed to the under developed mental health field, lack of government interest or support, and lack of professional resources available to couples in Pakistan (Gadit, 2006). Preliminary findings in Iqbal and Safdar (2014) suggest that the role of dyadic coping is associated with marital satisfaction among Pakistani couples, which warrants further research on this topic. It is necessary for mental health professionals and researchers to understand the type of dyadic coping strategies used by Pakistani couples, and how these strategies may vary depending on a number of factors, such as the type of stressor, gender, nature of the marriage (i.e., love, arranged, semi-arranged), age, education, and socio-economic status of the couple, in order to provide couples with more effective dyadic coping strategies to assist in increasing their marital satisfaction. Additionally, research should examine the role of dyadic coping in relation to other frequently used coping strategies among Pakistani couples, such as relying on family for support. Furthermore, studies could investigate potential associations between types of stressors and types of coping strategies (e.g., dyadic coping versus family support versus coping through prayer), and whether any of these associations vary in traditional versus modern Pakistani couples. Ideally, studies should collect longitudinal data and through both self-report and observations. Cross-cultural studies that include Pakistani samples might also show the extent to which Pakistani couples rely on dyadic coping versus other couples in the world.

Conclusion

Pakistan, predominantly a Muslim country and a patriarchal society, is rich in its cultural heritage. Marriages are arranged between men and women usually on the basis of compatibility rather than love. Stressors and coping methods among Pakistani couples can vary depending on several factors, such as ethnicity, religiosity, region, socio-economic status, and education. Couples engage in individual, dyadic, and relational coping methods depending on the type of stressor and gender of the spouse. However, very little is known about dyadic coping among Pakistani couples and a thorough exploration of this topic is needed. More research on dyadic coping would lead to identifying positive dyadic coping strategies used by couples in Pakistan and developing dyadic coping strategies which may be better suited to couples from Pakistan and other South Asian countries. Such research may lead to mental health professionals encouraging the use of more positive dyadic coping strategies among Pakistani couples, thus, increasing marital satisfaction among them (Iqbal & Safdar, 2014).

References

Abraham, M. (1998). Speaking the unspeakable: Marital violence against South Asian immigrant women in the United States. *Indian Journal of Gender Studies, 5,* 215–241.

Ali, T. (2014, July). Mental health situation in Pakistan. *Pakistan Observer.* Retrieved from www.pakobserver.net/detailnews.asp?id=247471

Ali, T. S., Krantz, G., Gul, R., Asad, N., Johansson, E., & Mogren, I. (2011). Gender roles and their influence on life prospects for women in urban Karachi, Pakistan: A qualitative study. *Global Health Action, 4,* 7448–7456.

Ayyub, R. (2000). Domestic violence in the South Asian Muslim immigrant population in the United States. *Journal of Social Distress and the Homeless, 9,* 237–248.

Babar, Q. (2012). Domestic violence—reasons for women to stay/leave an abusive relationship and the trauma attached to it. (Unpublished doctoral dissertation). University of Karachi, Karachi, Pakistan.

Batool, S. S., & Khalid, R. (2012). Emotional intelligence: A predictor of marital quality in Pakistani couples. *Pakistan Journal of Psychological Research, 27*(1), 65–88.

Blood, P. (Ed.) (1995). *Pakistan: A Country Study.* Washington: GPO for the Library of Congress.

Bodenmann, G. (1995). A systemic-transactional conceptualization of stress and coping in couples. *Swiss Journal of Psychology, 54*(1), 34–49.

Bodenmann, G. (2008). *Dyadic Coping Inventory (DCI): Test Manual.* Bern, Switzerland: Huber.

Critelli, F. M. (2012). Between law and custom: Women, family law, and marriage in Pakistan. *Journal of Comparative Family Studies, 43*(5), 673–693.

Dommaraju, P., & Jones, G. (2011). Divorce Trends in Asia. *Asian Journal of Social Science, 39,* 725–750.

Fikree, F. F., & Bhatti, L. I. (1999). Domestic violence and health of Pakistani women. *International Journal of Gynecology & Obstetrics, 65,* 195–201.

Fowers, B. J., & Olson, D. H. (1993). ENRICH Marital Satisfaction Scale: A brief research and clinical tool. *Journal of Family Psychology, 7*(2), 176–185.

Gadit, A. A. M. (2006). Mental health in Pakistan: Where do we stand? *The Journal of the Pakistan Medical Association, 56*(5).

Gallup Pakistan. (2009). *For 40 percent of Pakistanis, Practicing Religion is Very Important in Their Lives.* Gilani Research Foundation. Retrieved from www.gallup.com.pk/wp-content/uploads/2015/02/13-5-09.pdf

Gallup Pakistan. (2009). *Perspective on Gender Roles.* Gilani Research Foundation. Retrieved from www.gallup.com.pk/perspective-on-gender-roles/

Gallup Pakistan. (2010). *Views on Divorce Rate in Pakistan.* Gilani Research Foundation. Retrieved from www.gallup.com.pk/?s=divorce

Iqbal, N. & Safdar, H. (2014). Emotional stability, intimacy and dyadic coping and its relationship with marital satisfaction among love and arranged married couples. (Unpublished master's thesis). International Islamic University, Islamabad, Pakistan.

Khan, M. M. (1998). Suicide and attempted suicide in Pakistan. *Crisis, 19*(4), 172–176.

Khan, Z. H. (2007). Religiosity and coping in cancer patients. (Unpublished doctoral dissertation thesis). University of Karachi, Karachi, Pakistan.

Liu, C., Paul, E., Spector, P. E., & Shi, L. (2007). Cross-national job stress: A quantitative and qualitative study. *Journal of Organizational Behavior, 28,* 209–239.

Mir, M. (2013). Love, arranged, and in-between: Narratives of marriage in South Asian American couples (Doctoral dissertation). Retrieved from ProQuest Dissertations & Theses Global.

Mirza, I., & Jenkins, R. (2004). Risk factors, prevalence, and treatment of anxiety and depressive disorders in Pakistan: Systematic review. *British Medical Journal, 328*(7443).

Mullick, R., & Hraba, J. (2001). Ethnic attitudes in Pakistan. *International Journal of Intercultural Relations, 25*(2), 165–179.

Mumford, D. B., Minhas, F. A., Akhtar, I., Akhter, S., & Mubbashar, M. H. (2000). Stress and psychiatric disorder in urban Rawalpindi: Community survey. *British Journal of Psychiatry, 177*(6), 557–562.

Naheed, A., & Gah, S. (1997). No, I Don't: Arranged Marriages in Pakistan. *Women in Action, 2*, 24–27.

Niaz, U. (2004). Women's mental health in Pakistan. *World Psychiatry, 3*(1), 60–624.

Niaz, U., & Hassan, S. (2005). The psychosocial factors for depression in upper-middle-class urban women of Karachi. *Journal of Pakistan Psychiatric Society, 2*(2), 1–5.

Obeid, R. A. (1988). An Islamic theory of development. In T. R. Murray (Ed.), *Oriental Theories of Development*. New York: Peter Lang.

Pakistan Government. (2015). Pakistan Bureau of Statistics. Retrieved from www.pbs.gov.pk

Population Council. (2014). Pakistan 2012–13. *Studies in Family Planning, 45*(4).

Qadir, F., Khalid, A., Haqqani, S., Zill-e-Huma, & Medhin, G. (2013). The association of marital relationship and perceived social support with mental health of women in Pakistan. *BMC Public Health, 13*(1), 1150–1163.

Qadir, F., De Silva, P., Prince, M., & Khan, M. (2005). Marital satisfaction in Pakistan: A pilot investigation. *Sexual and Relationship Therapy, 20*(2), 195–209.

Quayes, S., & Ramsey, R. D. (2015). Gender disparity in education enrollment in Pakistan. *Asian Economic and Financial Review, 5*(3), 407–417.

Sarwar, A., & Aftab, H. (2011). Work stress and family imbalance in service sector of Pakistan. *International Journal of Business and Social Science, 2*(13), 250–261.

Stewart, S. M., Bond, M. H., Ho, L. M., Zaman, R. M., Dar, R., & Anwar, M. (2000). Perceptions of parents and adolescent outcomes in Pakistan. *British Journal of Developmental Psychology, 18*(3), 335–352.

Sultan, S. (2010). Marital discord: The hidden burden of infertility. *Pakistan Journal of Psychological Research, 25*(1), 31–43.

Yelsma, P., & Athappilly, K. (1988). Marital satisfaction and communication practices: Comparisons among Indian and American couples. *Journal of Comparative Family Studies, 19*(19), 37–54.

Zainab, F. Z. (2003). Marriage system and success in marriage in Pakistan. Bahria University. Retrieved from www.eprints.hec.gov.pk/2515/1/2446.htm

14

DYADIC COPING IN CHINESE COUPLES

Feng Xu and Danika N. Hiew

Introduction

China is the world's most populated country, with over 1.3 billion people (National Bureau of Statistics of China, 2013). Chinese have traditionally maintained strong family support networks (Shek, 2006). However, rapid economic development has eroded the traditional practice of extended family co-residence, with a large number of young Chinese migrating from rural areas to cities and from China to other countries (Chen, Hao, & Stephens, 2010; Ji, Xu, & Rich, 2002; Yang, 2013). In conjunction with this reduction in family support, Chinese couples are under increasing stress due to the soaring costs of urban accommodation in China (Chen et al., 2010), conflict between Western influences and traditional values (see e.g., Quek, Knudson-Marin, Rue, & Alabiso, 2010), and intergenerational stress resulting from the one child policy (Hesketh, Lu, & Xing, 2005). This means that Chinese couples have increased need for support at a time when partners are increasingly reliant on each other for support. Consequently, dyadic coping has emerged as an important issue for Chinese couples. The purpose of this chapter is to provide a reference for scholars and clinicians who wish to understand the use and appropriateness of dyadic coping for Chinese couples and do further research and practice in this area. We begin with a discussion of Chinese cultural characteristics of couple relationships and the stressors and resources available to these couples. This is followed by a presentation of the existing research on Chinese couples' dyadic coping with stress, including applications of the Systemic Transactional Model (STM; Bodenmann, 2008) to Chinese couples. Finally, implications for practice and research are discussed.

Review of the Literature

Couples' Relationships in China

Cultural Influences

To understand couples' relationships in China, it is necessary to understand the values of Confucianism and collectivism. Ethical and moral rules developed by the Chinese philosopher Confucius have influenced Chinese behavior for over 2,000 years (Huang & Grove, 2012). A central tenet of Confucian teachings was *Xian Dao* (filial piety)—the feelings of love and obligation children should have for their parents (Ebrey, 2006). Marriage was viewed as a filial duty, and failure to produce heirs was considered the worst of unfilial acts (Ebrey, 2006). Spouses resided with the husband's family and were expected to invest their energy in caring for their elders and children, rather than the couple's relationship (Shi & Wang, 2009). There is evidence that filial piety continues to be valued in Chinese cultures today. For example, in marital decision-making, Chinese place greater weight than Americans on a prospective partner's fulfillment of filial duties, and are more likely to comply with network members' wishes (Zhang & Kline, 2009).

Confucian doctrines promoted a patriarchal family system in which females obeyed their fathers, husbands and sons, and focused on domestic duties, while males provided for the family financially and glorified the family name with achievements (Huang & Grove, 2012; Lin & Ho, 2009). Although the Communist regime promoted gender equality and participation of women in the workforce (Zuo, 2003), there is evidence that traditional gender roles persist. For example, interviews with husbands and wives in Beijing revealed that the majority perceived greater domestic contributions from the wife and greater financial responsibility for the husband to be fair (Zuo & Bian, 2001).

China has been identified as a highly collectivistic culture (see Osyerman, Coon, & Kemmelmeier, 2002). Collectivistic cultures value the ability to work harmoniously within a network of interdependent relationships and fulfill one's role and obligations more highly than individual goal achievement (Markus & Kitayama, 1991; see Chapter 2). These values influence communication behavior between partners and family members. In contrast to the direct, explicit statements of thoughts and feelings which are considered good communication in Western countries, Chinese consider good communication to be *Han Xu* (contained, reserved, implicit, and indirect; Gao & Ting-Toomey, 1998). Chinese are socialized to suppress their emotions and express ideas hesitantly, in order to be able to negotiate meaning with their conversational partner and retreat if necessary to preserve relationship harmony (Gao & Ting-Toomey, 1998).

Chinese collectivistic views also shape different couple relationship standards. Couple relationship standards have been defined as beliefs about what partners and relationships should be like (Baucom, Epstein, Rankin, & Burnett, 1996).

Chinese couples have been found to place greater importance than Western couples on relations with the extended family, relational harmony, face maintenance, and traditional gender roles; whereas Western couples have been found to place greater importance than Chinese couples on intimacy and the demonstration of love and caring within couple relationships (Hiew, Halford, van de Vijver, & Liu, 2015). These differences may influence the provision of spousal support during times of stress. Research indicates that Chinese receive more informational and problem-solving support from their spouses than Americans, and Americans receive greater emotional support from their spouses than Chinese (Xu & Burleson, 2001). Compared with Americans, Chinese regard escaping and dismissing negative feelings and messages low in person-centeredness as more appropriate support strategies (Barbee & Cunningham, 1995). These findings have been attributed to a collectivistic cultural focus on avoidance of emotionality, recovery of composure, and restoration of social harmony (Burleson, 2003). In summary, in Chinese cultures, the values of Confucianism and collectivism have fostered prioritization of the family over the couple, traditional gender roles, and an emphasis on suppression of individual thoughts and emotions in order to preserve relationship harmony. These cultural influences are likely to have suppressed the use of dyadic coping by Chinese couples, particularly emotion-focused dyadic coping methods.

Stressors and Resources

Chinese couples are facing high levels of economic, environmental, and social stress. Rapid economic development over the last two decades has greatly improved Chinese living standards and quality of life (Shu & Zhu, 2009). However, this economic development has been accompanied by mass migration of rural people into the cities (Yang, 2013), with the result that urban housing has become difficult to obtain and extremely expensive (e.g., Chen et al., 2010). Family members frequently reside in separate cities in order to pursue economic advancement (Abbott & Meredith, 1994). Dangerous levels of air pollution have led to restriction of car ownership and usage in some cities (see Gan, 2003). A focus on quality improvement in state-owned enterprises has led to the practice of job shifting (transferring jobs to more highly skilled and younger workers and privatization of assets). Consequently, many urban Chinese couples are experiencing the disappointment of unrealized goals. The extent to which couples can engage in positive dyadic coping, rather than express their disappointment through recriminations towards each other or withdraw into self-focused coping strategies, may be important for relationship satisfaction and well-being.

The opening of Chinese domestic markets to Western investors in 1978 resulted in the introduction of Western values and ideas (Shek, 2006). Large numbers of young people have been inspired to pursue individualistic goals such as personal desires and interests (Shek, 2006). For example, increasing numbers of Chinese couples are engaging in non-traditional forms of marriage, such as marriage without children, naked marriages (getting married without any fixed assets), and flash marriages (engagement when the partners have known each other for less than three months). Extra-marital affairs are increasing (Zhang & Beck, 1999) and China's divorce rate has steadily risen over the past decade and now surpasses the marriage rate (Ministry of Civil Affairs of PRC, 2013). Dual-career couples are now the majority in urban areas, with the result that the division of household labor is gradually becoming more egalitarian (Zhang et al., 2013). Despite these developments, there is evidence that collectivistic and Confucian values such as relationship harmony, filial piety, and fulfillment of traditional gender roles remain important to Chinese couples (Quek et al., 2010; Zhang & Kline, 2009; Zuo & Bian, 2001). Therefore, couples can experience a push-and-pull conflict between Chinese and Western influences (see e.g. Quek et al., 2010). This could place the couple relationship under great stress, particularly if partners are unable to work together to resolve this conflict in a mutually satisfactory way, or there is family pressure to adhere to traditional ways.

In 1978, the Chinese government launched a population control policy of restricting urban couples to only one child. This molded the majority of families into a '4–2-1' structure (four grandparents, two parents, one child; Hesketh et al., 2005). This demographic shift has produced severe intergenerational stress for young urban Chinese couples, who must bear the responsibilities of caring for their child and four parents without sibling assistance (Hesketh et al., 2005). In addition, the hopes and expectations of two families are placed on one child, resulting in pressure for the child to succeed, over-indulgence of the child, and a child-focused life for the couple (Epstein et al., 2014).

In summary, in recent years China has undergone enormous social, environmental, and economic change, particularly in urban areas. These changes have resulted in young, urban Chinese couples facing the stressors of reduced family support; greater parental expectations; conflict between Chinese and Western cultural influences; difficulty obtaining housing, transport, and employment; and a large discrepancy between aspirations and achievements.

The large number of stressors faced by modern Chinese couples (described above) have led to research interest in Chinese couples' coping. This research has generally focused on the relationship outcomes of particular types of stressors, and individual coping processes, rather than dyadic coping processes. For example, economic stress (Lam, 2011) and work-family conflict (Zhang et al., 2013) have been found to be negatively associated with Chinese couples' relationship satisfaction. Chinese couples with lower quality marital and parent-child relationships report poorer physical and psychological health (Shek, 1996). Post-natal depression is more common in mainland Chinese couples with one depressed partner, lower social support, and higher perceived stress (Gao, Chan, & Mao, 2009). Decreased relationship satisfaction has been noted as occurring in Chinese couples after life crises (unanticipated situations that require change in family life), but not after life transitions (normative developmental changes in the family or family members; Chi et al., 2011). Greater perceived control (for female partners) and greater availability of social support have been found to buffer the adverse effect of life crises on Chinese couples' relationship satisfaction. Despite these demonstrations of adverse effects of stress on Chinese couple functioning, a culturally specific positive effect of stress on Chinese couples has been identified. Chinese husbands' sacrifices for the family and financial contributions appear to elicit higher levels of *enqing*—feelings of admiration and gratitude towards one's spouse—in their wives when the family has been under higher levels of stress (Chen & Li, 2007).

The research described above did not examine dyadic coping processes. However, using the STM, we can speculate that in a culture in which financially supporting the family is considered a male responsibility (Zhang & Kline, 2009), economic stress may be appraised by some spouses as a personal failure of the husband. This may lead to use of negative dyadic coping strategies such as criticism by the wife and withdrawal by the husband, and relationship deterioration. Conflict between the demands of work and family life may similarly provoke relationship-deteriorating coping behavior due to traditional gender roles. Wives' careers may not be considered important for the family, and therefore, wives struggling to balance work with family duties may not receive supportive and delegated dyadic coping from their husbands. If this occurs, wives are likely to negatively appraise their husband's appraisals of the situation and a vicious cycle of negative coping behavior and relationship deterioration may ensue. When husbands experience stress about work-family balance, a desire to uphold Confucian values may lead the couple to set unrealistic goals such as freeing the husband to focus only on his career, resulting in excessive amounts of delegated dyadic coping by the wife and increasing strain on the couple relationship.

The previously described research finding that the stress of low quality family relationships leads to poorer physical and psychological health can also be understood from an STM perspective. In a collectivistic culture where the ability to maintain harmonious relationships is prized above individual achievements (Markus & Kitayama, 1991), relationship problems seem likely to be appraised particularly negatively. When the couple relationship is problematic, negative dyadic coping seems likely to occur and exacerbate the situation. Similarly, when one partner is depressed, negative appraisals and negative dyadic coping are more likely to occur during the stressful early days of child-rearing, triggering post-natal depression in the other partner. Of note, the identification (in the research reported above) of a negative effect of lack of wider social support for the couple suggests that addition of the relationship network of the couple to the STM may be useful for understanding the effects of stress in collectivistic cultures. The utility of inclusion of the relationship network is supported by the finding (reported above) that greater social support buffers the adverse effect of life crises on Chinese couples' relationship satisfaction.

As reported above, the stress of unanticipated life crises has been found to have negative effects on Chinese couples, but the stress of normative developmental changes in the family has not. A possible explanation from an STM perspective is that Chinese couples may appraise normative changes positively, as part of the collective experience of family life. The normative nature of such stressors may also make goal-setting and dyadic coping easier for the couple due to the presence of cultural scripts for coping positively with such situations. The positive effect of high levels of stress on *enqing* also supports the importance of appraisals of stressors.

The above consideration of existing research from the perspective of the STM suggests that this model could provide insight into the associations between stressors and Chinese couple relationship outcomes. However, this model has not been explicitly tested with Chinese couples. Therefore, we conducted the first study on dyadic coping by Chinese couples and examined the associations between dyadic coping and relationship satisfaction.

Application of the STM to Chinese Couples

Participants in the current study were 474 couples (N = 948 individuals) recruited in urban (Beijing and Guangzhou) and rural areas of China (e.g., some counties of Guangdong and Jiangxi provinces).[1] Husbands' average age was 36.5 years (SD = 7.7), while wives' average age was 34.4 years (SD = 7.3). Couples had an average of one child (SD = 0.66, range = 0 to 3), and the average relationship duration was 9.4 years (SD = 7.9). Couples were mailed two copies of the Chinese translations of the Relationship Assessment Scale (RAS; Hendrick, S., Dicke, & Hendrick, C., 1998) and the Dyadic Coping Inventory (DCI; Bodenmann, 2008). The Chinese translation of the DCI has been validated by Xu and colleagues (in press), who demonstrated measurement invariance across genders (Chinese men and women) and cultures (China, Switzerland and the U.S.); convergent and discriminant validity of test scores; and good reliability of sub-scale and aggregated scale scores. Partners were instructed that they should complete their measures alone and mail them back separately from their partner's measures.

Dyadic Coping in Younger vs. Older Couples

Participants were separated into older (over 35 years) and younger (less than 35 years) age groups. *T*-tests were used to compare the DCI scores of older and younger husbands and older and younger wives (see Table 14.1). Notably, there was no significant difference between older and younger husbands' scores on any dyadic coping behavior. However, in comparison with younger wives, older wives reported lower levels of stress communication by self, problem-focused supportive dyadic coping by their partner, problem-focused common dyadic coping, total common dyadic coping and total dyadic coping, and higher levels of delegated dyadic coping by self. As discussed earlier in this chapter, traditional Chinese values emphasize suppression of thoughts and emotions in order to preserve relationship harmony. These values are likely to be held most strongly by older wives, whose ways of behaving in their relationships were established before China's doors opened to Western influences. Therefore, older wives may engage in less talk during stressful times and instead, demonstrate their support in practical ways such as by taking on their partner's tasks. They may not expect their husband to support them emotionally by talking through problems and their husbands may be less likely to do so, due to the more traditional values of their generation. The absence of age differences among husbands may be due to lack of generational change in males' values regarding the spousal relationship, possibly due to the greater gains for husbands of adherence to traditional gender roles, or reluctance by younger husbands to report engagement in dyadic coping behaviors that are not part of the traditional masculine role in China. Given that Chinese couples ($M = 3.54$) reported lower relationship satisfaction than Western samples (e.g., $M = 4.46$ for U.S. samples, Xu et al., in press), it may be that Chinese husbands and wives across the lifespan could benefit from higher levels of dyadic coping.

Dyadic Coping in Urban vs. Rural Couples

There are large differences in living standards and sources of stress between urban and rural areas in China that may be associated with differences in coping behaviors (Hesketh et al., 2005). Therefore, the dyadic coping behaviors of couples residing in major cities, other urban areas and rural areas were compared. There were significant regional differences in dyadic coping for both husbands and wives (see Table 14.2). Compared with husbands in urban areas, husbands in rural areas reported lower emotion-focused and problem-focused supportive dyadic coping by self, stress communication by partner, emotion-focused and problem-focused supportive dyadic coping by partner, negative dyadic coping by partner, problem-focused common dyadic coping, total common dyadic coping, and total overall dyadic coping. Wives in rural areas reported lower levels of problem-focused supportive dyadic coping by self and higher levels of negative dyadic coping by self than urban wives. These results may be explained by the higher levels of education and exposure to Western ideas and ways of living among urban Chinese. Traditional values regarding communication and gender roles are likely to be stronger among rural Chinese and may inhibit their ability to engage in many of the dyadic coping behaviors. Rural wives' higher levels of negative dyadic coping may also be due to greater endorsement of traditional values. As noted earlier in this chapter, the provision of support in collectivistic cultures is aimed at restoration of social composure. Therefore, rural wives may criticize their husbands' coping in an attempt to motivate them to compose themselves and behave in the culturally approved manner.

TABLE 14.1 Age differences in dyadic coping behaviors

Age differences for husbands	Older		Younger		t-test	
DCI scales	M	SD	M	SD	p	d
Oneself						
Stress communication	3.027	0.68	3.19	0.66	0.19	0.06
Emotion-focused SDC	3.53	0.72	3.60	0.77	0.34	0.04
Problem-focused SDC	3.57	0.67	3.54	0.69	0.71	0.01
Delegated DC	3.51	0.66	3.50	0.72	0.90	0.00
Negative DC	2.41	0.80	2.40	0.89	0.93	0.00
Partner						
Stress communication	3.37	0.65	3.41	0.70	0.48	0.03
Emotion-focused SDC	3.40	0.78	3.44	0.82	0.64	0.02
Problem-focused SDC	3.37	0.73	3.31	0.81	0.38	0.04
Delegated DC	3.38	0.81	3.27	0.85	0.15	0.07
Negative DC	2.42	0.76	2.41	0.87	0.84	0.01
Common						
Emotion-focused CDC	3.57	0.71	3.63	0.72	0.36	0.04
Problem-focused CDC	3.24	0.83	3.34	0.82	0.17	0.06
Total DC	3.19	0.36	3.19	0.39	0.19	0.06
Age differences for wives						
Oneself						
Stress communication	3.29	0.78	3.51	0.71	**0.00**	0.14
Emotion-focused SDC	3.47	0.73	3.51	0.78	0.57	0.03
Problem-focused SDC	3.36	0.74	3.41	0.76	0.51	0.03
Delegated DC	3.52	0.69	3.34	0.71	**0.01**	0.12
Negative DC	2.33	0.80	2.42	0.90	0.31	0.05
Partner						
Stress communication	3.17	0.78	3.24	0.70	0.36	0.04
Emotion-focused SDC	3.25	0.87	3.37	0.83	0.14	0.07
Problem-focused SDC	3.29	0.81	3.48	0.77	**0.01**	0.12
Delegated DC	3.24	0.81	3.35	0.79	0.14	0.07
Negative DC	2.47	0.78	2.46	0.85	0.87	0.01
Common						
Emotion-focused CDC	3.56	0.75	3.65	0.65	0.18	0.06
Problem-focused CDC	3.01	0.91	3.29	0.88	**0.00**	0.15
Total DC	3.10	0.41	3.19	0.39	**0.02**	0.11

Notes. DC = dyadic coping, SDC = supportive dyadic coping, CDC = common dyadic coping. Bold numbers are significant at $p < 0.001$. Couples rated dyadic coping behaviors on a 5-point Likert scale (1 = *not at all/very rarely* to 5 = *very often*). There were different numbers of participants in each group: Older husbands $n = 198$, younger husbands $n = 276$, older wives $n = 150$, younger wives $n = 324$.

TABLE 14.2 Regional differences in dyadic coping behaviors

Regional differences for husbands	Urban areas		Rural areas		t-test	
DCI scales	M	SD	M	SD	p	d
Oneself						
Stress communication	3.25	0.65	3.13	0.73	0.14	0.07
Emotion-focused SDC	3.61	0.72	3.39	0.82	**0.01**	0.12
Problem-focused SDC	3.59	0.69	3.38	0.66	**0.01**	0.12
Delegated DC	3.52	0.70	3.44	0.68	0.31	0.05
Negative DC	2.39	0.88	2.45	0.75	0.58	0.03
Partner						
Stress communication	3.44	0.66	3.19	0.71	**0.00**	0.14
Emotion-focused SDC	3.46	0.79	3.26	0.81	**0.04**	0.10
Problem-focused SDC	3.38	0.77	3.13	0.76	**0.01**	0.13
Delegated DC	3.33	0.86	3.23	0.72	0.28	0.05
Negative DC	2.38	0.83	2.59	0.79	**0.03**	0.09
Common						
Emotion-focused CDC	3.63	0.71	3.51	0.72	0.15	0.07
Problem-focused CDC	3.34	0.81	3.13	0.88	**0.03**	0.10
Total DC	3.21	0.37	3.11	0.42	**0.03**	0.10
Regional differences for wives						
Oneself						
Stress communication	3.46	0.74	3.36	0.73	0.24	0.05
Emotion-focused SDC	3.50	0.77	3.47	0.71	0.68	0.02
Problem-focused SDC	3.42	0.75	3.30	0.76	0.18	0.06
Delegated DC	3.41	0.70	3.32	0.72	0.27	0.05
Negative DC	2.37	0.87	2.47	0.88	0.35	0.04
Partner						
Stress communication	3.23	0.72	3.15	0.75	0.32	0.05
Emotion-focused SDC	3.33	0.85	3.34	0.83	0.87	0.00
Problem-focused SDC	3.43	0.80	3.38	0.70	0.60	0.02
Delegated DC	3.31	0.78	3.33	0.88	0.84	0.01
Negative DC	2.44	0.83	2.53	0.82	0.41	0.03
Common						
Emotion-focused CDC	3.62	0.69	3.62	0.65	0.98	0.00
Problem-focused CDC	3.20	0.89	3.20	0.94	0.98	0.00
Total DC	3.17	0.39	3.15	0.42	0.77	0.01

Notes. DC = dyadic coping, SDC = supportive dyadic coping, CDC = common dyadic coping. Bold numbers are significant at $p < 0.001$. Couples rated dyadic coping behaviors on a 5-point Likert scale (1 = *not at all/very rarely* to 5 = *very often*). There were different numbers of participants in each group: Urban husbands $n = 386$, rural husbands $n = 88$, urban wives $n = 386$, rural wives $n = 88$.

Dyadic Coping According to Income Level

Although the income of Chinese citizens has improved greatly, the average Chinese cannot afford to buy a house, which is considered an important step towards starting a family, or a car, or other highly priced consumer products (Chen et al., 2010). The financial stress is likely to be greater for Chinese couples with lower incomes, and therefore they may require higher levels of dyadic coping skills. To investigate this, three groups were compared: A high monthly income group (income above or equal to RMB10,001, which is approximately US$1,600), a medium monthly income group (above RMB2,001 or approximately US$335), and a low monthly income group (below RMB2,001 or approximately US$335). Results are presented in Table 14.3. Wives' reported dyadic coping did not differ between income groups. However, post hoc tests revealed that there were significant differences in use of problem-focused supportive dyadic coping by self (lower for high income) and delegated dyadic coping by self (lower for high income) between husbands of different income levels. This indicates that husbands with higher incomes were less likely than husbands with lower incomes to take on tasks to help their partner or support their partner by helping her to see the problem in a different light. It may be that husbands with higher incomes feel that they are fulfilling their culturally-prescribed duties to the family, and therefore do not need to provide other forms of support to their wives. Alternatively, it may be that husbands with lower incomes are engaging in higher levels of dyadic coping because these couples are facing higher levels of stress.

Dyadic Coping and Relationship Satisfaction

The association between use of dyadic coping strategies and relationship satisfaction was examined using the RAS. Participants responded to the seven items of this measure using a scale ranging from 1 (low) to 5 (high). The internal consistency of the Chinese translation was good for men (α =0.88) and women (α =0.92). As illustrated in Table 14.4, total dyadic coping scores and scores on all sub-scales of the DCI except negative dyadic coping by self and partner predicted relationship satisfaction. Effect sizes were moderate and the variance in relationship satisfaction explained by the scales ranged from 16 percent to 23 percent. Common dyadic coping explained the most variance in relationship satisfaction (23 percent for husbands and 22 percent for wives), suggesting that this may be the most important dyadic coping behavior for Chinese couples' satisfaction. Wives' dyadic coping behaviors explained more variance than those of husbands, suggesting that the behavior of wives during times of stress may be more important for couples' satisfaction than that of husbands. Common dyadic coping may be the most relationship-enhancing coping strategy for Chinese couples

TABLE 14.3 Differences in dyadic coping behaviors according to income level

Differences for husbands	High		Medium		Low		ANOVA	
DCI scales	M	SD	M	SD	M	SD	p	$\acute{\omega}^2$
Oneself								
Stress communication	3.39	0.69	3.45	0.77	3.46	0.60	0.78	−0.00
Emotion-focused SDC	3.47	0.73	3.50	0.79	3.51	0.58	0.92	−0.00
Problem-focused SDC	3.21	0.70	3.45	0.67	3.30	0.81	**0.01**	0.01
Delegated DC	3.22	0.76	3.45	0.67	3.30	0.79	**0.01**	0.01
Negative DC	2.46	0.89	2.38	0.88	2.34	0.76	0.68	−0.00
Partner								
Stress communication	3.14	0.67	3.24	0.76	3.17	0.61	0.48	−0.00
Emotion-focused SDC	3.28	0.79	3.34	0.87	3.38	0.76	0.81	−0.00
Problem-focused SDC	3.47	0.70	3.43	0.80	3.26	0.79	0.34	0.00
Delegated DC	3.41	0.75	3.30	0.83	3.21	0.67	0.33	0.00
Negative DC	2.47	0.87	2.44	0.82	2.59	0.81	0.57	−0.00
Common								
Emotion-focused CDC	3.61	0.65	3.63	0.69	3.55	0.74	0.80	−0.00
Problem-focused CDC	3.12	0.98	3.24	0.86	3.04	0.94	0.25	0.00
Total DC	3.14	0.40	3.18	0.40	3.12	0.31	0.56	0.00
Differences for wives								
Oneself								
Stress communication	3.25	0.57	3.24	0.68	3.45	0.38	0.72	−0.00
Emotion-focused SDC	3.40	0.69	3.58	0.73	3.17	0.66	0.24	0.00
Problem-focused SDC	3.41	0.60	3.55	0.69	3.62	0.70	0.25	0.00
Delegated DC	3.42	0.67	3.52	0.69	3.47	0.75	0.57	−0.00
Negative DC	2.53	0.73	2.40	0.85	2.35	0.92	0.53	−0.00
Partner								
Stress communication	3.32	0.57	3.39	0.68	3.44	0.75	0.63	−0.00
Emotion-focused SDC	3.37	0.72	3.44	0.79	3.37	0.88	0.69	−0.00

continued . . .

TABLE 14.3 Continued

Differences for husbands	High		Medium		Low		ANOVA	
DCI scales	M	SD	M	SD	M	SD	p	ὦ²
Partner continued . . .								
Problem-focused SDC	3.34	0.75	3.34	0.78	3.30	0.79	0.91	−0.00
Delegated DC	3.30	0.77	3.35	0.82	3.16	0.92	0.18	0.00
Negative DC	2.49	0.73	2.43	0.83	2.35	0.84	0.61	−0.00
Common								
Emotion-focused CDC	3.55	0.63	3.63	0.71	3.55	0.78	0.55	−0.00
Problem-focused CDC	3.24	0.86	3.30	0.80	3.32	0.91	0.88	−0.00
Total DC	3.17	0.32	3.20	0.38	3.16	0.42	0.65	−0.00

Notes. DC = dyadic coping, SDC = supportive dyadic coping, CDC = common dyadic coping. Bold numbers are significant at $p < 0.001$. Couples rated dyadic coping behaviors on a 5-point Likert scale (1 = not at all/very rarely to 5 = very often). There were different numbers of participants in each group: Husbands with high ($n = 93$), medium ($n = 340$), and low ($n = 41$) income; and wives with high ($n = 45$), medium ($n = 348$) and low ($n = 81$) income.

because collectivistic cultures place a high value on working harmoniously within a network of relationships. Wives' support behaviors may have greater impact on the couple's relationship satisfaction because as delineated in the STM, appraisals of the partner's coping are an important determinant of outcomes. Since Chinese women's culturally defined role is to support their husbands, dyadic coping behaviors by wives are likely to be appraised particularly positively by both partners and the absence of these is likely to provoke further distress and disappointment.

In summary, our administration of the DCI to mainland Chinese couples revealed generational, regional, and socio-economic group differences suggestive of an inhibitory effect of traditional values on dyadic coping behaviors. That is, lower levels of many of the dyadic coping behaviors were reported by rural husbands and wives, and older wives, whose values are likely to be more traditional than those of younger and urban Chinese. Husbands with higher incomes (who may be considered to be fulfilling their traditional provider role) were less likely than husbands with lower incomes to do their partner's tasks or help her to see a problem in a different light. However, higher levels of dyadic coping were associated with higher relationship satisfaction, particularly dyadic coping by wives.

TABLE 14.4 Prediction of Chinese couples' relationship satisfaction from dyadic coping behaviors

DCI scales	Husbands n = 474					Wives n = 474				
	ΔR^2	B	SE	β	p	ΔR^2	B	SE	β	p
Oneself										
Stress communication	0.06	0.13	0.02	0.24	**0.00**	0.10	0.15	0.02	0.31	**0.00**
Emotion-focused SDC	0.08	0.14	0.02	0.29	**0.00**	0.10	0.14	0.02	0.30	**0.00**
Problem-focused SDC	0.06	0.13	0.02	0.25	**0.00**	0.05	0.11	0.02	0.23	**0.00**
Delegated DC	0.06	0.12	0.02	0.24	**0.00**	0.03	0.09	0.02	0.18	**0.00**
Negative DC	0.01	−0.04	0.02	0.10	0.03	0.00	−0.01	0.02	0.03	0.54
Partner										
Stress communication	0.06	0.13	0.02	0.25	**0.00**	0.10	0.16	0.02	0.32	**0.00**
Emotion-focused SDC	0.11	0.15	0.02	0.33	**0.00**	0.14	0.16	0.02	0.37	**0.00**
Problem-focused SDC	0.07	0.12	0.02	0.27	**0.00**	0.09	0.14	0.02	0.30	**0.00**
Delegated DC	0.06	0.10	0.02	0.25	**0.00**	0.07	0.12	0.02	0.27	**0.00**
Negative DC	0.00	−0.03	0.02	0.08	0.06	0.00	−0.03	0.02	0.09	0.05
Common										
Emotion-focused CDC	0.14	0.18	0.02	0.37	**0.00**	0.13	0.20	0.02	0.37	**0.00**
Problem-focused CDC	0.23	0.20	0.01	0.46	**0.00**	0.18	0.17	0.02	0.43	**0.00**
Total										
DC total by Oneself	0.06	0.22	0.04	0.24	**0.00**	0.09	0.26	0.04	0.30	**0.00**
DC total by Partner	0.08	0.22	0.04	0.28	**0.00**	0.11	0.27	0.03	0.33	**0.00**
Total score of CDC	0.23	0.26	0.02	0.48	**0.00**	0.22	0.26	0.02	0.46	**0.00**
Total DC	0.16	0.36	0.04	0.39	**0.00**	0.20	0.41	0.04	0.44	**0.00**

Notes. DC = dyadic coping, SDC = supportive dyadic coping, CDC = common dyadic coping. Bold numbers are significant at $p < 0.001$. Couples rated dyadic coping behaviors on a 5-point Likert scale (1 = *not at all/very rarely* to 5 = *very often*). SE = standard error.

Implications for Practice

The research presented above has implications for couple therapists and relationship educators working with Chinese couples around the world who have been influenced by their heritage culture. The extent of this influence should be assessed at the commencement of therapy in order to determine the appropriateness of cultural adaptations. Stress is likely to be communicated indirectly in Chinese couple relationships due to the cultural emphasis on *Han Xu*. Although Chinese partners are likely to be more skilled in perception and interpretation of indirect communication than Western partners due to socialization in this communication style (see Chapter 2), there is still risk of misinterpretation. As discussed previously, Chinese are more likely to respond to support seeking with dismissal and escape from the negative feelings. However, perception of these responses as appropriate support strategies may reduce negative appraisals of such responses and lessen their negative impact on the couple relationship. In addition, a lower value on intimacy and greater valuing of face maintenance may reduce the likelihood of Chinese couples engaging in emotion-focused supportive dyadic coping. However, low levels of emotion-focused supportive dyadic coping may have a greater positive impact on Chinese partners than Western partners, because such behavior may be perceived as a greater support effort by the partner. These issues need to be considered when conceptualizing Chinese couples' responses to stress using the STM.

When working with couples in Mainland China, practitioners need to be aware of the stressors that the rapid pace of development has placed upon couples. In addition, Mainland Chinese couples appear to engage in relatively low levels of dyadic coping, particularly those from demographic backgrounds that indicate greater exposure to traditional Chinese values and lower exposure to Western values. This suggests that these couples face barriers to use of dyadic coping that need to be understood and overcome if the couple's current approach to stress is adversely affecting their relationship and well-being, potentially through re-appraisal of the meaning of dyadic coping. The positive association between dyadic coping and relationship satisfaction in Mainland Chinese couples suggests that they may benefit from learning about dyadic coping strategies, particularly common dyadic coping, which we found to be the best predictor of satisfaction. To increase engagement in common dyadic coping, couples could be encouraged to appraise stressors as concerning both partners and primarily caused by external conditions. This is compatible with the known Chinese tendency to engage in external attributions and perceive relationship partners as interdependent (Nisbett, 2003). Such an approach would be applicable to Chinese partners of all age groups and socio-economic backgrounds.

Couple therapy has only been practiced in China for two decades (Miller & Fang, 2012) and is therefore not an established pathway for seeking relationship assistance in Mainland China. Revelation of negative information about the family to outsiders is considered disloyal (Shi & Wang, 2009). Therefore, couples tend to seek professional help only when their situation is severe and shame may prevent them from fully disclosing their problems (Shi & Wang, 2009). This means that stress is likely to be a relevant issue for all couples seeking therapy and negative dyadic coping may not be disclosed. Accordingly, assessment of dyadic coping in a non-confrontational way, such as by use of self-report measures such as the DCI (Xu et al., in press), is an important part of intake assessment. Since education is highly valued by Chinese (Huang & Grove, 2012), relationship education programs may provide a socially acceptable way for Chinese couples to access professional relationship assistance.

Couples Coping Enhancement Training (CCET; Bodenmann & Shantinath, 2004) is a relationship education program which has been demonstrated to reduce marital distress and increase marital satisfaction in Western couples, and therefore may be beneficial for Chinese. However, we recommend caution when delivering the content designed to strengthen explicit communication about stress, including emotional self-disclosure and emotion-focused support. Educators should not imply that traditional Chinese ways of communicating and providing support are incorrect, since these are untested in research, and this may lead to feelings of invalidation and rejection of the program. Instead, educators could present CCET techniques as strategies couples could add to their repertoire of stress management approaches. Educators may need to explain the positive purposes that explicit communication strategies can serve, since Chinese communication norms may lead participants to interpret these negatively. CCET also encourages couples to establish boundaries around their relationship. Research has demonstrated lower desire for boundaries around the couple relationship among Chinese couples compared to Western couples (Epstein, Chen, & Beyder-Kamjou, 2005). Therefore, educators need to assist Chinese couples to identify a mutually satisfactory level of separation from the extended family and allow this to be low if partners' reports indicate that this is functional for them.

Implications for Research

Research findings suggest that younger age (for women), urban residence, and lower financial contribution to the household by the male partner are associated with more frequent use of dyadic coping. As discussed above, lower endorsement of traditional Chinese values is a potential cause of the more frequent dyadic coping of these groups. The associations between traditional Chinese values, Western values, socio-economic variables, and dyadic coping would be an interesting topic for further research. These socio-economic differences in dyadic coping also highlight the importance of recruiting couples from a variety of age groups, locations, and income levels, particularly in a country with vast geographic differences such as China. If the present research had recruited only young urban couples, a falsely high use of dyadic coping by Chinese couples would have been found.

Couples in the present research reported low relationship satisfaction. Despite this truncated range, we found associations between dyadic coping and relationship satisfaction, and between dyadic coping and age, location, and income level. However, future research with a wide range of satisfaction levels may reveal more and stronger associations. Furthermore, the cross-sectional design of the current study could not identify the direction of causality between dyadic coping behaviors and relationship satisfaction. Longitudinal studies are required to determine whether higher dyadic coping leads to higher relationship satisfaction or whether the reverse or both are true. Assessment of socio-demographic variables in longitudinal research could also provide data on the associations between the rapid economic developments in China and couple relationship processes. Research indicating that external social support plays an important role in Chinese couples' coping with stress suggests an extension of the STM to include the network of relationships within which the couple exists. Future studies could examine whether such a model explains a greater proportion of variance in collectivistic couples' satisfaction.

Conclusion

In conclusion, Chinese couples face a number of stressors due to the pressures of a rapidly developing economy (Chen et al., 2010) and conflict between Chinese and Western values (Quek et al., 2010). This chapter has described ways in which the STM may explain associations between stressors and Chinese couple relationship outcomes found in past research, and presented the first study of age, location, and income level differences in dyadic coping in China. Demographic differences in dyadic coping suggest potential cultural barriers to the use of dyadic coping strategies and the need to assist distressed couples to re-appraise the use of such strategies. The prediction of Chinese spouses' relationship satisfaction from dyadic coping suggests that educating Chinese couples about the use of these strategies may have powerful effects on their subjective well-being. These effects seem likely to become stronger with time, as the influence of Western values and lifestyle increases.

Note

1   Data were collected as part of a larger project entitled *An Investigation of Dyadic Coping in Chinese Couples* supported by China Scholarship Council and University of Zurich.

References

Abbott, D. A., & Meredith, W. (1994). Unintended marital separation in the Peoples Republic of China: A pilot study. *Journal of Comparative Family Studies*, 25(2), 269–277.
Barbee, A. P., & Cunningham, M. R. (1995). An experimental approach to social support communications: Interactive coping in close relationships. In B. R. Burleson (Ed.), *Communication Yearbook 18* (pp. 381–413). Thousand Oaks, CA: Sage.

Baucom, D. H., Epstein, N., Rankin, L. A., & Burnett, C. K. (1996). Assessing relationship standards: The Inventory of Specific Relationship Standards. *Journal of Family Psychology*, *10*, 72–88.

Bodenmann, G. (2008). *Dyadisches Coping Inventar (DCI)*. [*Dyadic Coping Inventory Manual, DCI*]. Bern/Göttingen: Huber/Hogrefe Tests.

Bodenmann, G., & Shantinath, S. D. (2004). The Couples Coping Enhancement Training (CCET): A new approach to prevention of marital distress based upon stress and coping. *Family Relations, 53*(5), 477–484.

Burleson, B. R. (2003). Emotional support skills. In J. O. Greene & B. R. Burleson (Eds.), *Handbook of communication and social interaction skills* (pp. 551–594). Mahwah, NJ: Erlbaum.

Chen, F. M., & Li, T. S. (2007). Marital enqing: An examination of its relationship to spousal contributions, sacrifices, and family stress in Chinese marriages. *The Journal of Social Psychology, 147*(4), 393–412.

Chen, J., Hao, Q., & Stephens, M. (2010). Assessing housing affordability for post-reform China: A case study of Shanghai. *Housing Studies, 25*(6), 877–901.

Chi, P., Tsang, S. K. M., Chan, K. S., Xiang. X., Yip. P. S. F., Cheung, Y. T., & Zhang, X. (2011). Marital satisfaction of Chinese under stress: Moderating effects of personal control and social support. *Asian Journal of Social Psychology, 14*(1), 15–25.

Ebrey, P. (2006). Confucianism. In D. S. Browning, M. C. Green, & J. Witte Jr, (Eds.), *Sex, marriage, and family in world religions* (pp. 367–450). New York: Columbia University Press.

Epstein, N. B., Chen. F., & Beyder-Kamjou, I. (2005). Relationship standards and martial satisfaction in Chinese and American couples. *Journal of Marital and Family Therapy, 31*, 454–465.

Epstein, N. B., Curtis, S. D., Edwards, E., Young, L. J., & Zheng, L. (2014). Therapy with families in China: Cultural factors influencing the therapeutic alliance and therapy goals. *Contemporary Family Therapy, 36*(2), 201–212.

Gan, L. (2003). Globalization of the automobile industry in China: Dynamics and barriers in greening of the road transportation. *Energy Policy, 31*(6), 537–551.

Gao, G., & Ting-Toomey, S. (1998). *Communicating effectively with the Chinese*. Thousand Oaks, CA: Sage Publications.

Gao, L. L., Chan, S, W., & Mao, Q. (2009). Depression, perceived stress, and social support among first-time Chinese mothers and fathers in the postpartum period. *Research in Nursing and Health, 32*(1), 50–58.

Hendrick, S. S., Dicke, A., & Hendrick, C. (1998). The Relationship Assessment Scale. *Journal of Social and Personal Relationships, 15*(1), 137–142.

Hesketh, T., Lu, L., & Xing, Z. W. (2005). The effect of China's one-child family policy after 25 years. *New England Journal of Medicine, 353*(11), 1171–1176.

Hiew, D. N., Halford, W. K., van de Vijver, F. J. R., & Liu, S. (2015). Relationship standards and satisfaction in Chinese, Western and intercultural Chinese-Western couples in Australia. *Journal of Cross-Cultural Psychology, 46*(5), 684–701.

Huang, G. H. C., & Grove, M. (2012). Confucianism and Chinese families: Values and practices in education. *International Journal of Humanities and Social Science, 2*(3), 10–14.

Ji, J., Xu, X., & Rich, S. L. (2002). Determinants of family life satisfaction in reforming China. *International Journal of Comparative Sociology, 43*(2), 169–191.

Lam, M. C. (2011). Psychological stress and parenting behavior among Chinese families: Findings from a study on parent education for economically disadvantaged families. *Social Indicators Research, 100*(3), 451–462.

Lin, L. H., & Ho, Y. L. (2009). Confucian Dynamism, culture and ethical changes in Chinese societies: A comparative study of China, Taiwan, and Hong Kong. *International Journal of Human Resource Management, 20*(11), 2402–2417.

Markus, H. R., & Kitayama, S. (1991). Culture and the self: Implications for cognition, emotion, and motivation. *Psychological Review, 98*(2), 224–253.

Miller, J. K., & Fang, X. (2012). Marriage and family therapy in the People's Republic of China: Current issues and challenges. *Journal of Family Psychotherapy, 23*, 173–183.

Ministry of Civil Affairs of PRC. (2013). Statistic on divorce rates in 2013. Beijing: Chinese Statistics Publisher. Retrieved from www.mca.gov.cn/article/sj/

Nisbett, R. E. (2003). *The geography of thought: How Asians and Westerners think differently . . . and why.* New York: Free Press.

Nolan, P., & Xiacquiang, W. (1999). Beyond privatization: Institutional innovation and growth in China's large state-owned enterprises. *World Development, 27*(1), 169–200.

Oyserman, D., Coon, H. M., & Kemmelmeier, M. (2002). Rethinking individualism and collectivism: Evaluation of theoretical assumptions and meta-analyses. *Psychological Bulletin, 128*, 3–72.

Quek, K. M., Knudson-Martin, C., Rue, D., & Alabiso, C. (2010). Relational harmony: A new model of collectivism and gender equality among Chinese American couples. *Journal of Family Issues, 31*(3), 358–380.

Shek, D. T. L. (1996). Perceptions of the value of children in Chinese parents in Hong Kong. *Journal of Psychology, 130*(5), 561–569.

Shek, D. T. L. (2006). Chinese family research: Puzzles, paradigms, and policy implications. *Journal of Family Issues, 27*(3), 275–284.

Shi, L., & Wang, L. (2009). A multilevel contextual model for couples from mainland China. In M. Rastogi & V. Thomas (Eds.), *Couple therapy with ethnic minorities* (pp. 297–318). Thousand Oaks, CA: Sage Publications.

Shu, X., & Zhu, Y. (2009). The quality of life in China. *Social Indicators Research, 92*(2), 191–225.

Xu, F., Hilpert, P., Randall, A. K., Li, Q., & Bodenmann, G. (in press). Validation of the Dyadic Coping Inventory with Chinese couples: Factorial structure, measurement invariance and construct validity. *Psychological Assessment.*

Xu, Y., & Burleson, B. R. (2001). Effects of sex, culture, and support type on perceptions of spousal social support: An assessment of the 'support gap' hypothesis in early marriage. *Human Communication Research, 27*(4), 535–566.

Yang, J. (2013). Social exclusion and young rural-urban immigrants' integration into a host country in China. *The Annals of the American Academy of Political and Social Science, 648*(1), 52–69.

Zhang, K., & Beck, E. J. (1999). Changing sexual attitudes and behavior in China: Implications for the spread of HIV and other sexually transmitted diseases, *AIDS Care: Psychological and Socio-medical Aspects of AIDS/HIV, 11*(5), 581–589.

Zhang, M., Foley, S., & Yang, B. Y. (2013). Work-family conflict among Chinese married couples: Testing spillover and crossover effects. *The International Journal of Human Resource Management, 24*(1), 3213–3231.

Zhang, S., & Kline, S. (2009). Can I make my own decision? A cross-cultural study of social network influence in mate selection. *Journal of Cross-Cultural Psychology, 40*, 3–23.

Zuo, J. (2003). From revolutionary comrades to gendered partners: Marital construction of breadwinning in post-Mao urban China. *Journal of Family Issues, 24*(3), 314–337.

Zuo, J., & Bian, Y. (2001). Gendered resources, division of housework, and perceived fairness: A case in urban China. *Journal of Marriage and Family, 63*(4), 1122–1133.

15

DYADIC COPING IN JAPANESE COUPLES

Akiko Kawashima and Tai Kurosawa

Introduction

Japan is an archipelago consisting of four main islands and 6,852 small islands with a total land area of 377,962 square kilometers, which is as large as Germany or Vietnam (Matsumoto, 2014; Statistics Bureau, Ministry of Internal Affairs and Communications, 2015). About 70 percent of the land is mountains or forests, so that the total population of 127 million of Japanese people are living in a quite limited area. Tokyo, the capital of Japan, has 12.6 million people, with a density of 6,000 people per square kilometer (Statistics Bureau, Ministry of Internal Affairs and Communications, 2015). Japan has been regarded as a homogeneous nation; however, there were 2.1 million foreign residents in 2013 (Statistics Bureau, Ministry of Internal Affairs and Communications, 2015).

Japanese culture is fundamentally influenced by Confucianism, which originated in China (see Chapter 14 for more information). Confucianism emphasizes 'propriety, reverence, courtesy, and ritual or ideal standards of conduct' (Kim, 2012, p. 89). Loyalty to the family and respect and care for parents (that is, the idea and practice of filial piety), are the principal virtues of Confucianism. Accordingly, it has been the eldest son's obligation to live with his parents when he gets married, in order to take care of them and to carry on the family name and property after their death. While these traditional customs are significantly weaker in Japanese urban areas, they are still followed quite strictly in rural areas, which is most of Japan (Kataoka, 2007).

Review of the Literature

Couples' Relationships in Japan

Japanese society used to be regarded as a 'marriage oriented society' in which marriage was the norm and most people were married (Tokuhiro, 2009). For women, in particular, there have been rigorous but implicit pressures to marry at a young age. During the 1980s, 'women in Japan used to be compared to Christmas cakes, which were eaten on the 25th and not after' (Tokuhiro, 2009, p. 3). However, similar to other societies such as the Swiss one (see Chapter 6), Japanese have now started to choose who they marry and when they marry, if at all, which has led to a general 'postponement of marriage.' Figure 15.1 shows that the age of first marriage in Japan has increased markedly since the 1970s for both men and women, but that this change has been more rapid for women. Today, the mean age for first marriage for men and women is 30.9 and 29.3 years respectively (Statistics and Information Department (Japan), 2014).

The government has attributed marriage postponement to the higher education levels of the Japanese men and women, as well as the slow disintegration of traditional marriage norms (Ministry of Health, Labour and Welfare (Japan), 2013). From a feminist perspective, however, traditional marriage characteristics (in other words, the Japanese patriarchal family tradition) may be viewed as the causal factors for the way in which young people view marriage in Japan today (Tokuhiro, 2009). In describing postwar Japanese women, Vogel (2012) said:

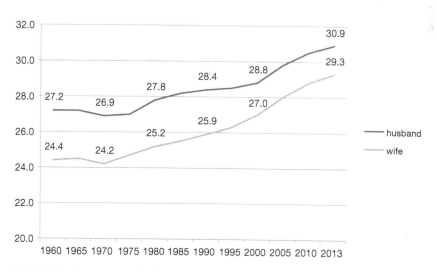

FIGURE 15.1 Average age for Japanese men and women at first marriage 1960 to 2013.

Ministry of Health and Welfare, Statistics and Information Department (Japan) (2014)

The woman's role was integrated into the traditional household (*ie*) system of the hierarchical extended family, with generations living together, a strict division of labor between the sexes, and middle-class housewives in charge of all household and family care yet subservient to husbands and/or mothers-in-law.

(Vogel, 2012, pp. 687–688)

As traditional marriage conventions in Japan focused on sustaining the family lineage and business over generations, which is known as the '*ie*' system (Ochiai, 2013), most marriages were arranged before the 1960s (National Institute of Population and Social Security Research, 2011). However, marriages based on personal choice have gradually increased and, in the 1990s, over 95 percent of all marriages were based on mutual love (National Institute of Population and Social Security Research (Japan), 2011). This shift away from the patriarchal '*ie*' system has resulted in a more egalitarian partnership between husband and wife. In a report from the Cabinet Office, Government of Japan (2005), it was noted that people got married as a way of gaining psychological comfort rather than the traditional gender-biased financial or instrumental satisfaction. Japanese couples are now setting their goals to be more egalitarian and intimate; however, without clear guidelines or norms, these goals produce new stressors by giving couples freedom and responsibility as it happens in many other individualist societies (Vogel, 2012).

Japanese Couples and Stressors

As noted above, Vogel (2012) warned Japanese society was now facing a huge transition 'from an insular, ethnocentric, self-styled homogeneous society emphasizing a commonly shared ethic, family structure, and social cohesion into a more diversified and international society with greater variation in moral guidelines, family patterns, and work conditions' (Vogel, 2012, p. 687), and the transition was a crisis causing a broad type of psychological effects. Although Vogel (2012) pointed out the psychological stresses caused by collapse of '*ie*' family system and prolonged economic recession, there is limited available literature in Japan on stress, and even more so on couples coping with stress.

External Stressors

Inconsistencies between changes in social values and the remnants of gender role practices have brought about stresses within families of Japanese couples. However, the traditional gender-role division among married couples in Japan has been found to be deeply rooted; that is, men act as breadwinners and women take care of the home. Moreover, since the 1990 economic recession, average incomes have decreased, forcing women to work as well as to manage the household. The average working hours of Japanese men are approximately fifty–fifty-one hours per week (Tsuya, Bumpass, Choe, & Rindfuss, 2012), with around 20 percent of men aged 30–44 years working over sixty hours a week. In contrast, wives are likely to hold temporary or part-time jobs; therefore, they only work for an average of thirty-two hours per week (Tsuya et al., 2012). In Japan, 80 percent of working men have full-time employment, while women tend to hold temporary or part-time jobs (Ministry of Health, Labor and Welfare (Japan), 2012). However, even if they do have full-time employment, Japanese women earn only 70 percent of the salaries of their male counterparts. Therefore, in general, husbands are the main income earners while wives look after the household and work shorter hours to supplement the household income. According to a diary study of 125 Japanese married men and women, Konjiki and colleagues (2014) revealed that husbands felt stressed mostly by work, followed by family relationships and childcare problems, while wives felt stressed mostly by family relationships, followed by childcare; regardless of their working status (Konjiki, Tsukamoto, Inoue, Andoh, & Takao, 2014). These results reflect that stressors among couples depend more on gender role division rather than on actual working status.

Besides the above, substantial studies among married couples have been on parenting stress, and its cause and effects on marital quality and parenting practice (e.g., Tanaka, 2010), because in the fields of family sociology and psychology, couples' parental roles have been regarded as more important than their role as partners (e.g., Egami, 2013; Ojima, Kikkawa, & Naoi, 1996). Studies showed that the marital quality could buffer the effect of parenting stress on children's outcome (e.g., Kazui, Muto, & Sonoda, 1996), and that marital quality could be a protective factor against parenting stress (e.g., Hisata, Miguchi, Senda, & Niwa, 1990). Several studies focusing on stressors during pregnancy showed that marital quality or husbands' support alleviate the negative effect of stressors on wives' depressive symptoms (e.g., Ogata, 2013).

There are only a few other stress related studies in Japan. These studies have focused on stress related to work-life balance or dual working couples (e.g., Koizumi, Sugawara, Maekawa, & Kitamura, 2003), traumatic stress and marital relationships (e.g., K. Kubo, Goto, & Shishido, 2013), and economic stress and marital relationships (e.g., Mifune, 2004). Close to the idea of work-life balance, but probably an indigenous stress in Japan, is 'relocation-induced separation (*Tanshin-funin*)' (e.g., Moriyama et al., 2012; Y. Tanaka, 1988). A *tanshin-funin* is a job transfer (usually of husbands) away from one's family, typically for a couple of years, and this working style is unique in Japan. Two studies (Moriyama et al., 2012; Y. Tanaka, 1988) showed the negative effects of *tanshin-funin* on individual and family well-being.

Internal Stressors

There are also several studies about stress inside married dyads (internal stress; Randall & Bodenmann, 2009); for example, the relationship between marital distress in middle-aged couples and subjective well-being (Hiraga, 2007). Those studies focusing on marital distress pointed out the relationship between husbands' adherence to traditional gender role practices and wives' marital distress (Hirayama & Kashiwagi, 2004; Nagatsu & Hamada, 1999). Wives' marital distress, in turn, could cause physical or psychological problems called retired husband syndrome (Johnson, 1984) or '*Shujin-zaitaku* (husbands being at home) stress syndrome' (Kurokawa, 2009); that is, wives' psychosomatic problems emerging after their husbands' retirements. There are also a few studies about caregiving in old couples, showing gender inequality enforcing wives to care for their husbands more (Hane, 2006; Nishimura, 2012).

A relatively new research area is about stress related to infertility (e.g., Murao, 2012). The later marriage age has been linked to the extremely low fertility rate in Japan, which has been recognized as a continuing problem by the government, researchers, and the media (Ishihara & Tabuchi, 2012; Ministry of Health, Labour and Welfare (Japan), 2013). Studies indicate that the stress from infertility problems is greater for wives because of the traditional belief that women are solely responsible for infertility (Matsubayashi et al., 2004; Murao, 2012).

In sum, Japanese couples' stress, especially wives' stress, is a result of traditional patriarchal principles that lead to specific gender role practices and the belief that 'women should fulfill the role of producing an heir to continue the family name' (Matsubayashi et al., 2004, pp. 398–399). Several studies suggest that the negative effects of stress could be moderated by marital quality (e.g., Tanaka, 2010); at the same time, marital problems could become sources of stress by themselves. Nonetheless, most of the studies have only reported simple correlations and have not examined the process of couples coping with stress. In the next section, we introduce some studies describing the couples' coping process.

Some studies in Japan focused on the benefits of support provided by the partner. One of these studies showed the unique contribution of partners' support, compared with other types of social support (Dainichi, 2012). This study found that partners' support was more effective for both men and women in coping with stress, whereas there were some buffering effects of other types of social support for women but not for men. However, in this study the partner's support was measured only by availability, and the types of supports (e.g., instrumental or emotional) provided by partners or other social network were unclear. In a different study on prevention of diabetes (Tomita, Ninomiya, & Fukuhara, 2010), it was found that some specific types of partner's support (e.g., preparing healthy meals, walking together, and showing consideration) had positive effects on keeping a healthy life style (Tomita, Ninomiya, & Fukuhara, 2010).

Two different studies examined partners' communication of stress to each other, one on nurses and another one on firefighters (Kubo, 1999; Yoo & Matsui, 2012). The study on nurses indicated that communication did not alleviate their burn-out symptoms (Kubo, 1999). On the other hand, the study with firefighters, using a mostly male sample, found that refraining from disclosing their stress to their partner led to psychological problems (Yoo & Matsui, 2012).

There has been another, more comprehensive, study using 'relationship-focused coping' (Coyne & Smith, 1991) in a Japanese sample (Kurosawa & Kato, 2013). Kurosawa and Kato (2013) developed an original measure to test relationship-focused coping in a Japanese sample, and found that active engagement, which includes open discussion and problem solving, was positively related to empathy, marital satisfaction, and well-being. In contrast, protective buffering was not associated with these aspects. They also found that the wives' active engagement was positively correlated with men's marital satisfaction and well-being, while the effects of men's support were not significant for their wives.

In sum, a few studies have suggested the importance of examining couples' coping in the Japanese population. Nonetheless, there was no study applying any comprehensive theory such as the systemic transactional model (STM; Bodenmann, 2005), considering both each partner's coping and the couple's coping as a dyad. If couples' coping is an important protective factor for one's mental health, as suggested by Dainichi's findings (2012), it is important to understand the process of dyadic coping (DC) in couples. Therefore, the first author and her colleagues conducted an online survey to examine dyadic coping process in a sample of Japanese couples.

Dyadic Coping: Cultural Differences

As noted in the previous section, the author and colleagues conducted the first study on dyadic coping from an STM perspective in Japan. The aim was to see if there were any particular cultural effects on dyadic coping in the Japanese sample. For that purpose we collected data from 251 married adults through an anonymous online/internet survey through an internet research company, Video Research Ltd. A total of 251 married adults out of 100,000 pooled informants across Japan responded to this survey individually (48 percent men and 52 percent women). The mean age was 36.7 years for men ($SD = 5.2$) and 35.5 years for women ($SD = 5.4$). Mean marital length was 8.1 years for men ($SD = 5.5$) and 8.2 years for women ($SD = 5.8$). Over half of the men (60 percent) in the sample had a university degree, 23 percent had completed junior college or vocational training, and 17 percent had completed high school. Thirty-five percent of women had a university degree, 38 percent completed junior college or vocational training, 24 percent graduated from high school and 3 percent completed the mandatory school years (nine years). Almost all of the men (90 percent) in the sample were full-time workers, 2 percent worked in part-time jobs, 6 percent were self-employed, and 2 percent were not working. Eighteen percent of women in the sample were full-time workers, 23 percent worked in part-time jobs, 8 percent were self-employed or other, and 50 percent were not working. On average, men in this sample used ten hours a day for their work (SD = 2.0), while women used seven hours a day for their work (SD = 2.1).

We measured couples' coping, their marital quality, and depressive symptoms, using the Japanese version of the Dyadic Coping Inventory (DCI) (Bodenmann, 2008), checked and approved by the original author (Dr. Bodenmann) (alpha = 0.93), the Japanese version of the Revised Dyadic Adjustment Scale (RDAS) (Busby, Christensen, Crane, & Larson, 1995), consisting of fourteen items with a six-point scale, (alpha = 0.90), and the Japanese version (Shima, Shikano, Kitamura, & Asai, 1985) of the Center for Epidemiologic Studies Depression Scale (CES-D) (Radloff, 1977), featuring twenty items and a four-point scale (alpha = 0.87).

Table 15.1 shows the means, and standard deviations for all dimensions of dyadic coping in this sample. There was an observed gender difference in negative dyadic coping: men showed greater negative dyadic coping than women (t (243) = 2.37, p < 0.05). Compared with the European means reported by Ledermann and colleagues (2010), the Japanese means for every subscale, except for the negative dyadic coping (which was higher), were lower. In other words, the Japanese couples seemed not to be as engaged in positive dyadic coping as the Swiss and Italian couples. Contrary to other studies (e.g., Falconier, 2013), no gender differences were found in supportive dyadic coping but rather in the negative dyadic coping, which would lead to wives' marital dissatisfaction with their partners. This result is in line with previous research in Japan, showing husbands more engaged in negative communication patterns such as intimidating and ignoring their wives (Hirayama & Kashiwagi, 2004).

Table 15.2 shows the correlations between dyadic coping and the demographic data. There were few significant correlations between the dyadic coping subscales and working hours or number of children. This indicates that the amount of stressors outside of marriage does not affect much the way couples cope as dyads. Rather, the age of respondents correlated with most of the subscales of dyadic coping; especially for men. This result supports that Japanese couples, especially husbands, are now coping with problems using a more egalitarian or 'we-ness' approach instead of the traditional stance (North, 2009).

In order to examine the relationship between dyadic coping and subjective perception of marital quality, the correlation coefficients between the subscales of dyadic coping and the scales of marital quality (RDAS and MLS) were calculated (Table 15.2). Most correlations between the dyadic coping subscales and the marital quality measure were significant and moderately high (with RDAS, r = −0.35 − 0.81, Table 15.2). However, unlike previous studies (e.g., Ledermann et al., 2010), correlations of marital quality with negative dyadic coping were not as strong as the ones with positive dyadic coping. It was found that the partners' support and common dyadic coping were strongly correlated with marital quality (Table 15.2).

TABLE 15.1 Japanese sample means and standard deviations (N = 251)

Variable	husbands n = 121		wives n = 130		gender
Subscales	M (SD)		M (SD)		difference (t)
Evaluations for oneself					
Stress communication	2.86	(1.07)	3.12	(1.01)	1.93
Supportive DC	3.02	(0.84)	2.94	(0.87)	0.81
Delegated DC	3.10	(0.85)	2.97	(0.89)	1.10
Negative DC	2.27	(0.92)	2.00	(0.85)	2.37★
Evaluations for the partner					
Stress communication	3.08	(0.92)	2.88	(1.03)	1.64
Supportive DC	2.95	(1.06)	2.81	(1.06)	1.04
Delegated DC	2.57	(0.96)	2.62	(0.93)	0.44
Negative DC	2.15	(0.99)	2.24	(0.85)	0.78
Joint DC	2.96	(0.96)	2.79	(1.03)	1.36
Evaluation of DC	3.25	(1.04)	3.22	(1.13)	0.21
Composite scales					
DC total by oneself	3.18	(0.59)	3.27	(0.57)	1.27
DC total by the partner	3.17	(0.66)	3.05	(0.72)	1.35
DC total	110.03	(21.54)	108.8	(22.04)	0.45

Note. DC = Dyadic Coping

The correlation analyses were again conducted to clarify the relationship between dyadic coping and subjective well-being, using the subscales of dyadic coping and depressive symptoms (CES-D) (Table 15.2). For women, negative correlations were found between supportive dyadic coping by oneself and one's partner and depressive symptoms ($r = -0.22$, -0.21, respectively, $ps < 0.05$). Evaluation of dyadic coping was negatively correlated with depressive symptoms for both men and women ($r = -0.25$, -0.31, respectively, $ps < 0.01$); however, the common dyadic coping was not significantly correlated with depressive symptoms ($r = -0.11$, -0.17, respectively, *n.s.*). There was positive correlation between partners' negative dyadic coping and depressive symptoms for both men and women ($r = 0.25$, 0.30, respectively, $ps < 0.01$), while one's negative dyadic coping positively correlated with depressive symptoms in the only male sample ($r = 0.26$, $p < 0.01$). In other words, for both men and women, the more their partners coped with stressors in a negative manner, the more depressive symptoms they experienced. Simultaneously, depressive men tended to cope negatively with stressors, while depressive women did not.

TABLE 15.2 Inter-correlations between dyadic coping, demographic background, and marital quality in Japanese samples

DCI		Age	Marital length	Number of children	Mean child age	Educational background	Work hour	RDAS	CES-D
Evaluation for oneself									
Stress communication	M	-0.18 *	-0.08	0.01	-0.13	-0.01	-0.12	0.26 *	0.06
	W	-0.14	-0.18 *	0.05	-0.17	0.06	-0.14	0.39 **	0.03
Supportive DC	M	-0.27 **	-0.15	-0.05	-0.20	-0.03	-0.12	0.58 **	-0.04
	W	-0.12	-0.17	-0.14	-0.12	0.12	-0.10	0.60 **	-0.22 *
Delegated DC	M	-0.19 *	-0.18 *	-0.03	-0.25 *	-0.03	-0.07	0.41 **	-0.06
	W	-0.20 *	-0.22 *	-0.05	-0.24 *	-0.01	0.04	0.27 *	-0.10
Negative DC	M	-0.09	0.01	0.19 *	0.00	-0.08	0.03	-0.21	0.26 **
	W	-0.01	0.15	0.11	0.05	-0.20 *	-0.02	-0.22	0.11

Evaluation for partner

Stress communication	M	-0.22 *	-0.09	-0.04	-0.11	0.00	-0.03	0.36 **	0.01
	W	-0.09	-0.11	-0.02	-0.17	-0.03	-0.12	0.58 **	-0.12
Supportive DC	M	-0.24 **	-0.16	-0.14	-0.22	0.05	-0.08	0.72 **	-0.13
	W	-0.10	-0.10	-0.08	0.00	0.07	-0.14	0.72 **	-0.21 *
Delegated DC	M	-0.26 **	-0.10	-0.09	-0.21	-0.05	-0.12	0.59 **	-0.09
	W	-0.05	-0.10	-0.14	-0.08	0.06	-0.15	0.51 **	-0.17
Negative DC	M	-0.10	0.04	0.07	-0.07	-0.18 *	-0.07	-0.32 *	0.25 **
	W	0.06	0.13	0.12	0.03	-0.18 *	0.04	-0.35 **	0.30 **
Joint DC	M	-0.25 **	-0.18	-0.02	-0.22	0.05	-0.07	0.54 **	-0.11
	W	-0.26 **	-0.23 **	-0.11	-0.21	0.09	-0.11	0.58 **	-0.17
Evaluation of DC	M	-0.13	-0.13	-0.08	-0.21	-0.02	-0.07	0.63 **	-0.25 **
	W	-0.20 *	-0.18 *	-0.17	-0.08	0.14	-0.17	0.81 **	-0.31 **

Note. DC = dyadic coping, M = men, W = women, RDAS = Revised Dyadic Adjustment Scale; 121 men and 130 women except for "mean child age" (71 men and 77 women), RDAS and MLS (63 men and 66 women).

In summary, Japanese couples seemed to be less engaged in positive dyadic coping including common dyadic coping, and more in negative dyadic coping than European couples (e.g., Ledermann et al., 2010). These results can be explained by several cultural factors. The most straightforward explanation is that the results reflect the reality of marital relationships in Japan; that is, couples are retaining their gender role practices in their dyads and are not emotionally helping each other. Consequently, lower positive coping was found. Another explanation is the cultural difference in the construction of the self. In Japan, characterized as an interdependent self-construal culture, one's partner is regarded as '*Uchi*' (in-group, (Kamei, 2006)), and '*Uchi*' should be introduced in front of '*Soto*' (out-group; in this case, the researchers) modestly, because modesty is an important virtue in interdependent culture (Markus & Kitayama, 1991). Therefore, participants may have underrated their own and their partners' positive dyadic coping and overrated their negative coping in the way of showing modesty.

From another perspective, the results could be interpreted using the concept of '*amae*' (psychological dependence): a child-like need to seek dependence on someone 'who senses one's need and can meet it' (Doi, 1992, p. 9). In this case, rating partners' positive coping lower and negative coping higher can be interpreted as a sign of *amae*; that is, these individuals want greater support from their partners without asking for it. Vogel (2012) mentioned 'this non-verbal sensing of another's feelings or state of mind (*sassuru*) is deeply embedded in relationships (Vogel, 2012, p. 713).' This non-verbal 'empathic understanding of others' can result in Japanese couples assuming that their partner would sense their feelings or needs (*sassite*) and comply with their demands, without any verbal communications.

Second, stressors such as number of children or work hours did not have a strong correlation with dyadic coping, but marital quality and subjective well-being did. These results might be due to the lack of more precise measures for external stressors (e.g., daily hassles or working stress); hence, it is necessary to study the relationship between their daily stressors further to know how dyadic coping works to protect couples from distress. Nevertheless, it is noteworthy that dyadic coping related to marital quality and subjective well-being, as this provides evidence for it being worthwhile for Japanese couples to learn effective dyadic coping.

Implications for Practice

Most studies on marital relationships in Japan have focused on the sociological implications (e.g., Suzuki, 2007), and are rooted in gender-role division between partners (Kashiwagi & Hirayama, 2003). As such, there have been few psychological studies or interventions concerning partners' dyadic processes (for an exception see Wakashima, 2003), and, to date, there have been no evidence-based studies regarding couple therapy. It is noteworthy that Japanese couples seek professional help to solve their children's problems rather than to improve their relationship. There are several case reports about treating individual problems, such as cancer, depression, or anxiety, in dyads (e.g., Fujitomi & Ueno, 2003). There are also several case reports about treating children's problems by de-escalating parents' marital problems using couple therapy (e.g., Sakata & Takeda, 2007). Kameguchi and Murphy-Shigematsu (2001) point out that the children's problems (e.g., school refusals and violence at home) caused the parents to seek psychological or psychiatric help, and, in turn, their family problem, (e.g., 'mothers' overinvolvement in their children's lives' and 'lack of intimacy as a couple') came to be uncovered. Unfortunately, because any universal prevention programs have not yet been examined or developed for couples in Japan (Horiguchi, 2005), professional interventions are provided only after children's problems have escalated. If the relationship between marital problems and children's well-being came to be known widely in Japan and attract more research attention, public policy would aim to pursue more universal programs to maintain healthy marital relationships and support the well-being of all family members.

According to Bodenmann and Shantinath (2004), the educational intervention to enhance couples' coping called the Couples Coping Enhancement Training (CCET), is suitable for those 'starting a new relationship' or those who 'may be experiencing early signs of distress' (p. 479). In Japan there has been a growing interest in marital relationships after the birth of the first child after a program focused on *Sango Kuraishisu* (relationship crisis after child birth; Uchida & Tshuboi, 2013), was broadcasted in 2012. Even though *Sango Kuraishisu* is almost the same phenomenon described by Belsky and Kelly (1994), its introduction brought new distress for Japanese couples, who began fearing that their newborns would disrupt their intimate relationships. As a result, new parents are interested in learning how to cope with childrearing as intimate dyads. Therefore, we suggest that professionals should provide psychoeducational sessions on coping with parenting as dyads at the maternity and parenting classes taken by most pregnant women, and some male partners. Couples could learn how to communicate verbally about their stress and reduce their distress at *Sango Kuraishisu*. Since Japanese parents, especially mothers, 'try to provide every possible competitive advantage to their one or two children (Shwalb, Kawai, Shoji, & Tsunetsugu, 1995, p. 631),' parents would be interested in obtaining information from reliable studies (e.g., Bodenmann, Cina, Ledermann, & Sanders, 2008) on how to cope with stress with their partners effectively as this can in turn promote their children's well-being.

According to Uchida and Tsuboi (2013), the phenomenon *Sango Kuraishisu* is mainly due to the conflict between wives' expectations of egalitarian parenting and traditional gender role reality. When Japanese women become pregnant, they are torn between work and children as it is still considered women's responsibility to rear their children. While parenting education programs for mothers during their pregnancies are typically given by many local governments (Shwalb et al., 1995), there should also be programs that include both parents and teach them to cope as dyads in their parenting in non-traditionally gender role ways (Horiguchi, 2005).

In addition, psychological problems in infertile couples, especially women, have been increasing due to the growing number of delayed marriages (Matsubayashi et al., 2004; Murao, 2012). Insufficient support from husbands during infertility treatments is associated with marital distresses of wives or decisions to divorce. It would therefore be helpful to administrate CCET for couples trying to conceive, in order to learn effective dyadic coping.

Because marriage in Japan is still assumed to be based on traditional gender roles, Japan lags behind in marital relationship research and clinical interventions. Nonetheless, as Japanese couples continue introducing non-traditional gender role views in their relationships, they could benefit from learning about effective dyadic coping strategies studied in Western psychology.

Implications for Research

As we discussed, Japanese society has been changing due to globalization and individualization and consequently marital relationship values are moving toward more egalitarian arrangements. However, in this shift, many young couples experience stress as they discover the gap between theory and practice (North, 2009). Young Japanese people are struggling with a contradiction between the idea of an intimate and equal relationship and maintaining traditional gender-role attitudes. The idea of dyadic coping is promising in enabling researchers to highlight how couples in Japan are changing and depict the results of this transition. According to our data (Kawashima, Yoshitake, Matsumoto, & Sugawara, 2014), positive dyadic coping could enhance marital quality and psychological well-being for both husbands and wives; however, not only correlational studies but also intervention studies would clarify how dyadic coping can help couples enhance their marital quality in stressful times (e.g., becoming parents, instable work conditions, and long economic recession). Despite its importance, dyadic coping has only just started to be studied in Japan.

Marriage trends indicate an egalitarianism that could assist young people to engage in closer relationships and, in turn, have more children to solve the low fertility problems. Hence, more research on close relationships' dynamics, including dyadic coping, in Japan is needed to clarify the mechanisms that maintain or enhance marital quality.

Conclusion

Japan is now facing a transition from a traditional, closed society to a more modern, international one. The transition brings a new set of stressors for Japanese couples, both internal (e.g., postponement of marriage, low fertility rate, problem with keeping intimacy, rise in divorce rate, and aging of population) and external (e.g., working long hours, job instability, and a prolonged recession) to their relationship. Due in part to the persistence of unequal gender-role division, Japanese couples are not yet fully able to cope as dyads with these internal and external stressors. Therefore, they could benefit from effective dyadic coping strategies, particularly those that enhance the communication between the partners. Because Japanese have grown up in a culture of 'non-verbal sensing of another's feelings or state of mind (*sassuru*)' (Vogel, 2012, p. 713), we have trouble with expressing one's feelings or state of mind verbally. However, the Japanese society is good at embracing foreign culture or practices and adapting them to a new style. As a result, we believe that dyadic coping could be incorporated into Japanese culture and that it could enhance couples' communication, benefiting couples' and children's well-being.

References

Belsky, J., & Kelly, J. (1994). *The transition to parenthood: How a first child changes a marriage: based on a landmark study*. London: Vermilion.

Bodenmann, G. (2005). *Dyadic coping and its significance for marital functioning*, in T. Revenson, K. Kayser, & G. Bodenmann (Eds.) (2005), Couples coping with stress: Emerging perspectives on dyadic coping (pp. 33–50). Washington DC: American Psychological Association.

Bodenmann, G. (2008). *Dyadisches Coping Inventar: Testmanual [Dyadic Coping Inventory: Test manual]*. Bern, Switzerland.

Bodenmann, G., Cina, A., Ledermann, T., & Sanders, M. R. (2008). The efficacy of the Triple P-Positive Parenting Program in improving parenting and child behavior: A comparison with two other treatment conditions. *Behaviour Research and Therapy, 46*(4), 411–427.

Bodenmann, G., & Shantinath, S. D. (2004). The Couples Coping Enhancement Training (CCET): A new approach to prevention of marital distress based upon stress and coping. *Family Relations, 53*(5), 477–484.

Busby, D. M., Christensen, C., Crane, D. R., & Larson, J. H. (1995). A revision of the Dyadic Adjustment Scale for use with distressed and nondistressed couples construct hierarchy. *Journal of Marital and Family Therapy, 21*, 289–308.

Cabinet Office, G. of J. (2005). Changes in marriage and birth trends. Retrieved from www5.cao.go.jp/seikatsu/whitepaper/h17/05_eng/pdf/chapter1

Coyne, J. C., & Smith, D. A. (1991). Couples coping with a myocardial infarction: a contextual perspective on wives' distress. *Journal of Personality and Social Psychology, 61*(3), 404–412.

Dainichi, Y. (2012). Uniqueness of Spousal Support. *Kazoku Syakaigaku Kenkyu, 24*(2), 189–199.

Doi, T. (1992). On the concept of amae. *Infant Mental Health Journal, 13*(1), 7–11.

Egami, S. (2013). Mothers' and fathers' adherence to 'maternal love': Interactions with their marital satisfaction and parenting style. *Japanese Journal of Educational Psychology, 61*(2), 169–180.

Falconier, M. K. (2013). Traditional gender role orientation and dyadic coping in immigrant latino couples: effects on couple functioning. *Family Relations, 62*(2), 269–283.

Fujitomi, Y., & Ueno, T. (2003). Programs and trials of psychological support for breast cancer patients. *Japanese Journal of Psychosomatic Medicine, 43*(12), 847–852.

Hane, A. (2006). Factors in murder or double suicide cases committed by male caregivers of the elderly. *Kazoku Syakaigaku Kenkyu, 18*(1), 27–39.

Hiraga, A. (2007). Positive and negative affect in middle-aged couples. *Contemporary Sociological Studies, 20*, 113–126.

Hirayama, J., & Kashiwagi, K. (2004). Communication patterns of married couples: association with couples' occupational statuses and marital Ideals. *The Japanese Journal of Developmental Psychology, 15*(1), 89–100.

Hisata, M., Miguchi, M., Senda, S., & Niwa, I. (1990). Childcare stress and postpartum depression: an examination of the stress-buffering effect of marital intimacy as social support. *Japanese Journal of Social Psychology, 6*(1), 42–51.

Horiguchi, M. (2005). Parenting education during prenatal period: A program with gender and developmental perspectives in the U.S. *F-GENS Journal, 4*, 13–20.

Ishihara, K., & Tabuchi, R. (2012). *Changing families in Northeast Asia: comparative analysis of China, Korea, and Japan*. Tokyo: Sophia University Press.

Johnson, C. C. (1984). The retired husband syndrome. *Western Journal of Medicine, 141*(4), 542–545.

Kameguchi, K., & Murphy-Shigematsu, S. (2001). Family psychology and family therapy in Japan. *The American Psychologist, 56*(1), 65–70.

Kashiwagi, K., & Hirayama, J. (2003). Marital norm, reality and satisfaction in middle-aged couples. *The Japanese Journal of Psychology, 74*(2), 122–130.

Kataoka, Y. (2007). A study of 'individualization in family' in a rural area: A case study in the hilly and mountainous areas of Shimane Prefecture. *Kazoku Syakaigaku Kenkyu, 19*(2), 32–44.

Kawashima, A., Yoshitake, N., Matsumoto, S., & Sugawara, M. (2014). Fuufu ko-pingu no kentou: Kodomo no fuufukan kattouji no joucho anteisei ni chakumoku shite. [Dyadic coping: Relation to the children's emotional security during parental conflicts]. In *Annual Child Science Conference* (p. 28). Tokyo: Japanese Society of Child Science.

Kazui, M., Muto, T., & Sonoda, N. (1996). The roles of marital quality and parenting stress in mother-preschooler relationships: A family systems perspective. *Japanese Journal of Developmental Psychology, 7*(1), 31–40.

Kim, J. N. (2012). Financial support to parents and parents-in-law: How the social status of married women affects financial support for parents in Korea, Japan, and China. In K. Ishihara & R. Tabuchi (Eds.), *Changing families in Northeast Asia: Comparative analysis of China, Korea, and Japan* (pp. 89—110). Tokyo: Sophia University Press.

Koizumi, T., Sugawara, M., Maekawa, K., & Kitamura, T. (2003). Direct and indirect effects of negative spillover from work to family, on depressive symptoms of Japanese working mothers. *The Japanese Journal of Developmental Psychology, 14*(3), 272–283.

Konjiki, F., Tsukamoto, N., Inoue, S., Andoh, T., & Takao, T. (2014). Stress factors of married couples observed in stress diaries. *Bulletin of Tokyo Kasei University. Cultural and Social Science, 54*, 79–84.

Kubo, K., Goto, K., & Shishido, M. (2013). Effects of Niigata-chuetsu earthquake disaster on marital relationship, mothers' stress and children's mental health, and clarification of support needed. *Journal of Child Health, 72*(6), 804–809.

Kubo, M. (1999). The relationships between burnout and social support among human service workers. *Memoirs of Osaka Kyoiku University. IV, Education, Pshychology, Special Education and Physical Culture, 48*(1), 139–147.

Kurokawa, N. (2009). The retired husband syndrome. *Japanese Journal of Psychosomatic Medecine, 49*(2), 99.

Kurosawa, T., & Kato, M. (2013). Development of a scale of relationship-focused coping for marital couple stress. *The Japanese Journal of Developmental Psychology, 24*(1), 66–76.

Ledermann, T., Bodenmann, G., Gagliardi, S., Charvoz, L., Verardi, S., Rossier, J., . . . Iafrate, R. (2010). Psychometrics of the dyadic coping inventory in three language groups. *Swiss Journal of Psychology, 69*(4), 201–212.

Markus, H. R., & Kitayama, S. (1991). Culture and the self: Implications for cognition, emotion, and motivation. *Psychological Review, 98*(2), 224–253.

Matsubayashi, H., Hosaka, T., Izumi, S. I., Suzuki, T., Kondo, A., & Makino, T. (2004). Increased depression and anxiety in infertile Japanese women resulting from lack of husband's support and feelings of stress, *General Hospital Psychiatry, 26*(5), 398–404.

Matsumoto, Y. (2014). *An introductory handbook to Japan and its people.* Tokyo: ALC Press.

Mifune, M. (2004). Fusai no Keizai Seikatsu/Ishiki to Otto no Sutoresu/Jouchoteki sapo-to [Couples' economic life, consciousness and husbands' stress and emotional supports]. *Kakei Keizai Kenkyu, 64*, 18–25.

Ministry of Health, Labour and Welfare (Japan). (2012). Chapter 3. Issues of the labour market for the promotion of employment: Demand for labour, supply of labour and its quality. Retrieved from www.mhlw.go.jp/wp/hakusyo/roudou/12/dl/03.pdf

Ministry of Health, Labour and Welfare (Japan). (2013). Annual health, labour and welfare report: Study of the aspirations of young people [Summary]. Retrieved from www.mhlw.go.jp/english/wp/wp-hw7/dl/summary.pdf

Moriyama, Y., Toyokawa, S., Kobayashi, Y., Inoue, K., Suyama, Y., Sugimoto, N., & Miyoshi, Y. (2012). A comparison of lifestyle, mental stress, and medical check-up results between Tanshin-funin workers and workers living with their families. *San Ei Shi, 54*(1), 22–28.

Murao, A. (2012). The impact of infertility-related stress to depression in infertile women: Focusing on marital relations and resilience. *Bulletin of Department of Psychology Teikyo University*, (16), 29–43.

Nagatsu, M., & Hamada, Y. (1999). Distress of middle aged women in their marital relations. *Journal of Home Economics of Japan, 50*(8), 793–805.

National Institute of Population and Social Security Research. (2011). *The Fourteenth Japanese National Fertility Survey in 2010 Marriage Process and Fertility of Japanese Married Couples Highlights of the Survey Results on Married Couples.* National Institute of Population and Social Security Research. Tokyo.

Nishimura, M. (2012). Stress process among spouse caregivers: A structural equation modeling test of gender differences. *Japanese Journal of Family Sociology, 24*(2), 165–176.

North, S. (2009). Negotiating what's 'natural': Persistent domestic gender role inequality in Japan. *Social Science Japan Journal, 12*(1), 23–44.

Ochiai, E. (2013). Paradigm shifts in Japanese family sociology. *International Journal of Japanese Sociology, 22*(1), 104–127.

Ogata, K. (2013). A study on the pregnant wife's marital relationship and mental stress: From the view point of husband's work-life balance and wife's occupation. *Bulletin of Aichi University of Education, 62* (Educational Sciences), 89–97.

Ojima, F., Kikkawa, T., & Naoi, A. (1996). Relationships between the Social Attitudes of Parents and Children. *Kazoku Syakaigaku Kenkyu*, *8*(8), 111–124, 206.

Radloff, L. S. (1977). The CES-D Scale: a self-report depression scale for research in the general population. *Applied Psychological Measurement*, *1*(3), 385–401.

Randall, A. K., & Bodenmann, G. (2009). The role of stress on close relationships and marital satisfaction. *Clinical Psychology Review*, *29*(2), 105–115.

Sakata, M., & Takeda, M. (2007). The attempt of the family therapeutic approach to the non-attendant. *Bulletin of the Faculty of Education, Wakayama University. Educational Science*, *57*, 9–14.

Shima, S., Shikano, T., Kitamura, T., & Asai, M. (1985). Reliability and validity of CES-D. *Clin Psychiatry*, *27*(6), 717–723.

Shwalb, D. W., Kawai, H., Shoji, J., & Tsunetsugu, K. (1995). The place of advice: Japanese parents' sources of information about childrearing and child health. *Journal of Applied Developmental Psychology*, *16*(4), 629–644.

Statistics and Information Department (Japan). (2014). Vital statistics 2013. Retrieved from www.e-stat.go.jp/SG1/estat/List.do?lid=000001127023

Statistics Bureau, Ministry of Internal Affairs and Communications, J. (2015). Japan Statistical Yearbook. Retrieved June 12, 2015, from www.stat.go.jp/english/data/nenkan/index.htm

Suzuki, F. (2007). Comparison of husbands' and wives' viewpoints regarding marital relationships. *Kazoku Syakaigaku Kenkyu*, *19*(2), 58–70.

Tanaka, K. (2010). Changes in father's behavior in child rearing and housekeeping and husband's satisfaction of the relationship between husband and wife and the correlation with the 6-th mother's stress in child rearing. *Annual Reports of Graduate School of Humanities and Sciences*, *25*, 125–134.

Tanaka, Y. (1988). The effects of relocation-induced separation on their families. *Japanese Journal of Educational Psychology*, *36*(3), 229–237.

Tokuhiro, Y. (2009). *Marriage in contemporary Japan*. New York: Routledge.

Tomita, S., Ninomiya, K., & Fukuhara, H. (2010). Effects of a specific health guidance program for prevention of diabetes. *Nihon Koshu Eisei Zasshi*, *57*(10), 921–931.

Tsuya, N. O., Bumpass, L. L., Choe, M. K., & Rindfuss, R. R. (2012). Employment and household tasks of Japanese couples, 1994–2009. *Demographic Research*, *27*, 705–718.

Uchida, S., & Tsuboi, K. (2013). *Sango Kuraishisu* [*Crisis after child birth*]. Poplar Paperback Shinsho (Vol. 9). Tokyo: Poplar Publishing Co., Ltd.

Vogel, S. H. (2012). Japanese society under stress. *Asian Survey*, *52*(4), 687–713.

Wakashima, K. (2003). The proposal of 'problem-interaction model' to predict the disqualification: on the analysis of the conflicting discourse of married couples. *Bulletin of St. Luke's College of Nursing*, (29), 22–31.

Yoo, S., & Matsui, Y. (2012). The influence of attitude of inhibiting spousal disclosure about stress on the mental health of firefighters. *The Japanese Journal of Psychology*, *83*(5), 440–449.

16

DYADIC COPING IN AFRICAN COUPLES

Peter Hilpert and Charles Kimamo

Introduction

Africa is the second largest and second most populous continent in the world (Sayre, 1999) with more than 1.1 billion inhabitants in fifty-four countries (Gudmastad, 2013). Although the African continent is generally rich in natural resources (e.g., precious metals, diamonds, wood) and receives around $150 billion in foreign aid each year, it is still the poorest continent. A substantial number of its countries have a GDP per capita income of less than US $2,000 per person (CIA World Factbook, 2012). In addition, political instability is prominent in many African countries. Since 1956, when African countries began to obtain independence from colonialism, there have been 142 plotted, 109 attempted, and 82 successful *coups d'état* (Collier & Hoeffler, 2005). Given that 50 percent of the African population is younger than 20 years of age (Njideka, 2013), it is important to understand the political-economic context in which hundreds of millions of people will be looking for jobs and spouses in the next decade.

Africans are by no means a uniform group, and the fifty-four countries that constitute the African continent certainly justify its diversity. In fact, according to UNESCO, there are up to 2,000 languages and more than 3,000 tribes in Africa—and every tribe has unique cultural and historical elements. For example, 400 languages are spoken in Nigeria alone (Mwamwenda, 1995). Moreover, rivalries and military conflicts (e.g., in Congo, Rwanda, Sierra Leone, Nigeria, Kenya, or Angola) prevail between some tribes, indicating cultural, economic, or religious differences. Other tribes coexist more peacefully, such as the 260 tribes in Tanzania. Furthermore, there are also racial differences in the African population. Even though a majority of Africans are black, there are also Arabs in the North and Caucasians in the South. Generalizing across African cultures is therefore not a simple task.

Although the African culture is quite diverse, Africans still tend to share cultural values across tribes and countries (Kanyongo-Male & Onyango, 1984), such as their collectivistic orientation (Triandis, 1989). People in a collectivistic culture establish their identities through group membership, emphasizing group goals, group conformity, and relationships—even at a high personal cost (Hofstede, 1980; Triandis, 1988, see Chapter 2). If group goals are more valued than individual goals in the African culture, it is reasonable to assume that this might impact the stress-coping process in couples and families.

Although we find great diversity in Africa, general living conditions for hundreds of millions of African individuals, couples, and families are highly stressful. On the one hand, many Africans suffer from stressors similar to what many people experience across the globe, such as unemployment, drug abuse, alcoholism (Kariuki, 2002), poverty (Warah, 2008), chronic diseases such as cancer (MOH, 2013), HIV/AIDS, loss (Maranga, Muya, & Ogila, 2008), problems within family members, and work-related conflict (Kimamo, 2015). On the other hand, many Africans experience stressors that are typical for Africa but less common for Western couples, such as dowry and polygamy (Wanjohi & Wanjohi, 2005), arranged marriages (Mwololo, 2015), strict gender norms (Kimamo, 2009), hard physical labor (e.g., digging minerals; Kimamo, 2015), incompetent and corrupt governments, political infightings, war, high crime rates, inappropriate education systems, brain drain, lack of affordable health care, epidemics, pollution, and drought (Mills, 2010; Kimamo, 2007).

Review of the Literature

General Marital Culture in African Couples

Extended Family Influence on Mate Selection

Based on the principles of collectivism (Triandis, 2001), choosing the right partner is not just an individual affair, but involves the extended family as well (Kanyongo-Male & Onyango, 1984). Although this structure is starting to change as family members scatter in search of work, mate selection for most Africans is a choice of the extended family. Traditionally, African couples live in an extended family set-up, which includes the husband, wife, and children, as well as grandparents, uncles, aunts, and cousins (Mbiti, 1969). Furthermore, marriages across tribes, clans, political perspectives, and religions are often discouraged by the extended family. This is a problem if an individual falls in love with someone who does not meet the family criteria insofar that such relationships are often impeded by the family. Supporting the members of one's ethnicity is considered a noble obligation, and does not fall under the realm of tribalism (Lamb, 1985). This contrasts with the Western assumption that an emotional bond connects a couple together (Coontz, 2007).

Marriage and Dowry

Dowry, or the payment of a bride price, is very common in Africa. Traditionally, dowry was paid in the form of goats and cows, but nowadays it mostly consists of cash payments (Wanjohi & Wanjohi, 2005). Dowry is often high for middle income families such that it leaves the new couple in debt, and increases the financial problems of the couple in the long run—especially if the debt included a bank loan. However, if a woman later seeks separation or divorce, the dowry is supposed to be reimbursed. If a woman's family is unable or unwilling to refund the dowry, she might be forced by her family of origin to return to her husband's family (Kimani, 2007), which is certainly problematic.

Bridal Age and Marriage

At the time of marriage, brides can be very young—sometimes as young as 12 (Mwololo, 2015). In most cases, onset of puberty is used to determine readiness for marriage (Kariuki, Ginsberg, & Kimamo, 2014), though this trend is changing through law enforcement to protect minors. In Kenya, the 2014 Marriage Act outlaws marriage below the age of 18, though the practice is still rampant (Mwololo, 2015). In such cases, parental consent to the marriage is more important than the young woman's agreement.

Polygamy

In more than 50 percent of the countries in Africa, polygamy is legal, and in nearly all others it is illegal, yet common practice and hardly criminalized. Monogamy, though present and practiced in traditional Africa, is not as widespread as polygamy (Waruta, 2005). Polygamy is fairly common for those men who can afford it. Modern education and religion seem to have not discouraged this practice (Kanyongo-Male & Onyango, 1984; Yasuko & Liaw, 1997). In such cases, the senior wives induct the young bride to the marriage set-up. When the wives live together, conflicts may escalate, or the wives may provide social support for each other.

Patriarchal Family Structure

Traditionally, the African family culture is patriarchal (Kariuki, 2010). The husband has final authority over all important decisions related to the family, whereas the wife's role is submissive. However, in many urban areas in Africa, women, compared to men, receive an equal quality education as well as equal jobs and salaries (Kimani, 2012). Nonetheless, being successful, respected at the job, and financially independent often collides with the cultural expectations of an obedient and submissive home life. Similar to the women's rights movement in the last century in the West, African women have started to claim equal rights at home (Kimani, 2012). Even though these claims are understandable, they place the husband in a challenging position, as the husband's cultural expectation is to rule the family. Giving the partner equal rights in decision making is culturally seen as a weakness (Kimani, 2012). A recent study shows that women who claim for equal rights in a relationship face more domestic violence and a higher divorce rate as men fight to regain authority (Keya, 2014). This is concerning in a continent where there are a large number of women who are victims of domestic violence. Indeed, a study conducted by the World Health Organization (WHO) found that 56 percent of women in Tanzania and 71 percent of women in Ethiopia's rural areas reported beatings or other forms of violence by husbands or other intimate partners (WHO, 2005). However, domestic violence in Africa is beginning to change. There are also a substantial number of reported cases where the husband is beaten or injured by his wife (Okeyo, 2015). Taking all of this into consideration, it seems that there is a dearth of research on violence instigated by either spouse—male or female (Okeyo, 2015).

Labor Division in Marriage

Finally, labor division between husbands and wives is clearly defined (Kimamo, 2009). To date, husbands are expected to be the primary breadwinners and provide physical resources such as food, clothing, and shelter for their families (Kimamo, 2009). On the one hand, husbands can be proud of their work if they can satisfy cultural expectations, and provide the financial resources for their families to flourish (Kimamo, 2009). On the other hand, this is a huge burden for many Africans, as there are not enough jobs and millions of husbands struggling to be able to feed their families. As many husbands cannot fulfill the cultural expectations in such difficult circumstances, it is challenging for them, as their families demand financial support (Kimamo, 2015). Wives, on the other hand, are culturally expected to be the homemakers and mothers (Kanyongo-Male & Onyango, 1984). However, the roles of African women are not limited to domestic chores. In some communities they are expected to participate economically and in community affairs (Safiya & Dallalfar, 2012). In more modernized areas of Africa, women receive a high quality education, maintain good jobs, and are now able to cater to their personal needs. As these women gain more respect and empowerment in the workplace, they start to challenge their submissive role in the family (Kimani, 2012).

In summary, couples in Africa are squeezed into a relatively tight corset of cultural norms dictating mate selection and behavior in the relationship. This is quite different for couples in the West, where the prominent idea is that love should emotionally connect the two members of a couple (Coontz, 2007). Moreover, the workload distribution is defined mainly by each couple individually, and the relationships are less hierarchical but more egalitarian. There are also differences between African couples and couples in other collectivistic cultures.

Even though in India and China, arranged marriages are still common but polygamy is culturally not accepted.

The Stress-Coping Process in African Couples: A Theoretical Perspective

The Systemic Transactional Model (STM; Bodenmann, 1995, 1997, 2005; see Chapter 1) suggests that stress occurring outside of the relationship can spill over into the relationship and affect the relationship negatively (Repetti, 1989; Hilpert, Nussbeck, & Bodenmann, 2013), but it is an open question how the 'African culture' affects the stress-coping process in couples. The stress-coping process in couples subsumes who seeks support and who provides support after one member of a couple undergoes a stressful experience. According to the general life situation, many Africans struggle with stressors (e.g., job stress, rearing, lack of leisure time, and finance). Now, in individualistic cultures, where people live only with their nuclear families, their most important and frequent support provider is the partner (Bodenmann, 2000). However, this is not the case for individuals in collectivistic cultures, as they often live with the extended family, which allows them to seek support from any of the family members (e.g., partner, parents, parents-in-law, cousins; Kanyongo-Male & Onyango, 1984). Yet, cultural expectations regulate which support seeker can turn to which support provider. For example, African men are not supposed to seek support from their wives, and even though their wives might be willing to offer support, most African men may not open up in fear of being perceived as weak (Kimamo, 2015). Rather, men discuss their problems either with male friends or choose to regulate their stress levels by using drugs or alcohol. The cultural expectation for women, however, is very different. Women can show vulnerability to the partner (Kimamo, 2015). If a woman faces a stressful situation, she either turns to her husband, to some family members, or to female friends (Oketch-Oboth, 1997). Because experiences can be shared only from one side, this demonstrates that culture can shape the stress-coping process as specific behaviors are culturally expected or scorned.

Empirical Findings

The stress-coping process in couples has been studied in the Western culture for more than two decades (see Chapter 1). However, to date, only two studies have examined the stress spillover effect and stress-coping process in African couples. Their findings start to provide evidence that stress-coping processes may be different in comparison with findings based on Western couples.

Study 1

In the first study, Modie-Moroka (2014) examined how support moderates the link between stress and well-being in 388 low income urban residents in

Francistown, Botswana (South Africa). Overall, 140 men and 248 women ($N =$ 388 individuals) participated in the study with an age range between 18 to 88 years. Forty-eight percent of the sample received no formal education, 36 percent had received primary education, and the rest had received junior certificates or higher degrees. Participants were asked about stressful life events such as serious accidents or injuries, losses, deaths, illnesses, evictions, work related problems, and financial burdens. Further, social support from family and partner, as well as well-being was assessed. Results show that social support was not only positively associated with physical and mental well-being, but also moderated the link between stress and mental well-being. However, Modie-Moroka (2014) did not find a buffering effect, but rather, an amplification effect; the link between stress and mental well-being was greater for people with more support.

Study 2

The second study aimed to examine how dyadic coping and gender affect relationship satisfaction in a larger study of thirty-five countries (Hilpert et al., submitted). In this study, four samples were from Africa (i.e., Ghana, Kenya, Nigeria, and Uganda). Uganda and Kenya are part of East Africa, and are characterized by a shared border, predominantly agricultural communities, and tribes along the border. A major difference in culture is that male and female circumcision is more common in Kenya than in Uganda. Conversely, Ghana and Nigeria are countries from West Africa, and are characterized by predominantly agricultural communities, a shared official language (English) and common cultural practices such as polygamy. Yet, these four countries do maintain some similarities, such as traditional foods like yams and cassava, the traditional female child-bearing role, and polygamous practices. In order to participate, individuals had to be at least 18 years of age and married. In each country, researchers[1] recruited participants on their own. All data were assessed by a paper pencil approach and participants did not receive incentives for participation.

Sample

In total, 900 people from Africa participated in the study ($n_{Ghana} = 104$; $n_{Kenya} = 94$; $n_{Nigeria} = 602$; $n_{Uganda} = 100$). Table 16.1 shows the demographic background of the four samples separately for men and women. Most participants were between 30 to 50 years of age and had been married for 2 to 25 years, indicating that the samples were heterogeneous. On average, participants had two to three children. Overall, there were no significant gender differences in demographics and the four countries are representative for East and West Africa (see Table 16.1).

Measures

Participants completed a long survey for the larger study, but the measures, which were relevant for the current study include positive dyadic coping and marital

TABLE 16.1 Samples' demographics

	Ghana		Kenya		Nigeria		Uganda	
	Men (N = 53) M (SD)	Women (N = 51) M (SD)	Men (N = 47) M (SD)	Women (N = 47) M (SD)	Men (N = 304) M (SD)	Women (N = 298) M (SD)	Men (N = 62) M (SD)	Women (N = 36) M (SD)
Age	37.5 (8.4)	43.3 (9.7)	32.8 (7.0)	31.8 (6.6)	37.7 (8.9)	40.2 (9.0)	35.3 (8,8)	34.1 (12.7)
Marital duration	10.2 (8.5)	13.9 (10.3)	8.6 (6.9)	6.5 (5.0)	10.8 (8.9)	9.8 (8.5)	8.3 (7.0)	8.1 (10.2)
Children	2.3 (1.6)	2.7 (2.3)	1.9 (1.1)	1.8 (1.3)	2.4 (1.8)	2.6 (1.8)	3.0 (2.0)	2.6 (2,0)
Financial situation	2.02 (0.7)	2.04 (0.8)	2.7 (0.7)	2.6 (0.7)	2.0 (1.0)	2.1 (1.0)	2.4 (0.8)	2.9 (1.0)

satisfaction. In order to assess dyadic coping, two subscales (supportive and common dyadic coping) were assessed with two items each (Bodenmann, 2008). But because supportive and common dyadic coping were nearly identical in predicting relationship satisfaction, Hilpert and colleagues (submitted), we used an aggregated subscale of these subscales known as positive dyadic coping. Internal consistency ranged from 0.85 to 0.88 across the different countries. In addition, marital satisfaction was assessed with the Marriage and Relationships Questionnaire (MARQ; Russell & Wells, 1986) with a nine-item scale. The internal consistency of the MARQ ranged from 0.88 to 0.93 across the different countries.

Statistical Analysis

The hypotheses were tested in a multilevel modeling approach, as individuals were nested in countries (Raudenbush & Bryk, 2002). As individuals from a specific country share the same environment, Hilpert and colleagues (submitted) separated further between-country variability $(\overline{DC_j})$ and within-country variability $(DC_{ij}-\overline{DC_j})$, where i indexes individuals and j indexes countries (Eid & Lischetzke, 2013). The following equation was tested, controlling for age, marital duration, amount of children, and education:

$$\hat{y}_{ij} = \beta_0 + \beta_1 (\overline{DC_j}) + \beta_2 (DC_{ij}-\overline{DC_j}) + \beta_3 (\text{gender}_{ij}) + \beta_4 (\text{age}_{ij}) + \beta_5 (\text{marital duration}_{ij}) + \beta_6 (\text{children}_{ij}) + \beta_7 (\text{education}_{ij}) + r_i + u_{0ij} + u_{1ij}$$

In a second model, Hilpert and colleagues (submitted) included the interaction between supportive dyadic coping (within-country variability) and gender into the aforementioned question.

Results

Table 16.2 shows mean and standard deviations of supportive dyadic coping and marital satisfaction. Results show that dyadic coping behavior and marital satisfaction were relatively high in all four samples (range 1–5). On average, participants reported to be very satisfied with their relationships and they also reported relatively frequent dyadic coping behavior. Only women in Uganda reported significantly lower levels of relationship satisfaction and dyadic coping behavior.

Results of the multilevel analysis show that the association between dyadic coping and relationship satisfaction is significant in all thirty-five countries ($\beta = 0.35$), but the effects in the African samples were significant lower: Uganda ($\beta = 0.24$), Ghana ($\beta = 0.16$), Nigeria ($\beta = 0.11$), and Kenya ($\beta = 0.25$). Furthermore, the effects for the four African nations were in the bottom eight in comparison with all thirty-five countries, indicating that the effect of supportive dyadic coping on relationship satisfaction is significant, but lower in all four samples in comparison to most countries outside of Africa. Finally, Hilpert and colleagues (submitted) further tested if gender moderates the association between positive

TABLE 16.2 Means and standard deviations for all study variables

Scales	Ghana		Kenya		Nigeria		Uganda	
	Men (N = 53) M (SD)	Women (N = 51) M (SD)	Men (N = 47) M (SD)	Women (N = 47) M (SD)	Men (N = 304) M (SD)	Women (N = 298) M (SD)	Men (N = 62) M (SD)	Women (N = 36) M (SD)
Dyadic coping	3.9 (0.9)	3.7 (1.0)	3.7 (1.1)	3.9 (1.0)	3.9 (1.0)	3.9 (1.0)	3.7 (0.9)	3.5 (1.0)
Marital satisfaction	4.7 (0.6)	4.7 (0.4)	4.6 (0.6)	4.7 (0.5)	4.7 (0.5)	4.7 (0.5)	4.6 (0.4)	4.2 (0.7)

dyadic coping and relationship satisfaction. Findings show that on average, gender does not moderate this association across the thirty-five nations. However, a significant moderation effect of gender was found in Uganda and Nigeria, and the effect of positive dyadic coping on relationship satisfaction is stronger for men in Uganda ($\beta = 0.23$), whereas a stronger effect was found for women in Nigeria ($\beta = -0.06$).

Study 3

The findings in study 2 raise the question of why the association between positive dyadic coping and relationship satisfaction is so low in Africa. In order to answer this, the second author asked a group of primary school teachers (N = 75) for a causal explanation. The seventy-five teachers were advancing their studies by pursuing a bachelor's degree in education at the University of Nairobi in Kenya. On average, these teachers were 30 years of age and came from diverse regions and communities in Kenya. The sample comprised of thirty-eight males and thirty-seven females, and a majority of them were married.

In a human development class, the teachers were taught the concept of dyadic coping. Their homework was to think about explanations, and consider why the link between dyadic coping and relationship satisfaction is lower for couples in Africa in comparison to Western couples. The next day, the teachers were asked to write down the causes that they believed might explain the low linkage based on their own experiences. Finally, all the causes were qualitatively analyzed. Results showed that the teachers had four main explanations: African marital culture, patriarchy, poverty, and religion.

African Marital Culture and Patriarchy

Most teachers (37.5 percent) reported that both the African marital culture combined with the patriarchic system could explain the small association between dyadic coping and relationship satisfaction. According to the teachers, the dowry systems leads to the perception that women can be bought and are, therefore, part of the husband's property. Consequently, a wife is not really seen as an equal partner facilitating mutual exchange and support. The main task for a woman is to give birth to children, raise them, and cook for the husband. The African man's most important duty is to protect the patriarchal image in a culture that does not allow him to appear weak.

Poverty

In addition, 31.3 percent of all the teachers mentioned poverty as a cause. Unemployment or low payments often lead to conflict as basic needs cannot be fulfilled. The obvious issue is that lack of money is a huge problem, and we can assume that this is stressful for the husband. Culturally, the man is responsible to earn enough money, but if there are no jobs available, he might not be able to fulfill his family expectations. Not having enough money is such a severe problem that it is difficult for the wife to show empathy and understanding. In addition, many jobs are physically exhaustive (e.g., working in mines), which then undermines the ability for the husband to connect with the wife after work. Finally, one cannot take leave in many jobs without fear of being replaced. Not having time or money for spending quality time together hinders the bonding process between the husband and wife.

Religion

Third, 22.5 percent of the study participants suggested that religion is another factor explaining the weak link. Participants thought that the two widespread religions in Africa, Christianity and Islam, teach that the wife's position is inferior to the husband's. This then reiterates a similar problem mentioned in the previous section. If the husband and wife cannot meet each other on an equal level, mutual emotional support is difficult if the situation is perceived as unfair.

General Discussion of the Findings

In summary, there are many possible explanations for the lower association between dyadic coping and relationship satisfaction, such as African marital culture, polygamy, traditional gender roles, the dowry system, poverty, and religion. However, it is most likely that an interaction between different factors might explain the lower association best. If we compare, for example, African couples with Romanian couples, we find some overlap. Couples from Africa and couples from Romania struggle financially (for more about Romanian couples see Chapter 12) and are religious. However, although we find a significantly lower association between dyadic coping and relationship satisfaction in African couples than on average across the thirty-five nations, we find a significantly higher association for Romanian couples (Hilpert et al., submitted). Thus, coping dyadically seems to pull Romanian couples close together, as they live in nuclear families, have no cultural boundaries to sharing their vulnerabilities, and have, on average, good education levels. The interaction between previously mentioned factors (e.g., living in nuclear families, polygamy, hierarchical marital culture, religious beliefs of female inferiority, low education levels, and restricted cultural acceptance for male vulnerability) in combination with poverty, seems to undermine the general positive effect of dyadic coping on relationship outcomes.

Implications for Practice

In the last two decades, several couples' interventions were developed, which in theory can be extended for use with African couples. However, these couples' interventions (i) were developed based on studies examining behaviors in Western, white middle-class couples (Kariuki, 2002) and (ii) the effectiveness of these couple interventions were tested on Western white middle-class couples (Shadish & Baldwin, 2003) with few exceptions (Falconier, 2015; Johnson, 2012). Concepts, theories, and methodology in African studies still reflect a Western orientation (Kariuki, 2002). As we provided evidence that the current African (marital) culture is in many aspects fundamentally different to the Western culture, we conclude that couples' interventions cannot be simply transferred to the African context. Rather, more research is needed in order to understand and adapt a culturally sensitive intervention to deal with the hierarchical structure of the relationship, where husbands cannot show their vulnerabilities.

Implications for Research

As there have not been many studies on couple and family mechanisms on the African continent thus far, we suggest that couples in Africa, their marital culture, and family traditions should be studied more rigorously. In order to understand Africans, one must be familiar with their culture, history, and socio-economic situations (Kariuki, 2002). Overall, four areas should be examined more closely.

Dyadic Coping

As there are hardly any studies about the stress-coping processes based on couples living in Africa, more studies are needed to examine different aspects of these processes. We need to better understand the effect of stressors unique to African culture. Thus far, we can only speculate that addressing dowry and polygamy (Wanjohi & Wanjohi, 2005), arranged marriage (Mwololo, 2015), corrupt governments, political infightings, war, lack of affordable healthcare, epidemics, pollution, and drought (Kimani, 2007; Mills, 2010) might require fundamentally different skills for the partner than dealing with common stressors such as parenting or job stress. Furthermore, it is clear that support-seeking as well as selecting a support provider is strongly influenced by culture (Kariuki, 2002). More studies are needed to understand how this cultural influence works in traditional and more modern couples.

Culture and Cultural Changes

Couple interactions are influenced by many cultural aspects such as the dowry system (Wanjohi & Wanjohi, 2005), religion (Mbiti, 1969) gender role, and patriarchy (Kimamo, 2009). Future research should examine couple interactions in respect to these cultural influences. Furthermore, some of these cultural aspects are in transition. For example, some women advocate for more equality in their relationships. Such transitions can be very difficult, as the increase in couple violence seems to suggest, and more research could help us understand this transition. This, in turn, allows researchers to give better suggestions. As gender inequality seems to play a huge role for African couples, and we can assume that the next generation of newlywed women will continue to fight for equal rights, more research is needed on how this problem can be solved. Currently, it appears to be a very complicated problem, as husbands will be culturally perceived as weak if they give equal rights to their wives. On the other hand, however, economically successful women now desire an equal role in a relationship. Conflicts are, therefore, unavoidable in this context. As we have seen, this problem is already associated with partner violence, and, therefore, should be a focus in research. This is crucial in order to provide reasonable and culturally adapted solutions to make the transition from a traditional to a more modern culture less hurtful for the next generation of intimate relationships.

Diversity

In contrast to our current perspective in this book chapter on cultural similarities across the African continent, it is reasonable to assume that couples across different countries and tribes may differ widely. More research is needed in order to differentiate between dyadic coping processes across African countries and tribes. Although in the current article we focused on cultural similarities (for example, collectivism, patriarchy, and extended family structure) across Africa, this was necessary in order to make a generalizable conclusion. However, future research should focus on examining differences across different countries, tribes, age, social economic standards, and sexual orientation.

Study Design

Finally, we would like to make an argument about the study design for future research. Stress and coping processes occur on a daily basis. As the main phenomena are about the processes within individuals across time, cross-sectional study designs may not be ideal for capturing these specific phenomena. In the last decade, cross-sectional studies have provided us with insight into the stress-coping phenomenon (Falconier, Jackson, Hilpert, & Bodenmann, 2015), but these studies are limited in that they cannot inform us about the causal mechanism. Therefore, we suggest that the stress-coping process be studied with data generated through longitudinal studies (e.g., daily diaries; see Bolger & Laurenceau, 2014).

Conclusion

In this book chapter we discussed the influence of African culture on the stress-coping process in couples. Thus far, few studies have examined the stress-coping process and therefore, more research is needed. This new knowledge could be used to adapt couples' interventions to the African culture. However, another strategy could be to scrutinize some of the current cultural approaches and draw out their inherent pros and cons. This approach could enable us to generate better solutions, which could be more appropriate and helpful for a cultural transition. For example, *family influence on mate selection* and the *dowry system* are common in Africa. Both aspects are aimed at establishing a stable foundation for a couple, which is essential in an environment where resources are limited. Further, family influence and dowry prevent young people from marrying when they just fall in love, only to realize later that the chosen partner is not the right one. On the other hand, parents could forbid potentially satisfying relationships due to arguments about group membership, religion, education level, or dowry. The practice of dowry needs to be evaluated as well, as dowry often commercializes women, hindering more egalitarian-based relationships.

In addition, some cultural aspects such as *patriarchy* and *inequality* between genders seem to be in transition. If a couple can accept the traditional role model, where the husband is the breadwinner and the main decider and the wife is more obedient, it might work just fine, as it has worked for centuries in Africa and also in Europe. However, in the modern world, where women have equal education and claim equal rights, the traditional model leads to tension in couples, which might be comparable to emancipation in the Western world some decades ago. Even though most husbands and wives in the Western world see each other as equal, the emancipation has not resulted in a panacea to make couples happy, as is demonstrated by the high divorce rate in the Western world. Rather, it works for some couples, who feel very close to each other, whereas many other couples struggle to find compromises acceptable for both of them. Solving this transition and trying to avoid an increase in couple violence seems to be a complex problem requiring intensive and interdisciplinary research. However, it is worth exploring solutions as the next decade approaches, and millions of people will be seeking marital partners, and navigating their way in a world where cultures and traditions are in transition.

Note

1 The following researchers assisted with data collection in Ghana, Kenya, Nigeria, and Uganda: Aryeetey, R., Inogbo, C. F., James, B., Laar, A., Kimamo, C. O. N., Ntayi, J., Ojedokun, O., & Onyishi, I. E.

References

Bodenmann, G. (1995). *Bewältigung von Stress in Partnerschaften. Der Einfluss von Belastungen auf die Qualität von Paarbeziehungen* [Coping with stress in relationships. The effect of stress on relationship quality]. Bern: Verlag Hans Huber.

Bodenmann, G. (1997). Dyadic coping—a systemic-transactional view of stress and coping among couples: Theory and empirical findings. *European Review of Applied Psychology*, 47, 137–140.

Bodenmann, G. (2000). *Stress und Coping bei Paaren* [*Stress and coping in couples*]. Göttingen, Germany: Hogrefe.

Bodenmann, G. (2005). Störungen von interpersonellen Systemen [Problems in interpersonal systems]. In M. Perrez & U. Baumgartner (Hrsg.), *Lehrbuch: Klinische Psychologie— Psychotherapie* (S. 1105 –1138). Bern: Huber Bodenmann.

Bodenmann, G. (2008). *Dyadisches Coping Inventar (DCI). Manual. [Dyadic Coping Inventory, DCI]*. Bern/Goettingen: Huber/Hogrefe Tests.

Bolger, N., & Laurenceau, J. P. (2014). *Intensive longitudinal methods: An introduction to diary and experience sampling research*. New York: The Guilford Press.

CIA World Fact book, (2012). Retrieved: www.cia.gov/library/publications/the-world-factbook/rankorder/2004rank.html

Collier, P., & Hoeffler, A. (2005). *Coup Traps: Why does Africa have so many Coups d'Etat?* Paper presented at the annual meeting of the American Political Science Association, Washington DC.

Coontz, S. (2006). *Marriage, a history: From obedience to intimacy, or how love conquered marriage*. Penguin.

Eid, M., & Lischetzke, T. (2013). Statistische Methoden der Auswertung kulturver-gleichender Studien [Statistical Methods of Cross-cultural Studies]. In T. Ringeisen, P. Genkova, & F. Leong, *Stress und Kultur: interkulturelle und kulturvergleichende Perspektiven [Cultural comparison in social support within relationships and families]*. Springer: Wiesbaden.

Falconier, M. K., Jackson, J., Hilpert, J., & Bodenmann, G. (2015). Dyadic coping and relationship satisfaction: A meta-analysis. *Clinical Psychology Review, 42*, 28–46.

Gudmastad, E (2013). 2013 *World Population Data Sheet*. Retrieved from http://www.prb.org/pdf13/2013-WPDS-infographic_MED.pdf

Hayase, Y., & Liaw, K. (1997). Factors on polygamy in Sub-Saharan Africa: Findings based on the demographic and health survey. *The Developing Economies, 35*(3), 293–327.

Hilpert, P., Sorokowski, P., et al., (in preparation). The association between dyadic coping behavior and marital satisfaction worldwide: A multi-national study in 35 nations.

Hilpert, P., Bodenmann, G., Nussbeck, F. N., & Bradbury, T. N. (2013). Predicting relationship satisfaction in distressed and non-distressed couples based on a stratified sample: a matter of conflict, positivity, or support? *Family Science, 4*, 110–120. doi:10.1080/19424620.2013.830633

Hofstede, G. (1980). *Culture's consequences: International differences in work-related values*. Beverly Hills, CA: Sage Publications.

Johnson, M. D. (2012). Healthy marriage initiatives: On the need for empiricism in policy implementation. *American Psychologist, 67*(4), 296–308.

Kanyongo-Male, D., & Onyango, P. (1984). *The sociology of the African family*. London: Longman.

Kariuki, G. C. (2010). Women participation in the Kenyan society. *The African Executive, 296*(3), 1–8.

Kariuki, P. W. (2002). The challenge and role of psychology to development in Africa, *Journal of Education, 1*, 73–80.

Kariuki, P. W., Ginsberg, P., & Kimamo, C. O. N. (2014). The Changing Concept of Adolescence in Kenya. *Psychology Thought, 7*(1), 55–65.

Keya, L. (2014, January 6). Why Nairobi marriages flop. *The Nairobian*, Retrieved from www.standardmedia.co.ke

Kimamo, C. O. N. (2007). *University of Nairobi student's views about why Africans are not famous in Inventions*. Proceeding of Annual KDSA Conference. pp. 120–126.

Kimamo, C. O. N. (2009). College students' views concerning purported male chauvinism. *Journal of Education, 3*, 39–46.

Kimamo, C. O. N. (2015). *Causes of Poor dyadic coping among Africans*. Paper presented at the University of Nairobi First year Bachelor of Arts Students Seminar, 2015.

Kimani, M. (2007). Taking on violence against women in Africa: International norms, local activism starts to alter laws, attitudes. *Africa Renewal, 21*(2), 4.

Lamb, D. (1985). *The Africans.* New York: Vintage Books.

Maranga, R. O., Muya, S. M., & Ogila, K. A. (2008). *Fundamentals of HIV/AIDS education.* JKUAT: Juja.

Mbiti, J. (1969). *African religions and philosophy.* London: Heinemann Educational Books.

Mills, G. (2010). *Why Africa is poor.* CATO: Centre for Global Liberty and Prosperity.

Modie-Moroka, T. (2014). Stress, social relationships and health outcomes in low-income Francistown, Botswana. *Social Psychiatry and Psychiatric Epidemiology, 49*(8), 1269–1277.

MOH (2013). *National Palliative Care Guidelines.* Nairobi: Ministry of Health.

Mwamwenda, T. S. (1995). *Educational psychology: An African perspective.* Durban: Butterworths.

Mwololo, M. (2015). Study shows child marriage still rampant in Kenya despite being outlawed. *Daily Nation,* 31.

Njideka, H. U. (2013). African youth, innovation and the changing society. *Huffington Post.* Retrieved from www.huffingtonpost.com

Oketch-Oboth, J. W. B (1997). Emotional Expression and Health Outcomes. Paper presented at the International Conference on Psychology and Counseling at the United States International University, Nairobi.

Okeyo, V. (2015). The silent abuse of Kenyan men and how society abets it, *Daily Nation,* 2. Retrieved from www.nation.co.ke

Raudenbush, S. W. & Bryk, A. S. (2002). *Hierarchical Linear Models* (Second ed.). Thousand Oaks: Sage Publications.

Repetti, R. (1989). Effects of daily workload on subsequent behavior during marital interaction—the roles of social withdrawal and spouse support. *Journal of Personality and Social Psychology, 57*(4), 651–659.

Russell, R., & Wells, P. (1993). *Marriage and relationship questionnaire: MARQ handbook.* Kent, UK: Hodder and Stoughton.

Safiya, A. J., & Dallalfar, A. (2012). *Sex and Gender Roles.* Retrieved from www.lesley.edu/ journal-pedagogy-pluralism-practice/safiya-jardine-arlene-dallalfar/sex-gender-roles/

Sayre, April Pulley (1999). *Africa.* Twenty-First Century Books.

Shadish, W. R. & Baldwin, S. A. (2003). Meta-analysis of MFT interventions. *Journal of Marriage and Family, 29*(4), 547–570.

Triandis, H. C. (1989). The self and social behaviour in differing cultural contexts. *Psychological Review, 96*(3), 506–520.

Triandis, H. C. (2001). Individualism-collectivism and personality. *Journal of Personality, 69*(6), 907–924.

Wanjohi, G. S., & Wanjohi, G. W. (2005). *Social and religious concerns of East Africa.* Gerald: Nairobi.

Warah, R. (2008). *Missionaries, mercenaries and misfits.* Central Milton Keyes: Author House UK Ltd.

Waruta, D. W. (2005). Marriage and family in contemporary African society: challenges in pastoral counseling. In D. W. Waruta and H. W. Kinoti, (Eds.), *Pastoral care in African Christianity,* 101–119. Nairobi: Acton Publishers.

WHO (2005). WHO Multi-country study on women's health and domestic violence against women. Retrieved from www.who.int/gender/violence/who_multicountry_study/en/

Yasuko H., & Liaw, K. L. (1997). Factors on polygamy in sub-Saharan Africa: Findings based on the demographic and health surveys. *Development Economics, 35,* 293–327.

17

DYADIC COPING IN AUSTRALIAN COUPLES

Melissa G. Bakhurst and William K. Halford

Introduction

This chapter explores the ways in which dyadic coping influences the adjustment of Australian couples and reports on the first study to assess dyadic coping and apply the systemic-transactional model (STM; Bodenmann, 2005) in Australian couples, within a sample of Australian military couples. We begin by describing the characteristics of Australian couple relationships, followed by the distinctive benefits and challenges of the military lifestyle for couples. The relevance of dyadic coping to understanding how couples adapt to the military lifestyle is explored, and then data is presented on the association of dyadic coping with relationship adjustment. We conclude by analyzing the implications of a dyadic coping focus for couple relationship education.

Review of the Literature

Couples' Relationships in Australia

Australian couples have some characteristics that are distinctive from other countries. Relative to the U.S., where a significant amount of couple research has been conducted, there are low levels of religiosity in marriage among Australians (Australian Bureau of Statistics, 2010; United States Census, 2012). Specifically, nearly 70 percent of all Australian couples marry in civil ceremonies rather than religious ceremonies; whereas only 30 percent of U.S. marriages are civil ceremonies (Australian Bureau of Statistics, 2010; United States Census, 2012).

Relative to the twenty-seven member countries of the Organisation for Economic Co-operation and Development (OECD), Australia has a relatively high fertility rate (1.9 children per woman), which is above the OECD average (1.7) and close to the replacement rate (2.1) (OECD, 2011). The rate of adult women in the workforce is 66.2 percent, which has been rising steadily since the 1960s, is now well above OECD average (59.6 percent), and is similar to the U.S. (62.2 percent). However, part-time work is more common among Australian women with young children than in other developed countries (OECD, 2011).

Cohabiting couples constitute about 17 percent of Australian couple households, which is substantially higher than in the U.S. (about 12 percent), and similar to countries such as Denmark, France, and Finland (OECD, 2011). Moreover, more than 80 percent of Australian couples married in the last twenty years cohabited before marriage (Hewitt & Baxter, 2015). For most couples, cohabitation is a transitional phase as within five years couples tend to either marry (40 percent of couples) or separate (45 percent of couples), with only 15 percent of couples continuing long-term cohabitation beyond a five-year period (Hewitt & Baxter, 2015).

Under Australian law, couples who live together for two years are of very similar status to married couples, with regards to financial and legal matters (Hewitt & Baxter, 2015). For example, cohabiting partners are recognized for spouse entitlements in terms of employment benefits, death, and disability entitlements, retirement benefits, and access to the Family Court to resolve separation disputes. At the same time, cohabiting and marital couple relationships have some distinctions. In Australia, cohabiting couples break up at much higher rates than married couples, which is suggested to reflect less partner commitment to cohabiting than married relationships, and lower constraints of commitment (i.e., separate assets, less likely to have children together) (Hewitt & Baxter, 2015).

Same-sex marriage is not recognized in Australia; although Australian cohabiting same-sex couples have the same legal rights as cohabiting heterosexual couples. In the 2011 Australian census, there were 33,714 self-identified same-sex couples, a threefold increase since the 1996 census. This increase likely reflects the increasing willingness of same-sex couples to make their relationships public, both by living together and by reporting (Australian Bureau of Statistics, 2012). Same-sex couples make up 1.6 percent of all couple households for partners between ages 18–35 years, but only consist of 0.1 percent of couple households for partners of ages 55 and older (Australian Bureau of Statistics, 2012), suggesting a generational change in the likelihood of openly cohabiting in same-sex relationships. Assuming these trends continue, the number of same-sex couples is likely to increase substantially in Australia across the next two decades.

Australia is a multicultural society with people tracing their ancestry to more than 140 other countries, with the three most widely spoken languages being English, Chinese, and Italian (Australian Bureau of Statistics, 2012). Australia's population is growing quite quickly relative to most other developed countries, in part due to the high fertility rate and in part from relatively high rates of immigration with more than 30 percent of the population born outside of

Australia (Australian Bureau of Statistics, 2012). Australia's multicultural nature is underscored by the fact that more than 30 percent of Australian couples are classified as intercultural (i.e., consisting of partners from different cultural backgrounds), which is similar to the rates of intermarriage in the most culturally diverse regions of the world such as Singapore, Taiwan, and Hawaii (Hiew, Halford, & Liu, 2014).

In summary, Australian couples can be characterized as low on religiosity, high on rates of cohabitation, high on numbers of children and dual career families, and high on cultural diversity with high rates of intercultural relationships. Cohabitation is the most common pathway into committed couple relationships, with high rates of break up among such couples. There is a rapidly increasing number of cohabiting same-sex couples.

Support in Romantic Relationships

These couple characteristics suggest a particular importance for dyadic coping in Australian couples. Support from family and friends for less religious couples, cohabiting couples, same-sex couples, and intercultural couples is often lower than for religious, married, heterosexual, and intracultural couples (Halford, 2011). Consequently, partners are often more reliant on each other for support in the face of stress, as they lack supplementary support. Moreover, other characteristics suggest Australian couples often face significant external stresses that they must manage together. For example, the high Australian fertility rates combined with workforce participation rates result in large numbers of dual career families (OECD, 2011), who often struggle with balancing work and family demands. Intercultural couples sometimes struggle with reconciling different cultural standards for how couple relationships should be, as well as different cultural-based styles of intimate communication, which might explain elevated rates of separation relative to intercultural couples (Hiew, Halford, & Liu, 2014). Same-sex couples often are exposed to homophobic discrimination that is associated with high risk of relationship distress (Frost & Meyer, 2009) in the face of external judgment and disapproval of their relationship.

In the current chapter, we present the first research study that looked at dyadic coping behaviors in Australian couples. As noted previously, data were collected in a sample of Australian military couples. As military couples have a unique lifestyle and experience challenges distinctive from those of the broader population of Australian couples, we discuss these unique characteristics before presenting the results of the study.

Australian Military Couples

Military couples in Australia have a number of protective relationship factors that include stable employment, financial benefits, and access to healthcare (Defence

Force Recruiting, 2014). Military personnel are screened for mental and physical health problems during recruitment (Cardona & Ritchie, 2007), and members have good health in comparison to the general population (Waller & McGuire, 2011). Military couples are, nonetheless, exposed to a number of stressors that have the potential to erode couple relationships (Allen, Rhoades, Stanley, & Markman, 2011). Military couples relocate frequently, causing potential social and employment difficulties for spouses and children (Castaneda & Harrell, 2008). These frequent relocations are disruptive to military spouses' careers, with Australian Defense spouses out of work on an average of 5.4 months following relocation (Department of Defence, 2012). Frequent absences and irregular hours mean the non-military spouse often has to take primary responsibility for childcare (Faber, Willerton, Clymer, MacDermid, & Weiss, 2008). Military personnel are often away on training exercises and deployments, putting couples at risk of emotional disconnect (Everson & Herzog, 2011).

A number of Western countries (the U.S., the U.K., Australia, Canada, New Zealand, Denmark, Spain, the Netherlands, and others) have deployed large numbers of troops to Iraq or Afghanistan since 2001. Australia, with a relatively small military, has deployed approximately 33,000 members (Waller, Kanesarajah, Zheng, & Dobson, 2013). Wartime deployments put members at risk of serious injury or death, as spouses at home fear for the safety of their loved ones (Allen et al., 2011). Personnel who return home with physical disabilities may experience strain in their couple relationship, as both spouses deal with the loss of independence associated with the caregiver-patient relationship (Centre for Military and Veterans' Health, 2010). Deployments also put personnel at risk of mental health problems and other trauma-related issues, such as intimate partner violence and substance abuse (Jacobson et al., 2008; Taft, Walling, Howard, & Monson, 2011). In particular, there are high rates of Post-traumatic Stress Disorder (PTSD) among returning military personnel, and the presence of PTSD is associated with low relationship satisfaction among military couples (Allen et al., 2011; Miller, Schaefer, Renshaw, & Blais, 2013) and elevated psychological distress in spouses (McGuire et al., 2012). In addition to personnel with clinical PTSD, many more military personnel retiring from deployment experience sub-clinical elevations of trauma stress symptoms (e.g., emotional numbing, hyperarousal) that are associated with low relationship satisfaction (Nelson Goff, Crow, Reisbig, & Hamilton, 2007; Renshaw, Blais, & Caska, 2011).

Although most Western armed forces share similar strengths and challenges as a result of service, the situation for military couples varies somewhat across different countries. For example, military couples in the U.S. often have the opportunity to live on military bases with support from other military personnel close at hand (U.S. Army, 2014). In contrast, Australian military couples most often live in the community and are at higher risk of becoming isolated following relocation, and consequently relying more on their spouse for support. On the other hand, Australian military personnel earn higher wages than many other international forces (Defense Force Recruiting, 2013) and are likely to have fewer financial stressors than military families in countries like the U.S., where the baseline military income is much lower (Defense Finance and Accounting Service, 2014).

In summary, Australian couples differ from couples around the world in a number of important ways. Overall low religiosity, paired with high prevalence of cohabitation, same-sex and intercultural couples, put some Australian couples at increased risk of relationship distress. Australian military couples have unique strengths and challenges to their relationships in addition to those faced by civilian couples, such as financial stability, frequent relocations, and time apart. These stressors differ slightly from those experienced by other Western military couples, giving Australian military couples a distinctive risk and resiliency profile.

Couples Coping with Stress

Dyadic coping has been consistently linked to high couple relationship satisfaction (Bodenmann, Meuwly, & Kayser, 2011; Herzberg, 2013; Papp & Witt, 2010). Dyadic coping skills may prove especially useful for military couples, because they face a number of external stressors; external stressors are those due to factors outside of the relationship (e.g., work stress) that can spill over into the relationship and cause negative interactions (Bodenmann & Randall, 2012). Although there is currently no research in this area, in this section we discuss the ways that military couples might use dyadic coping to deal with the stresses of the military lifestyle.

As noted earlier, military personnel are typically relocated every few years (Castaneda & Harrell, 2008). Dyadic coping could involve spouses each expressing their feelings about these relocations to their partners, developing a shared understanding of the challenges for them as a couple, and then jointly developing and implementing agreed-on solutions. For example, after such a discussion the military spouse might help their partner to find new social connections by introducing them to the partners of fellow military personnel. In this way, both spouses work together to cope with relocation challenges, ensuring one partner does not feel alone in coping with their situation.

Deployment is a major stressor for military personnel, who must live and work in a war zone, as well as their spouses and families who fear for their safety (Allen et al., 2011). One area in which couples can dyadically cope is by jointly deciding what to communicate about while apart. Military personnel are often exposed to traumatic experiences during deployment. Some personnel might wish to discuss these experiences with their spouse, but some personnel might avoid such disclosure (Balderrama-Durbin et al., 2013). Spouses may seek disclosure from their partner, or may feel unable to deal emotionally with these stories and avoid such discussion. Moreover, personnel might feel guilt and helplessness if their spouse is struggling to cope with loneliness, childrens' difficulties, or other crises while they are overseas on deployment. If couples talk about expected challenges before deployment and discuss ground rules for communication when separation occurs, they can reach a mutually acceptable agreement about how to best cope dyadically. For example, couples may agree to only discuss deployment experiences in general terms rather than focusing on details of events. Similarly, there might be agreement to only discuss major problems (e.g., a serious illness) and leaving less critical issues (e.g., minor child misbehavior) until they are reunited.

Reintegration after deployment is another key time for military couples to utilize dyadic coping. Military personnel often struggle to reintegrate into family life after a long separation, while civilian spouses have become accustomed to a new lifestyle and can find it difficult to readjust to living with their partner. Couples can use dyadic coping here by speaking openly to each other about what they are finding stressful and come up with joint strategies for coping during this adjustment period. Military personnel dealing with trauma-related symptoms who discuss their experiences during deployment with their spouse tend to adjust better (Monson et al., 2012), and couples who discuss the military spouse's combat experiences have higher relationship satisfaction (Balderrama-Durbin et al., 2013). It seems likely that civilian spouses who show empathy can aid in the recovery process by allowing their partner to emotionally process their traumatic experiences and feel supported. Civilian spouses can also contribute to their partners' recovery by ensuring that they support graded exposure to feared situations. For example, if the military spouse is anxious in large crowds, the civilian spouse might prompt and support graduated attempts to enter and manage that anxiety-eliciting situation. In contrast, a civilian spouse's well-intended offer to support military personnel to avoid feared situations (e.g., the spouse doing all the shopping alone) may inadvertently prevent exposure and hinder their partner's recovery. Military couples can benefit from psycho-education, which addresses these issues and provides guidelines for couples on how to dyadically cope with the challenges of deployment and reintegration.

Supportive and Common Dyadic Coping in Australian Military Couples

As described in Chapter 1, the STM perspective of dyadic coping (Bodenmann, 2005) differentiates between supportive and common dyadic coping. *Supportive dyadic coping* refers to behaviors displayed by an individual in an attempt to support their partner. *Common dyadic coping* involves the couple working together to overcome stressors, by developing potential strategies and deciding together on an appropriate solution. Here, we present new data attained from a sample of Australian military couples, which assessed the association of supportive and common dyadic coping with relationship satisfaction.

Couples were recruited as part of a larger program of research evaluating *Couple CARE in Uniform* in a randomized controlled trial (Halford & Bakhurst, 2013). *Couple CARE in Uniform* is an adaptation of the Couple CARE relationship education program (Halford, 2011), with the adaptation paying particular attention to the external challenges faced by military couples such as separations, relocations, and deployment. The Couple CARE programs are similar to the Couple Coping Enhancement Training (CCET) of Bodenmann and Shantinath (2004) (see Chapter 6 for more information). Both programs use cognitive-behavioral techniques to facilitate change in couples, with Couple CARE focusing on self-regulation in partners, while CCET places an emphasis on how dyads manage stress. Data reported here are based on assessments completed by couples before they began relationship education. The male and female partner in each couple rated their own and their spouse's dyadic coping behaviors, and each partner reported on their relationship satisfaction. This enabled us to use one partner's reports of dyadic coping to predict the other partner's relationship satisfaction. This method circumvents the limitations of common method variance, in which one person's report of behavior is used to predict their own outcome. Positive associations were expected between (a) an individual's dyadic coping behaviors, as reported by their partner, and their relationship satisfaction (an actor effect), (b) an individual's self-reported dyadic coping behaviors and their partner's relationship satisfaction (a partner effect), and (c) an individual's self-evaluation of the couple's conjoint dyadic coping behaviors and their partner's relationship satisfaction.

Study Sample

Participants were thirty-two couples in which one or both partners were members of the Australian Defence Force (ADF). Inclusion criteria for the study were that couples had been married or cohabiting for at least six months, and that neither partner was currently receiving psychological therapy for an individual or couple-related issue. Participants were recruited through articles in ADF newsletters and magazines, flyers, presentations to military units, and radio interviews.

Participants' mean age was 34.3 years ($SD = 9.0$) for men and 32.8 years ($SD = 9.0$) for women. Twenty-seven couples were married (84.4 percent), and five were cohabiting (15.6 percent). Couples had been married/cohabiting for an average of 5.9 years ($SD = 7.9$), with relationship length varying from zero to thirty-eight years. Four couples were dual military couples (both partners were members of the ADF), with the remaining twenty-eight couples consisting of one military member and a civilian spouse. All but one of these couples consisted of a male military member and a female civilian spouse. Of the military personnel who took part in the study, there were eighteen army (50 percent), eleven air force (31 percent), and seven navy personnel (19 percent).

Measures

As part of a broader program of research, couples completed a battery of assessment measures assessing the couple relationship, dyadic coping, and individual adjustment. Here we only describe the measures relevant to the current study. Relationship satisfaction was measured by the sixteen-item Couples Satisfaction Index of Funk and Rogge (2007). Individuals obtain a global satisfaction score ranging from 0–81, with higher scores indicating high satisfaction with the relationship. Scores below 52 are considered to indicate clinical levels of couple distress. Internal reliability was high at $\alpha = 0.96$.

The Depression Anxiety Stress Scales—21 (DASS21) (Lovibond & Lovibond, 1995) were administered to describe the individual adjustment of the partners. The twenty-one items were rated from 0 (*Did not apply to me at all*) to 3 (*Applied to me very much, or most of the time*) and consisted of statements such as 'I felt that I had nothing to look forward to' and 'I felt scared without any good reason.' Participants received a score for each sub-scale, as well as a total score reflecting their overall distress. Higher scores reflect a greater number of symptoms. Internal reliability was high, $\alpha = 0.89$ for males and $\alpha = 0.88$ for females.

The Dyadic Coping Inventory (DCI) (Bodenmann, 2008) was administered to assess the individual's supportive dyadic coping, their evaluation of their partner's supportive dyadic coping, and the couple's common dyadic coping. For a description of the DCI, see Chapter 3. Internal reliabilities were high for all three sub-scales: $\alpha = 0.75$ for males and $\alpha = 0.82$ for females on self-report of own supportive dyadic coping, $\alpha = 0.85$ for males and $\alpha = 0.87$ for females on report of partner supportive dyadic coping, and $\alpha = 0.81$ for males and $\alpha = 0.89$ for females on common dyadic coping.

Procedure

Couples expressed interest in the study by contacting the researchers by email or telephone. The lead researcher then contacted couples by phone for an initial screening interview, to discuss what participation would involve, and to assess their suitability for the study. Eligible couples who chose to proceed were sent informed consent documents by post. Once consent was received, couples were emailed a link to the online survey. Each partner was instructed to complete the survey individually. Ethical approval for the study was received by the Human Research Ethics Committee at the University of Queensland and the Australian Defence Human Research Ethics Committee.

Data Analysis

In order to examine the association of dyadic coping with relationship satisfaction in military couples, we conducted a gender-specific, couple-level multi-level model (MLM) analysis using MLwiN (Rasbash, Charlton, Browne, Healy, & Cameron, 2005). We first analyzed the association between supportive dyadic coping and satisfaction, and then analyzed common dyadic coping and satisfaction. In order to reduce the possibility of spurious associations resulting from common method variance, we used one partner's report of dyadic coping to predict the other partner's satisfaction. Specifically, we predicted male relationship satisfaction from the female partner's reports of the male spouse's dyadic coping (an actor effect), the female partner's report of her own dyadic coping (a partner effect), and the female partner's report of the couple's common dyadic coping. Conversely, we predicted female relationship satisfaction from the male partner's reports of the female spouse's dyadic coping (an actor effect), the male partner's report of his own dyadic coping (a partner effect), and the male partner's report of the couple's common dyadic coping. The equations for the model tested are as follows:

$$\text{Relationship satisfaction}_{ij} = [\beta \; male_{0i} + \beta \; female_{1i}] + [\text{male.male\_dyadic coping}_i + \text{female.female\_dyadic coping}_i + \text{male.female\_dyadic coping}_i + \text{female.male\_dyadic coping}_i + \text{male.conjoint\_dyadic coping}_i + \text{female.conjoint\_dyadic coping}_i]$$

In the above equation male and female are dummy variables that create the gender specific estimates, and $\beta \; male_{0i} + \beta \; female_{1i}$ represent the intercepts of satisfaction for men and women, respectively. Male. male_dyadic coping$_i$ and female. female_dyadic coping$_i$ are the actor effects of male and female dyadic coping, respectively. Male. female_dyadic coping$_i$ and female. male_dyadic coping$_i$ are the partner effects of male and female dyadic coping, respectively. Male. conjoint_dyadic coping$_i$ and female. conjoint_dyadic coping$_i$ are the effects of common coping on male and female relationship satisfaction, respectively.

Study Results

Table 17.1 presents the means, standard deviations, and correlations between dyadic coping and relationship satisfaction in the sample. Mean scores on relationship satisfaction are similar to the population means described by Funk and Rogge (2007). Scores on the DASS reflect low levels of anxiety, depression, and stress. Male and female relationship satisfaction was highly correlated, as was common dyadic coping. There was no correlation within couples between male and female psychological distress, and small to moderate correlation between partners on individual dyadic coping. Dyadic coping showed high correlation with relationship satisfaction, but dyadic coping and psychological distress were not correlated.

As is conventional with MLM (Singer & Willett, 2003), we developed the model sequentially. We began first by estimating the unconditional model. Men had an overall mean CSI satisfaction of 62.0 ($SE = 2.0$), and women had a mean of 61.0 ($SE = 2.1$). As we had both cohabiting and married couples, we wanted to test if this variable influenced couples' relationship satisfaction. We entered marital status as a dummy variable (cohabiting = 0, married = 1), and found it did not significantly predict relationship satisfaction, $\chi^2 (2) = 0.090$ $p = 0.955$. Following usual MLM conventions (Singer & Willett, 2003), we removed the non-significant marital status term.

TABLE 17.1 Correlation between dyadic coping and relationship satisfaction in Australian military couples

Variable	Male Mean	SD	Female Mean	SD	1	2	3	4	5
1. Satisfaction	62.0	11.8	61.0	12.2	0.66*	-0.34	0.40*	0.56*	0.57*
2. Distress	8.8	7.3	8.9	6.9	-0.33	-0.23	-0.01	-0.22	-0.17
3. Actor supportive dyadic coping	40.8	7.3	40.8	6.6	0.45*	-0.25	0.32	0.63*	0.72*
4. Partner supportive dyadic coping	43.3	5.1	42.5	5.0	0.36*	-0.24	0.74*	0.42*	0.70*
5. Common dyadic coping	16.3	4.7	15.8	3.5	0.63*	-0.11	0.58*	0.58*	0.74*

*$p < .05$; correlations above the diagonal are for male partners, below the diagonal for female partners, and on the diagonal show correlation between male and female partners on the same variable; relationship satisfaction and psychological distress are self-report, dyadic coping variables are all spouse report.

TABLE 17.2 Multilevel model prediction of couple relationship satisfaction from supportive and common dyadic coping

Block	Block entry statistic		Predictor	MLM Coefficients (standard error)	
	Chi-square	df		Male	Female
Supportive dyadic coping	18.38*	4	Actor	0.122 (.302)	0.710 (.431)*
			Partner	1.172 (.428)*	0.191 (.580)
Common dyadic coping	11.92*	2	Actor	-0.193 (.333)	0.098 (.422)
			Partner	0.794 (.455)*	-0.133 (.525)
			Common	1.042 (.563)*	2.150(.680)*
Common dyadic coping		2	Common	1.435 (.363)*	2.168 (.481)*

*$p < .05$—one tailed tests; df = degrees of freedom

We entered the supportive dyadic coping terms as a block, and then the common dyadic coping as a block, to predict relationship satisfaction. Table 17.2 presents the results of these analyses. As shown, supportive dyadic coping significantly predicted satisfaction, and then entering common dyadic coping further enhanced prediction of satisfaction. However, once common dyadic coping was entered, none of the supportive dyadic coping terms predicted satisfaction. We then entered common dyadic coping first, and then entered supportive dyadic coping actor and partner effects after common dyadic coping. Adding supportive dyadic coping actor and partner effects after common dyadic coping did not significantly enhance prediction of satisfaction, χ^2 (4) = 3.01 p = 0.556. Thus, the final equation was the one shown at the bottom of Table 17.2, in which both male and female relationship satisfaction are significantly predicted by common dyadic coping. It is important to remember these associations are not due to common method variance resulting from reports by just one person, as male reports of common dyadic coping are predicting female satisfaction, while female reports of common dyadic coping are predicting male satisfaction.

In order to give an estimate of effect size for the effect of common dyadic coping on relationship satisfaction, we used the final equation in Table 17.2, to estimate the male and female relationship satisfaction for couples with common dyadic coping 1 SD above and 1 SD below the sample mean on dyadic coping. Figure 17.1 displays the estimated satisfaction levels. The difference between the high and low dyadic coping couples in relationship satisfaction was 13.4 points for men and 19.3 points for women. Based on a standard deviation of 17 on the CSI, as reported by Funk and Rogge (2007), these differences correspond to large effect size differences, d = 0.79 and d = 1.14, for male and female satisfaction, respectively.

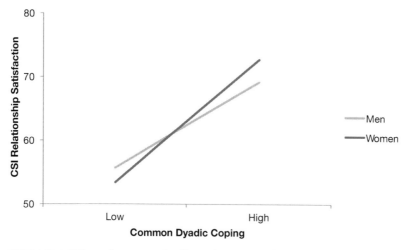

FIGURE 17.1 Effect of common dyadic coping on couple relationship satisfaction

The study replicated prior research (Bodenmann et al., 2011; Herzberg, 2013; Ruffieux, Nussbeck, & Bodenmann, 2014) showing a robust association between dyadic coping and couple relationship satisfaction. The current study suggests that common dyadic coping is more strongly associated with relationship satisfaction than supportive dyadic coping. Implementing joint coping strategies might result in feelings of teamwork and togetherness that contribute further to the enhancement of relationship satisfaction. For military couples, working together to overcome the challenges of military service likely results in the development of strategies that suit both partners. Due to the distinctive challenges faced by military couples, it is not clear whether these results generalize to all Australian couples.

Implications for Practice

Most existing couple relationship education (RE) programs encourage spouses to provide support to one another during times of stress. Adding promotion of common dyadic coping might enhance the benefit of RE for couples. Specifically, it seems potentially useful to teach couples techniques, which involve discussing problems together, developing a shared understanding of the situation (i.e., we-stress) and the various options available to them, and deciding together on which approach to take. Future research should seek to test whether changes in common dyadic coping mediate enhanced satisfaction in couples after RE.

As mentioned previously, this sample was recruited as part of a randomized controlled trial of couple relationship education tailored to address the distinctive challenges for military couples. The adapted program, Couple CARE in Uniform (Halford & Bakhurst, 2013), contained several additional exercises on military-specific stressors and various strategies that couples could use to cope with these stressors together. The exercises encouraged couples to use their time together to develop strategies that they could implement during their next separation. For example, one exercise explored how the couple communicated while separated; couples discussed the pros and cons of different approaches, before agreeing on an approach that worked best for them as a couple. Similar techniques were used to explore challenges of the homecoming phase, such as re-establishing intimacy and reintegrating into the family routine. Thus, our adaptation of Couple CARE for military couples tries to promote common dyadic coping to help couples manage military life. Minor adaptation of this dyadic coping focus could also be used with non-military couples. For example, couples managing the transition to parenthood can benefit from dyadic coping with the considerable demands of caring for a baby (Petch, Halford, Creedy, & Gamble, 2012).

Implications for Research

The data with Australian military couples extended prior work in three important ways. First, by using one partner's report of dyadic coping to predict the other partner's relationship satisfaction, the association of dyadic coping with relationship satisfaction is not just an artifact of common method variance resulting from having one person's report to assess the predictor and criterion variables. Second, data showed that the prior work on dyadic coping and relationship satisfaction generalizes to Australian military couples, a population of couples with significant external stresses to manage. Third, it considered the relative contribution of supportive dyadic coping and common dyadic coping, showing the latter has the strongest association with relationship satisfaction.

A key limitation of the current study was the cross-sectional design, which prevents any conclusion on the causal effects of dyadic coping on relationship satisfaction over time. However, as noted previously, incorporating promotion of common dyadic coping into RE and testing its effect could test causal models. The sample was made up of largely married, heterosexual couples, limiting generalizability to the wider population. Future studies should look to include cohabiting, intercultural, and same-sex couples in order to be more representative of the Australian population. The couples in the current study were also presenting for RE, and therefore might not be representative of all Australian military couples. Across studies evaluating RE, couples who present typically over-represent the couples at high-risk of future relationship problems (Halford & Bodenmann, 2013). However, high-risk couples are those most likely to show the largest benefits from RE (Halford & Bodenmann, 2013), so the predictors of satisfaction in these couples are of particular relevance to planning interventions.

Conclusion

Couples in Australia face a number of distinctive challenges, such as those faced by dual career families and high rates of intercultural relationships. There has been a dearth of research on dyadic coping in Australian couples, but the data presented in this chapter is a start to such research. Consistent with earlier research, we found a strong association between common dyadic coping behaviors and relationship satisfaction. The sample consisted of Australian military couples, who face distinctive challenges in navigating the relocations, separations, and deployments characteristic of military life. Given the distinctiveness of military couples, the generalizability of the current results to the wider Australian population is unclear. However, couples who cope with stress together appear to have healthier and happier relationships, therefore including these techniques in relationship education may be important in enhancing and maintaining relationship quality.

References

Allen, E. S., Rhoades, G. K., Stanley, S. M., & Markman, H. J. (2011). On the home front: Stress for recently deployed Army couples. *Family Process, 50*(2), 235–247.

Australian Bureau of Statistics. (2010). *Marriages and divorces, Australia, 2009 (Cat no. 3310.0).* Retrieved from www.abs.gov.au/ausstats/abs@.nsf/0/094C7CFFDA274E61CA2577ED0014617C

Australian Bureau of Statistics. (2012). *Reflecting a nation: Stories from the 2011 Census (Cat no. 2071.0).* Retrieved from www.abs.gov.au/ausstats/abs@.nsf/Latestproducts/2071. 0Main%20Features852012%E2%80%932013?opendocument&tabname=Summary& prodno=2071.0&issue=2012%962013

Balderrama-Durbin, C., Snyder, D. K., Cigrang, J., Talcott, G. W., Tatum, J., Baker, M., . . . Smith Slep, A. M. (2013). Combat disclosure in intimate relationships: Mediating the impact of partner support on posttraumatic stress. *Journal of Family Psychology, 27*(4), 560–568.

Bodenmann, G. (2005). Dyadic coping and its significance for marital functioning. In T. A. Revenson, K. Kayser, & G. Bodenmann (Eds.) (2005), *Couples coping with stress: Emerging perspectives on dyadic coping* (pp. 33–49). Washington DC: American Psychological Association.

Bodenmann, G. (2008). *Dyadisches Coping Inventar (DCI)* [Dyadic Coping Inventory]. Test manual. Bern, Switzerland: Huber & Hogrefe Tests.

Bodenmann, G., Meuwly, N., & Kayser, K. (2011). Two conceptualizations of dyadic coping and their potential for predicting relationship quality and individual wellbeing. *European Psychologist, 16*, 255–266.

Bodenmann, G., Plancherel, B., Beach, S. R. H., Widmer, K., Gabriel, B., Meuwly, N., . . . Schramm, E. (2008). Effects of coping-oriented couples therapy on depression: A randomized clinical trial. *Journal of Consulting and Clinical Psychology, 76*, 944–954.

Bodenmann, G., & Randall, A. K. (2012). Common factors in the enhancement of dyadic coping. *Behavior Therapy, 43*(1), 88–98.

Bodenmann, G., & Shantinath, S. D. (2004). The Couples Coping Enhancement Training (CCET): A new approach to prevention of marital distress based upon stress and coping. *Family Relations, 53*(5), 477–484.

Cardona, R. A., & Ritchie, E. C. (2007). U.S. Military enlisted accession mental health screening: History and current practice. *Military Medicine, 172*(1), 31–35.

Castaneda, L. W., & Harrell, M. C. (2008). Military spouse employment. *Armed Forces & Society, 34*(3), 389–412.

Centre for Military and Veterans' Health. (2010). Readjustment to 'normal': Literature review. Retrieved from www.cmvh.org.au/docs/ThinkTank/2010_TT_Lit_Rev_ Final.pdf

Defence Force Recruiting. (2013). *ADF Permanent Pay Rates.* Retrieved from www. content.defencejobs.gov.au/pdf/triservice/DFT_Document_PayRates.pdf

Defence Force Recruiting. (2014). Benefits (Navy). Retrieved from www.defencejobs.gov. au/navy/PayAndBenefits/benefits.aspx

Defense Finance and Accounting Service. (2014). *Military Pay Tables.* Retrieved from www.dfas.mil/militarymembers/payentitlements/militarypaytables.html

Department of Defence. (2012). *Department of Defence Census 2011 Public Report.* Canberra, Australia: Department of Defence.

Everson, R. B., & Herzog, J. R. (2011). Structural strategic approaches with army couples. In R. B. Everson & C. R. Figley (Eds.), *Families under fire* (pp. 55–78). New York: Routledge.

Faber, A. J., Willerton, E., Clymer, S. R., MacDermid, S. M., & Weiss, H. M. (2008). Ambiguous absence, ambiguous presence: A qualitative study of military reserve families in wartime. *Journal of Family Psychology, 22*(2), 222–230.

Frost, D. M., & Meyer, I. H. (2009). Internalized homophobia and relationship quality among lesbians, gay men, and bisexuals. *Journal of Counseling Psychology, 56*, 97–109.

Funk, J. L., & Rogge, R. D. (2007). Testing the ruler with item response theory: Increasing precision of measurement for relationship satisfaction with the Couples Satisfaction Index. *Journal of Family Psychology*, *21*(4), 572–583.

Halford, W. K. (2011). *Marriage and relationship education: What works and how to provide it.* New York: The Guilford Press.

Halford, W. K., & Bakhurst, M. G. (2013). *Couple CARE in Uniform: A guidebook for life partners serving in the military.* The University of Queensland. Brisbane, Australia.

Halford, W. K., & Bodenmann, G. (2013). Effects of relationship education on maintenance of couple relationship satisfaction. *Clinical Psychology Review*, *33*(4), 512–525.

Herzberg, P. Y. (2013). Coping in relationships: The interplay between individual and dyadic coping and their effects on relationship satisfaction. *Anxiety, Stress, & Coping*, *26*, 136–153.

Hewitt, B., & Baxter, J. (2015). Relationship dissolution. In G. Heard & D. Arunachalam (Eds.), *Family formation in 21st century Australia* (pp. 77–99). The Netherlands: Springer.

Hiew, D. N., Halford, W. K., & Liu, S. (2014). Loving diversity: Living in intercultural couple relationships. In A. Abela & J. Walker (Eds.), *Contemporary issues in family studies: Global perspectives on partnerships, parenting and support in a changing world.* Oxford: John Wiley & Sons, Ltd.

Jacobson, I. G., Ryan, M. A. K., Hooper, T. J., Smith, T. C., Amoroso, P. J., Boyko, E. J., . . . Bell, N. S. (2008). Alcohol use and alcohol-related problems before and after military combat deployment. *Journal of the American Medical Association*, *300*(6), 663–675.

Lovibond, S. H., & Lovibond, P. F. (1995). *Manual for the Depression Anxiety Stress Scales* (2nd ed.). Sydney, Australia: Psychology Foundation.

McGuire, A. C. L., Runge, C., Cosgrove, L., Bredhauer, K., Anderson, R., Waller, M., . . . Nasveld, P. (2012). *Timor-Leste Family Study: Technical Report.* Brisbane, Australia: Centre for Military and Veterans' Health, The University of Queensland.

Miller, A. B., Schaefer, K. E., Renshaw, K. D., & Blais, R. K. (2013). PTSD and marital satisfaction in military service members: Examining the simultaneous roles of childhood sexual abuse and combat exposure. *Child Abuse & Neglect*, *37*(11), 979–985.

Monson, C., Fredman, S. J., Macdonald, A., Pukay-Marin, N. D., Resick, P. A., & Schnurr, P. P. (2012). Effect of cognitive-behavioral couple therapy for PTSD: A randomized controlled trial. *Journal of the American Medical Association*, *308*, 700–709.

Nelson Goff, B. S., Crow, J. R., Reisbig, A. M. J., & Hamilton, S. (2007). The impact of individual trauma symptoms of deployed soldiers on relationship satisfaction. *Journal of Family Psychology*, *21*(3), 344–353.

Organisation for Economic Co-operation and Development. (2011). *Doing Better for Families.* Retrieved from www.oecd.org/els/soc/doingbetterforfamilies.htm

Papp, L. M., & Witt, N. L. (2010). Romantic partners' individual coping strategies and dyadic coping: Implications for relationship functioning. *Journal of Family Psychology*, *24*, 551–559.

Petch, J. F., Halford, W. K., Creedy, D. K., & Gamble, J. (2012). A randomized controlled trial of a couple relationship and co-parenting program (Couple CARE for Parents) for high- and low-risk new parents. *Journal of Consulting and Clinical Psychology*, *80*(4), 662–673.

Rasbash, J., Charlton, C., Browne, W. J., Healy, M., & Cameron, B. (2005). MLwiN Version 2.02. University of Bristol: Centre for Multilevel Modelling.

Renshaw, K. D., Blais, R. K., & Caska, C. M. (2011). Distress in spouses of combat veterans with PTSD: The importance of interpersonally based cognitions and behaviors.

In S. MacDermid Wadsworth & D. Riggs (Eds.), *Risk and resilience in U.S. Military families* (pp. 69–84). New York: Springer.

Ruffieux, M., Nussbeck, F. W., & Bodenmann, G. (2014). Long-term prediction of relationship satisfaction and stability by stress, coping, communication, and well-being. *Journal of Divorce & Remarriage, 55*(6), 485–501.

Singer, J. D., & Willett, J. B. (2003). *Applied longitudinal data analysis: Modeling change and event occurrence.* New York: Oxford University Press.

Taft, C. T., Walling, S. M., Howard, J. M., & Monson, C. (2011). Trauma, PTSD, and partner violence in military families. In S. MacDermid Wadsworth & D. Riggs (Eds.), *Risk and resilience in U.S. Military families* (pp. 195–212). New York: Springer.

U.S. Army. (2014). Benefits. Retrieved from www.goarmy.com/benefits

United States Census. (2012). *Population.* Retrieved from www.census.gov/compendia/statab/cats/population.html

Waller, M., Kanesarajah, J., Zheng, W., & Dobson, A. (2013). The Middle East Area of Operations (MEAO) mortality and cancer incidence study. Brisbane, Australia: The University of Queensland, Centre for Military and Veterans' Health.

Waller, M., & McGuire, A. C. L. (2011). Changes over time in the 'healthy solider effect.' *Population Health Metrics, 9*(7), 1–9.

18

INCLUDING THE CULTURAL CONTEXT IN DYADIC COPING

Directions for Future Research and Practice

Karen Kayser and Tracey A. Revenson

Theorists developed the concept of dyadic coping to describe how spouses or partners together manage common stressors (Bodenmann, 1997; Revenson, Kayser, & Bodenmann, 2005) and many framed this in terms of coping with a chronic illness (Coyne & Fiske, 1992; Revenson, 1994). The chapters in this volume afford a state-of-the-art review of the research on dyadic coping being conducted worldwide, providing us with tantalizing insights about how aspects of national culture affect dyadic coping. Given the diverse and global context in which mental health and healthcare practitioners work, identifying these influences is important for providing culturally sensitive psychosocial care to patients, their partners, and their families.

Cultural Aspects of Dyadic Coping: Models and Concepts

The original Systemic Transactional Model (STM; Bodenmann, 1997) did not explicitly include the cultural context. A number of approaches embryonically included cultural factors in dyadic coping models but focused on generalities vs. specifics. In her social ecological framework for studying both individual-level (Revenson, 1990) and dyadic coping (Revenson, 2003), Revenson suggested that the choice of coping strategies and their influence on psychological and health outcomes are shaped by the larger sociocultural context. The socio-cultural context was defined as including molar variables such as age, gender, socioeconomic status, and education level. These demographic markers were hypothesized to serve as moderators of the relationship between stress and coping, or serve as coping resources in their own right. Sociocultural factors also defined the acceptability of a particular coping strategy; for example, gender colors the acceptability of emotional expression. However, Revenson only examined gender and gender roles as socio-demographic factors in her empirical research on couples coping with chronic illness.

Berg and Upchurch (2007) proposed a developmental model of dyadic coping specific to illness that also includes aspects of the sociocultural context, namely, culture and gender. Specifically, they noted that sociocultural factors affect the norms and expectations for the level of interdependence among spouses, with collectivistic cultures and women more likely to represent the self in relation to others. Chapter 2 reintroduces these two dimensions as important aspects of culture; specifically, they suggest that low-context communication styles in European cultures would result in less interpersonal stress communication and fewer common dyadic coping efforts. They also suggest that in couples who cling to more traditional gender roles, women are more responsible for the emotional aspects of the relationship and thus engage in more emotion-focused coping.

Kayser, Watson, and Andrade (2007) maintained yet expanded the STM into a Relational-Cultural Coping framework by adding three relationship components —relationship awareness, mutuality, and authenticity—that assist the couple in moving through the process of coping. The model acknowledged the cultural context but no specific cultural factors were identified. However, drawing on data from their study of couples in America, China, and India, Kayser and her colleagues (2014) identified four cultural dimensions that influenced couples' coping with the stressor of breast cancer, which will be described in more detail below.

The minimal attention paid to specific aspects of the cultural context in studies of dyadic coping may be due to the homogeneity of samples in existing research. Primarily middle-class European and American couples have participated in research on dyadic coping. The majority of couples are happily married, with only a relatively small portion experiencing major life stressors (e.g., cancer) or marital discord.

Cultural Aspects of Dyadic Coping

It is widely accepted that culture is best understood as a multidimensional concept. Simply defining a person as belonging to a particular ethnic or religious group, speaking a particular language, or living in a particular country minimizes the complexity of the concept. We often think of cultures as geographical (place dependent) but they can also refer to ethnicities (e.g., Latino culture) or populations (e.g., gay culture, military culture, the culture of the elderly). Most conceptualizations of culture include external referents, such as customs, artifacts, and social institutions, and internal referents such as ideologies, belief systems, attitudes, expectations, and epistemologies. These cultural constructs are organizing principles that influence all other aspects of our daily lives and interpersonal relationships. Examples of these constructs include cultural complexity, honor, collectivism, individualism, and vertical-horizontal relationships (Triandis, 1996). Approaching cultural variation by these organizing constructs forces the researcher to ask questions about the couple's cultural customs, values, or beliefs instead of relying on categories of race and ethnicity.

With regard to dyadic coping, it is useful to think of cultural contexts as supplying a blueprint for how to cope: how meaning is given to events, what is considered stressful, which coping behaviors are acceptable, and what roles and competencies are valued. These cultural blueprints offer a lens through which the boundaries of dyadic coping are defined, for example, whether one perceives the stressor as an individual versus family stressor. Culture also defines the acceptability of particular coping responses, such as emotional expression or anger, and thus defines their value as adaptive mechanisms. It is important to reiterate that most individuals are members of multiple cultural groups, which may not share the same values or beliefs.

To complicate this even further than an examination of culture and coping (Kuo, 2011), spouses/partners may come from different backgrounds or cultures requiring them to negotiate around different norms and values and creating their unique dyadic culture. As a result, we cannot assume that any couple holds a unified cultural value system.

An Exemplar: Dyadic Coping with Illness in China, India, and the U.S.

A study by the first author (Kayser, Cheung, Rao, Chan, Chan, & Lo, 2014) of twenty-eight couples from China (Hong Kong), India (Chennai), and the U.S. (Boston) illustrates how dyadic coping is embedded in culture. Using a qualitative methodology, Kayser and her colleagues identified the unique ways in which couples from different ethnic cultures cope with the wife's breast cancer and how cultural norms both encourage and constrain particular forms of dyadic coping as defined by the Systemic Transactional Model (Bodenmann, 1997).

Stress Appraisals and Stress Communication

Clear differences emerged in how the stressors of illness were perceived by couples from the different cultural groups and how stress was communicated to one's partner. Couples in all three cultural groups were in agreement that treatment side effects constitute one of the most stressful aspects of cancer. In contrast, financial stress and lifestyle changes, including changed living arrangements (i.e., living far away from one's home and community during treatment) were much more likely to be cited as stressors by the Indian and Chinese couples. For the Chinese couples, conflict with their in-laws over treatment decisions and conflict between spouses that emerged when support needs were not met were identified as most stressful. American couples more frequently reported changes in their relationship (sex life, social life, communication and closeness, and interdependence of couple) as the most stressful aspects of living with the illness. Similar appraisal patterns have emerged in studies of coping in collectivistic and individualistic cultures (see Chung et al., 2006; Zhan & Montgomery, 2003 in Chapter 2).

Dyadic Coping—It's Not What You Do But Why You Do It

The types of dyadic coping behaviors used were quite similar across the three cultural groups, but the explanations for why they used these strategies and the meanings attached to their coping behaviors differed among cultures. Often, these explanations reflected cultural norms for behavior, although at times the couples purposively used dyadic coping strategies that worked against those norms. For example, the Chinese and Indian couples specifically mentioned that the husbands were going beyond their traditional male roles and responding to the stressors of illness with behaviors that were more typical of women. The American couples described the husbands doing more household tasks as well, but did not mention that these tasks were different from what the husbands would normally be doing. Couples in all three cultures reported the dyadic coping strategies of reassigning family responsibilities and joint problem solving but, once again, cultural differences were evident in how these strategies were implemented. We will illustrate this with three modes of dyadic coping: allowing family involvement, accepting the illness, and finding benefits.

Family Involvement

One distinct difference between the couples from the Asian cultures compared to the American couples lay in the degree to which they involved their extended families in their coping efforts. Among Chinese couples, it was apparent that the disease not only affected the couple but the entire family. Although the notion of 'we-stress' is used in dyadic coping research to refer to both partners 'owning' the stress, when Chinese couples used the word 'we,' it was often in reference to the whole family. The Chinese couples openly disclosed the cancer diagnosis to the extended family, whereas American couples were more selective in whom they would tell. Chinese couples also routinely included extended family in making treatment decisions and expected practical support from the extended family during treatment. It is worth noting that this family involvement was apparent during relatively less stressful times during the illness and was not initiated only during medical crises, as was often the case with the American couples. Hence, the term 'we-stress' or a 'we-disease' (Kayser et al., 2007) becomes even broader in some non-Western cultures that interpret the 'we' as including parents, children, siblings, and other family members, not simply the spouse or partner.

Accompanying the outpouring of care and support in these Chinese families, however, were conflicts over how to deal emotionally with the cancer in the context of a group of people. One Chinese wife described her difficulty in disclosing her diagnosis to the whole family:

> When the doctor told me at that time I didn't cry, the first thing on my mind was, how can I tell them, because my mom and my mother-in-law appeared and when everyone got there, seeing my older sister really frantic, my nephew looked like he just cried, it was then I started to cry, because I felt really guilty.

Some of the Chinese husbands were torn between taking care of their wives and taking care of their own parents or children. They attributed their dilemma to the Chinese tradition that emphasizes the parent-child relationship and obligations to one's parents as more important. Attending to the wife rather than a parent at times could elicit criticism from other family members.

Some Chinese couples had to be assertive in order to have their own voice in the treatment decision. While they treasured the relationship with the supportive extended family, they also wanted their autonomy. This reflected some new values about privacy and boundaries that conflicted with the prevailing cultural norms and created relationship conflict. Although the American couples in crisis appreciated extended family support, the Chinese couples expressed the desire and the difficulty in maintaining a balance between the need for privacy and the involvement of their extended families.

For the Indian couples, extended family played a major role in their handling many practical challenges related to the cancer. Unlike the Hong Kong-Chinese couples that interacted with extended family on a daily basis, many of the Indian couples had to leave their families to move to the city for treatment. However, this did not minimize the critical role their families played in taking care of the children left behind at home.

Illness Acceptance

Another cultural difference in dyadic coping was the degree to which the couple accepted the illness vs. trying to control it. In Western cultures, acceptance can sometimes be seen as passive and conflicts with the basic tenets of Lazarus and Folkman's (1984) stress and coping model, with its emphasis on individual coping efforts, personal control, agency, and direct action (Kuo, 2011).

The Asian (Chinese and Indian) couples conveyed the notion that they were dealing with a situation beyond their control; their spiritual beliefs incorporated a different meaning to the illness that placed it meaningfully in their life course (Fadiman, 1997, provides an extended and compelling description of this in her narrative about the clash of cultures between a Hmong family with an ill child who immigrated to the U.S. and Western medicine). Chinese couples described a sense of acceptance, the essence of which was that they were unable to change things and tried to see whatever was positive. American couples, in contrast, were more likely to believe that they could or should manage the cancer without much emotional fallout, or at least, have some control over it. In the words of one American husband:

> Well, we need to fix this [cancer] before we go back and attend to everyone else . . . We're still going to see my mother, we're still taking care of her needs, we're dealing with her mother, we're dealing with our children. But in the foreground is this issue.

Among the Asian spouses, there was not this desperation to 'do' something. In contrast, they would explain how through pulling back and accepting, more was to be gained. In addition to accepting the effects of cancer, one Chinese wife reported how she used acceptance in coping with her husband's lack of disclosure about his emotions. The wife accepted the disappointment that her husband could not be as expressive as she was in matters of emotions and would not express his care and love for her in words. According to her, that was the way he has been since the time of courtship. The wife's acceptance helped her not to focus on the disappointment from the unrealistic expectations, find space to appreciate her husband's expressions of love in actions, and eventually gain more from the relationship. Compared with their American counterparts, Chinese couples may be more flexible in the face of difficult situations (see Cheng, Lee, & Chiu, 1999), by reframing their experiences (Ching et al., 2009) and reconstructing meaning (Ching et al., 2012; Leung 2007).

Finding Benefits in Stressful Experiences

Within the U.S. stress and coping research, an expanding trend has been to examine personal growth or resilience resulting from the stressor and actively finding positive ways to reframe the stressor or find benefits in negative experiences (Lepore & Revenson, 2006; Tedeschi & Calhoun, 2004). When asked about any positive things that had resulted from the cancer experience, the Chinese, Indian, and American couples all mentioned the lifestyle changes that are typically mentioned in cancer studies: less attention to work and a greater attention to their health and families. More importantly, couples in all three groups spontaneously mentioned benefits that focused on the couple's relationship, such as greater understanding and respect for each other, greater intimacy, a sense of 'we-ness' as a couple, and an increased value of the relationship.

Yet differences emerged. Most of the American couples reported that a benefit was that the cancer brought them closer together and more dependent on each other. The Chinese women said that they learned about their own needs and how to express their need more openly to their husbands. In an individualistic Western society, a stressful event may help couples to realize their interdependence. In a society that already emphasizes interdependence, partners may become more aware of their individual needs and learn to voice them.

Although couples from different cultures may demonstrate similar coping behaviors, such as turning to a loved one for support, the behavior may take on different meanings depending on the cultural context. For couples in a Chinese culture, taking care of one's wife over caring for parents may mean to others in the family that the husband was not fulfilling his obligation to his parents. For Indian men, taking care of the children, cooking, and doing housework may be interpreted by family members who value traditional gender roles that he is less of a man since that is a woman's work.

A Blueprint for Incorporating the Cultural Context in Research and Practice

For those who want to incorporate culture into their research or clinical practice, we would like to recommend that four dimensions that appear to influence dyadic coping be considered: Family boundaries; gender roles; personal control; and interdependence. Note that we have not included the dimension of collective vs. individualistic cultures, as described in Chapter 2 and Kuo's work (2011, 2013) as it is reflected in all four of the cultural dimensions we describe.

Family Boundaries (Open—Closed)

A boundary in the family system is a rule or norm that guides who interacts with whom, the frequency of interaction between individuals, and the roles of individuals in the family system (Kayser et al., 2014). For example, in some cultures, older siblings, grandparents, and members of the village or community may be involved in raising a child, and in other cultures, it is left primarily to one or two parents. In the former case, the boundaries are open and in the latter case they would be referred to as closed. In open families, interaction is fluid and contact among family members can be frequent; it is not unusual for a person to see or talk with a sibling, a parent, or cousin on a daily basis. In a closed system the contact may be limited to occasions such as a birthday, holiday, or a personal crisis, such as a serious illness or a death. Thus, family boundaries may shape many aspects of dyadic coping, from disclosure (who is told about the stressor) to asking for and receiving help, to how one feels about the help that is received.

Asian cultures such as those found in Pakistan, China, and Japan are examples of more open family boundaries. For example, in Chapter 13, the authors refer to a study on Pakistani couples in which the husbands and wives solved their small issues with each other but large stressors such as financial loss were discussed with the parents of the husbands or wives. Hence, dyadic coping occurred within the context of a much larger family system. Similarly, in the Japanese culture (see Chapter 15) filial piety (loyalty to family and respect for parents) is highly valued, and within this larger family system a couple is obligated to attend to the stress of parents as well as their own stressors. In contrast, Westernized countries such as Switzerland and Germany are characterized as more closed family boundaries and, as the research in Chapters 7 and 8 illustrates, couples cope as isolated systems with less dependence on extended family in managing daily stresses.

Gender Roles (Differentiated—Flexible)

Cultural norms dictate how acceptable it is for men and women to engage in similar behaviors and roles in society. Cultures that condone distinct roles for men and women will fall on the differentiated end of the dimension while cultures that are tolerant of men and women playing the same roles will be on the flexible end of the continuum. At times, responding in a crisis situation requires actions that may challenge prevailing cultural gender roles and require flexibility.

Spouses from cultures with very differentiated roles do not need to spend extensive time discussing these roles—it is clear which gender does what during a stressful situation. For example, when an Indian couple is faced with breast cancer, a male member of the family (usually the husband) is designated as the person to communicate with the physician, even when the woman is the patient, often leaving the woman (patient) in the dark as to the seriousness of her condition and her treatment. Similarly, the gender roles of *machismo* for men and *marianismo* for women in Latino cultures dictate that the men take the lead and 'fight' for the well-being of the family while women tend to the emotional support and caretaking of children (Chapter 5). Another illustration can be found in Greek culture where roles for men and women clearly are divided along traditional norms of masculinity and femininity. This has implications for dyadic coping. In their sample of Greek couples, Karademas and Rousi (Chapter 10) found that couples in which men and women were highly congruent in using positive coping behaviors tended to report high overall marital satisfaction and low levels of depressed mood. High levels of marital satisfaction and low levels of depressed mood were also reported by couples where women used exclusively emotional-focused coping and men used both problem- and emotion-focused coping. The lowest levels of marital satisfaction and highest levels of depressed mood were reported by spouses exhibiting non-traditional gender roles: Women reporting more problem-focused coping and men reported primarily emotion-focused coping (venting their emotions and disengaging mentally).

When talking about dyadic coping, in particular, many cultural differences intersect with culturally sanctioned gender roles. For example, a hallmark of mental health in the U.S. is that an individual uses active, instrumental, problem-solving efforts to cope with stress, that is, drawing on one's inner resources and self-reliance to minimize or eliminate the stressor (Lazarus & Folkman, 1984). The finding that women are comforted more by expressing and processing emotions rather than solving problems (Stanton et al., 2000) is not recognized or valued as an acceptable way of coping in many cultures. To illustrate, the Greek society highly values masculinity and meeting expectations of a good provider for one's family (Chapter 10). The recent economic crises in Greece had a negative impact on the parental self-efficacy of Greek men in that they were no longer able to provide for the material needs of their families and fulfill the traditional role as breadwinners.

Drawing strength from interpersonal relationships and relying on them for practical support are essential components of women's coping processes (Helgeson, 2012). Women rely on their support networks more often; these interpersonal contacts serve as a place to express emotions, acquire feedback on coping choices, and obtain assistance with life tasks, such as childcare. Women are more likely to ask for support, use support, and not feel demeaned by it (Shumaker & Hill, 1991). Thus, coping through interpersonal means often confers benefits for women. At the same time, this mode of coping may result in additional stresses and poorer health (Helgeson, 2012) as women are often taking care of others while they are coping with family stressors (Abraído-Lanza & Revenson, 2006; Revenson, Abraído-Lanza, Majerovitz, & Jordan, 2005).

It is often difficult to isolate the effect of gender on dyadic coping. For example, most studies of dyadic coping with myocardial infarction involve male patients and female spouses and studies of breast cancer involve female patients and male spouses. It is difficult to tease out the effects of gender or role (patient/caregiver). After a heart attack, men tend to reduce their work activities and responsibilities and are nurtured by their wives. In contrast, after returning home from the hospital, women resume household responsibilities more quickly, including taking care of other family members, and report receiving a greater amount of help from adult daughters and neighbors than from their healthy husbands (Rose, Suls, Green, Lounsbury, & Gordon, 1996).

Although clear gender roles may eliminate extensive discussion and be more efficient, adhering rigidly to roles can be problematic when one of the partners is not able to fulfill the respective gender role. For example, coping with a wife's serious illness may require a husband to become more flexible in gender-related activities such as housework, or childcare (Revenson et al., 2005). Similarly, the wife may need to change her expectations of being self-sacrificing and the primary caregiver to her family. She may need to be more assertive of her needs for support. Transcending gender roles in order to compensate for a partner's limitations is a salient issue among couples from differentiated cultures in which dyadic coping may be constrained by these roles.

Personal Control (Acceptance—Mastery)

Culture can influence the attitudes and beliefs about how much control individuals have over the things that happen to them. An individual can approach stress with a sense of acceptance of one's fate or a sense of mastery over it. The choices range from coping with stress through reflective thought, mindfulness, and acceptance of the situation to an attitude that one can solve a problem through determination and action. The frustration of dealing with a situation beyond one's control can lead to an awareness that the traditional way of coping is not going to work with the problem. It can facilitate an openness for a new approach to a fact of life that will not be resolved through determination to master and control.

A belief related to acceptance is the notion of fatalism or *fatalismo*, the belief that most of what happens in our lives is beyond our control and that we are not in charge of our destiny (Falicov, 2014). Usually this is connected to a faith-based belief that God controls our destiny and it is through religious practices such as prayer that we cope. This spiritual orientation is common among Latinos but similarly can be found among Chinese in the Confucian value of harmony. The Chinese life orientation promotes a way of coping in which partners accept each other's coping efforts as opposed to trying to change each other. In other words, partners may not agree with each other but will work together to maintain harmony. The emphasis is on a harmonious relationship and, as illustrated in Chapter 14, positive dyadic coping among Chinese couples plays a significant role in their relationship satisfaction. Furthermore, common dyadic coping was the type of coping that explained most of the variance in the relationship satisfaction among the Chinese couples. As defined in Chapter 2, common dyadic coping is a shared coping process that involves both partners jointly trying to reframe the stress, find solutions, or mutually make meaning of it. According to the STM, it often occurs when the stressor affects both partners.

Among Romanian couples, a strong religious faith can play a significant role in a couple's marital satisfaction and dyadic coping (Chapter 12). Over the past decades, Romania has endured very high rates of poverty and social exclusion compared to other European Union countries. Turning to the church for support under times of stress (86 percent are Christian Orthodox) and maintaining one's religious faith and practices are ways to deal with stressors over which they have little control. Interestingly, the husband's religiosity appears to have more bearing on the relationship satisfaction and supportive dyadic coping than the wife's religiosity (Chapter 12), suggesting that gender can also play a role in this coping behavior.

Interdependence (Dependence—Independence)

This dimension refers to the degree to which an individual's identity is embedded in their interpersonal relationships or is separate from their relationships. It has implications for the identity of a couple—their sense of 'we-ness'—and, thus, for dyadic coping. Couples who are able to see themselves as part of a collective unit when coping with a stressor are more effective in coping (Berg & Upchurch, 2007). Interdependence theory (Lewis, McBride et al., 2006) posits that relationship-enhancing behaviors involve a movement away from individual self-interest to focus on long-term relational goals that promote both one's own and one's partner's well-being. This also has been called *cognitive interdependence*, in which each partner regards her or himself as part of a collective unit (Agnew, Van Lange, Rusbult, & Langston, 1998).

We suggest that this value of interdependence will shape dyadic coping. In a culture that values individualism in relationships, each partner is more likely to view oneself as an independent, self-determining person pursuing his/her own purpose. In more collective societies, each partner considers herself or himself as embedded in a relationship network and a shared identity. An extreme example of this latter concept is the social exclusion experienced by an Indian wife when her husband dies. In India, losing a husband means the woman no longer has an identity as a whole person—in some respects, her identity has died along with her husband since she was defined by her marriage. She is abandoned by her family and shunned by members of society who consider her impure and inauspicious.

In a culture that emphasizes interdependence, decision-making about stressors involves taking into account the needs of others. For example, with Chinese couples a wife would consult the husband about having a mastectomy because his marital sex will be affected. She may consult him about going to a private doctor for diagnosis or for treatment, because family finance is involved. Many chapters in this volume provide examples of the dimension of interdependence, ranging from Chinese spouses where wives 'play an obedient role in family life' to more individualistic German, Swiss, and American cultures where spouses tend to express their emotions and individual needs in their intimate relationships. In these latter countries, couples may value a more mutual type of dyadic coping characterized by we-ness and joint coping.

In Chapter 7, Vedes and colleagues describe how we-ness was related to greater use of common dyadic coping and higher relationship satisfaction among Portuguese couples. In particular, wives' outcomes were more strongly related with husband's dyadic coping and we-ness. We suggest that the key factor may not be the overall amount of we-ness (low vs. high) but whether the level of we-ness fits with the couple's expectation for interdependence, given the cultural context.

Coping *Against* Culture

Although dyadic coping is conditioned and shaped by distal and proximal aspects of culture, during times of crisis couples can also cope in ways contrary to prevailing cultural patterns in order to manage the overwhelming stress in their lives (Kayser et al., 2014). Although by adulthood partners or spouses in intimate relationships have internalized their cultural norms, when a potentially life-threatening situation or crisis occurs, couples may need to go outside cultural scripts and norms.

If prevailing cultural norms prove to be barriers to adaptation, they will need to be changed or transcended to give way to something that will enable adaptation to the situation. For example, the cultural norms of silencing the self and putting others' interests before one's own interest may become barriers for a woman who is required to take care of herself, make decisions based on her own situation, and access the support that she needs from others. The concept of coping flexibility, namely, the ability to use diverse types of coping behavior according to the demands of different situations also may contribute to our understanding of the transcendence of cultural patterns in coping (Bonanno, Pat-Horenczyk, & Noll, 2011). When faced with a traumatic event, couples with coping flexibility can rise to the challenge, irrespective of whether or not the action taken is prescribed by the culture.

Applications to Clinical Practice

The lion's share of couple-based interventions that currently exist have been developed and evaluated with couples from Western industrialized countries. Although these interventions have produced promising results, are they similarly culturally appropriate for couples from other non-Western countries or for cultural groups that historically have had limited financial and social resources?

We do not want to throw the baby out with the bath water. The field of dyadic coping is only in its adolescence. Existing interventions can be modified to be culturally-anchored; for example in their book on helping couples cope with cancer, Kayser and Scott (2008) make suggestions how the therapeutic intervention could be modified in light of sociocultural factors such as the couple's economic status, education, and race/ethnicity. Although the couples in their research were from Australia and the U.S., the authors recognized that cultural differences exist within these countries that must be attended to.

One option is to adapt couple-based interventions developed with White, Western middle-class couples for other cultural groups, with attention to the unique aspects of a particular cultural context. The clinician working with the couple will need to balance a respect for the couple's cultural values and a course of action that empowers the couple to handle the stressor in the most effective way. This latter course of action may require them at times to go beyond the prevailing cultural norms and will need to address the 'secondary stressors' that may erupt within the extended family, for example. A second option is to develop interventions based on cultural values. Respecting the couple's cultural values and tapping into cultural values as a resource requires an awareness of the cultural dimensions of family boundaries, gender roles, acceptance and mastery, and interdependence. For example, sensitivity to open family boundaries may require the clinician to include more family members in conversations about a couple's coping and how the family can be a source of support. For a couple in a culture that emphasizes mastery, the practitioner may want to assist a couple to tap into their inner abilities to accept a non-controllable situation.

Cultural sensitivity to prevailing norms needs to be balanced with recognition of certain cultural limits that may hinder effective coping. An example of this would be helping a couple to transcend rigid gender roles that do not permit flexible sharing of tasks. It is hoped that by recognizing certain cultural practices as constraints will facilitate an understanding of how cultural contexts can become challenges to the couple's coping and prevent cultural value issues from becoming personal or interpersonal issues. A therapist who is familiar with or is of the same culture as the couple may be better suited to help the couple rethink their coping strategies in order to more effectively manage their stress. Furthermore, offering programs or workshops for couples managing similar stressors may be helpful in building supportive relationships with other couples facing common cultural conflicts. In the U.S., many marriage enrichment programs are sponsored by religious institutions and appeal to couples who are trying to live according to the values of their religion and ethnic heritage within a larger society that does not necessarily share the same values.

Conclusion

Using the Systemic Transactional Model (STM) as the overarching framework, the authors in this volume have shown how variations of dyadic coping can emerge in couples across fourteen countries. Despite cultural differences, the research also illustrates some commonalities among couples coping. For example, there was a consistent finding between positive types of dyadic coping and relationship satisfaction. The studies make a compelling case for incorporating a cultural lens when conducting research or working clinically with couples. How we achieve this goal still remains a challenge.

A strength of this volume is that all of the chapters used the STM as the theoretical framework and the Dyadic Coping Inventory (DCI) as the measure of couples' coping. This approach allowed the comparison of couples from different countries on the same measure of dyadic coping. In this chapter, we have suggested that future research may want to look more closely at potential differences in meanings of dyadic coping. Building on this research, our measures of dyadic coping may need to include additional items especially relevant to individuals from other cultures.

While there are numerous aspects to the cultural context of coping, we selected four concepts for analyzing the cultural impact on couples coping: family boundaries, gender roles, personal control, and interdependence. By applying these concepts to the different ways that couples can cope, we offer a lens to further understand dyadic coping within a specific cultural context and to help couples as they navigate the stresses of daily living in contemporary societies.

References

Abraído-Lanza, A. F., & Revenson, T. A. (2006). Illness intrusion and psychological adjustment to rheumatic diseases: A social identity framework. *Arthritis and Rheumatism: Arthritis Care & Research, 55*, 224–232.

Agnew, C. R., Van Lange, P. A. M., Rusbult, C. E., & Langston, C. A. (1998). Cognitive interdependence: Commitment and the mental representation of close relationships. *Journal of Personality and Social Psychology, 74*(4), 939.

Berg, C. A., & Upchurch, R. (2007). A developmental-contextual model of couples coping with chronic illness across the adult life span. *Psychological Bulletin, 133*(6), 920–954.

Bodenmann, G. (1997). Dyadic coping: A systemic-transactional view of stress and coping among couples: Theory and empirical findings. *European Review of Applied Psychology, 47*(2), 137–140.

Bonanno, G. A., Pat-Horenczyk, R., & Noll, J. (2011). Coping flexibility and trauma: The perceived ability to cope with trauma (PACT) Scale. *Psychological Trauma: Theory, Research, Practice and Policy, 3*(2), 117–129.

Cheng, C., Lee, S., & Chiu, C. (1999). Dialectic thinking in daily life. *Hong Kong Journal of Social Sciences, 15*, 1–25.

Ching, S. S. Y., Martinson, I. M., & Wong, T. K. S. (2009). Reframing: Psychological adjustment of Chinese women at the beginning of the breast cancer experience. *Qualitative Health Research, 19*(3), 339–351.

Ching, S. S. Y., Martinson, I. M., & Wong, T. K. S. (2012). Meaning making: Psychological adjustment to breast cancer by Chinese women. *Qualitative Health Research, 22*(2), 250–262.

Chun, C., Moos, R. H., & Cronkite, R. C. (2006). Culture: A fundamental context for the stress and coping paradigm. In P. T. P. Wong, L. C. Wong, & C. Scott (Eds.), *Handbook of multicultural perspectives on stress and coping* (pp. 29–53), New York: Springer.

Coyne, J. C., & Fiske, V. (1992). Couples coping with chronic and catastrophic illness. In M. A. P. Stephens, S. E. Hobfoll, & J. Crowther (Eds.), *Family Health Psychology* (pp. 129–149). Washington DC: Hemisphere.

Fadiman, A. (1997). *The spirit catches you and you fall down: A Hmong child, her American doctors, and the collision of two cultures.* Macmillan.

Falicov, C. J. (2014). *Latino families* (2nd ed.). New York: The Guilford Press.

Helgeson, V. S. (2012). Gender and health: A social psychological perspective. In A. Baum, T. A., Revenson, & J. E. Singer (Eds.) *Handbook of health psychology*, 2nd ed. (pp. 519–537). New York: Psychology Press.

Kayser, K., & Scott, J. (2008). *Helping couples cope with women's cancers: An evidence-based approach for practitioners.* New York: Springer.

Kayser, K., Cheung, P. K. H., Rao, N., Chan, Y. C. L., Yu Chan, Y., & Lo, P. (2014). The influence of culture on couples coping with breast cancer: A comparative analysis of couples from China, India, and the United States. *Journal of Psychosocial Oncology, 32*(3), 264–288.

Kayser, K., Watson, L. E., & Andrade, J. T. (2007). Cancer as a 'we-disease': Examining the process of coping from a relational perspective. *Families, Systems & Health, 25*(4), 404–418.

Kuo, B. C. (2011). Culture's consequences on coping theories, evidences, and dimensionalities, *Journal of Cross-Cultural Psychology, 42*(6), 1084–1100.

Kuo, B. C. (2013). Collectivism and coping: Current theories, evidence, and measurements of collective coping. *International Journal of Psychology, 48*(3), 374–388.

Lazarus, R. S., & Folkman, S. (1984). *Stress, appraisal, and coping*. New York: Springer.

Lepore, S. J., & Revenson, T. A. (2006). Resilience and posttraumatic growth: Recovery, resistance, & reconfiguration. In L. Calhoun, & R. G. Tedeschi (Eds.), *The handbook of posttraumatic growth: Research and practice* (pp. 24–46). Mahwah, NJ: Erlbaum.

Leung, P. Y. P. (2007). Experiences and meaning reconstruction among Chinese women with breast cancer in Hong Kong (Unpublished doctoral dissertation), The University of Hong Kong.

Lewis, M. A., McBride, C. M., Pollak, K. I., Puleo, E., Butterfield, R. M., & Emmons, K. M. (2006). Understanding health behavior change among couples: An interdependence and communal coping approach. *Social Science & Medicine, 62*(6), 1369–1380.

Revenson, T. A. (1990). All other things are *not* equal: An ecological perspective on the relation between personality and disease. In H.S. Friedman (Ed.), *Personality and disease* (pp. 65–94), New York: John Wiley.

Revenson, T. A. (1994). Social support and marital coping with chronic illness. *Annals of Behavioral Medicine, 16*(2), 122–130.

Revenson, T. A. (2003). Scenes from a marriage: Examining support, coping, and gender within the context of chronic illness. In J. Suls & K. Wallston (Eds.), *Social psychological foundations of health and illness* (pp. 530–559). Oxford, England: Blackwell Publishing.

Revenson, T. A., Abraído-Lanza, A. F., Majerovitz, S. D., & Jordan, C. (2005). Couples coping with chronic illness: What's gender got to do with it? In T. A. Revenson, K. Kayser, & G. Bodenmann (Eds.) (2005), *Couples coping with stress: Emerging perspectives on dyadic coping* (pp. 137–156). Washington DC: American Psychological Association.

Revenson, T. A., Kayser, K., & Bodenmann, G. (Eds.) (2005). *Couples coping with stress: Emerging perspectives on dyadic coping*. American Psychological Association.

Rose, G., Suls, J., Green, P. J, Lounsbury, P., & Gordon, E. (1996). Comparison of adjustment, activity, and tangible social support in men and women patients and their spouses during the six months post-myocardial infarction. *Annals of Behavioral Medicine, 18*(4), 264–272.

Shumaker, S. A., & Hill, D. R. (1991). Gender differences in social support and physical health. *Health Psychology, 10*(2), 102.

Stanton, A. L., Danoff-Burg, S., Cameron, C. L., Bishop, M., Collins, C. A., Kirk, S. B., et al. (2000). Emotionally expressive coping predicts psychological and physical adjustment to breast cancer. *Journal of Consulting and Clinical Psychology, 68*(5), 875–882.

Tedeschi, R. G., & Calhoun, L. G. (2004). Posttraumatic growth: Conceptual foundations and empirical evidence. *Psychological Inquiry, 15*(1), 1–18.

Triandis, H. C. (1996). The psychological measurement of cultural syndromes. *American Psychologist, 51*(4), 407–415.

Appendix: Dyadic Coping Inventory (DCI)

This scale is designed to measure how you and your partner cope with stress. Please indicate the first response that you feel is appropriate. Please be as honest as possible. Please respond to any item by marking the appropriate case, which is fitting to your personal situation. There are no false answers.

This section is about how you communicate your stress to your partner.

	very rarely	rarely	some-times	often	very often
1. I let my partner know that I appreciate his/her practical support, advice, or help.	❑	❑	❑	❑	❑
2. I ask my partner to do things for me when I have too much to do.	❑	❑	❑	❑	❑
3. I show my partner through my behavior when I am not doing well or when I have problems.	❑	❑	❑	❑	❑
4. I tell my partner openly how I feel and that I would appreciate his/her support.	❑	❑	❑	❑	❑

This section is about what your partner does when you are feeling stressed.

	very rarely	rarely	some-times	often	very often
5. My partner shows empathy and understanding to me.	❑	❑	❑	❑	❑
6. My partner expresses that he/she is on my side.	❑	❑	❑	❑	❑
7. My partner blames me for not coping well enough with stress.	❑	❑	❑	❑	❑
8. My partner helps me to see stressful situations in a different light.	❑	❑	❑	❑	❑

Continued

	very rarely	rarely	some-times	often	very often
9. My partner listens to me and gives me the opportunity to communicate what really bothers me.	❏	❏	❏	❏	❏
10. My partner does not take my stress seriously.	❏	❏	❏	❏	❏
11. My partner provides support, but does so unwillingly and is unmotivated.	❏	❏	❏	❏	❏
12. My partner takes on things that I normally do in order to help me out.	❏	❏	❏	❏	❏
13. My partner helps me analyze the situation so that I can better face the problem.	❏	❏	❏	❏	❏
14. When I am too busy, my partner helps me out.	❏	❏	❏	❏	❏
15. When I am stressed, my partner tends to withdraw.	❏	❏	❏	❏	❏

This section is about how your partner communicates when he/she is feeling stressed.

	very rarely	rarely	some-times	often	very often
16. My partner lets me know that he/she appreciates my practical support, advice, or help.	❏	❏	❏	❏	❏
17. My partner asks me to do things for him/her when he/she has too much to do.	❏	❏	❏	❏	❏
18. My partner shows me through his/her behavior that he/she is not doing well or when he/she has problems.	❏	❏	❏	❏	❏
19. My partner tells me openly how he/she feels and that he/she would appreciate my support.	❏	❏	❏	❏	❏

This section is about what you do when your partner lets you know about his/her stress.

	very rarely	rarely	some-times	often	very often
20. I show empathy and understanding to my partner.	❑	❑	❑	❑	❑
21. I express to my partner that I am on his/her side.	❑	❑	❑	❑	❑
22. I blame my partner for not coping well enough with stress.	❑	❑	❑	❑	❑
23. I tell my partner that his/her stress is not that bad and help him/her to see the situation in a different light.	❑	❑	❑	❑	❑
24. I listen to my partner and give him/her space and time to communicate what really bothers him/her.	❑	❑	❑	❑	❑
25. I do not take my partner's stress seriously.	❑	❑	❑	❑	❑
26. When my partner is stressed I tend to withdraw.	❑	❑	❑	❑	❑
27. I provide support, but do so unwillingly and am unmotivated because I think that he/she should cope with his/her problems on his/her own.	❑	❑	❑	❑	❑
28. I take on things that my partner would normally do in order to help him/her out.	❑	❑	❑	❑	❑
29. I try to analyze the situation together with my partner in an objective manner and help him/her to understand and change the problem.	❑	❑	❑	❑	❑
30. When my partner feels he/she has too much to do, I help him/her out.	❑	❑	❑	❑	❑

This section is about what you and your partner do when you are both feeling stressed.

	very rarely	rarely	some-times	often	very often
31. We try to cope with the problem together and search for ascertained solutions.	❑	❑	❑	❑	❑
32. We engage in a serious discussion about the problem and think through what has to be done.	❑	❑	❑	❑	❑
33. We help one another to put the problem in perspective and see it in a new light.	❑	❑	❑	❑	❑
34. We help each other relax with such things such as massage, taking a bath together, or listening to music together.	❑	❑	❑	❑	❑
35. We are affectionate to each other, make love and try that way to cope with stress.	❑	❑	❑	❑	❑

This section is about how you evaluate your coping as a couple.

	very rarely	rarely	some-times	often	very often
36. I am *satisfied* with the support I receive from my partner and the way we deal with stress together.	❑	❑	❑	❑	❑
37. I am satisfied with the support I receive from my partner and I find as a couple, the way we deal with stress together is *effective*.	❑	❑	❑	❑	❑

CONCLUSION

Mariana K. Falconier, Ashley K. Randall, and Guy Bodenmann

The main goal of this book was two-fold: First, we wanted to present what we know about how couples cope with stress in different parts of the world using the conceptual framework of Bodenmann's systemic-transactional model (STM; Bodenmann, 1995, 1997); second, we wanted to understand the role of the cultural context in the stress and coping process. Each of the cultural chapters (4 through 17) presented research that indicates that partners do engage, to various degrees in dyadic coping strategies, and that this type of coping has positive effects for both individual and relational well-being. In other words, these chapters suggest that the STM dimensions of dyadic coping of stress communication, supportive, delegated, negative, and common dyadic coping are relevant in a wide range of cultures. Furthermore, in several chapters when demographic factors such as age, gender, education, length of the relationship, area of residence (e.g., rural versus urban), and income level affected dyadic coping, the effect was in the same direction across the different cultural groups (see Table C1). Younger, more educated, and more affluent couples who had been together for shorter periods of time living in urban areas seemed to rely on dyadic coping more frequently than couples who were older, less educated and affluent, had been together for longer, and lived in rural areas. Women were also found to use more positive dyadic coping strategies, particularly emotion-focused ones, whereas men in many cultures used more negative dyadic coping strategies.

Despite the similarities, each of the cultural chapters also reveal that there may be some variations in the dyadic coping process across different cultures, suggesting that the cultural context may affect the extent to which couples prefer dyadic coping over other coping strategies, the potential benefits of dyadic coping over other coping mechanisms, the specific factors that favor dyadic coping, and the preference for relying more on some dyadic coping dimensions versus others.

For example, the chapter on African couples (Chapter 16) reported that these couples tended to engage in dyadic coping less frequently than non-African couples and the chapters on Italian (Chapter 9) and Latino (Chapter 5) couples suggested that common dyadic coping was a better predictor of relationship satisfaction than supportive dyadic coping was. For some couples such as the Romanian (Chapter 12) or Latino ones, religion seemed to favor the use of dyadic coping whereas for couples from other cultures, such as African couples, the Islamic religion was seen as unsupportive of the use of dyadic coping strategies. These cultural differences also suggest, as Chapter 18 points out, that the same dyadic coping behavior may have different meanings across cultures, which may play a role in the likelihood of relying on dyadic coping as well as on its effects on relational and individual well-being.

Table 1 highlights some of the similarities and differences in dyadic coping across different cultural groups based on the main findings in dyadic coping reported in each of the chapters. Table C1 also lists the applications, either clinical or programmatic, that have been developed for that specific population based on an STM framework. Additionally, the dominant value orientation for each cultural group is included together with the dimensions that each value orientation encompasses. These are the cultural dimensions, which were recommended in Chapter 18 to use when examining the effects of the cultural context in dyadic coping: Closed/open boundaries, flexible/differentiated gender roles, mastery/acceptance, and independence/interdependence. Even though we tried to include the dominant value orientation of the cultural group, it is important to remember that wide variations exist within a culture. As several of the chapters discuss (e.g., Chapters 5, 7, 9, 10, 11, 12, 14, 15, and 16), many cultures, which were considered to be collectivistic have been incorporating individualistic values particularly among younger generations, and therefore, these cultures should no longer be viewed as purely collectivistic (e.g., Portuguese, Chinese, Japanese, etc.).

In addition to bringing most of the findings together in a comparative way, Table 1 also shows significant differences in the volume and type of research studies conducted with each cultural group. Dyadic coping has been studied more extensively in some populations such as Swiss (Chapter 6) or Portuguese (Chapter 7) couples whereas only a few studies have been conducted for Pakistani (Chapter 13), Greek (Chapter 10), and Latino (Chapter 5) couples. Even though most research has examined the influence of demographic variables on dyadic coping and the effects of dyadic coping on relationship satisfaction and there have been many validation studies of the Dyadic Coping Inventory, some variables have only been examined in some cultural groups but not in others. For example, the association between parents' and children's dyadic coping has only been assessed in Italian couples or psychological aggression has only been studied as an outcome variable in Latino couples. Furthermore, studies have also differed in terms of the stressor that couples have to cope with ranging from specific medical conditions such as diabetes, breast cancer, and chronic obstructive pulmonary disease to economic pressure, daily hassles, or military stressors. These dissimilarities in research studies across the various cultural groups included in this book reveal that there are still many areas to be examined in each population. Most importantly, further studies that assess specific cultural values (e.g., Chapters 5, 12, and 18) are needed if we want to expand our understanding of the role of cultural factors in the dyadic coping process. In this regard, the cultural dimensions presented and discussed in Chapter 2 and Chapter 18 can be useful guidelines for such research. But given that a majority of the studies on dyadic coping use cross-sectional data and self-report measures, it is equally important to conduct longitudinal studies that combine self-report with observational and physiological data. Qualitative studies are also needed to explore partners' experience of dyadic coping in terms of perception and meaning.

Despite the need for further research on dyadic coping in different cultural contexts, the studies presented in this book indicate that couples in different parts of the world do cope dyadically and that overall, dyadic coping is beneficial for couples. This book also highlights culture as a key contextual factor in the stress and dyadic coping process. We hope that the studies and discussions presented in this book inspire further research on dyadic coping from a culturally informed perspective. Furthermore, we invite clinicians and program developers to translate the accumulated knowledge into interventions (e.g., CCET or TOGETHER) that assist couples to cope with stress in different parts of the world.

TABLE C.1 Value orientations and dyadic coping research and programs in different cultural groups

Cultural Group (Chapter)	Value Orientations	Dyadic Coping Research	Available Programs
American Couples (Chapter 4)	Individualism: • Flexible gender roles • Open family boundaries • Mastery • Independence	DC associated with relationship satisfaction and better predictor than individual coping. DC associated with lower perceptions of stress and less anxiety in the workplace for same sex couples. Diabetes: CDC associated with diabetes efficacy and higher adherence to dietary and exercise requirements. Breast cancer: mutuality, awareness, authenticity, and previous depression treatment contribute to PDC. NDC predicts men's intrusiveness and DC predicts greater dyadic adjustment. *DCI Validation:* Randall, Hilpert, Jiménez-Arista, Walsh, & Bodenmann, 2015	*Partners in Coping Program:* Couples with women diagnosed with breast cancer. *TOGETHER:* couples coping with economic stress. TOGETHER reduces economic stress and psychological aggression and improves CDC and relationship satisfaction.
Latino Couples in the U.S. (Chapter 5)	Collectivism: • Differentiated gender roles (*machismo & marianismo*) • Closed family boundaries (*familismo*) • Acceptance • Interdependence • Spirituality	Both partners agree that women provide more emotion-focused SDC than men do. Spirituality contributes to dyadic coping in both partners and men's traditional gender role reduces the likelihood of DC. DC associated positively with relationship satisfaction, negotiation in the couple, individual engagement coping strategies, and negatively with psychological aggression. CDC moderates women's negative effect of immigration stress on each partner's relationship satisfaction, but has the opposite effect for men's immigration stress. *DCI Validation:* Falconier, Nussbeck, & Bodenmann, 2013	

continued . . .

TABLE C.1 Continued

Cultural Group (Chapter)	Value Orientations	Dyadic Coping Research	Available Programs
Swiss Couples (Chapter 6)	Individualism: • Flexible gender roles • Open family boundaries • Mastery • Independence	DC contributes to relationship quality, psychological well-being, quality of life, grief work, and adjustment to bereavement. Partner's SDC contributes to faster recovery from stress, but less beneficial from anxiously attached women. Older couples, severely depressed individuals, and people having experienced trauma are less likely to use dyadic coping. Securely attached couples more likely to use PDC and less likely to use negative DC. Partner's SDC more predictive of one's own relationship satisfaction that one's own SDC. Higher partner's SDC in lesbian couples than in heterosexual couples. Chronic obstructive pulmonary disease: more negative DC than healthy couples. DC moderates effect of chronic external stress on chronic internal stress. *DCI Validation:* Bodenmann, 2008	*Couples Coping Enhancement Training (CCET):* stress prevention program. CCET improves relationship quality, problem-solving behaviors, PDC, personal happiness, life satisfaction, psychological well-being. CCET outperformed both the Individual Coping Training (ITP) and a waiting-list control group. Women benefit more from CCET. *Coping Oriented Couple Therapy (COCT):* decreases depressive symptoms and as effective as cognitive–behavioral treatment and ITP.
Portuguese Couples (Chapter 7)	Collectivism: • Both flexible & differentiated gender roles *(maternalism)*	Both partners report women communicating stress more frequently but women perceive themselves as providing more PDC than men whereas men view themselves as providing more NDC than them. Better education predicts more DC and lower education is associated with NDC.	

	• Closed family boundaries (*familialism*) • Acceptance • Interdependence	PDC associated with better quality of sex, romance, and passion, constructive conflict processes, high shared meaning and consensus, cohesion, affectional expression, and relationship satisfaction. But one study found that women's SDC and CDC contributes to men's dyadic adjustment but not their own. However, men's NDC affects negatively women's dyadic adjustment. We-ness mediates DC and relationship satisfaction. Economic pressure: NDC mediates association between economic pressure and couple's conflict and psychological distress. Death of child: Lower grief levels linked to higher CDC, in turn linked to better dyadic adjustment. *DCI Validation*: Vedes, A., Nussbeck, F. W., Bodenmann, G., Lind, W., & Ferreira, A., 2013.	
German Couples (Chapter 8)	Individualism: • Flexible gender roles • Open family boundaries • Mastery • Independence	Relationship-focused standards predict dyadic coping and this association is stronger for men than women. Secure couples report more DC than fearful-avoidant couples but same as mixed couples. Secure couples report more SDC and less NDC than fearful-avoidant and mixed couples. In older couples, the association between marital satisfaction and DC is higher for women than for men. For men, income distribution associated with problem-focused CDC but not with emotion-focused CDC, which is associated with men's relationship satisfaction more strongly than problem-focused CDC.	*Side-by-Side*: A couple-based psycho-oncological intervention program for women diagnosed with breast cancer. *Side-by-Side* reduces women's fear of cancer progression, reduces couple's avoidance strategies, increases post-traumatic grown, improves relationship skills, and maintains DC. Changes are more pronounced in women than men.

continued . . .

TABLE C.1 Continued

Cultural Group (Chapter)	Value Orientations	Dyadic Coping Research	Available Programs
		Problem-focused DC associated with relationship satisfaction whereas individual coping is not. Problem-focused DC fully mediates the link between individual task-oriented coping and relationship satisfaction. The men's individual emotional DC predicts women's DC, which in turn predicts their own relationship satisfaction. Men's individual emotion-oriented coping negatively associated with women's relationship satisfaction and DC. Women's perception of CDC mediates the link between their individual coping and the men's relationship satisfaction. Cancer: CDC reduces child distress.	
Italian Couples (Chapter 9)	Individualism and Collectivism: • Differentiated gender roles but emphasis on fairness • Both open & closed family boundaries • Mastery • Independence & interdependence	Partner's stress communication, PDC, and CDC predict relationship satisfaction and CDC is the strongest predictor. NDC negatively related to relationship satisfaction. PDC and CDC also associated with partners' affection, sexual satisfaction, and lower tension while NDC is negatively associated. DC attenuates effects of common stressors (e.g., sexual dissatisfaction) on relationship satisfaction. Partners' perceived similarity higher than partners' actual similarity in DC. Men's understanding of DC was higher for NDC than PDC. Perceived similarity in PDC predicts relationship satisfaction. Perceived stereotypical similarity in DC higher for younger couples whereas stereotypical and unique understanding of DC are higher for more mature couples. Stereotypical understanding associated with relationship quality in mature couples.	*Groups for Family Enrichment (couple version)*: information and training on relational competencies for couples. The program is not focused on DC but does include DC as one of the competencies.

		More similarities between parents and children in NDC than in PDC, particularly for daughters. For PDC stereotypical similarities between children and parents but both unique and stereotypical similarities between partners. Cardiac Illness: partner's NDC associated with patient's engagement in treatment. *DCI Validation:* Donato, Iafrate, Barni, Bertoni, & Bodenmann, 2009.
Greek Couples (Chapter 10)	Collectivism: • Mostly differentiated gender roles but flexible in younger, urban couples • Closed family boundaries • Acceptance/ Mastery • Interdependence	Women report higher emotion-focused SDC by oneself and higher NDC by men. For both men and women DC by oneself and by partner associated with their own relationship satisfaction. Each DC dimension related negatively (except for NDC) to psychological symptoms for both men and women for their own reports. However, men's psychological symptoms also related to women's report of DC dimensions. *DCI Validation:* Roussi & Karademas (Chapter 10)
Hungarian Couples (Chapter 11)	Individualism: • Differentiated and flexible gender roles • Closed family boundaries	DC associated with life and relationship satisfaction for both men and women. Couples with both partners high on every DC dimension are younger, less time in relationship, more satisfied with DC and relationship in general. Couples with both partners lower on every DC dimension are less satisfied with DC and relationship

continued . . .

TABLE C.1 Continued

Cultural Group (Chapter)	Value Orientations	Dyadic Coping Research	Available Programs
	• Mastery • Independence	in general. Couples with only one partner high on every DC dimension close in satisfaction with DC and relationship to couples with both partners high on every DC dimension. Child with disability: couples use less SDC and more NDC and are less satisfied with DCD compared to community couples. *DCI Validation:* Martos, Sallay, Nistor, & Józsa, 2012.	
Romanian Couples (Chapter 12)	Individualism and Collectivism: • Differentiated and flexible gender roles • Both open & closed family boundaries • Mastery • Independence & interdependence • Religiosity	Length of marriage associated negatively with PDC and positively with NDC whereas education is associated positively with PDC and negatively with NDC. Both partners report that women engage more frequently in stress communication and SD than men do. Daily stress and economic strain negatively related to self and partner's SDC and CDC and positively associated with self and partner's NDC. Women's daily stress influences both partners' DC and marital satisfaction more than men's. Religious faith, religious cognitions, positive religious coping associated with PDC. SDC mediates the influence of sanctification on marital satisfaction and well-being. Individual cognitive coping related to PDC and dysfunctional individual coping related to NDC. Male and female PDC mediates association between individual cognitive coping and marital satisfaction. *DCI Validation:* Rusu, Hilpert, Turliuc, & Bodenmann (under review).	

Pakistani Couples (Chapter 13)	Collectivism: • Differentiated gender roles • Closed family boundaries • Acceptance • Interdependence	PDC associated positively with relationship satisfaction and NDC associated negatively with marital satisfaction. Wives are more likely to engage in PDC, particularly emotion-focused SDC and delegated DC than husbands are and husbands tend to engage in more NDC than wives do. Both men and women engage more in problem-focused DC than any other form of coping.
Chinese Couples (Chapter 14)	Confucianism: • Filial piety • Patriarchal family system Collectivism: • Differentiated gender roles • Closed family boundaries • Acceptance • Interdependence	Older wives show lower stress communication by self, problem-focused SDC by partner, problem-focused CDC, and total CDC and DC compared with younger wives. No differences in any DC dimension for husbands. Urban marriages tend to engage in less PDC and more NDC than rural marriages. Income level has no effect on wives' DC but higher income husbands report less problem-focused SDC and delegated DC. All dimensions of DC, except for NDC, predict relationship satisfaction for both wives and husbands. Wives' DC more strongly associated with relationships satisfaction than men's DC. _DC Validation:_ Xu, Hilpert, Randall, Li, & Bodenmann (under review).
Japanese Couples (Chapter 15)	Confucianism: • Filial piety • Patriarchal family system Collectivism: • Differentiated gender roles	Men report more use of NDC than women. Less frequent PDC and more frequent NDC than Swiss and Italian couples. Age is negatively related to DC, particularly for men. However, few DC dimensions are affected by number of working hours or number of children for either men or women. All DC dimensions are positively associated with marital quality, especially SDC and CDC. Less strong correlations for NDC.

continued . . .

TABLE C.1 Continued

Cultural Group (Chapter)	Value Orientations	Dyadic Coping Research	Available Programs
	• Closed family boundaries • Acceptance • Interdependence (Less collectivism in urban areas)	Women's depressive symptoms negatively associated with SDC and evaluation of DC by either partner. Men's NDC associated with their own depressive symptoms. NDC by the partner associated with depressive symptoms for both men and women.	
African Couples: (Chapter 16)	Collectivism: • Differentiated gender roles • Closed family boundaries • Acceptance • Interdependence	DC relatively high and associated with relationship satisfaction but association is lower than other 31 non-African countries. Weaker relationship attributed to patriarchal system, the dowry system and women seen as property, poverty, influence of Christianity and Islam subordinating wife's position to the husband's. The association between DC and relationship satisfaction is stronger for men in Uganda and women in Nigeria.	
Australian Couples (Chapter 17)	Individualism: • Flexible gender roles • Open family boundaries • Mastery • Independence	Military couples: DC associated with SDC and CDC for both men and women. CDC more strongly associated with relationship satisfaction than SDC. No association between DC and psychological distress.	*Couple CARE in Uniform:* Helps couples apply strategies to cope with military specific stressors.

Note. DC = Dyadic Coping; PDC = Positive Dyadic Coping; NDC = Negative Dyadic Coping; SDC = Supportive Dyadic Coping; CDC = Common Dyadic Coping.

AUTHOR INDEX

SUBJECT INDEX

Taylor & Francis eBooks

Helping you to choose the right eBooks for your Library

Add Routledge titles to your library's digital collection today. Taylor and Francis ebooks contains over 50,000 titles in the Humanities, Social Sciences, Behavioural Sciences, Built Environment and Law.

Choose from a range of subject packages or create your own!

Benefits for you

>> Free MARC records
>> COUNTER-compliant usage statistics
>> Flexible purchase and pricing options
>> All titles DRM-free.

REQUEST YOUR **FREE** INSTITUTIONAL TRIAL TODAY	**Free Trials Available** We offer free trials to qualifying academic, corporate and government customers.

Benefits for your user

>> Off-site, anytime access via Athens or referring URL
>> Print or copy pages or chapters
>> Full content search
>> Bookmark, highlight and annotate text
>> Access to thousands of pages of quality research at the click of a button.

eCollections – Choose from over 30 subject eCollections, including:

Archaeology	Language Learning
Architecture	Law
Asian Studies	Literature
Business & Management	Media & Communication
Classical Studies	Middle East Studies
Construction	Music
Creative & Media Arts	Philosophy
Criminology & Criminal Justice	Planning
Economics	Politics
Education	Psychology & Mental Health
Energy	Religion
Engineering	Security
English Language & Linguistics	Social Work
Environment & Sustainability	Sociology
Geography	Sport
Health Studies	Theatre & Performance
History	Tourism, Hospitality & Events

For more information, pricing enquiries or to order a free trial, please contact your local sales team: www.tandfebooks.com/page/sales

 Routledge
Taylor & Francis Group

The home of Routledge books

www.tandfebooks.com